Birds of the Southwest

Number Thirty
W. L. Moody, Jr., Natural History Series

TEXAS A&M UNIVERSITY PRESS: COLLEGE STATION

Birds of the Southwest

Arizona

New Mexico

Southern California

& Southern Nevada

John H. Rappole

With Photographs by

Barth Schorre

Vernon Grove

David Parmelee

William Paff

and VIREO

(Philadelphia Academy of Sciences)

The paper used in this book
meets the minimum requirements
of the American National Standard
for Permanence of Paper
for Printed Library Materials, z39.48-1984.
Binding materials have been chosen for durability.

Library of Congress Cataloging-in-Publication Data

Rappole, John H.
    Birds of the Southwest : Arizona, New
  Mexico, Southern California, and southern
  Nevada / John H. Rappole ; with photographs
  by Barth Schorre ... [et al.].—1st ed.
      p. cm.—(W.L. Moody, Jr., natural
  history series ; no. 30)
    Includes bibliographical references (p.).
    ISBN 0-89096-957-4 (cloth)—
    ISBN 0-89096-958-2 (pbk.)
  1. Birds—Southwest, New. I. Title. II. Series.
  QL683.S75R36   2000
  598'.0979—dc21   00-044315

To my children:

Brigetta Bartlett Stewart,

John Hilton Rappole, Jr.,

& Nathaniel Brian Rappole

"My babe so beautiful! it thrills my heart
With tender gladness, thus to look at thee, . ."

Frost at Midnight by S. T. Coleridge

Contents

Illustrations

Preface

Why? Why should you own a field guide to the birds of the Southwest? Aren't the numerous national guides enough? Yes, they are more than sufficient if your goal is to log as many birds as possible from across the continent in as short a time as possible. The field guide market is filled with excellent books directed toward the continental and national levels—the Peterson series, Audubon series, National Geographic, Golden Guides, Masters guides, Stokes guides, etc. There is little need for more such guides. In addition, most places also now have detailed handbooks explaining precisely which county road to turn on to in order to find a particular rarity. But there is a need that neither the national guides nor handbooks can satisfy. If you want to develop some sense of what a particular bird is about within a relatively confined geographical area, the regional guide is essential. In addition to identification data, a regional guide gives you necessary and particularly satisfying bits of information about a species that makes birding such a popular pastime. National guides don't have the space to tell you whether or not you are likely to hear an Elegant Trogon in April in southeastern Arizona's Cave Creek Canyon. Using a national guide, you'll be lucky to find Arizona, and for many of these extra-limital specialties, it won't help if you do, because there is little or no information on breeding localities distant from the normal range of the species. How could there be? Such detailed information would require several volumes.

National guides are good, particularly for the novice who dreams of finding Phainopeplas in New York. They have everything—serving as a stimulus to find weird birds or visit exotic places. But once in an exotic place, you need more precise information. You need a Baedeker to direct you to the right spot at the right times, or to tell you what to look for at this particular moment. The regional guide can fill this need, as well as help to satisfy a more refined taste. The seasoned birder comes to recognize the singular beauties of a choice habitat, one containing its own special set of inhabitants. Every region has its share of choice habitats; obvious ones like the Grand Canyon or Death Valley, and less obvious ones like southern California's Joshua Tree National Monument or New Mexico's Guadalupe Canyon. With a key to time and place, you can find them. That is what the regional guide is all about.

When visiting a new part of the country, many people like to purchase things that can serve as both introduction and souvenir to that particular location: the Rand-McNally map book, the AAA guide to places to stay and see, the Park Service guide to scenic spots. A regional bird guide satisfies the same kind of need. In places like New Mexico's Sangre de Cristo Mountains or Arizona's Organ Pipe National Monument, a guide to the birds and habitats of these new areas is a handy reference while there, and a delightful reminder of the trip at home.

Acknowledgments

Nate Rappole, Eric Fleischmann, Tom Small, and Jeff Diez provided help with computer graphics. Several of the most outstanding wildlife photographers in North America donated slides for this venture, including Dr. W. A. Paff, Dr. Vernon E. Groves, Dr. David W. Parmelee, and Barth Schorre. Lynn and Denis O'Pray and Jean and David Parmelee provided hospitality and information on birding sites in southern California and southern Nevada, respectively. Keith Arnold did a thorough review of early drafts and made a number of comments and corrections that greatly improved the quality of the manuscript. Certain sections of this guide (e.g., some species and range descriptions) are taken from John H. Rappole's and Gene W. Blacklock's *Birds of Texas: A Field Guide,* published by Texas A&M University Press, 1994. Material from that work reprinted herein is used with the kind permission of my coauthor, Gene W. Blacklock. Finally, I thank my wife, Bonnie Rappole, who provided invaluable encouragement and support throughout the long evolutionary history of the project.

Birds of the Southwest

Introduction

The vast southwestern corner of the United States covers 320,000 square miles of some of the most spectacular scenery to be found anywhere in the world: mountains, deserts, seacoast, forest, prairie, and chaparral. The area encompasses the highest point in the lower forty-eight states (Mount Whitney—14,494 feet above sea level), as well as the lowest point (Death Valley—282 feet below sea level). This remarkable diversity presents a rich experience for those who want to explore a bit. One of the most accessible and rewarding aspects of that diversity is the region's more than 450 species of birds, as distinctive as the landscape. There are roadrunners, magpies, and prairie chickens; White-tailed Kites and spotted owls; Scissor-tailed Flycatchers and Red-faced Warblers; and more hummingbirds than are found in all the rest of the United States taken together.

Europeans first came to the Southwest seeking riches of other kinds. In 1536, Alvar Nuñez Cabeza de Vaca led a party of soldiers up from Mexico into present-day New Mexico and Arizona. They found extraordinary indigenous cultures whose ancestors had inhabited the region for ten thousand years, including advanced agricultural societies, such as the Hokoam and Anasazi, as well as the Zuni, Hopi, Navajo, Pueblo, and Apache. They also found hints and rumors of rich cities with streets of gold and silver. Accounts from this journey stimulated other explorers, and in 1540 Coronado led his famous expedition into the same area searching for the "seven cities of gold." Though no such riches were found, the invaders soon recognized other opportunities, and colonists followed shortly.

Europeans established their first settlement at San Juan de los Caballeros in the Chama River valley in northern New Mexico in 1598 and founded Santa Fe in 1609. These early explorers were searching for gold, souls to save, and routes to the East Indies.

The first Europeans to reach "upper" California arrived by ship in 1542, after overland routes across the Sonora Desert proved too inhospitable. Though Baja California was colonized in the mid-1600s, the region that now constitutes the state of California was not settled until much later. They built their first mission on the shores of San Diego Bay in 1769, and by 1823 there were twenty missions along the California coast.

European exploration and colonization of what is now Nevada was later still, delayed until 1775 by the harsh environment and stiff resistance from the region's indigenous peoples to the loss of their lands and inundation of their culture by settlers. In 1680, Indians revolted against the Spanish and drove them out of what is now Arizona and New Mexico. The Spanish put down the revolt and reestablished control during fighting from 1692 to 1696, but conflicts between settlers and indigenous peoples continued in the Southwest until the capture of the Chiricahua Apache leader Geronimo in 1886.

The lands that are now California, New Mexico, and Arizona were under Spanish suzerainty until the 1820s, when they became provinces of the newly independent Mexican Republic. Rapid influx of settlers from the United States into Texas and other parts of the Southwest during the next twenty years created political turmoil in the region, and, in 1846, Mexico and the United States went to war to resolve the conflicting claims. This war ended with Mexico ceding control of most all the lands now constituting the southwestern United States to the American government in the Treaty of Guadalupe Hidalgo on February 2, 1849. California became a state in 1850; Nevada in 1864; New Mexico and Arizona in 1912.

Ornithological exploration of the Southwest took much longer than its political, social, and economic exploitation. Though Coronado's chronicler made some mention of "cranes," "wild geese," "starlings," "cocks," and "tame eagles," no systematic study of the region's natural history was begun until the early to mid-1800s. An increasing number of trained observers investigated and reported on the animal and plant life, beginning with Major Stephen Harriman Long's expedition into New Mexico in 1820 (James 1823). Many of these early scientists were army surgeons; men like Samuel Washington Woodhouse, Thomas Charlton Henry, Dewitt Clinton Peters, Caleb Burwell Kennerly, Charles Emil Bendire, Adolphus Heerman, and Elliott Coues. Florence Merriam Bailey (1928), H. C. Oberholser (1974), and J. Stokley Ligon (1961) provide summaries of their pioneering ornithological studies.

Landforms

It is said that when Cortes was asked by his royal sponsors to describe Mexico, he grasped a piece of parchment, crushed it in his hands, and displayed it to them, saying, "This is Mexico." The same could be said for the Southwest, where much of the earth's surface is broken, crumpled, and folded in rugged peaks, cliffs, canyons, and crags. In some places along the eastern slope of the Sierra Nevada, the land rises ten thousand feet in less than ten miles. Such contrasts make for spectacular scenery. Southwestern landforms are divided into six principal physiographic prov-

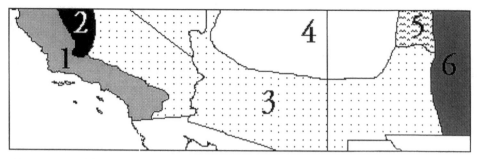

Figure 1. Map of the Southwest showing principal landforms. 1) Pacific Border, 2) Sierra Nevada, 3) Basin and Range, 4) Colorado Plateau, 5) Rocky Mountain, 6) Great Plains.

inces, based on their characteristics. From west to east, these are as follows: (1) Pacific Border, (2) Sierra Nevada, (3) Basin and Range, (4) Colorado Plateau, (5) Rocky Mountains, and (6) Great Plains. (figure 1).

The Great Plains Province stretches hundreds of miles across the heartland of the continent, reaching its western edge at the foot of the Rocky Mountains in New Mexico. There, the province is divided into two sections, the High Plains in the northeastern portion and the Staked Plains (Llano Estacado) in the southeast. The Staked Plains region, whose name, according to some accounts, derives from stakes used by travelers to mark trails across the featureless waste, is one of the largest flat areas on the continent.

West of the Great Plains is the Rocky Mountain Province, whose Southern Rockies Section reaches into north-central New Mexico in the form of the Sangre de Cristo range. The general trend of the roughly parallel ranges making up the province is north-south, forming a jagged backbone for both North and South America that stretches more than ten thousand miles from Canada to Chile.

The Colorado Plateau Province covers the northwestern section of New Mexico and much of northern Arizona. It is a region of high tablelands sliced and carved by deep canyons with layered, multi-colored walls. The province's dominant feature is the Grand Canyon, a vast gorge more than one hundred miles long and a mile deep, cut through the plateau by the Colorado River.

Southern Nevada, Arizona, New Mexico, and eastern California are included in the Basin and Range Province. Worn peaks rising thousands of feet above desert basins characterize the province.

The Sierra Nevada Province is long and narrow, extending roughly four hundred miles north to south at a width of forty to sixty miles. Steep-sided peaks, U-shaped valleys, numerous lakes, horns, aretes, and cirques characterize the Sierra Nevada. Its bedrock is grooved, sculpted, and polished by more than sixty ancient glaciers.

The Pacific Border Province consists of coastal mountain ranges bordered on the east by the broad, dry, sediment-filled lowlands collectively referred to as the Great Valley of California. The San Joaquin River flows northward and empties into the Sacramento River and San Francisco Bay, draining the southern California portion of the valley. However, sections of the valley have internal drainage, and water collects in shallow, ephemeral playa lakes during rainy periods.

Climate

Three major climatic types occur in the Southwest: Arid, Semiarid, and Montane. High mean annual temperatures and low precipitation characterize arid climate, with evaporation greatly exceeding its average annual precipitation of less than eight inches per year. Semiarid climate is similar, though not as extreme. Precipitation averages eight to twenty inches per year. Montane climates are subject to marked variation in temperature and precipitation, depending on elevation, aspect, slope, and season. The highest elevations, those above 11,500 feet, have polar climates, with mean highs below 50 degrees F. in the warmest month, and a growing season of less than two months. Areas west of the highest peaks can receive significant precipitation in the form of rain or snow, while areas south and east of these ranges receive much less precipitation.

Habitat

The varied geography of the Southwest forms the basis for the wonderful diversity of plant and animal communities or habitats that occur in the region. Specific associations or communities of plants and animals constitute a habitat for a given species, and, with experience, one can learn to recognize these communities and know which birds to expect in them. However, there are differences among the habitat classifications provided by biologists. For instance, C. Hart Merriam (1890) described seven major terrestrial habitats or life zones for the Southwest, while the plant ecologist A. W. Kuchler (1975) described thirty two. The difference is largely from considerations of scale. At one end of the spectrum, we could place all the planet's creatures in a single habitat called Earth, while at the other, we could assign the space occupied by each individual organism as its own particular habitat. In the nine major categories presented below, I have attempted to select groupings of plant associations that are easily recognizable and possess characteristic bird communities.

Figure 2. Marine, Coastal Waters, and Shoreline Habitat. The tidal marsh, mudflats, and open ocean of Morro Bay, California, are home to a rich variety of coastal marine life including loons, grebes, pelicans, and shorebirds.

Marine, Coastal Waters, and Shoreline

The ocean seems to stir something deep in people, from Homer's "wine-dark sea" to Melville's "all pervading azure" and Coleridge's "sultry main." A little time spent contemplating the Pacific provides some understanding of this feeling. California's coast is among the most beautiful in the world and offers outstanding birding possibilities. The coastal marine habitat can be broken into three major subdivisions, each with its own characteristic group of avian species: (1) Pelagic (open ocean); (2) Beaches and Dunes; and (3) Salt Marshes and Tidal Flats.

Freshwater Wetlands

Water is a precious commodity in much of the desert Southwest, and its sudden discovery in deep canyons carved in the sun-baked rock can be, as Edward Abbey says, like a "miraculous mirage" to the traveler. Freshwater wetland habitat includes lakes, ponds, impoundments, rivers, and marshes. The defining characteristic is the presence of fresh water, which stimulates the growth of such plants as cattails (*Typha*), sedges (*Carex*), and bulrushes (*Scirpus*).

Figure 3. Freshwater Wetland Habitat. Corn Creek ponds form a tiny, anomalous portion of the immense Desert National Wildlife Range, Nevada. These small oases draw a disproportionate number of species, including many transients, to the cottonwoods and tules bordering the ponds including Black Phoebe, Merlin, Cinnamon Teal, Virginia Rail, Solitary Sandpiper, and Yellow-billed Cuckoo.

Southeastern California's Salton Sea, created by a failed Colorado River water project in 1916, is a strange combination of salt and freshwater habitats. Most parts of the Salton Sea are too saline to support any type of freshwater plant or animal community. As a result, the kinds of birds and other flora and fauna are similar to those found in marine and coastal habitats. However, there are places where fresh water flows into the sea, such as Barnacle Marsh near the Salton Sea National Wildlife Refuge headquarters, where small, freshwater communities occur.

Grassland and Savanna

The vast grasslands of the North American continent reach a portion of their western boundary in eastern New Mexico where the grassy, treeless plains of the heartland give way to the woodlands and desert scrub of the West. William Cullen Bryant referred to the prairies as, "gardens of the desert . . . unshorn fields, boundless and beautiful for which the speech of England has no name." Much of this habitat in

New Mexico originally was shortgrass prairie, dominated by grama (*Bouteloua*) and galleta (*Hilaria*) or buffalo grass (*Buchloe*). Overgrazing, farming, exotic introductions, and other human changes have altered this once rich and varied habitat, and in many parts of the region, grassland habitats are represented by "improved" pasture, golf courses, and lawns. Nevertheless, some of the bird species characteristic of natural grasslands and savannas can be found in these areas, including Western Meadowlark, Northern Harrier, and Horned Lark. But you will have to look harder, and in special places, to find others, such as White-tailed Kite, Mountain Plover, Burrowing Owl, Golden Eagle, and Prairie Falcon. Much of California's great Central Valley was once unbroken native grassland. However, as elsewhere, agriculture, grazing, and introduction of exotic species has changed this habitat. Parts of the desert as well become grasslands during wet periods, if they are not overgrazed, and there also are natural meadows in the highlands.

Figure 4. Grassland and Savanna Habitat. The prairies of the Great Plains reach their western border in the foothills of the Rockies at Las Vegas, New Mexico, though some of the bird species typical of the habitat can be found in other grassland types elsewhere in the region. Characteristic birds include Western Meadowlark, Mountain Plover, Burrowing Owl, Horned Lark, and, in winter, McCown's, Chestnut-collared, and occasionally, Lapland longspurs.

Desert Scrub

"Below, below . . . beneath a sea, not of brine, but of heat, of shimmering simmering waves of light and a wind as hot and fierce as a dragon's teeth." So Edward Abbey describes the desert in his essay, "Death Valley." It was not his favorite place. Nevertheless there is an attraction, especially if you're completely unfamiliar with the desert. The openness, brightness, and all–around strangeness can be a completely new and fascinating experience, so long as you are within easy reach of a good supply of fresh water. Much of the terrestrial habitat below four thousand feet in the Southwest is a variation on this theme: barren areas of sand, gravel, and rock, more or less covered with sparse, low shrubs, herbs, and grasses. The dominant plant of these regions in the Southwestern United States is creosote bush (*Larrea*), though saltbush (*Atriplex*), greasewood (*Sarcobatus*), or bur sage (*Franseria*) can be dominant species depending on local variations in soil salinity, slope, aspect, elevation, and rainfall. Typical birds include Verdin, Rock Wren, Common Raven, Western Screech-Owl, Lesser Nighthawk, LeConte's Thrasher, and House Finch.

Figure 5. Desert Scrub Habitat. Saguaro National Park provides a beautiful setting for a variety of typical desert species including Harris's Hawk, Greater Roadrunner, Cactus Wren, Curve-billed Thrasher, and Gambel's Quail. When spring rains occur, blooms of poppy, opuntia, ocotillo, and other desert flowers can be spectacular.

Figure 6. Highland Desert Habitat. Though this site is mainly famous as an ancient Indian cultural center, Bandelier National Monument's Frijoles Canyon in New Mexico has excellent pinyon-oak-juniper habitat of the high desert, and there is highland coniferous forest within the monument's boundaries as well. Some birds that can be found here include Juniper Titmouse, Pygmy Nuthatch, Bushtit, Brown Creeper, Black-chinned Hummingbird, and Hammond's Flycatcher.

Highland Desert

The highland desert regions of the Southwest are those areas found roughly between four thousand and seven thousand feet, depending on local topography, soils, rainfall, and latitude. They include three relatively distinct subcategories: (1) Lower Sonoran Desert; (2) Upper Sonoran Desert; and (3) Great Basin Sagebrush. The Lower Sonoran Desert habitat is found at four thousand to six thousand feet and is characterized by paloverde (*Cercidium*), ocotillo (*Fouquieria*), opuntia cactus (*Opuntia*), and, in some areas, saguaro (*Cereus*) or joshua trees (*Yucca brevifolia*). Birds of this habitat are those we usually think of as "typically Southwestern," such as Pyrrhuloxia, Phainopepla, Greater Roadrunner, Harris's Hawk, Cactus Wren, Gambel's Quail, Common Poorwill, Curve-billed Thrasher, and Gila Woodpecker.

Great Basin Sagebrush habitat is found at elevations similar to that of the Lower

Sonoran, but is located farther north under somewhat drier conditions. Sagebrush (*Artemesia*) is the dominant plant species, and typical birds include Sage Thrasher, Brewer's Sparrow, Red-tailed Hawk, Black-throated Sparrow, Golden Eagle, Poorwill, Loggerhead Shrike, Say's Phoebe, and Mourning Dove.

Upper Sonoran is distinct and easily recognizable because the dominant plant species are familiar shrubs and small trees: oaks (*Quercus*), junipers (*Juniperus*), and pinyon pines (*Pinus*). Characteristic birds include Black-throated Gray Warbler, Canyon Wren, Pinyon Jay, Acorn Woodpecker, Canyon Towhee, Ash-throated Flycatcher, Black-billed Magpie, Gray Vireo, and Common Bushtit.

California Mediterranean Scrub and Oak Woodland

Neither wet enough to be a forest nor arid enough to be a desert, the scrub and oak woodlands of California's coast and foothills are unique in North America. Similar associations are found in the Mediterranean region, hence the name, as well as in Chile, South Africa, and Australia.

There are three major types of Mediterranean scrub or chaparral in southern California: (1) Coastal Sage, (2) Dry Chaparral, and (3) Montane Chaparral. Coastal sage is a low, dense, fragrant scrub dominated by sagebrush (*Salvia*) and wild buckwheat (*Eriogonum*). It is home to the California Gnatcatcher, Wrentit, California Thrasher, Rufous-crowned Sparrow, Chestnut-backed Chickadee, Pacific-slope Flycatcher, Nuttall's Woodpecker, and Hutton's Vireo.

Chamise (*Adenostoma*) and wild lilac (*Ceanothus*) dominate dry chaparral. Some typical birds are California Quail, Bewick's Wren, California Towhee, Lazuli Bunting, Anna's Hummingbird, MacGillivray's Warbler, and Sage Sparrow.

Montane Chaparral is found at higher elevations of four thousand to nine thousand feet and is dominated by manzanita (*Arctostaphylos*), chinquapin (*Castanopsis*), and wild lilac (*Ceanothus*). Birds include Green-tailed Towhee, Black-chinned Sparrow, Mountain Quail, Fox Sparrow, Black-throated Gray Warbler, and Dusky Flycatcher.

Oak Woodland is found mostly on the northern and eastern slopes of the California Coastal Ranges and often more or less intergrades with chaparral habitats. Evergreen oaks such as California live oak (*Quercus agrifolia*) and interior live oak (*Quercus wislizenii*) dominate the lower, hotter, drier portions of this habitat. At moister, higher elevations, California black oaks (*Quercus keloggii*) and blue oaks (*Quercus douglasii*) are dominant, intergrading with pines at the upper end of their elevational range. Birds of the oak woodlands include Bushtit, House Wren, Acorn Woodpecker, Band-tailed Pigeon, Western Scrub-Jay, Red-shouldered Hawk, Oak Titmouse, Warbling Vireo, Black-headed Grosbeak, and Western Wood-Pewee.

Figure 7. California Mediterranean Scrub and Oak Woodland Habitat. Endangered California Gnatcatchers share dwindling coastal scrub habitat with wealthy landowners on California's Palos Verdes Peninsula. Other species that can be found here include Allen's Hummingbird, Marsh Wren, Bewick's Wren, and California Towhee.

Riparian Scrub and Woodland

This designation contains a wide variety of different plant associations whose principal shared characteristic is their restriction to the borders of water courses. Human land use has been hard on these habitat types. Damming, channeling, cutting, polluting, and replacement of native species with exotics like salt cedar (*Tamarix*) make native riparian zones among the most endangered of Southwestern plant communities, along with birds such as Bell's Vireo and other animals that live in them. Somewhat arbitrarily, I have subdivided this grouping into two main categories: (1) Desert Wash, and (2) Riparian Woodland. Desert wash is characterized by shrubs and low trees, greener (in season) and at higher density than is seen in surrounding desert habitats. Typical wash plant species include honey mesquite (*Prosopis glandulosa*), acacias (*Acacia*), and paloverdes (*Cercidium*). Birds include Gambel's Quail, Black-chinned Hummingbird, Ladder-backed Woodpecker, Bullock's Oriole, Black-tailed Gnatcatcher, and Crissal Thrasher. In some

Figure 8. Riparian Scrub and Woodland Habitat. In addition to regular summer residents like the Thick-billed Kingbird, Swainson's Hawk, Mississippi Kite, and Vermilion Flycatcher, the Patagonia-Sonoita Reserve has been a good location for finding Mexican rarities such as Green Kingfishers and Gray Hawks.

areas, drainages have created broad floodplains that are inundated at least once or twice every few years, and in these areas there can be extensive growths of desert wash–type habitat known as "bosques" (literally, "woods" in Spanish). The once–extensive mesquite stands along the Gila River south of Phoenix represented such a bosque.

There is no sharp division between what constitutes a wash versus what can be classified as riparian woodland. The principal difference is that more water for longer periods produces more plants of greater stature in riparian woodland. Thus, intermittent streams have wash–type growth, while woodlands or even gallery forests border more permanent flows. Trees such as cottonwoods (*Populus*), sycamores (*Plantanus*), willows (*Salix*), and alders (*Alnus*) characterize riparian woodlands in the Southwest. Similar in structure in some respects to broadleaf forests, these habitats attract many species of songbirds that breed in the deciduous and mixed broadleaf forests of northern and eastern North America. This is especially true in eastern and central New Mexico where Broad-winged Hawk, Ovenbird, American Redstart, Least Flycatcher, Red-eyed Vireo, Black-throated Blue Warbler, and Tennessee Warbler can be found on late-April to early-May migrations.

Highland Coniferous and Mixed Coniferous/Deciduous Forest

John Muir found the coniferous forest of the southwestern mountains to be a religious experience, "The horizon is bounded and adorned by a spiry wall of pines, every tree harmoniously related to every other; definite symbols, divine hieroglyphics written with sunbeams" (Muir 1911). Many others have found the cool, scented air, lofty trees, and deep blue skies similarly inspiring. There are four principal habitat divisions in the region: (1) Transitional Zone, (2) Canadian Zone, (3) Hudsonian Zone, and (4) Arctic or Alpine Zone.

The transitional zone is seven thousand to eight thousand feet, down to four thousand feet on the wetter, western slopes of the Sierras. Its dominant plant species is the ponderosa pine (*Pinus ponderosa*) throughout most of the Southwest, though in the Sierras there are also white fir (*Abies concolor*) and, in some areas,

Figure 9. Highland Coniferous and Mixed Coniferous/Deciduous Forest Habitat. Sequoia National Park, California, is a revelation to many. Like stars in the desert night, Sequoias dwarf human experience. Specialties of the park include Blue Grouse, Pileated Woodpecker, Winter Wren, and Hermit Warbler.

giant sequoia (*Sequoiadendron giganteum*). Birds found here include Northern Goshawk, Spotted Owl, Rufous Hummingbird, Lewis' Woodpecker, Hammond's Flycatcher, Steller's Jay, Virginia's Warbler, and Hepatic Tanager.

The Canadian zone is eight thousand to nine thousand feet, down to six thousand feet in the Sierras. The zone's dominant trees are douglas fir (*Pseudotsuga*) and aspen (*Populus*), though on the western slope of the Sierras, red fir (*Abies magnifica*) and lodgepole pine (*Pinus contorta*) are dominants. Characteristic birds include Northern Saw-whet Owl, Broad-tailed Hummingbird, Williamson's Sapsucker, Gray Jay, Mountain Chickadee, Hermit Thrush, Ruby-crowned Kinglet, Pine Siskin, and Red Crossbill.

The Hudsonian zone is nine thousand to ten thousand feet, down to eight thousand feet in the Sierras. Dominant trees are spruce (*Picea*) and fir (*Abies*) and in some areas, bristlecone pine (*Pinus aristata*). In the Sierras, the dominants are mountain hemlock (*Tsuga mertensia*), lodgepole pine, limber pine (*Pinus flexilis*), and whitebark pine (*Pinus albicaulis*). Typical birds in this habitat are Blue Grouse, Calliope Hummingbird, Olive-sided Flycatcher, Clark's Nutcracker, Red-breasted Nuthatch, Swainson's Thrush, Townsend's Warbler, and Cassin's Finch.

The arctic or alpine zone is above ten thousand feet. Conditions here above the tree line are harsh most of the year. Lichens, mosses, grasses, and small shrubs of the tundra are the predominant cover types during August and September when the snow cover is reduced. Birds of this habitat are Common Raven, American Pipit, and Brown-capped Rosy Finch.

Agriculture/Residential

Unfortunately, many of the beautiful, bizarre, and distinctive areas of the Southwest have been converted to agriculture or residential habitats. These habitats share common species in many parts of the world, such as European Starlings, House Sparrows, and Rock Doves. Still, there are some species native to the region's grasslands, savannas, and woodlands that also are found in such improved or altered environments. Representatives include White-tailed Kite, Loggerhead Shrike, Inca Dove, House Finch, Killdeer, Common Nighthawk, Horned Lark, Northern Mockingbird, and many hummingbird species where there are feeders or flowers.

There are three additional habitat types found in the Southwest that, while restricted in distribution, are nonetheless significant in their distinctiveness. Shinnery Oak is a shrub–dominated type found in eastern New Mexico's Canadian River valley. Pine-Cypress Forest is found along the California coast at the south end of Monterrey Bay and north of San Luis Obispo. Redwood Forest is in the Big Sur area of the southern California coast.

Figure 10. Agriculture/Residential Habitat. Ploughed fields outside Lenmore, California, appear pretty desolate baking in the mid-day sun. Still, Horned Larks, pipits, and other open-country species can be found in this generic habitat during the proper season.

Migratory Movements

Ninety species of birds occur in the Southwest, principally or solely as transients en route to breeding or wintering areas. The majority of these birds breed in the northwest portion of the continent and winter in Mexico or the Pacific slope of Central America. Typical of these species are the Western Tanager, Virginia's Warbler, and Rufous Hummingbird. However, the outside edge of the main migration routes of eastern North America touches the eastern portions of the Southwest as well. In places like Carlsbad Caverns National Park and woodlands along the lower Pecos River valley in southeastern New Mexico, you can find such eastern rarities as Ovenbirds, Magnolia Warblers, Chestnut-sided Warblers, Black-throated Green Warblers, Hooded Warblers, and Northern Waterthrushes.

It has been well known since at least the early 1900s (Cooke 1915) that the Gulf of Mexico exerts a major influence on routes taken by long-distance migrants in eastern North America. The Southwest's extremes of elevation, climate, and habitat likely exert a similar influence on the routes migrants take across the region.

However, very little has been done to determine the shapes of migration routes in the region. One exception is the excellent summary reported by Phillips et al. (1964:63–64) in which they describe the elliptical migration route followed by the Rufous Hummingbird, which is an easterly route in fall across New Mexico and eastern Arizona, and a westerly route in spring, across western Arizona and California. Many other species that migrate across the Southwest likely follow different routes in fall and spring to take advantage of prevailing winds, avoid harsh mountain or desert barriers, or exploit seasonally available resources, but documentation of such changes has yet to be made for most species.

The Pacific Ocean also plays a major role in shaping migration routes. It is a barrier to many species, causing large numbers to collect along the shore and follow the coastline in both fall and spring. As a result, these areas are excellent places for viewing migrating herons, egrets, waterfowl, shorebirds, and hawks as they parallel the coastline on their migratory flights. Often hundreds or thousands of birds will pass along the beaches or just offshore during the course of a single day during peak migratory periods. Young songbirds lacking experience in preparation and navigation also back up in coastal habitats during migration.

For other species, the eastern Pacific is an important pathway. Major seabird migrations brush the Pacific coast and can be viewed from such places as Goleta Point in Santa Barbara and La Jolla in San Diego.

Using the Guide

Each account begins with the species' common name followed by the scientific name in italics. Nomenclature follows the American Ornithologists' Union Checklist, 7th Edition (1998). The size of the bird is given in parentheses—L = length from tip of the bill to tip of the tail in inches, W = wingspread in inches. A description of the adult male breeding plumage follows. Other plumages are described where necessary. In most cases, the juvenile plumage (immediate post-fledging period) is not described since an adult is usually in attendance. Immature (First Basic, i.e., first winter after hatching), female, and other plumages are described when they differ significantly from the breeding male. The plumage description necessarily involves the use of a few arcane morphological terms. These areas of the bird are shown in figure 11. At least one photo depicting each species is provided. While photos can be misleading in terms of plumage coloration, they capture an essence of the way the bird carries itself that is peculiar to that particular species, which is difficult to capture in a painting. In addition, photos often place the bird in a fairly typical environment.

Habits—This category is included only when some peculiarity of the bird's behavior can be useful in identifying the species, e.g., "hangs upside down while foraging," or "flicks tail."

Voice—This section usually consists of two parts: (1) description of the song, which often is given only by the male during the breeding season, and (2) the call, which normally is given by both sexes at any time during the year. A typical song is described based on field notes, recorded songs, or, where necessary, descriptions in the literature (author credited). It should be remembered that songs vary among regions and among individuals. Also, one person's interpretation of what a song sounds like will differ from another's. To some people "chip" is "ship" or "tschip" or "slip," etc.

Similar Species—This category is omitted unless there is a bird similar in size, pattern, and coloration.

Habitat—Those habitats most often used by the bird in the Southwest and on its North American breeding grounds are given here. No attempt is made to describe tropical habitats used by birds when they are away from our region. Transients are found in a variety of habitats in which they would not normally forage,

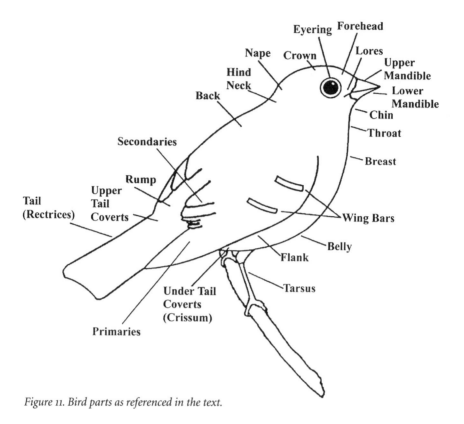

Eyering Forehead

Nape Crown

Lores

Upper
Mandible

Hind
Neck

Lower
Mandible

Back

Chin

Throat

Breast

Secondaries

Rump

Upper
Tail
Coverts

Tail
(Rectrices)

Wing Bars

Belly

Flank

Under Tail
Coverts
(Crissum)

Tarsus

Primaries

Figure 11. Bird parts as referenced in the text.

and no attempt is made to catalog all such habitats. A discussion of major Southwest habitat types, their appearance, characteristics, and location in the region is provided in the special section on habitats of the Southwest.

Abundance and Distribution—The abundance, principal time of occurrence and place of occurrence for the bird in the Southwest are presented here. Normally, only regular (common, uncommon, rare) occurrences of the bird within the region are reported. As an example, the Ovenbird is a rare transient in eastern New Mexico and casual or accidental elsewhere in the region. Only its status in New Mexico is provided. For more detailed distribution information, see specific, state-wide summaries, e.g., Ligon (1961) for New Mexico; Monson and Phillips (1981) for Arizona; Alcorn (1988) for Nevada; and Garrett and Dunn (1981) for southern California. If the species is known to have bred in the region, an asterisk (*) is shown following the bird's residency status.

The meaning of the abundance categories used are as follows:

COMMON—Ubiquitous in specified habitat; high probability of finding several individuals in a day.

UNCOMMON—Present in specified habitat; high probability of finding at least one individual in a day.

RARE—Scarce in specified habitat, with only a few records per season; low probability of finding the bird.

CASUAL—A few records per decade.

ACCIDENTAL—Not expected to recur.

HYPOTHETICAL—Recorded for the region, but not accepted by the state records committees.

Where to Find—In this section at least one locality from each of the four states represented is provided whenever possible. In selecting these localities, I have leaned heavily on the various bird-finding guides for the region. The reader should consult these guides to obtain further information on the best places to find birds, which may have ten or fifteen widely distributed localities where a bird may be found in a given state. The principal sources for bird-finding sites are listed below and in the bibliography:

Figure 12. Offshore islands, like Santa Catalina, provide nesting habitat for several pelagic species including Xantus's Murrelet, Brown Pelican, Tufted Puffin, and Cassin's Auklet. Boat trips to the islands can be productive for shearwaters, petrels, albatrosses, and other birds of the open ocean.

Figure 13. Nearly every species of waterbird recorded for the Southwest's interior has been found in the ponds and flooded fields of Bosque del Apache National Wildlife Refuge along the Rio Grande in central New Mexico. Regular visitors during spring and fall migration include bitterns, night herons, egrets, Common Snipe, American Avocet, Ross' Goose, and Wilson's Phalarope. Bald Eagles, Sandhill Cranes, and a few Whooping Cranes (from the U.S. Fish and Wildlife Service's cross-fostering program) can be found in winter.

Southern California—Holt (1990); Childs (1993); Garrett and Dunn (1981)
Arizona—McMillon (1995); Monson and Phillips (1981)
Southeastern Arizona—Taylor (1995); Edison et al. (1995)
New Mexico—Zimmerman et al. (1992)
Southern Nevada—Titus (1991)

Not all of the locality information used in this book was derived from these sources. With the exception of Titus, which is mainly a checklist, all of these books have extensive information on exactly where and when to go to find most of the species that occur in the regions that they cover, and how to get there. Hunting down specialties and rarities using these guides can be challenging, exciting, and fun. The intrepid bird seeker should be advised, however, that Southwestern terrain can be unforgiving. Blizzards in the highlands, flash floods in the deserts, and breakdowns anywhere in the back country can be life-threatening if you are not prepared.

When considering localities for listing in this guide, I have attempted to choose those that are well-known public-use areas requiring relatively little familiarity with the region to locate. However, this procedure has not been possible always and there are some localities listed that will require fairly adventurous navigating.

There also is no guarantee the bird will be there when you arrive. In most cases, I have tried to pinpoint the best places to find the bird. However, there are many species that simply are not found anywhere with any degree of regularity, and even in well-known regions there are places that have escaped the notice of bird watchers.

Some species are ubiquitous. There is an old story about a bird-watching newspaper columnist who, when called and asked, "What's this bird in my yard?" answered, "House Sparrow." Good guess. Some birds are almost everywhere, but for most species, you will have a much better chance of finding them if you are given a particular place.

Range—Total world range of the bird is provided in abbreviated form, based on information from the A.O.U. Checklist, 7th Edition (1998).

Color Plates

1. Red-throated Loon

2. Pacific Loon

3. Common Loon

4. Pied-billed Grebe

5. Horned Grebe

6. Eared Grebe

7. Western Grebe

8. Clark's Grebe

9. Black-footed Albatross

10. Pink-footed Shearwater

11. Flesh-footed Shearwater

12. Sooty Shearwater

13. Short-tailed Shearwater

14. Leach's Storm-Petrel

15. Ashy Storm-Petrel

16. Black Storm-Petrel

17. American White Pelican

18. Brown Pelican

19. Brandt's Cormorant

20. Neotropic Cormorant

21. Double-crested Cormorant

22. Pelagic Cormorant

23. American Bittern

24. Least Bittern

25. Great Blue Heron

26. Great Egret

27. Snowy Egret

28. Little Blue Heron

29. Cattle Egret

30. Green Heron

31. Black-crowned Night Heron

32. White-faced Ibis

33. Wood Stork

34. Black Vulture

35. Turkey Vulture

36. California Condor

37. Black-bellied Whistling-Duck

38. Fulvous Whistling-Duck

39. Greater White-fronted Goose

40. Snow Goose

41. Ross' Goose

42. Canada Goose

43. Brant

44. Tundra Swan

46. Gadwall

45. Wood Duck

47. Eurasian Wigeon

48. American Wigeon

49. Mallard

50. Blue-winged Teal

51. Cinnamon Teal

52. Northern Shoveler

53. Northern Pintail

54. Green-winged Teal

55. Canvasback

56. Redhead

57. Ring-necked Duck

58. Greater Scaup

59. Lesser Scaup

60. Surf Scoter

61. White-winged Scoter

62. Black Scoter

63. Bufflehead

64. Common Goldeneye

65. Barrow's Goldeneye

66. Hooded Merganser

67. Common Merganser

68. Red-breasted Merganser

69. Ruddy Duck

70. Osprey

71. White-tailed Kite

72. Mississippi Kite

73. Bald Eagle

74. Northern Harrier

75. Sharp-skinned Hawk

76. Cooper's Hawk

77. Northern Goshawk

78. Gray Hawk

79. Common Black-Hawk

80. Harris's Hawk

81. Red-shouldered Hawk

82. Swainson's Hawk

83. Zone-tailed Hawk

84. Red-tailed Hawk

85. Ferruginous Hawk

86. Rough-legged Hawk

87. Golden Eagle

88. Crested Caracara

89. American Kestrel

90. Merlin

91. Aplomado Falcon

92. Peregrine Falcon

93. Prairie Falcon

94. Ring-necked Pheasant

95. Sage Grouse

96. White-tailed Ptarmigan

97. Blue Grouse

98. Lesser Prairie-Chicken

99. Wild Turkey

100. Mountain Quail

101. Scaled Quail

102. California Quail

103. Gambel's Quail

104. Northern Bobwhite

105. Montezuma Quail

106. Black Rail

107. Clapper Rail

108. Virginia Rail

109. Sora

110. Common Moorhen

111. American Coot

112. Sandhill Crane

113. Black-bellied Plover

114. American Golden-Plover

115. Pacific Golden-Plover

116. Snowy Plover

117. Semipalmated Plover

118. Killdeer

119. Mountain Plover

120. American Black Oystercatcher

121. Black-necked Stilt

122. American Avocet

123. Greater Yellowlegs

124. Lesser Yellowlegs

125. Solitary Sandpiper

126. Willet

127. Wandering Tattler

128. Spotted Sandpiper

129. Upland Sandpiper

130. Whimbrel

131. Long-billed Curlew

132. Marbled Godwit

133. Ruddy Turnstone

134. Black Turnstone

135. Surfbird

136. Red Knot

137. Sanderling

138. Semipalmated Sandpiper

139. Western Sandpiper

140. Least Sandpiper

141. Baird's Sandpiper

142. Pectoral Sandpiper

143. Dunlin

144. Stilt Sandpiper

145. Short-billed Dowitcher

146. Long-billed Dowitcher

147. Common Snipe

148. Wilson's Phalarope

149. Red-necked Phalarope

150. Red Phalarope

151. Pomarine Jaeger

152. Parasitic Jaeger

153. Laughing Gull

154. Franklin's Gull

155. Bonaparte's Gull

156. Heerman's Gull

157. Mew Gull

158. Ring-billed Gull

159. California Gull

160. Herring Gull

161. Thayer's Gull

162. Yellow-footed Gull

163. Western Gull

164. Glaucous-winged Gull

165. Glaucous Gull

166. Sabine's Gull

167. Black-legged Kittiwake

168. Gull-billed Tern

169. Caspian Tern

170. Royal Tern

171. Elegant Tern

172. Common Tern

173. Arctic Tern

174. Forster's Tern

175. Least Tern

176. Black Tern

177. Black Skimmer

178. Common Murre

179. Xantus's Murrelet

180. Craveri's Murrelet

181. Ancient Murrelet

182. Cassin's Auklet

183. Rhinoceros Auklet

184. Tufted Puffin

185. Rock Dove

186. Band-tailed Pigeon

187. White-winged Dove

188. Mourning Dove

189. Inca Dove

190. Common Ground-Dove

191. Yellow-billed Cuckoo

192. Greater Roadrunner

193. Barn Owl

194. Flammulated Owl

195. Western Screech-Owl

196. Whiskered Screech-Owl

197. Great Horned Owl

198. Northern Pygmy-Owl

199. Ferruginous Pygmy-Owl

200. Elf Owl

201. Burrowing Owl

202. Spotted Owl

203. Long-eared Owl

204. Short-eared Owl

205. Northern Saw-whet Owl

206. Lesser Nighthawk

207. Common Nighthawk

208. Common Poorwill

209. Buff-collared Nightjar

210. Whip-poor-will

211. Black Swift

212. Chimney Swift

213. Vaux's Swift

214. White-throated Swift

215. Broad-billed Hummingbird

216. White-eared Hummingbird

217. Violet-crowned Hummingbird

218. Blue-throated Hummingbird

219. Magnificient Hummingbird

220. Lucifer Hummingbird

221. Black-chinned Hummingbird

222. Anna's Hummingbird

223. Costa's Hummingbird

224. Calliope Hummingbird

225. Broad-tailed Hummingbird

226. Rufous Hummingbird

227. Allen's Hummingbird

228. Elegant Trogon

229. Belted Kingfisher

230. Green Kingfisher

231. Lewis's Woodpecker

232. Red-headed Woodpecker

233. Acorn Woodpecker

234. Gila Woodpecker

235. Williamson's Sapsucker

236. Red-naped Sapsucker

237. Red-breasted Sapsucker

238. Ladder-backed Woodpecker

239. Nuttall's Woodpecker

240. Downy Woodpecker

241. Hairy Woodpecker

242. Strickland's Woodpecker

243. White-headed Woodpecker

244. Three-toed Woodpecker

245. Black-backed Woodpecker

246. Northern Flicker

247. Pileated Woodpecker

248. Northern Beardless-Tyrranulet

249. Olive-sided Flycatcher

250. Greater Pewee

251. Western Wood-Pewee

252. Willow Flycatcher

253. Least Flycatcher

254. Hammond's Flycatcher

255. Gray Flycatcher

256. Dusky Flycatcher

257. Pacific-slope Flycatcher

258. Cordilleran Flycatcher

259. Buff-breasted Flycatcher

260. Black Phoebe

261. Eastern Phoebe

262. Say's Phoebe

263. Vermillion Flycatcher

264. Dusky-capped Flycatcher

265. Ash-throated Flycatcher

266. Brown-crested Flycatcher

267. Sulphur-bellied Flycatcher

268. Tropical Kingbird

269. Cassin's Kingbird

270. Thick-billed Kingbird

271. Western Kingbird

272. Eastern Kingbird

273. Scissor-tailed Flycatcher

274. Rose-throated Becard

275. Loggerhead Shrike

276. Northern Shrike

277. Bell's Vireo

278. Gray Vireo

279. Plumbeous Vireo

280. Cassin's Vireo

281. Hutton's Vireo

282. Warbling Vireo

283. Red-eyed Vireo

284. Gray Jay

285. Steller's Jay

286. Blue Jay

287. Western Scrub-Jay

288. Mexican Jay

289. Pinyon Jay

290. Clark's Nutcracker

291. Black-billed Magpie

292. Yellow-billed Magpie

293. American Crow

294. Chihuahuan Raven

295. Common Raven

296. Horned Lark

297. Purple Martin

298. Tree Swallow

299. Violet-green Swallow

300. Northern Rough-winged Swallow

301. Bank Swallow

302. Cliff Swallow

303. Cave Swallow

304. Barn Swallow

305. Black-capped Chickadee

306. Mountain Chickadee

307. Mexican Chickadee

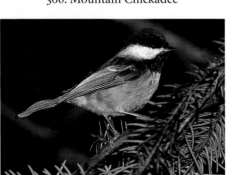

308. Chestnut-backed Chickadee

309. Bridled Titmouse

310. Oak Titmouse

311. Juniper Titmouse

312. Verdin

313. Bushtit

314. Red-breasted Nuthatch

315. White-breasted Nuthatch

316. Pygmy Nuthatch

317. Brown Creeper

318. Cactus Wren

319. Rock Wren

320. Canyon Wren

321. Bewick's Wren

322. House Wren

323. Winter Wren

324. Marsh Wren

325. American Dipper

326. Golden-crowned Kinglet

327. Ruby-crowned Kinglet

328. Blue-gray Gnatcatcher

329. California Gnatcatcher

330. Black-tailed Gnatcatcher

331. Eastern Bluebird

332. Western Bluebird

333. Mountain Bluebird

334. Townsend's Solitaire

335. Veery

336. Swainson's Thrush

337. Hermit Thrush

338. American Robin

339. Varied Thrush

340. Wrentit

341. Gray Catbird

342. Northern Mockingbird

343. Sage Thrasher

344. Brown Thrasher

345. Bendire's Thrasher

346. Curve-billed Thrasher

347. California Thrasher

348. Crissal Thrasher

349. LeConte's Thrasher

350. European Starling

351. American Pipit

352. Sprague's Pipit

353. Bohemian Waxwing

354. Cedar Waxwing

355. Phainopepla

356. Olive Warbler

357. Tennessee Warbler

358. Orange-crowned Warbler

359. Nashville Warbler

360. Virginia's Warbler

361. Lucy's Warbler

362. Yellow Warbler

363. Yellow-rumped Warbler

364. Black-throated Gray Warbler

365. Black-throated Green Warbler

366. Townsend's Warbler

367. Hermit Warbler

368. Grace's Warbler

369. Black-and-white Warbler

370. American Redstart

371. Ovenbird

372. Northern Waterthrush

373. MacGillivray's Warbler

374. Common Yellowthroat

375. Wilson's Warbler

376. Red-faced Warbler

377. Painted Redstart

378. Yellow-breasted Chat

379. Hepatic Tanager

380. Summer Tanager

381. Western Tanager

382. Green-tailed Towhee

383. Spotted Towhee

384. Canyon Towhee

385. California Towhee

386. Abert's Towhee

387. Rufous-winged Sparrow

388. Cassin's Sparrow

389. Botteri's Sparrow

390. Rufous-crowned Sparrow

391. Five-striped Sparrow

392. American Tree Sparrow

393. Chipping Sparrow

394. Clay-colored Sparrow

395. Brewer's Sparrow

396. Field Sparrow

397. Black-chinned Sparrow

398. Vesper Sparrow

399. Lark Sparrow

400. Black-throated Sparrow

401. Sage Sparrow

402. Lark Bunting

403. Savannah Sparrow

404. Grasshopper Sparrow

405. Baird's Sparrow

406. Fox Sparrow

407. Song Sparrow

408. Lincoln's Sparrow

409. Swamp Sparrow

410. White-throated Sparrow

411. Harris's Sparrow

412. White-crowned Sparrow

413. Golden-crowned Sparrow

414. Dark-eyed Junco

415. Yellow-eyed Junco

416. McCown's Longspur

417. Lapland Longspur

418. Chestnut-collared Longspur

419. Northern Cardinal

420. Pyrrhuloxia

421. Rose-breasted Grosbeak

422. Black-headed Grosbeak

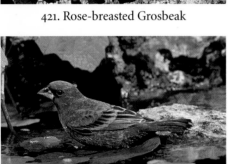

423. Blue Grosbeak

424. Lazuli Bunting

425. Indigo Bunting

426. Varied Bunting

427. Painted Bunting

428. Dickcissel

429. Red-winged Blackbird

430. Tricolored Blackbird

431. Eastern Meadowlark

432. Western Meadowlark

433. Yellow-headed Blackbird

434. Brewer's Blackbird

435. Common Grackle

436. Great-tailed Grackle

437. Bronzed Cowbird

438. Brown-headed Cowbird

439. Orchard Oriole

440. Hooded Oriole

441. Baltimore Oriole

442. Bullock's Oriole

443. Scott's Oriole

444. Gray-crowned Rosy-finch

445. Brown-capped Rosy-Finch

446. Pine Grosbeak

447. Purple Finch

448. Cassin's Finch

449. House Finch

450. Red Crossbill

451. Pine Siskin

452. Lesser Goldfinch

453. Lawrence's Goldfinch

454. American Goldfinch

455. Evening Grosbeak

456. House Sparrow

Species Accounts

Order Gaviiformes
Family Gaviidae
Loons
Mallard-sized or somewhat larger waterbirds with tapered body and chisel-shaped bill. Legs set far back for swimming and diving. Awkward on land, they require considerable flapping and running on water to become airborne. In flight, rapid wing beats, hump-backed silhouette, and feet extending beyond tail are characteristic.

1. Red-throated Loon
Gavia stellata (L—25 W—42)
Black mottled with gray on back; gray, rounded head; gray neck

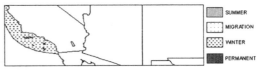

striped with white on nape; rufous throat; red eye; white below with barring on flanks; relatively thin, slightly upturned bill. *Winter:* Black back with indistinct white spots; head grayish with some white below eye; throat and underparts white. *Similar Species:* White spotting on black back; lack of white patch on flank; thin, upturned bill and usual upward tilt of head separate this bird from other winter loons. *Habitat:* Marine, bays, lakes, rivers. *Abundance and Distribution:* A fairly common winter visitor (Nov.–Mar.) and occasional summer vagrant along the coast in southern California; casual in winter on lakes and rivers elsewhere in the region. *Where to Find:* Ocean Beach County Park and Guadalupe Dunes County Park in southern California; Middle Rio Grande Conservancy District, New Mexico. *Range:* Breeds in the high arctic; winters in coastal temperate and boreal regions of the Northern Hemisphere.

2. Pacific Loon
Gavia pacifica (L—24 W—39)
Black back with barred white patches; head gray; purple throat

with white streaking on neck; white below with black streaks on flanks; red eye;

slim, pointed bill. *Winter:* Gray back, nape and crown; white throat and cheek with dark gray edging; often shows a grayish line across upper throat. *Similar Species:* Winter Pacific Loon has a dagger-shaped bill and holds head level, not upturned as in Red-throated Loon; also differs from Common and Red-throated loons by its white flank patch and lack of distinct white spotting on back. *Habitat:* Marine, bays, estuaries, large lakes, rivers. *Abundance and Distribution:* Uncommon winter visitor (Nov.–Mar.) mainly along coast; rare to casual at large, inland lakes and rivers; has occurred in summer. *Where to Find:* Upper Newport Bay in southern California; Lake Perris, California; Middle Rio Grande Conservancy District, New Mexico. *Range:* Breeds in high arctic; winters along boreal and temperate coasts of Northern Hemisphere, primarily along west coast in North America.

3. Common Loon
Gavia immer (L—31 W—54)
Checked black and white on back;
black head with a white streaked col-

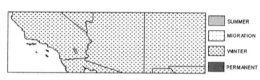

lar; white below with black streaking on breast and flanks; thick, heavy bill; red eye. *Winter:* Dark gray above; white below; dark gray crown and nape; white face and throat with a partial collar of white around neck. *Similar Species:* See Pacific Loon. *Habitat:* Marine, bays, lakes, rivers. *Abundance and Distribution:* Common winter visitor (Nov.–Mar.) mainly along coast; uncommon to rare at large, inland lakes and rivers; occasionally summers. *Where to Find:* Upper Newport Bay and Morro Bay in southern California; Middle Rio Grande Conservancy District, New Mexico; Havasu Lake, Arizona/California. *Range:* Breeds in northern North America south to northern United States; winters coastal North America and on large lakes inland south to Baja California, Sonora, and south Texas.

Order Podicipediformes
Family Podicipedidae
Grebes
Loon-like birds the size of a small to medium-sized duck; dagger-shaped bill and lobed toes are distinctive. Seldom seen in flight though most species are migratory.

4. Pied-billed Grebe
Podilymbus podiceps (L—13 W—22)
Grayish-brown body; short, pale bill
with dark black ring; black throat;

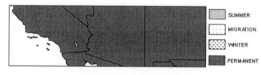

dark brown eye with white eyering. *Winter:* Whitish throat; no black ring on bill. *Juvenile:* Prominently striped in dark brown and white (Mar. to as late as Oct.).

Habits: This bird has the curious facility of sinking when disturbed. Carries newly hatched young on its back. *Voice:* A cuckoo-like "hoodoo hoo hoo hoo hoo kow kow kow kow." *Similar Species:* The dark eye and stubby, pale bill of the Pied-billed Grebe distinguish this bird from the smaller and extremely rare Least Grebe, which has a golden eye and thin, dark bill. The other grebes have relatively long, thin bills. *Habitat:* Ponds, lakes, swales, marshes, estuaries, bays. *Abundance and Distribution:* Uncommon resident* in southwestern California; summer resident* in the Sierras; winter resident along Colorado River and southern New Mexico and Arizona; transient throughout. *Where to Find:* Jackson Lake Refuge, New Mexico; Maitre Lake, Arizona; Lake Mead, Nevada; Upper Newport Bay, California (winter). *Range:* Breeds across most of Western Hemisphere from central Canada south to southern Argentina; West Indies; winters in temperate and tropical portions of breeding range.

5. Horned Grebe

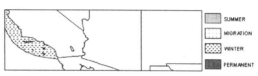

Podiceps auritus (L—14 W—23)
Dark back; rusty neck and sides; whitish breast; black head with buffy orange ear patch and eyebrow; red eye. *Winter:* Upper half of head dark with white spot in front of eye; cheek, throat and breast white; nape and back dark. *Similar Species:* Winter Horned Grebe has white cheek and neck not grayish as in Eared Grebe; also Horned Grebe has whitish spot in front of eye, which Eared Grebe lacks. Not all individuals of these two species are readily separable in winter plumage. *Habitat:* Bays, estuaries, larger lakes. *Abundance and Distribution:* Locally common (along coast) to rare (inland) transient and winter resident (Nov.–Mar.). *Where to Find:* Lake Perris State Recreation Area, California; Clayton Lake State Park, New Mexico; Lake Mead, Nevada; Goose Lake, Arizona/California. *Range:* Breeds in boreal and north temperate regions; winters mainly along coast in boreal and temperate regions of the Northern Hemisphere.

6. Eared Grebe

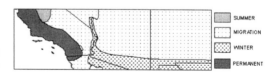

Podiceps nigricollis (L—12 W—22)
Dark back; black neck and rusty sides; whitish breast; black head with buffy orange ear tufts; red eye. *Winter:* Dark gray throughout except grayish chin and ear patch, whitish on breast and throat. *Voice:* "kip kip kip kuweep kuweep", etc. *Similar Species:* See Horned Grebe. *Habitat:* Lakes and ponds (breeding), bays, estuaries, larger lakes (winter). *Abundance and Distribution:* Common to uncommon winter resident (Nov.–Mar.), mainly along coast or on larger lakes; locally common summer resident* at highland lakes and ponds. *Where to Find:* Lake Mead, Nevada; Lake Perris State Recreation Area, California (winter); Goose Lake,

Arizona/California; Dulce Lake, New Mexico (summer); Salton Sea, California. *Range:* Breeds locally in southern boreal, temperate and tropical regions of the world; in North America mainly in west.

7. Western Grebe *Aechmophorus occidentalis* (L—25 W—34)
A very large, long-necked grebe; dark gray above, white below; front half

of neck and chin are white; back half of neck, face, and crown are dark gray; red eye; long, pointed, yellow-green bill. *Voice:* Two-note courtship call (single note in the similar Clark's Grebe). *Similar Species:* The Western Grebe has cheeks, lores, and superciliary stripe black not white as in Clark's Grebe, which was long considered a light color phase of the Western Grebe. Fall and winter birds can be difficult to separate. *Habitat:* Lakes, marshes; bays in winter. *Abundance and Distribution:* Transient throughout; common winter resident along the California coast, on larger lakes in California and western New Mexico, and along the Colorado River; local summer resident* in California on larger lakes and impoundments and on Lake Havasu along the Colorado River. *Where to Find:* Clayton Lake State Park, New Mexico; Havasu Lake, Arizona/California; Overton Wildlife Management Area, Nevada; Lake Elsinore, California (winter). *Range:* Breeds in central and southwestern Canada and western half of United States south to western Mexico; winters mainly along Pacific Coast from southwestern Canada to southern Mexico. Western Grebe is more common in northern and eastern portions of the range replaced by Clark's Grebe in southern and western portions.

8. Clark's Grebe
Aechmophorus clarkii (L—25 W—34)
Very similar to Western Grebe but lighter in color; bill yellow-orange:

superciliary stripe, lores, and cheeks white. *Voice:* Single-note courtship call. *Similar Species:* See Western Grebe. *Habitat:* See Western Grebe. *Abundance and Distribution:* See Western Grebe. *Where to Find:* Upper Newport Bay, California (winter); Lopez Lake County Park, California (winter); Salton Sea National Wildlife Refuge, California (breeding); Overton Wildlife Management Area, Nevada; Alamo Lake State Park, Arizona. *Range:* See Western Grebe.

Order Procellariiformes

Family Diomedeidae

Albatrosses

Large seabirds with exceptionally long, narrow wings, relatively short tail, heavy, hooked bill, and tubed nasal passages.

9. Black-footed Albatross

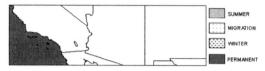

Phoebastria nigripes (L—32 W—89)
Mostly dark brown throughout; white at base of bill, under eye, and base of tail; white under-tail coverts and ventral area. *Immature:* White areas on adult can be grayish and indistinct or dark brown in immatures, perhaps depending on age. *Habits:* The long, hooked bill of albatrosses is an adaptation for grasping their principal prey—cephalopods (squids, octopuses, cuttlefish). *Similar Species:* This species is the only albatross seen regularly off the Pacific coast of the United States. *Habitat:* Pelagic. *Abundance and Distribution:* Rare offshore; most numerous in summer months (May–Aug.). *Where to Find:* Follows fishing boats and ships but seldom seen from shore. Boat trips to Channel Islands National Park provide the best chance to see pelagic species. Call the park headquarters in Ventura, California, for details. *Range:* Ranges over much of the northern Pacific Ocean; breeds in Hawaiian Islands, Marshall Islands, and other islands of the central and western Pacific.

Family Procellariidae

Shearwaters

Dove-sized seabirds with long, narrow wings, short legs and tail, tubed nose, and hooked bill; rapid fluttering flight with frequent glides.

10. Pink-footed Shearwater

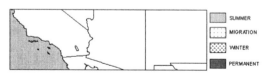

Puffinus creatopus (L—19 W—43)
Dark above; white below mottled with brown on flanks and underwing; pink feet; pink bill with dark tip. *Habits:* Flies with a measured wing beat and occasional glides; solitary or in mixed flocks with other species. *Similar Species:* White underparts and pink bill with dark tip are distinctive. *Habitat:* Pelagic. *Abundance and Distribution:* Common offshore in summer and fall (Jul–Oct.). *Where to Find:* Boat trips to Channel Islands National Park provide the best chance to see pelagic birds. Call the park headquarters in Ventura, California, for details.

Summer is the best time to find this species. *Range:* Breeds on islands of the southwestern Pacific off the coast of Chile during austral summer (Nov.–Jan.); migrates to northwestern Pacific for boreal summer.

11. Flesh-footed Shearwater
Puffinus carneipes (L—20 W—43)
Dark brown throughout; pink legs
and feet; pink bill with dark tip; pri-

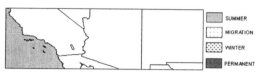

maries silvery from below. *Habits:* Alternately glides and flaps with slow, deep strokes; often occurs in loose flocks. *Similar Species:* Dark underparts, pinkish feet, pinkish bill with dark tip are distinctive. *Habitat:* Pelagic. *Abundance and Distribution:* Rare offshore—Apr. to Oct. *Where to Find:* Boat trips to Channel Islands National Park provide the best chance to see pelagic birds. Call the park headquarters in Ventura, California, for details. Summer is the best time to find this species. *Range:* Breeds on islands in the southern Pacific and Indian Oceans during the austral summer (Oct.–Mar.); migrates mainly into the northern Pacific for the boreal summer.

12. Sooty Shearwater
Puffinus griseus (L—19 W—42)
Entirely dark gray except for paler
wing linings; dark bill and legs. *Hab-*

its: Flaps and glides like other shearwaters; when foraging, drops from a yard or so above the water, wings out; often in large, loose flocks. *Similar Species:* Long bill and pale wing linings contrasting with dark flight feathers separate the Sooty Shearwater from the nearly identical, but much rarer Short-tailed Shearwater, which usually has dark underwing linings (no contrast between wing lining and flight feathers). Also, peak numbers for the Short-tailed Shearwater occur from Nov. to Feb., not in summer. *Habitat:* Pelagic; coastal waters. *Abundance and Distribution:* Common in summer (Apr.–Sep.) offshore. *Where to Find:* Though the best chance to see these birds is on a boat trip, the Sooty Shearwater can be seen with a spotting scope in coastal waters from viewing spots like Guadalupe Dunes County Park, Ocean Beach County Park, and Montaña de Oro State Park where flocks numbering in the millions can sometimes be seen (Harrison 1983:260). *Range:* Breeds on islands near Cape Horn and New Zealand during austral summer (Oct.–Mar.); disperses widely across the oceans of the world during migration; spends boreal summer mainly in oceans of Northern Hemisphere.

13. Short-Tailed Shearwater

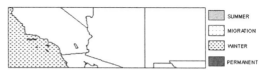

Puffinus tenuirostris (L—14 W—38)
Dark throughout, though slightly
paler below. *Similar Species:* See Sooty
Shearwater. *Habitat:* Pelagic. *Abundance and Distribution:* Rare in winter (Nov.–
Feb.) offshore. *Where to Find:* Boat trips to Channel Islands National Park provide
the best chance to see pelagic birds. Call the park headquarters in Ventura, California, for details. Winter (Nov.–Feb.) is the best time to find this species. This bird
occasionally can be seen from shore at spots like the Point La Jolla Lifeguard Station. *Range:* Breeds on islands off southern Australia (Sep.–Mar.); migrates north
to the northern Pacific in the Aleutian region during the non-breeding season.

Family Hydrobatidae
Storm-Petrels
Dark, swallow-like seabirds that feed by hopping and skipping over the waves.

14. Leach's Storm-Petrel

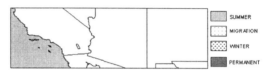

Oceanodroma leucorhoa
(L—8 W—19)
Dark gray; white rump with dark cen-
tral stripe; slightly forked tail. *Habits:* Flight is erratic, with sudden alterations of
speed and direction, low over water. *Similar Species:* Leach's Storm-Petrel has a dark
central stripe across the white rump band and slightly forked tail, which the extremely
rare Wilson's Storm-Petrel lacks. Also, these two species are quite different in behavior. The Leach's Storm-Petrel glides and darts erratically over the water surface while
the Wilson's Storm-Petrel skims and flutters, often dabbling feet in water. *Habitat:*
Pelagic. *Abundance and Distribution:* Uncommon offshore (June–Sep.). *Where to Find:*
Boat trips to Channel Islands National Park provide the best chance to see pelagic
birds. Call the park headquarters in Ventura, California, for details. Summer (June–
Sep.) is the best time to find this species. *Range:* Breeds on islands in the northern
Atlantic and Pacific oceans; winters in temperate and tropical seas of the world.

15. Ashy Storm-Petrel

Oceanodroma homochroa
(L—8 W—19)
Dark throughout; forked tail. *Habits:*
Fluttering flight with shallow wing beats. *Similar Species:* Feet do not extend beyond
tail in Ashy Storm-Petrel as they do in the larger and somewhat darker Black Storm-

Petrel. Shallow, fluttery wing beats of the Ashy contrast with deep, graceful strokes of the Black. *Habitat:* Pelagic; nests on offshore islands. *Abundance and Distribution:* Breeding colonies for this species are located on the Channel Islands off the southern California coast (egg dates from Jan. to June). Otherwise uncommon to rare offshore during the remainder of the year. *Where to Find:* Boat trips to Channel Islands National Park provide the best chance to see this bird. Call the park headquarters in Ventura, California, for details. Summer (May–Sep.) is the best time to find this species. *Range:* Apparently restricted to the northeastern Pacific. Principal breeding colonies are found along the California coast (Farallon Islands, Channel Islands).

16. Black Storm-Petrel

Oceanodroma melania (L—9 W—20) Dark throughout; forked tail; pale bar on upper wing surface. *Similar Spe-*

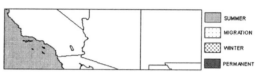

cies: See Ashy Storm-Petrel. *Habitat:* Pelagic; nests on offshore islands. *Abundance and Distribution:* Common to uncommon offshore in summer (May–Oct.). Breeding colonies for this species are located on the Channel Islands off the southern California coast (May–Oct.). *Where to Find:* Summer boat trips to Channel Islands National Park provide the best chance to see this bird. Call the park headquarters in Ventura, California, for details. *Range:* Breeds on islands in the northeastern Pacific, including several off the California Coast. Winters at sea in the southeastern Pacific.

Order Pelecaniformes
Family Pelecanidae
Pelicans
Extremely large, heavy-bodied water birds with long bill and gular pouch.

17. American White Pelican
Pelecanus erythrorhynchos
(L—62 W—105)
White body; black primaries and

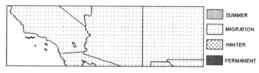

secondaries; enormous orange bill and gular pouch; often with a horn-like growth on upper mandible (breeding); orange-yellow feet. *Habits:* Does not dive from the air for fish like Brown Pelican. Forages by dipping for prey, often in groups. Migrates in large flocks. *Voice:* Various coughs and croaks. *Similar Species:* Immature Brown Pelicans can appear a dusty brownish-white, but the American White Pelican is bright white in all plumages. *Habitat:* Large lakes, impoundments. *Abun-*

dance and Distribution: Common to uncommon transient (Apr.–May; Aug.–Oct.); smaller numbers remain on lakes during summer and winter months; not known to breed in the region. *Where to Find:* Salton Sea, California; Havasu Lake, Arizona/ California; Lake Mead, Nevada; Bosque del Apache National Wildlife Refuge, New Mexico. *Range:* Breeds locally at large lakes and marshes in central and western Canada south through western half of the United States; winters southwestern United States to Nicaragua, and from Florida around the Gulf of Mexico to Yucatan.

18. Brown Pelican
Pelecanus occidentalis
(L—48 W—78) **Endangered**
Grayish above; brownish below with

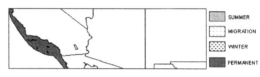

dark chestnut nape and neck; whitish head tinged with yellow; enormous bill and gular pouch. *Immature:* Entirely brownish-gray. *Habits:* Dives from a considerable height to catch fish. *Voice:* Occasional croaks. *Similar Species:* See American White Pelican. *Habitat:* Marine. *Abundance and Distribution:* Suffered serious declines in 1950's and 1960's but now uncommon and increasing permanent residents* along coast; breeds on Channel Islands; rare or casual inland at large lakes and impoundments. *Where to Find:* Shell Beach; Upper Newport Bay; Guadalupe Dunes County Park. *Range:* Coastal Western Hemisphere from North Carolina to eastern Brazil including West Indies in east and California to southern Chile in west.

Family Phalacrocoracidae
Cormorants
Dark water birds the size of a small goose with tapered body, long, hooked bill, small gular pouch, and webbed feet. They generally fly in small flocks with necks extended.

19. Brandt's Cormorant
Phalacrocorax penicillatus
(L—35 W—48)
Entirely black with an iridescent

green tinge; gular pouch blue; buff throat patch bordering pouch; long, sparse white plumes on head, neck, and back. *Winter:* White plumes lacking; gular pouch a brownish blue. *Immature:* Dark brown above, paler below; buffy throat. *Habits:* Often occurs in large flocks. *Similar Species:* Dark facial skin and gular pouch with buffy lining separate adult Brandt's from adult Double-crested and Pelagic cormorants, which have orange facial skin and pouch. Immature Brandt's is uniformly brown with pale throat; immature Double-crested is brown above with paler throat and breast; immature Pelagic is brown throughout. *Habitat:* Coastal marine; cliffs; rocky shores. *Abundance and Distribution:* Common resident* along coast; breeds (Mar.–Aug.) on Channel Islands and on rocky cliffs along shore. *Where to Find:* Shell Beach; Morro Rock (breeding); Point Fermin Park. *Range:* Resident along the west coast of North America from southeastern Alaska to Baja California; wanders south to Sinaloa during non-breeding season.

20. Neotropic Cormorant
Phalacrocorax brasilianus
(L—26 W—42)

Entirely black with an iridescent green tinge; gular pouch is yellowish tinged with greenish or brownish, edged in white feathers. *Immature:* Brownish; darker brown on back, wings and tail. *Voice:* An occasional croak. *Similar Species:* The smaller, more delicate Neotropic Cormorant has a relatively longer tail; it also has a yellowish gular pouch with a greenish or brownish tinge that ends in a point on the cheek; the gular pouch of the Double-crested Cormorant is orange-yellow and has a rounded edge. The gular pouch is edged with white feathers in adult Neotropic, but not in the Double-crested. *Habitat:* Rivers, ponds, lakes. *Abundance and Distribution:* Uncommon to rare resident* on ponds and lakes of southwestern New Mexico; rare or casual elsewhere in region. *Where to Find:* Bill Evans Lake; Bosque del Apache; Elephant Butte Reservoir. *Range:* Resident in lowlands from Texas, New Mexico, and northwestern Mexico south to southern South America; Cuba.

21. Double-crested Cormorant
Phalacrocorax auritus
(L—32 W—51)

Entirely iridescent black; whitish or dark ear tufts during breeding season; gular pouch of bare orange skin. *Immature:* Buffy head and neck. *Habits:* Forages by swimming low in water and diving for long periods. Sits on snags and posts with wings spread to dry. *Voice:* Various croaks. *Similar Species:* See Neotropic Cormorant. *Habitat:* Estuaries, marine, lakes, ponds. *Abundance and Distribution:* Common transient and winter resident (Oct.–Apr.) along coast and at large lakes and impoundments throughout; uncommon to rare summer resident*. *Where to Find:* Morro Bay (breeding), California; Lake Mead, Nevada; Havasu Lake and impoundments, Arizona/California; Bosque del Apache, New Mexico. *Range:* Breeds locally across central and southern Canada and northern and central United States, along both coasts from Alaska to southern Mexico on the west, and Newfoundland to east Texas on the east, also Cuba; winters in coastal breeding range to south Texas, Greater Antilles, Yucatan Peninsula, and Belize.

22. Pelagic Cormorant

Phalacrocorax pelagicus

(L—28 W—38)

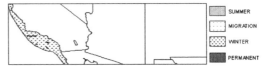

Body black with bright greenish
tinge; neck with purplish tinge and thin, white plumes; short, dark crests jut from
forehead and nape; facial skin and gular pouch bright orange; white flank patch.
Winter: Facial skin and pouch dull orange; lacks plumes and white flank patch.
Immature: Uniformly brown. *Similar Species:* Adult Pelagic in breeding plumage
has white flank patch, which Brandt's and Double-crested lack; in flight, the Pelagic holds head and neck straight, not crooked as in Double-crested and Brandt's;
head is noticeably smaller and bill is thinner in the Pelagic Cormorant than in the
larger Brandt's and Double-crested cormorants. Immature Pelagic is entirely brown;
Brandt's is brown with pale throat; immature Double-crested is brown above with
paler throat and breast. *Habitat:* Coastal marine; rocky shores, cliffs, breakwaters.
Abundance and Distribution: Uncommon winter resident along coast; rare in summer; breeds on Channel Islands (May–Aug.) and on rocky cliffs along shore. *Where
to Find:* Morro Rock (breeding); Cabrillo National Monument; Point Fermin Park.
Range: Breeds on islands and rocky coasts of the northern Pacific south to Japan
and California; winters mainly in breeding range.

Order Ciconiiformes

Family Ardeidae

Herons, Egrets, and Bitterns

Long-billed, long-necked, long-legged wading birds.

23. American Bittern

Botaurus lentiginosus (L—26 W—39)

A chunky, relatively short-legged
heron; buffy brown above and below
streaked with white and brown on throat, neck, and breast; dark brown streak on
side of neck; white chin; greenish-yellow bill and legs; yellow eyes. *Habits:* A very
secretive bird; often, rather than fly when approached, it will "freeze" with its neck
extended in an attempt to blend into the marsh reeds and rushes. *Voice:* A deep
"goonk glunk-a-lunk," like blowing on an empty soft drink bottle. *Similar Species:*
Could be mistaken for an immature night heron in flight, but dark brown primaries and secondaries contrast with light brown back and upper wing coverts; night
herons lack prominent dark streak on side of neck. *Habitat:* Marshes. *Abundance
and Distribution:* Uncommon to rare transient throughout; uncommon winter

Figure 14. Dulce Lake on the Jicarilla Apache Reservation in northwestern New Mexico is readily accessible from U.S. Highway 64, and a magnet for waterbirds, including White-faced Ibis, Canvasbacks, mergansers, and cormorants.

Figure 15. Lake Mead, which straddles the Arizona/Nevada border, is the largest human-made lake in the United States. Obviously, the open water provides habitat for ducks, geese, swans, cormorants, and the like. Less obvious is that, despite its generally sterile appearance, the hundreds of miles of shoreline provide a myriad of hidden wetland nooks and crannies ideal for many shorebirds, especially at times of low water.

resident (Sep.–Apr.) in California coastal region; uncommon to rare permanent resident* at Salton Sea, lower Colorado River valley, and in Rio Grande marshes; secretive habits and patchy distribution of wetland habitat in the desert Southwest make status of this species unclear over much of the region. *Where to Find:* Jackson Lake Refuge, New Mexico (breeding); Las Vegas Wash, Nevada (breeding); Buena Vista Lagoon, California (winter). *Range:* Breeds central and southern Canada south to southern United States and central Mexico; winters southern United States to southern Mexico and Cuba.

24. Least Bittern
Ixobrychus exilis (L—14 W—17)
A very small heron; dark brown with white streaking on back; tan wings,

head, and neck; dark brown crown; white chin and throat streaked with tan; white belly; yellowish legs and bill; yellow eyes; extended wings are half tan (basally) and half dark brown. *Habits:* Like the American Bittern, this bird will often "freeze" with neck extended when approached. *Voice:* A rapid, whistled "coo-co-co-co-coo." *Similar Species:* Immature Green Heron is heavily streaked below and lacks buff shoulders. *Habitat:* Marshes. *Abundance and Distribution:* Uncommon to rare transient (Mar–Apr., Sep.–Oct.) throughout; uncommon to rare permanent resident* in coastal southwestern California, Salton Sea, the Colorado valley of Arizona, California, Nevada, and elsewhere in marshes of the southern portions of the region. As with the American Bittern, the Least Bittern's secretive habits and the patchy distribution of its wetland habitat in the desert Southwest make its status unclear. *Where to Find:* Imperial National Wildlife Refuge, California/Arizona; Bosque del Apache, New Mexico. *Range:* Breeds in the eastern half of United States and southeastern Canada; locally in the western United States, south through lowlands to southern Brazil; West Indies; winters through breeding range from the southern United States southward.

25. Great Blue Heron
Ardea herodias (L—48 W—72)
A very large heron; slate gray above and on neck; white crown bordered

with black stripes that extend as plumes (breeding); white chin and throat streaked with black; gray breast and back plumes; white below streaked with chestnut; chestnut thighs; orange-yellow bill; dark legs. *Immature:* Dark cap; brownish-gray back; buffy neck. *White Phase:* Entirely white with yellow bill and legs; this phase is extremely rare except in southern Florida and the Caribbean. *Voice:* A low "krarrrk." *Habitat:* Lakes, rivers, marshes, bays, estuaries. *Abundance and Distribution:* Common permanent resident* in south; common summer resident* in northern portions, uncommon to rare in winter. *Where to Find:* Cibola National Wildlife Refuge, California; Hassayampa River Preserve, Arizona; Lake Mead, Nevada; Elephant Butte Reservoir, New Mexico. *Range:* Breeds from central and southern Canada south to coastal Colombia and Venezuela; West Indies; winters southern United States southward through breeding range.

26. Great Egret

Ardea alba (L—39 W—57)
Entirely white, with shaggy plumes on breast in breeding season; long, yellow bill; long, dark legs that extend well beyond tail in flight. *Voice:* Various "krrank"s and "krronk"s. *Similar Species:* The Great Egret has yellow bill and black legs; the smaller Snowy Egret has black bill, black legs, and yellow feet; immature Little Blue Heron has two-tone bill (dark tip, pale base), pale legs, and usually some gray smudging on white plumage; Cattle Egret is half the size; has short, thick yellow bill and yellowish legs that barely extend beyond tail in flight; rare white phase of Great Blue has yellow legs (not dark); white phase of the rare Reddish Egret has dark or two-tone bill (dark tip, pinkish base) and dark legs. *Habitat:* Lakes, ponds, rivers, marshes, estuaries, bays. *Abundance and Distribution:* Common resident* along lower Colorado River impoundments in Arizona/California and elsewhere in appropriate habitat in southern California; uncommon to rare and local resident* elsewhere in southern portions of the region; uncommon to rare transient (Mar–Apr., Sep.–Oct.) throughout. *Where to Find:* Bosque del Apache, New Mexico; Morro Bay, California; Imperial National Wildlife Refuge, California/Arizona. *Range:* Breeds in temperate and tropical regions of the world; winters mainly in subtropical and tropical portions of breeding range.

27. Snowy Egret

Egretta thula (L—23 W—45)
Small, entirely white heron; black legs with yellow feet; black bill; yellow lores; white plumes off neck and breast (breeding). *Immature:* Has yellow line up back of leg. *Habits:* Occasionally arches wings to form a canopy while foraging; also puts foot forward and shakes it on bottom substrate. *Voice:* A crow-like "caaah." *Similar Species:* See Great Egret. *Habitat:* Marshes, ponds, lakes, estuaries, bays. *Abundance and Distribution:* Common to uncommon resident* in southern California lowlands, the Colorado River valley, and Rio Grande impoundments; uncommon summer resident* (Apr.–Sep.) in southeastern Arizona and southwestern New Mexico; uncommon to rare transient (Mar–Apr., Sep.–Oct.) elsewhere.

Where to Find: Imperial National Wildlife Refuge, Arizona/California; Bosque del Apache, New Mexico. *Range:* Breeds locally across United States and extreme southern Canada south in lowlands to southern South America; West Indies; winters from coastal southern United States southward through breeding range.

28. Little Blue Heron

Egretta caerulea (L—23 W—39)
A smallish heron; dark blue body;
maroon neck and head; two-tone bill,

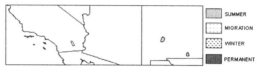

black at tip, pale gray or greenish at base; plumes on neck, breast and head; dark legs. *Winter:* Mainly navy blue on neck with maroon tinge; no plumes. *Immature:* Almost entirely white in first year with some gray smudging; greenish legs; two-tone bill; more smudging in second year. *Voice:* Pig-like squawks. *Similar Species:* See Great Egret. *Habitat:* Mainly inland marshes, lakes, ponds. *Abundance and Distribution:* Rare and local summer resident* in New Mexico; rare to casual postbreeding wanderer and transient (June–Sep.) elsewhere in the region. *Where to Find:* Laguna Grande, New Mexico; Bosque del Apache, New Mexico. *Range:* Breeds along coastal plain of eastern United States from Maine to Texas south through lowlands to Peru and southern Brazil; West Indies; winters from southern United States south through breeding range.

29. Cattle Egret

Bubulcus ibis (L—20 W—36)
A small, entirely white heron; yellow-
orange bill and legs; buff coloration

and plumes on crest, breast and back (breeding). *Immature:* Like adult but lacks buff coloration, and legs are dark. *Similar Species:* See Great Egret. *Habitat:* The Cattle Egret is not an aquatic species, though it occasionally nests on bay islands. It prefers savanna and grasslands where it feeds on insects, mainly grasshoppers. *Abundance and Distribution:* Common but local resident* in coastal southern California, Salton Sea, lower Colorado and Rio Grande valleys; rare transient and postbreeding wanderer elsewhere. *Where to Find:* Salton Sea National Wildlife Refuge, California; Bosque del Apache, New Mexico. *Range:* Once strictly an Old World species, the Cattle Egret appeared in South America in the late 1800's and has expanded steadily northward, reaching Texas in 1955. Current distribution includes most temperate and tropical regions of the world. Northern populations are migratory.

30. Green Heron

Butorides virescens (L—19 W—28)

A small, dark heron; olive back; black
cap; chestnut neck; white throat with

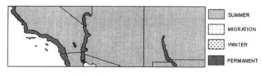

chestnut striping; yellow eye and yellow lores; white malar stripe; grayish belly; greenish legs; bill dark above, yellowish below. *Immature:* Heavily streaked below. *Habits:* Forages in a slow, deliberate manner. *Voice:* A loud "kyoook." *Similar Species:* Least Bittern is buffy, not dark, and has two-tone wings; Green Heron wings are uniformly dark in flight. *Habitat:* Streams, rivers, lakes, marshes. *Abundance and Distribution:* Uncommon resident* along coast, Salton Sea, Colorado and Rio Grande valleys, and southeastern Arizona; uncommon transient and summer resident* (Apr.–Oct.) elsewhere except in highlands where rare or absent. *Where to Find:* Bosque del Apache, New Mexico; Mittry Lake Wildlife Area, California; Lake Mead, Nevada. *Range:* Breeds from southern Canada south to northern Argentina (including Green-backed Heron form, *B. striatus*); absent from dryer plains and deserts; West Indies; winters from southern United States through breeding range.

31. Black-Crowned Night-Heron

Nycticorax nycticorax

(L—26 W—45)

A rather squat heron; black on back

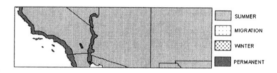

and crown with long, trailing white plumes (breeding); gray wings; pale gray breast and belly; white forehead, cheek and chin; red eye; dark beak; pale legs. *Immature:* Dark brown above, heavily streaked with white; whitish below streaked with brown; red eye; bluish lores; pale legs. *Habits:* Nocturnal. *Voice:* "kwark." *Similar Species:* Immature Yellow-crowned Night-Heron has longer legs that extend well beyond end of tail in flight; Blackcrown's legs barely reach beyond end of tail; also the Blackcrown is streaked on back, not spotted as in Yellowcrown. *Habitat:* Bays, lakes, marshes. *Abundance and Distribution:* Uncommon permanent resident* in coastal California, Salton Sea, and Colorado River valley; uncommon to rare transient and summer resident* (Mar.–Oct.) elsewhere. *Where to Find:* Imperial National Wildlife Refuge, Arizona/California; Bosque del Apache, New Mexico; Morro Bay, California; Roosevelt Lake, Arizona. *Range:* Breeds locally in temperate and tropical regions of the world; withdraws from seasonally cold portions of breeding range in winter.

Family Threskiornithidae
Ibises and Spoonbills
Ibises are small to medium-sized, heron-like birds with long, decurved bills.

32. White-faced Ibis

Plegadis chihi (L—22 W—36)
Body entirely dark purplish brown
with green sheen on wings and back;

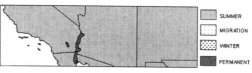

bare pinkish skin on face, edged with white feathers (present only briefly during height
of breeding); pale bill; pinkish legs; red eyes. *Immature:* Brownish throughout with
white streaking on head and neck; dark bill and legs. *Voice:* "kruk." *Similar Species:*
White-faced Ibis has pinkish loral skin, reddish legs and red eyes; extremely rare Glossy
Ibis has dark loral skin, dark legs, and brown eyes; immatures of these species are
indistinguishable in the field. *Habitat:* Bays, marshes, lakes, ponds. *Abundance and Dis-
tribution:* Uncommon permanent resident* along lower Colorado River impound-
ments and Salton Sea, California; common to uncommon transient (Apr.–June, Aug.–
Sep.) and local summer resident* elsewhere. *Where to Find:* Salton Sea, California;
Imperial Wildlife Refuge, Arizona/California; Dulce Lake, New Mexico; Lake Mead,
Nevada. *Range:* Breeds locally in western United States, and from south Texas through
Mexico and along the Pacific Coast to El Salvador, locally in north and south-central
South America; winters from southwestern United States south through breeding range.

Family Ciconiidae
Storks
Tall, long-legged, heavy-billed, long-necked wading birds.

33. Wood Stork

Mycteria americana
(L—41 W—66) **Endangered**
A large white-bodied bird with long,
heavy, bill, down-turned towards the

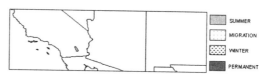

tip; black primaries and secondaries; naked, black-skinned head and neck; pale
legs with pinkish feet. *Immature:* Patterned like adult but with grayish feathering
on neck and head; yellowish bill. *Habitat:* Lakes, coastal marshes, bays. *Abundance
and Distribution:* Rare to casual post-breeding wanderer (July–Sep.) to the Salton
Sea, California; casual during this period elsewhere in the region. *Range:* Georgia,
Florida and Gulf states southern in coastal regions to central Argentina; West Indies.

Family Cathartidae
New World Vultures
Large, black, diurnal raptors with long, hooked bills and featherless heads that forage mostly from the air for carrion.

34. Black Vulture

Coragyps atratus (L—26 W—57)
Entirely black with naked, black-skinned head; primaries appear sil-

very from below. *Habits:* Black Vultures do not normally soar; they alternate flapping and gliding, usually at low levels. *Similar Species:* Turkey Vultures soar, seldom flapping, and normally hold their wings at an angle while Black Vultures hold their wings horizontal during glides; Black Vultures have silvery primaries while Turkey Vultures have silvery primaries and secondaries. *Habitat:* Savanna, thorn forest, second growth. *Abundance and Distribution:* Rare permanent resident* of southern Arizona. *Where to Find:* Organ Pipe National Monument; Picacho Peak; Santa Cruz River valley. *Range:* Breeds from eastern (New Jersey) and southwestern (Arizona) United States south to central Argentina; winters from southern United States south through breeding range.

35. Turkey Vulture

Cathartes aura (L—26 W—69)
Black with naked, red-skinned head; relatively long tail; silvery flight feath-

ers (outlining black wing lining). *Immature:* Black head. *Habits:* Soars for long periods with wings held at an angle above horizontal. *Similar Species:* See Black Vulture. *Habitat:* Nearly ubiquitous except in extensive agricultural areas. *Abundance and Distribution:* Common summer resident* (Mar.–Oct.) throughout; Salton Sea, Colorado River Valley, and southern Arizona in winter. *Where to Find:* San Jacinto Wildlife Area, California; Aubrey Valley, Arizona; Carlsbad Caverns National Park, New Mexico; Desert National Wildlife Range, Nevada. *Range:* Breeds from southern Canada south to southern South America, Bahamas and Cuba; winters from southern United States south through breeding range.

36. California Condor

Gymnogyps californianus (L—47 W—108)
Huge black bird; white wing linings; orange bill; naked orange head and neck except for black feathers on forehead and face; flesh-colored legs and feet. *Immature:* Wing linings are grayish rather than white; head is dark (adult coloration is not

achieved until fourth year). *Habits:* Soars one hundred to one hundred fifty miles per day in search of large mammal carcasses (elk, deer, buffalo, cattle). *Habitat:* Arid mountains, grasslands, and savannas. *Abundance and Distribution:* Probably throughout the region prior to European settlement. Bones have been found from Arizona, New Mexico, Nevada, and west Texas. The last extant population was in the Sespe Wildlife Area of Los Padres National Forest in Ventura County, California. The last known wild-born bird was taken into captivity on April 19, 1987. Since then the U.S. Fish and Wildlife Service has run a captive breeding/re-introduction program, and forty-two individuals have been released as of February 1999 into the Sespe Wildlife Area in Big Sur's Ventana Wilderness, Lion Canyon in the San Rafael Wilderness Area, and the Vermilion Cliffs in Arizona. No breeding has yet taken place in this reintroduced population. *Where to Find:* Vermilion Cliffs, Arizona. *Range:* Formerly from British Columbia south to southern Baja California east to Nevada and west Texas.

Order Anseriformes
Family Anatidae
Ducks, Geese, and Swans
Heavy-bodied water birds with short legs, webbed feet, and broad, flat bills. Johnsgard (1979) and Hines (1985) provide in-depth identification information for members of this group.

37. Black-bellied Whistling-Duck
Dendrocygna autumnalis
(L—21 W—36)
A long-necked, long-legged duck;

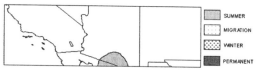

SUMMER
MIGRATION
WINTER
PERMANENT

neck and breast a rich, tawny buff; black belly; gray head with brown crown; dark streak running from crown down nape to back; red-orange bill and legs; dark wings with broad white stripe; dark tail. *Voice:* A shrill, whistled "per-chee-chee-chee." *Similar Species:* Black-bellied Whistling-Duck has black belly, orange bill and extensive white in wings visible in flying bird; the extremely rare Fulvous Whistling-Duck has buff belly, gray bill, and dark wings. *Habitat:* Lakes, marshes, grasslands, croplands. *Abundance and Distribution:* Rare summer resident* (May–Sep.) in southern Arizona. *Where to Find:* Nogales Sewage Ponds; Kino Springs. *Range:* Breeds from south Texas and northwestern Mexico south in lowlands to Peru and southern Brazil.

38. Fulvous Whistling-Duck

Dendrocygna bicolor

(L—20 W—36)

A long-necked, long-legged duck;

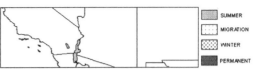

body a rich, tawny buff; mottled black and tan on back; dark streak running from crown down nape to back; whitish streaking on throat; white on flanks; gray bill and legs; dark wings; dark tail with white base. *Voice:* A shrill, whistled "ker-chee." *Similar Species:* See Black-bellied Whistling-Duck. *Habitat:* Lakes, marshes, grasslands, croplands. *Abundance and Distribution:* Uncommon to rare summer resident* (May–Sep.) along the lower Colorado River valley. *Where to Find:* Imperial Valley National Wildlife Refuge, California/Arizona. *Range:* Breeds locally from southern California, Arizona, Texas, Louisiana, and Florida south in coastal regions to Peru and central Argentina; West Indies; also in the Old World from East Africa, Madagascar, and India.

39. Greater White-fronted Goose

Anser albifrons (L—28 W—57)

Grayish-brown body; barred with buff on back; speckled with black on

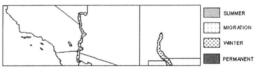

breast and belly; white lower belly and under-tail coverts; pinkish bill with white feathering at base, edged in black; orange legs; in flight white rump and gray wings are key. *Immature:* Lacks white feathering at base of bill and speckling on breast and belly; pale legs and bill. *Voice:* A tremulous, high-pitched "ho-ho-honk." *Similar Species:* Other dark geese of the region have white heads or chin straps clearly visible in flight. *Habitat:* Lakes, marshes, grasslands, croplands. *Abundance and Distribution:* Common to uncommon winter resident (Sep.–Apr.) at Salton Sea and Colorado and Rio Grande valleys; rare transient at large lakes throughout; mostly fall (Sep.–Oct.). *Where to Find:* Bosque del Apache, New Mexico; Salton Sea, California; Lake Mead, Nevada. *Range:* Breeds in arctic regions; winters in temperate regions of Northern Hemisphere.

40. Snow Goose

Chen caerulescens (L—28 W—57)

A medium-sized white goose with black primaries; red bill with dark

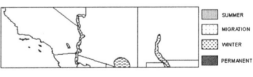

line bordering mandibles; red legs. *Immature:* Patterned like adult but with gray bill and legs and grayish wash on back. *Blue Phase:* Dark gray body with white head, neck, and belly; red legs and bill. *Immature:* Dark brownish-gray throughout with white chin and belly; dark legs and bill. *Voice:* A shrill, high-pitched, "honk." *Similar Species:* White phase Snow Goose has dark line on mandible edges ("grin patch") that Ross' Goose lacks; Snow Goose bill is longer than head while Ross' is shorter. The immature Greater White-fronted Goose has no white on chin and has pale legs and bill (not dark as in blue phase immature). *Habitat:* Lakes, marshes, grasslands, croplands. *Abundance and Distribution:* Common to uncommon winter resident (Sep.–Apr.) at Salton Sea, Colorado; Rio Grande valleys; and lakes in southeastern Arizona; rare transient at large lakes throughout; mostly in fall (Sep.–Oct.). *Where to Find:* Bosque del Apache Refuge, New Mexico; Lake Mead, Nevada; Imperial National Wildlife Refuge, California/Arizona. *Range:* Breeds in Canadian arctic; winters in the west along Pacific Coast from southwestern Canada to central Mexico, and in the east from Chesapeake Bay through southeastern United States to northeastern Mexico, also east Asia.

41. Ross' Goose
Chen rossii
(L—23 W—48)
A small white goose with black pri-

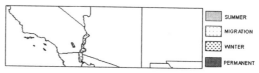

maries; red bill and legs. *Immature:* Patterned like adult but with grayish wash on back. *Blue Phase:* Dark gray body with white head and belly; red legs and bill. *Voice:* Soft "kek-kek." *Similar Species:* See Snow Goose. *Habitat:* Lakes, marshes, grasslands, croplands. *Abundance and Distribution:* Uncommon to rare winter resident (Nov.–Feb.) at Salton Sea and lower Colorado River valley; rare to casual elsewhere. *Where to Find:* Salton Sea, California; Imperial National Wildlife Refuge, California/Arizona. *Range:* Breeds in central Canadian high arctic; winters in central California and sparingly along the Gulf coast.

42. Canada Goose
Branta canadensis
(L— 26 to 48 W— 54 to 84)
Subspecies of this goose vary consid-

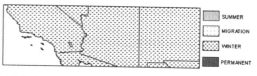

erably in size; grayish-brown above; grayish below; black neck and head with white chin strap; white rump, belly and under-tail coverts; black tail. *Habits:* These geese often fly in large "v"s. *Voice:* A medium or high-pitched, squeaky "honk" at different pitches by different flock members. *Similar Species:* The Brant has black across breast and lacks white chin strap of the Canada Goose. *Habitat:* Lakes, estuaries, grasslands, croplands. *Abundance and Distribution:* Common to uncommon transient (Oct.–Nov., Mar–Apr.) throughout; uncommon and local winter resident (Oct.–Apr.) at large lakes.In recent years, there has been a return of breeding populations to northern New Mexico. *Where to Find:* Bill Williams Delta National Wildlife Refuge, Arizona; Bosque del Apache, New Mexico; Lake Mead, Nevada; Cibola National Wildlife Refuge, California. *Range:* Breeds across northern half of North

America; winters from northern United States south to northern Mexico, farther north along coasts; also introduced in various Old World localities.

43. Brant
Branta bernicla
(L—24 W—39)

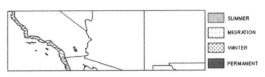

A small goose; dark above, barred with brown; white upper-tail coverts nearly obscure dark tail; white below with gray barred flanks; black breast, neck, and head with white bars on side of throat; dark bill and legs. *Immature:* Lacks barring on throat. *Habits:* Feeds by dabbling for sea grasses in shallows of bays and estuaries. *Voice:* A rolling, guttural "krrrronk." *Similar Species:* Black breast contrasting with white belly, and white upper-tail coverts are distinctive even in flight. *Habitat:* Bay shores, estuaries. *Abundance and Distribution:* Uncommon transient and winter resident along coast (Nov.–Apr.) and at Salton Sea; somewhat more common in spring (Mar.–Apr.). *Where to Find:* Montaña de Oro State Park; Goleta Point; Salton Sea National Wildlife Refuge. *Range:* Breeds in high arctic; winters along northern coasts of Northern Hemisphere.

44. Tundra Swan
Cygnus columbianus
(L—52 W—81)

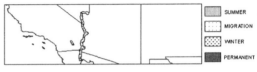

Very large, entirely white bird; rounded head; black bill, often with yellow, pre-orbital spot. *Immature:* Brownish-gray with orangish bill. *Voice:* A mellow "hoonk" repeated. *Similar Species:* The larger Trumpeter Swan has an angular, wedge-shaped rather than rounded head; Trumpeter lower mandible also has orange base and lacks yellow eye spot; immature Tundra Swans have orangish bill with black tip while immature Trumpeter has black base of orange bill. *Habitat:* Lakes, bays. *Abundance and Distribution:* Rare winter resident in Colorado River valley and Salton Sea; casual elsewhere. *Where to Find:* Imperial Valley National Wildlife Refuge; Salton Sea National Wildlife Refuge. *Range:* Breeds in arctic regions of Northern Hemisphere; winters in coastal boreal and north temperate areas.

45. Wood Duck
Aix sponsa
(L—19 W—29)

Green head and crest streaked with white; red eye, face plate, and bill; white throat; purplish breast; iridescent dark bluish back; beige belly with white flank stripes. *Female:* Deep, iridescent blue on back; brownish flanks; grayish belly; brownish-gray head and crest; white eyering

Figure 16. Tidal marshes rim Buena Vista Lagoon at Oceanside, California. Birds to be seen here include a number of dabbling duck species (such as wigeon, teal, shoveller, Gadwall) as well as many other kinds of waterfowl.

Figure 17. Located on the University of California at Santa Barbara campus, Goleta Point provides an excellent site from which to scan the open ocean for inshore species including scoters and Brant. Rock-loving shorebirds like turnstones and surfbirds also can be found here.

and postorbital stripe; white chin. *Voice:* A high, whistling "aweek aweek aweek." *Similar Species:* The shrill flight call, relatively short neck, large head, and long square tail are distinctive for the birds in flight. *Habitat:* Mainly rivers and swamps. *Abundance and Distribution:* Uncommon to rare and local winter resident (Oct.– Apr.) in coastal and lowlands of southern California, Salton Sea, Colorado River valley, southern Arizona and New Mexico. Uncommon to rare summer resident at Kaweah and other inland lakes in southern California. *Where to Find:* Corn Creek, Desert National Wildlife Range, Nevada; Fairmount Park, California; Bosque del Apache, New Mexico. *Range:* Breeds across southeastern Canada and eastern half of United States, and in west from southwestern Canada to central California, also Cuba and Bahamas; winters in southeastern United States south through northeastern Mexico, and in the west from Oregon, California, and New Mexico south through northwestern Mexico.

46. Gadwall

Anas strepera (L—20 W—34)

A dapper, medium-sized duck; gray above; scalloped gray, black, and

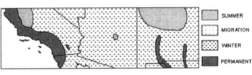

white on breast and flanks; brownish head; white belly; black hindquarters; chestnut, black, and white patches on wing. *Female:* Brown body mottled with buff and dark brown; orange bill marked with black; distinctive white wing patch when visible. *Voice:* A nasal "ack." *Similar Species:* Female Mallard has mottled (not white) belly, white tail, and lacks white patch on wing. *Habitat:* Lakes, estuaries, ponds, bays. *Abundance and Distribution:* Uncommon transient and winter resident (Oct.– Mar.) across most of region; summer resident* in northern New Mexico; permanent resident in lowlands and foothills of southern California, Salton Sea, Rio Grande and Pecos River valleys. *Where to Find:* Navajo Lake State Park, New Mexico; San Jacinto Wildlife Area, California; Allen Severson Wildlife Area, Arizona; Pahranagat Lake, Nevada. *Range:* Breeds in boreal and north temperate steppe regions; winters temperate and northern tropical areas of Northern Hemisphere.

47. Eurasian Wigeon

Anas penelope (L—19 W—32)

Medium-sized duck; gray above and on flanks; pinkish breast; chestnut

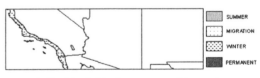

head with creamy forehead and crown; white belly; black hindquarters; white and black patches on wing; green speculum. *Female:* Brown body mottled with buff and dark brown; grayish bill; black wing patch; green speculum. *Similar Species:* Female Eurasian Wigeon has gray axillaries visible in flight (white in female American Wigeon) and a brownish head (paler in American, contrasting with brown back). *Habitat:* Estuaries, lakes, marshes, crops, fields, lawns. *Abundance and Distribution:* Rare winter visitor (Nov.–Mar.) along the coast; casual inland. *Where to Find:* Upper Newport Bay; Morro Bay; Buena Vista Lagoon. *Range:* Breeds in northern Eurasia; winters in temperate and subtropical Eurasia, but regular along coasts of North America.

48. American Wigeon
Anas americana (L—19 W—33)
Medium-sized duck; gray above; purplish-brown on breast and flanks;

white crown and forehead; broad, iridescent green stripe through and past eye; densely mottled black and white on cheek, chin and throat; pale blue bill with black tip; white belly; black hindquarters; green speculum. *Female:* Brown body mottled with buff and dark brown; grayish bill; black wing patch; green speculum. *Voice:* A wheezy "whip" or "wheep." *Similar Species:* See Eurasian Wigeon. *Habitat:* Lakes, estuaries, bays, ponds, crops, fields, lawns. *Abundance and Distribution:* Common winter resident (Nov.–Mar.) in southern California, southern Nevada, southern Arizona, and southern New Mexico; resident at Salton Sea; rare summer resident* occasionally nesting in mountain lakes. *Where to Find:* Bitter Lake National Wildlife Refuge, New Mexico; Nogales Sewage Ponds, Arizona; Davis Dam, Nevada. *Range:* Breeds northern North America south to northern United States; winters along Atlantic and Pacific coasts, and inland from southern United States to northwestern Colombia; West Indies.

49. Mallard
Anas platyrhynchos (L—23 W—36)
A large duck; iridescent green head; yellow bill; white collar; rusty breast;

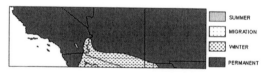

gray scapulars and belly; brownish back; purple speculum; black rump and under-tail coverts; curling black feathers at tail; white tail. *Female:* Brown body mottled with buff; orange bill marked with black; white outer tail feathers; blue speculum. *Voice:* A nasal "quack" (male) or series of "quack"s (female). *Similar Species:* The "Mexican Duck" (*Anas platyrhynchos diazi*) currently is considered a subspecies of the Mallard by the American Ornithologists' Union, though this is subject to change. At any event, the Mexican Duck is a rare summer resident* in extreme southwestern New Mexico and southeastern Arizona. Both sexes of the Mexican Duck resemble a dark, female Mallard. The best field mark to distinguish the Mexican Duck from the Mallard is the occurrence of a close association between two apparently female Mallards (in fact, a pair of Mexican Ducks). *Habitat:* Ponds, lakes, marshes, estuaries, bays. *Abundance and Distribution:* Permanent resident* nearly throughout; common to uncommon in winter (Oct.–Mar.); uncommon to rare and local in summer (especially scarce in southern Arizona). *Where to Find:* Bitter Lake National Wildlife Refuge, New Mexico; Allen Severson Wildlife Area, Arizona; San Jacinto Wildlife Area, California. Mexican Duck—San Pedro Riparian National Conservation Area, Arizona. *Range:* Breeds across boreal and temperate regions of the Northern Hemisphere; winters in temperate and subtropical regions.

50. Blue-winged Teal

Anas discors (L—16 W—25)

A small duck; brown mottled with dark brown above; tan marked with spots below; light blue patch on wing; green speculum; dark gray head with white crescent at base of bill. *Female:* Mottled brown and dark brown above and below; tan under-tail coverts spotted with brown; yellowish legs. *Voice:* A high-pitched "eeeee" (male); a series of soft "quack"s (female). *Similar Species:* Female Blue-winged Teal often shows some light blue on wing, has yellowish legs (not grayish); female Green-winged Teal has smaller bill than other teal and white (not spotted) under-tail coverts; female Cinnamon Teal is a dark rusty brown, rather than the grayish brown of Bluewing and buffy brown of the Greenwing. *Habitat:* Lakes, estuaries, marshes, ponds. *Abundance and Distribution:* Uncommon to rare transient throughout (Mar.–Apr., Sep.–Oct.); rare resident at Salton Sea and lower Colorado and Rio Grande valleys; rare to casual at other times of the year elsewhere; principally a spring transient in Arizona (Mar.–May). *Where to Find:* Bosque del Apache, New Mexico; Las Vegas Wash, Nevada; Havasu Lake, Arizona/California. *Range:* Breeds across boreal and temperate North America south to central United States; winters southern United States to northern South America; West Indies.

51. Cinnamon Teal

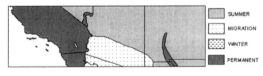

Anas cyanoptera (L—16 W—25)

Dark chestnut head and underparts; red eye; dark brown and chestnut on back; light blue on wing; green speculum; black under-tail coverts. *Female:* Mottled brown and dark brown above and below; tan under-tail coverts spotted with brown; yellowish legs. *Voice:* A low "quack." *Similar Species:* See Blue-winged Teal. Some female and eclipse plumage Bluewings cannot be safely distinguished from female Cinnamon Teal. *Habitat:* Ponds, marshes, lakes, estuaries. *Abundance and Distribution:* Common to uncommon transient and summer resident* (Mar.–Sep.) across much of the region (not southern Arizona where found mainly as a transient);

uncommon to rare or casual in winter in southern California and Colorado and Rio Grande river valleys. *Where to Find:* Louis Rubidoux Nature Center, California; Holloman Lakes Wildlife Refuge, New Mexico; Corn Creek, Desert National Wildlife Range, Nevada; Allen Severson Wildlife Area, Arizona. *Range:* Breeds from southwestern Canada south through western United States to northwestern Mexico; winters southwestern United States south locally through Middle and South America; some South American populations resident.

52. Northern Shoveler

Anas clypeata (L—19 W—31)

Medium-sized duck with large, spatulate bill; green head; golden eye;

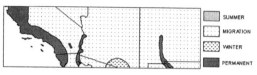

black back; rusty sides; white breast and belly; black rump and under-tail coverts; blue patch on wing; green speculum. *Female:* Mottled brown and dark brown above and below; brown eye; orange "lips" on dark bill. *Voice:* A low, hoarse "kuk kuk." *Similar Species:* The heavy, flattened bill is distinctive. *Habitat:* Lakes, estuaries, bays, ponds. *Abundance and Distribution:* Common to uncommon resident* in lowlands and foothills of southern California, Salton Sea, and Rio Grande and lower Colorado River valleys; uncommon to rare, mainly as a transient, in most of Arizona and New Mexico; common transient and winter resident (Sep.–Mar.) in southeastern Arizona. *Where to Find:* Roosevelt Lake Wildlife Area, Arizona; Holloman Lakes, New Mexico; Lake Mead, Nevada; Buena Vista Lagoon, California. *Range:* Breeds across boreal and north temperate regions (mainly in west in North America); winters along temperate coasts south to subtropics and tropics of Northern Hemisphere.

53. Northern Pintail

Anas acuta (L—26 W—36)

A long-necked, long-tailed duck; gray back and sides; brown head; white

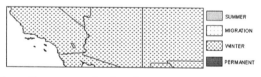

neck, breast, and belly; black rump, under-tail coverts and tail with extremely long central feathers; speculum iridescent brown. *Female:* Brownish mottled with dark brown throughout; grayish bill; pointed tail. *Voice:* A high-pitched "quip" (male); a series of "quack"s (female). *Similar Species:* Female resembles other female dabblers but shape is distinctive (long neck and relatively long, pointed tail).*Habitat:* Flooded fields, swales, shallow ponds, bays. *Abundance and Distribution:* Common to uncommon transient (Aug.–Sep., Feb.–Mar.) throughout; uncommon to rare and local winter resident, mainly in southern portions of region. Breeds* occasionally in highlands. *Where to Find:* Bosque del Apache, New Mexico; Havasu Lake and impoundments, Arizona/California; Lake Mead, Nevada. *Range:* Breeds in arctic, boreal, and temperate grasslands and tundra; winters in temperate, subtropical and tropical areas of Northern Hemisphere.

54. Green-winged Teal
Anas crecca (L—15 W—24)
A small, fast-flying duck; chestnut head with broad, iridescent green

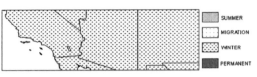

stripe above and behind eye; gray body; beige breast with black spots; white bar on side of breast; white tail; black rump and under-tail coverts. *Female:* Mottled brown and white above and below; whitish under-tail coverts; green speculum. *Voice:* A high-pitched "teet" or a nasal "kik quiik kik kik." *Similar Species:* See Blue-winged Teal. *Habitat:* Lakes, estuaries, marshes, ponds. *Abundance and Distribution:* Common to uncommon transient and winter resident throughout (Sep.–Apr.); has bred* irregularly. *Where to Find:* Buena Vista Lagoon, California; Bosque del Apache, New Mexico; Hassayampa River Preserve, Arizona; Lake Mead, Nevada. *Range:* Breeds in boreal and arctic areas; winters in temperate and subtropical regions of Northern Hemisphere.

55. Canvasback
Aythya valisineria
(L—21 W—33)
A medium-sized, heavy-bodied duck

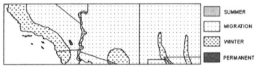

with steeply, sloping forehead; rusty head; red eye; black breast; gray back and belly; black hindquarters. *Female:* Grayish body, brownish neck and head. *Voice:* A gabbling "kup kup kup." *Similar Species:* The sloping forehead is distinctive for both sexes; female Redhead has bluish bill with black tip (Canvasback is all black); also Canvasback female shows contrast between brown head and gray body that is lacking in the all brown female Redhead. *Habitat:* Lakes, bays. *Abundance and Distribution:* Uncommon transient throughout; winter resident (Oct.–Mar.) in lowlands and foothills of southern California, southeastern Arizona, and Colorado, Rio Grande, and Pecos River valleys; resident at Salton Sea; rare to casual in summer elsewhere; has bred* (Overton Wildlife Management Area, Nevada). *Where to Find:* Bluewater Lake State Park, New Mexico; Salton Sea, California; Lake Mead, Nevada; Willcox Lake, Arizona. *Range:* Breeds across northwestern North America south to California and Iowa; winters locally from southern Canada south through the United States to southern Mexico.

56. Redhead

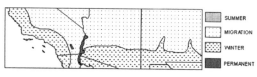

Aythya americana (L—20 W—33)
Rusty head; red eye; bluish bill with
white ring and black tip; black breast;
gray back and belly; dark brown hindquarters. *Female:* Brownish throughout; bluish
bill with black tip. *Voice:* A soft, catlike "yow," repeated. *Similar Species:* See Canvasback. *Habitat:* Bays, lakes, ponds. *Abundance and Distribution:* Common to
uncommon transient throughout; winter resident (Oct.–Apr.) in southern California (except mountains and deserts), southern Arizona, and southern New
Mexico; resident at Salton Sea and the lower Colorado River valley (has bred*);
rare to casual in summer in highland areas, has bred*. *Where to Find:* Cholla Lake,
Arizona; Salton Sea, California; Rio Grande Nature Center, New Mexico; Lake
Mead, Nevada. *Range:* Breeds in western Canada and northwestern United States,
locally in Great Lakes regions; winters central and southern United States south to
Guatemala; also Greater Antilles.

57. Ring-necked Duck

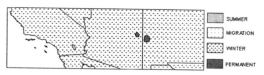

Aythya collaris (L—17 W—28)
A smallish duck with characteristically pointed (not rounded) head;
black back, breast, and hindquarters; dark head with iridescent purple sheen; gray
flanks with white bar edging breast; golden eye; white feather edging at base of
bill; white band across dark bill. *Female:* Brown body and head; white eyering; bill
with whitish band. *Voice:* "Caah," repeated. *Similar Species:* The pointed head shape
of Ring-necked Ducks is distinctive. Scaup have rounded heads; male scaup have
light (not dark) backs; female scaup have distinct white face patch at base of bill.
Habitat: Lakes, ponds. *Abundance and Distribution:* Common to uncommon transient and winter resident (Oct.–Apr.) throughout; uncommon summer resident*
at lakes in the White Mountains of Arizona and the Mogollon Mountains of New
Mexico. *Where to Find:* Dulce Lake, New Mexico; Lake Mead, Nevada; Willcox
Lake, Arizona; Lake Cachuma, California. *Range:* Breeds across central and southern Canada, northern United States; winters along both United States coasts, southern United States south to Panama; West Indies.

58. Greater Scaup

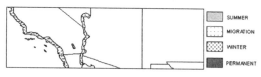

Aythya marila (L—19 W—31)
Rounded head; gray mottled with
black back; black breast and hind-
quarters; dark head with iridescent green sheen; gray flanks; golden eye; bluish
bill with dark tip. *Female:* Brown body and head; white patch at base of bluish-

gray bill. *Voice:* A soft cooing or rapid, whistled "week week week" (male); a guttural "caah" (female). *Similar Species:* Male Greater Scaup has green sheen on a more rounded head (male Lesser has purple sheen on a more pointed head); Lesser Scaup has white band on secondaries only, Greater Scaup has white band on primaries and secondaries (both sexes, visible only in flight). *Habitat:* Large lakes, bays. *Abundance and Distribution:* Uncommon to rare winter resident (Nov.–Mar.) along the coast, Salton Sea, and the Colorado River; rare or casual at lakes in northern Arizona and New Mexico; casual or absent from southern portions. *Where to Find:* Davis Dam, Nevada; Lake Perris State Recreation Area, California; Conchas Lake, New Mexico; Imperial National Wildlife Refuge, Arizona/California. *Range:* Breeds in Old and New World arctic; winters along temperate and northern coasts and large lakes in Northern Hemisphere.

59. Lesser Scaup

Aythya affinis (L—17 W—28)
A smallish duck; gray back; black
breast and hindquarters; dark head

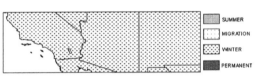

with iridescent purple sheen (sometimes greenish); gray flanks; golden eye; bluish bill with dark tip. *Female:* Brown body and head; white patch at base of grayish bill. *Voice:* A soft "wheeooo" or single whistled "weew" (male); a weak "caah" (female). *Similar Species:* See Greater Scaup. *Habitat:* Bays, lakes. *Abundance and Distribution:* Common to uncommon winter resident (Nov.–Feb.); rare or casual in summer*. *Where to Find:* Upper Newport Bay, California; Kino Springs, Arizona; Conchas Lake, New Mexico; Lake Mead, Nevada. *Range:* Breeds in Alaska, western and central Canada, and northern United States; winters coastal and central inland United States south to northern South America; West Indies.

60. Surf Scoter

Melanitta perspicillata
(L—19 W—34)
Black with white patches on nape,

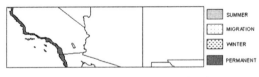

and forehead; orange bill with bull's-eye on side (white circle, black center); white eye. *Female:* Entirely brown with white patches in front of and behind eye; dark bill. *Voice:* A guttural croak. *Similar Species:* Surf Scoter female has distinct white pre- and postorbital patches on otherwise brown head and brown throat; female White-winged Scoter has feathering almost to nostrils on bill (lacking on Black and Surf Scoters); female Black Scoter has white cheek and throat contrasting with dark brown head and neck. *Habitat:* Marine, bays, lakes. *Abundance and Distribution:* Common winter resident (Oct.–May) and uncommon to rare summer resident, principally along the California coast. Especially common in spring (Apr.)

when large numbers can be observed flying northward just offshore. Rare to casual inland, mainly as a fall transient. *Where to Find:* Upper Newport Bay; Goleta Point; Ocean Beach County Park. *Range:* Breeds northern North America south to central Canada; winters mainly along coasts from Alaska to northwestern Mexico, and Nova Scotia to Florida; also Great Lakes.

61. White-winged Scoter

Melanitta fusca (L—22 W—39)

Black with white eye and wing patches; dark bill with black knob at base and

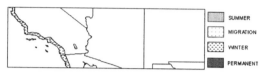

orange tip. *Female:* Entirely dark brown (sometimes with whitish pre- and post-orbital patches); bill dark orange with black markings; feathering on bill extends nearly to nostrils; white secondaries sometimes visible on swimming bird. *Voice:* A plaintive whistle or low growl. *Similar Species:* See Surf Scoter. *Habitat:* Bays, lakes. *Abundance and Distribution:* Uncommon to rare winter visitor (Oct.–Mar.), rare to casual in summer along California coast; numbers vary considerably from year to year; rare to casual in winter inland. *Where to Find:* Upper Newport Bay; Goleta Point; Ocean Beach County Park. *Range:* Breeds in bogs, ponds, and lakes in boreal and arctic regions of Old and New World; winters mainly along northern coasts, south to northwestern Mexico and South Carolina in North America.

62. Black Scoter

Melanitta nigra (L—19 W—33)

Entirely black with orange knob at base of bill. *Female:* Dark brown with

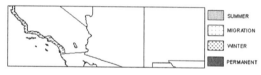

whitish cheek and throat contrasting with dark crown and nape. *Immature:* Patterned similarly to female but whitish belly. *Voice:* A rattle-like "quack." *Similar Species:* See Surf Scoter. *Habitat:* Marine, bays, lakes. *Abundance and Distribution:* Rare to casual winter visitor (Oct.–Mar.) along coast, mostly immatures and females. Scattered records inland. *Where to Find:* Upper Newport Bay; Shell Beach. *Range:* Breeds locally in tundra regions of Eurasia and North America; winters in northern and temperate coastal waters of Northern Hemisphere, south to California and South Carolina in United States

63. Bufflehead

Bucephala albeola (L—14 W—23)

A small, plump, short-billed duck; head white from top of crown to nape,

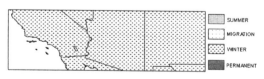

the rest iridescent purple; black back; white breast, belly and sides; gray bill; pink legs. *Female and Immature:* Dark back; grayish-white below; dark head with large white patch extending below and behind eye. *Voice:* A weak, nasal "eeh." *Similar Species:* The much larger male Hooded Merganser also has white back of crown and nape but the white is edged in black; also has golden eye (dark in Bufflehead), thin, pointed bill, rusty sides. *Habitat:* Bays, lakes, estuaries. *Abundance and Distribution:* Uncommon to rare winter resident (Nov.–Feb.) throughout; rare to casual in summer. *Where to Find:* Buena Vista Lagoon, California; Davis Dam, Nevada/ Arizona; Picacho Reservoir, Arizona; Holloman Lakes, New Mexico. *Range:* Breeds across Canada and extreme northern United States; winters from subarctic along both coasts of North America, and inland from central United States south to central Mexico.

64. Common Goldeneye

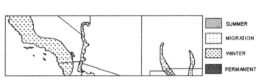

Bucephala clangula (L—18 W—30)
Iridescent green head (sometimes purplish); golden eye; white patch at base of bill; black back and hindquarters; white breast, sides and belly; black and white scapulars; white wing patch visible in flight. *Female:* Gray body; brown head; golden eye; gray bill yellowish at tip (mostly yellow in some birds). *Voice:* A high-pitched, nasal "eeh." *Similar Species:* Common Goldeneye bill appears to be nearly as long as head, while that of the Barrow's Goldeneye appears to be half the length of the head; Barrow's show less white in wing than Common; male Barrow's Goldeneye has purplish sheen on head and crescent-shaped preorbital patch; most female Barrow's have an orange bill (gray or mostly gray in most female Common Goldeneyes). *Habitat:* Bays, lakes. *Abundance and Distribution:* Uncommon to rare winter resident (Nov.–Feb.) in coastal, lowland, and foothill wetlands of southern California, the Salton Sea, and the Colorado, Rio Grande, and Pecos River valleys; rare to casual in summer. *Where to Find:* Salton Sea, California; Parker Dam, Arizona/California; Davis Dam, Nevada/Arizona; Bosque del Apache National Wildlife Refuge, New Mexico. *Range:* Breeds across boreal and north temperate regions of Old and New World; winters along northern coasts south to temperate and subtropical regions of the Northern Hemisphere.

65. Barrow's Goldeneye

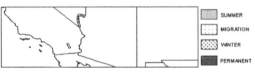

Bucephala islandica (L—18 W—29)
Iridescent purple head (sometimes greenish); white crescent-shaped patch at base of bill; golden eye; black back and hindquarters; white breast, belly, and sides; black and white scapulars. *Female:* Gray body; brown head; golden eye; orange bill (partially gray in some birds). *Voice:* "Eck eck eck." *Similar Species:* See Common Goldeneye. *Habitat:* Coastal waters, lakes. *Abundance and Distribution:*

Rare and local winter resident along Colorado River (Nov.–Feb.); casual elsewhere. *Where to Find:* Davis Dam, Nevada/Arizona; Parker Dam, California/Arizona. *Range:* Breeds locally in northern United States, Canada, Greenland, and Iceland; winters along coastal North America (Alaska to California and Nova Scotia to New York).

66. Hooded Merganser

Lophodytes cucullatus (L—18 W—26)
Head with white crest from top of
crown to nape broadly edged in black,

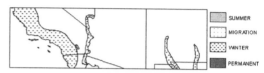

the rest black; golden eye; black back and tail; white breast with prominent black bar; rusty sides; sharp, black bill. *Female and Immature Male:* Body brownish; head a pale orange with dusky crown; pale orange crest off back of crown and nape; upper mandible dark; lower mandible orangish. *Voice:* A trilled "crrroooo" (male); low grunt (female). *Similar Species:* Other female mergansers (Common and Red-breasted) are much larger and have dark russet heads, bright orange bills, grayish bodies. *Habitat:* Ponds, lakes, estuaries, bays. *Abundance and Distribution:* Rare to casual winter resident (Nov.–Feb.) in coastal, lowland, and foothill wetlands of southern California, the Salton Sea, and the Colorado, Rio Grande, and Pecos River valleys; some summer records. *Where to Find:* Bosque del Apache National Wildlife Refuge, New Mexico; Parker Dam, Arizona/California; Las Vegas Wash, Nevada; Lopez Lake County Park, California. *Range:* Breeds across central and southern Canada and northern United States, farther south in Rockies and Appalachians; winters mainly along coasts from southern Canada to northern Mexico; West Indies.

67. Common Merganser

Mergus merganser (L—25 W—36)
Iridescent green head; sharp, red-
orange bill; black back; gray rump

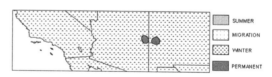

and tail; white breast, sides and belly. *Female and Immature Male:* Rufous, crested head; white chin; rufous throat and neck ending abruptly at white breast; gray back and sides; orange bill. *Voice:* A low "uu-eek-wa" (male); a harsh "karr" (female). *Similar Species:* The female Common Merganser lacks white wing patch that is evident in female Red-breasted Merganser; female Common has distinct boundary between white throat and rufous neck; female Red-breasted has a whitish neck and throat with no abrupt line between rufous neck and throat. *Habitat:* Lakes, rivers, bays. *Abundance and Distribution:* Common to uncommon or rare winter resident (Nov.–Mar.) throughout; rare summer resident* in highlands of Mogollon Plateau and White Mountains. *Where to Find:* Pharanagat Refuge, Ne-

Figure 18. The Aubrey Cliffs, located just off Route 66, east of Kingman, Arizona, offer an impressive backdrop for a huge prairie dog town (several miles in length and breadth) in a beautiful expanse of native sagebrush. Birds typical of the area include Golden Eagle, Sage Thrasher, Prairie Falcon, and Common Raven.

Figure 19. The Tesuque River bottom at Pojoaque, New Mexico, provides desert riparian habitat for a variety of species including Scaled Quail, Loggerhead Shrike, and Northern Rough-winged Swallow.

vada; Conchas Lake, New Mexico; Parker Dam, California/Arizona. *Range:* Breeds in Old and New World subarctic and boreal regions south in mountains into temperate areas; winters from northern coasts south inland through temperate and subtropical zones of the Northern Hemisphere.

68. Red-breasted Merganser

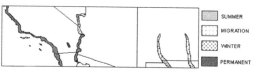

Mergus serrator (L—22 W—32)
Iridescent green, crested head; sharp, red-orange bill; white collar; buffy breast streaked with brown; gray back, rump and tail; black shoulder with white chevrons; white scapulars; grayish sides. *Female and Immature Male:* Rufous, crested head; white chin and throat; gray back and sides; white wing patch. *Voice:* "Eeoww" (male); a harsh "karr" (female). *Similar Species:* See Common Merganser. *Habitat:* Bays, lakes, marine. *Abundance and Distribution:* Common winter resident along coast (Nov.–Apr.), rare in summer; uncommon winter resident in the Colorado, Rio Grande, and Pecos River valleys and Salton Sea, rare in summer on the lower Colorado River and at Salton Sea; rare to casual on large lakes elsewhere. *Where to Find:* Upper Newport Bay, California; Parker Dam, Arizona/California; Lake Mead, Nevada; Conchas Lake, New Mexico. *Range:* Breeds in arctic and boreal regions of Old and New World; winters mainly along coasts in southern boreal and temperate areas.

69. Ruddy Duck

Oxyura jamaicensis
(L—15 W—23)
A small duck; chestnut body; stiff black tail held at a 45-degree angle; black cap; white cheek; blue bill. *Winter:* Grayish-brown body; dark cap; white cheek. *Female:* Mottled grayish and white body; stiff black tail; dark cap and dark line below eye. *Voice:* A staccato, cicada-like "tsk-tsk-tsk-tsk quark." *Similar Species:* Female Ruddy Duck has dark cap extending below eye; extremely rare female and winter male Masked Ducks have a whitish line above eye. *Habitat:* Lakes, ponds, bays. *Abundance and Distribution:* Common winter resident (Oct.–Apr.); uncommon to rare in summer*. *Where to Find:* Upper Newport Bay, California; Willcox Lake, Arizona; Lake Mead, Nevada; Dulce Lake, New Mexico. *Range:* Breeds locally from northern Canada through the United States to central Mexico, West Indies, and South America; winters coastal and southern United States south to Nicaragua and elsewhere in tropical breeding range.

Order Falconiformes
Family Accipitridae
Kites, Hawks, Ospreys, and Eagles

A diverse assemblage of diurnal raptors, all of which have strongly hooked bills and powerful talons. Clark and Wheeler (1987) and Dunne and Sutton (1989) provide identification guides for advanced students of this difficult group.

70. Osprey

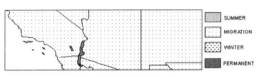

Pandion haliaetus (L—23 W—63)
Dark brown above; white below, often with dark streaking (females); white crown with ragged crest from occiput; broad dark line extending behind yellow eye; white chin and cheek; extended wings are white finely barred with brown with prominent dark patches at wrist. *Habits:* Feeds mainly on fish snatched from water surface. *Voice:* A shrill "kew," repeated. *Habitat:* Estuaries, lakes, rivers, bays. *Abundance and Distribution:* Uncommon to rare transient (Sep.–Oct., Apr.–May) throughout; rare to casual summer and winter resident (Sep.–Apr.) at Salton Sea and the lower Colorado River valley; most numerous in fall along coast; rare to casual summer resident* along streams of the Mogollon Rim in Arizona and New Mexico. *Where to Find:* Upper Newport Bay, California; Patagonia Lake State Park, Arizona; Las Vegas National Wildlife Refuge, New Mexico; Lake Mead, Nevada. *Range:* Breeds in boreal, temperate, and some tropical localities of Old and New World, particularly along coasts; winters mainly in tropical and subtropical zones.

71. White-tailed Kite

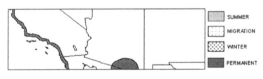

Elanus leucurus (L—16 W—42)
Gray above; white below; red eyes and yellow legs; black shoulders; in flight note white tail and silvery wings with black wrist mark. *Immature:* Rusty wash on back, head and breast. *Habits:* Often hovers while foraging. *Voice:* A shrill "kee kee kee." *Habitat:* Prairie, savanna, thorn forest, meadows, agricultural areas. *Abundance and Distribution:* Uncommon permanent resident* in valleys and coastal plain of California and locally in southeastern Arizona; rare spring (Apr.) transient through Sandia Mountains in New Mexico; scattered records elsewhere. *Where to Find:* Santa Rosa Plateau Preserve, California; Buenos Aires National Wildlife Refuge, Arizona; Cibola National Forest Hawk Watch, New Mexico (migration). *Range:* Resident from Oregon, California, Oklahoma, and Louisiana south to central Argentina. The closely related (conspecific?) Black-shouldered Kite is resident in the Old World tropics and subtropics.

72. Mississippi Kite

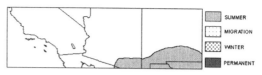

Ictinia mississippiensis (L—15 W—35)
Dark gray above; pale gray below
with black primaries and tail; red eye;
orange-yellow legs; gray cere; in flight note pointed wings, uniform gray underparts and dark, slightly forked tail. *Immature:* Streaked rusty below; barred tail;
red or yellow eye. *Habitat:* Riparian and oak woodlands; deciduous forest and
swamps; savanna. *Abundance and Distribution:* Rare and local summer resident*
in central and southern New Mexico and southeastern Arizona. *Where to Find:*
Roswell Spring River Golf Course, New Mexico; Aravaipa Canyon, Arizona. *Range:*
Breeds southern United States; winters central South America.

73. Bald Eagle

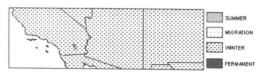

Haliaeetus leucocephalus
(L—35 W—84) **Endangered**
Huge size; dark brown body; white
head and tail; yellow beak and legs. *Immature:* Entirely brown with whitish wing
linings and base of tail. *Habits:* Feeds primarily on fish. *Voice:* A descending "keee
chip-chip-chip-chip." *Similar Species:* Immature Golden Eagle has well-defined
white (not whitish) base of tail and white wing patches at base of primaries; also
has golden head. *Habitat:* Lakes, rivers, estuaries. *Abundance and Distribution:*
Uncommon to rare and local winter resident (Nov.–Mar.) along coast and at large
bodies of water throughout; formerly bred*. *Where to Find:* Maxwell National
Wildlife Refuge, New Mexico; Lopez Lake, California; Coleman Lake, Arizona; Lake
Mead, Nevada. *Range:* Breeds across Canada and northern United States, south
along coasts to Florida, California, and Texas; winters throughout breeding range
from southern Canada southward, particularly along the coasts and at larger inland lakes.

74. Northern Harrier

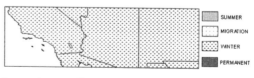

Circus cyaneus (L—19 W—42)
A slim, long-tailed, long-winged
hawk; gray above; pale below with
dark spots; white rump; yellow eye and cere; long, yellow legs. *Female:* Streaked
dark brown and tan above; whitish below heavily streaked with brown; yellow
eyes; pale yellowish cere; yellow legs; barred tail; white rump. *Habits:* Flies low
over open areas, usually within a few feet of the ground, alternately flapping and
gliding; wings at an angle during glides; often hovers just above the ground. *Voice:*
A rapid, descending "cheek-cheek-cheek-cheek-cheek." *Similar Species:* Similar
haunts and habits as Short-eared Owl, but white rump is distinctive; Harris's Hawk

has white rump but usually is dark below (except immature) and is mainly a sit-and-wait predator in thorn forest—doesn't flap and glide or hover like the harrier. *Habitat:* Marshes, prairies, estuaries, savanna, agricultural areas. *Abundance and Distribution:* Uncommon to rare and local winter resident (Sep.–Apr.); rare to casual in summer*. *Where to Find:* Maxwell National Wildlife Refuge, New Mexico; Sonoita, Arizona; Louis Rubidoux Nature Center, California. *Range:* Breeds across boreal and temperate regions of Northern Hemisphere; winters in temperate and tropical zones.

75. Sharp-shinned Hawk
Accipiter striatus
(L—12 W—24)

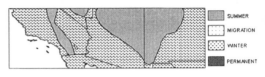

Slate gray above; barred rusty and white below; gray crown with rusty face; red eye; yellow cere; barred tail; long, yellow legs; as in other accipiters, the female is much larger than the male. *Immature:* Brown above; streaked brown and white on head, breast, and belly. *Habits:* All three accipiters (Sharpshin, Cooper's, and Northern Goshawk) are distinguished from other hawks by their relatively short, broad wings, and long tails, and by their behavior in flight, which is characterized by a series of rapid wing beats followed by a short, flat-winged glide. They seldom soar except during migration. All three species are forest bird hunters. *Voice:* A rapid, high-pitched "kew-ki-ki-ki-ki-ki." *Similar Species:* The calls of the three similar species of accipiters are different; Sharpshin has a squared tail (slightly rounded in the larger Cooper's Hawk); immature Sharpshin tail has narrow and indistinct terminal white band (immature Cooper's terminal white tail band is broader and more distinct); immature Sharpshin has heavy streaking on breast (immature Cooper's has finer streaking). The immature Merlin also is similar to the immature Sharpshin, but has dark eyes (not red) and dark tail with thin, light bands (not broad light bands as in Sharpshin). *Habitat:* Forests. *Abundance and Distribution:* Uncommon permanent resident* in mountains of southern California and Nevada, northern Arizona, and New Mexico; common to uncommon winter resident (Oct.–Mar.) elsewhere in region. *Where to Find:* NM 511, Reese Canyon, New Mexico; Bill Williams Delta National Wildlife Refuge, Arizona; Louis Rubidoux Nature Center, California; Kyle Canyon, Nevada. *Range:* Breeds from subarctic Alaska and Canada to northern Argentina (except prairie regions and most of southern United States), also in Greater Antilles; winters from northern coastal regions and southern Canada south through breeding range.

76. Cooper's Hawk

Accipiter cooperii (L—18 W—32)

Slate gray above; barred rusty and white below; gray crown with rusty face; red eye; yellow cere; barred tail; long, yellow legs. *Immature:* Brown above; streaked brown and white on head, breast, and belly. *Habits:* See Sharp-shinned Hawk. *Voice:* A wheezy "peeew," repeated. *Similar Species:* See Sharp-shinned Hawk. Adult Northern Goshawk is barred gray and white below, and has a prominent white eyebrow; immature Northern Goshawk closely resembles immature Cooper's but has white eyebrow. *Habitat:* Forests. *Abundance and Distribution:* Uncommon to rare or casual resident*; more common in mountain forests and northern regions in summer, in valleys and southern areas in winter; most numerous as a transient (Sep.–Oct.) in coastal regions. *Where to Find:* Crystal Cove State Park, California; Bandelier National Monument, New Mexico; Organ Pipe Cactus National Monument, Arizona; Red Rock Canyon National Conservation Area, Nevada. *Range:* Breeds from southern Canada to northern Mexico; winters from northern United States to Honduras.

77. Northern Goshawk

Accipiter gentilis (L—23 W—39)

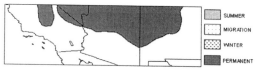

Slate gray above; barred gray and white below; gray crown with prominent white eyebrow; dark patch behind eye; red eye; yellow cere; unevenly barred tail; long, yellow legs. *Immature:* Brown above; streaked brown and white on head, breast, and belly; white eyebrow; uneven tail barring. *Habits:* See Sharp-shinned Hawk. *Voice:* "Tew tew tew tew tew tew." *Similar Species:* See Sharp-shinned and Cooper's Hawks. *Habitat:* Montane forests, especially aspen and ponderosa pine. *Abundance and Distribution:* Uncommon to rare resident* in mountains of Nevada, Arizona, New Mexico, and California; rare or casual in winter in lowlands. *Where to Find:* Canjilon Mountain, New Mexico; Kaibab Plateau Parkway, Arizona; Mount Charleston, Nevada; Generals Highway, Sequoia National Park, California. *Range:* Breeds in boreal regions of Northern Hemisphere, south in mountains to temperate and tropical zones; winters in breeding range and irregularly southward and in lowlands.

78. Gray Hawk

Asturina nitida (L—17 W—35)

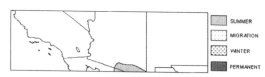

Gray above; whitish below finely barred with gray; white under-tail coverts; yellow legs and cere; brown eyes; in flight—wings are whitish finely checked with gray, black-tipped; tail is barred gray and white; shows white rump bar. *Immature:* Brown above; buffy with dark markings below; head streaked in distinctive pattern—whitish line over eye, dark bar through the eye, whitish cheek, and dark malar stripe; also shows a pale whitish rump in flight. *Voice:* A plaintive "*cree-eer.*" *Similar Species:* The distinctive vocalization, facial marks, and whitish rump bar distinguish the immature Gray Hawk from immature Broad-winged Hawks and Roadside Hawks, both of which are casual or accidental in the region. *Habitat:* Riparian forest, open woodlands; pastures with scattered trees and hedgerows. *Abundance and Distribution:* Uncommon to rare summer resident* (Mar.–Oct.) in southeastern Arizona and perhaps southwestern New Mexico. *Where to Find:* Aravaipa Canyon, Arizona; Muleshoe Ranch Preserve, Arizona; Kino Springs, Arizona. *Range:* Southern Arizona and Texas south to northern Argentina.

79. Common Black-Hawk
Buteogallus anthracinus
(L—21 W—48)
Black; black tail with broad white bar

and thin, white terminal band; yellow cere and legs; in flight note the single white bar and white at base of primaries. *Immature:* Brown above; streaked brown and white on head, breast, and belly; prominent dark malar stripe; several sinuous bars on tail; buffy wing linings. *Voice:* A distinctive "keeeeeeeee" first rising in pitch, then trailing off, repeated, often given in flight. *Similar Species:* Zone-tailed Hawk has three white tail bands plus terminal strip, and shows whitish primaries and secondaries in flight. *Habitat:* Riparian forest, woodlands, second growth, swamps. *Abundance and Distribution:* Uncommon to rare resident* in southeastern and central Arizona and southwestern New Mexico. *Where to Find:* Aravaipa Canyon, Arizona; Bill Evans Lake, New Mexico; Muleshoe Ranch Preserve, Arizona. *Range:* Breeds in lowlands from southwest United States (Arizona, Texas) to northern South America; Cuba.

80. Harris's Hawk
Parabuteo unicinctus (L—21 W—45)
Dark brown; chestnut shoulders and
thighs; yellow cere and legs; dark tail

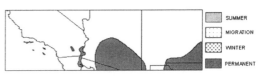

with broad white band at base and narrow white terminal strip; white under-tail coverts; brown eyes. *Immature:* Dark below variably streaked with buff and white; in flight—wing linings and flight feathers are whitish finely barred with brown, but chestnut shows at wrist; tail whitish finely barred with brown. *Habits:* Mainly a "sit-and-wait" predator, often seen perched on telephone poles, fence posts, and dead snags. *Voice:* A short, dry scream. *Similar Species:* Northern Harrier has white rump but is long-winged, long-tailed, and much paler (Harris's Hawk usually appears black in flight, not brownish or grayish). *Habitat:* Thorn forest, arid scrub. *Abundance and Distribution:* Rare resident* in southern Arizona and southeastern New Mexico; formerly resident in the Colorado River valley and southern Salton Sea area of California; reintroduced to these regions in the 1980s. *Where to Find:* Mittry Lake, Arizona; Harroun Lake, New Mexico; Imperial Dam, California; Saguaro National Park, Arizona. *Range:* Resident from southwestern United States to central Argentina.

81. Red-shouldered Hawk
Buteo lineatus (L—19 W—39)
Mottled dark brown and white above
with rusty shoulders, head and up-

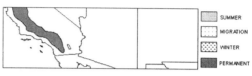

per breast; barred rusty below; tail dark with three or four narrow, whitish bars; brown eye; pale yellowish cere; yellow legs; in flight note brown and white barring on flight feathers, pale white patch at base of primaries ("window"), and rusty wing linings. *Immature:* Brown mottled with white above; buff streaked with brown on breast, barred on belly; rusty shoulders. *Voice:* A strident "ki-cheek ki-cheek ki-cheek keeew." *Similar Species:* Voice is distinctive. Immature is similar to other immature buteos but usually shows rusty shoulders, crescent-shaped wing "window" in flight, tail appears to be dark with light bars. In this region, the Red-shouldered Hawk overlaps with only four species of buteos (the "broad-winged, short-tailed" hawks): the Red-tailed Hawk, Swainson's Hawk, Ferruginous Hawk, and Rough-legged Hawk. The immature Red-tailed Hawk has unstreaked breast and light-colored tail with dark bars; the immature Swainson's Hawk shows two-toned wings in flight—lighter underwing coverts contrasting with darker flight feathers; immature Ferruginous Hawk appears uniformly pale from below in flight with some mottling; immature Rough-legged Hawk shows dark belly and light tail with dark, subterminal band. *Habitat:* Riparian forest, woodlands, swamps. *Abundance and Distribution:* Uncommon to rare resident* in southern California foothills; expands into coastal plain during migration and winter. *Where to Find:* O'Neill Regional Park, Tapia County Park, Santa Rosa Plateau Preserve. *Range:* Breeds southeastern Canada and eastern United States south to central Mexico, also California; winters from central United States south through breeding range.

82. Swainson's Hawk
Buteo swainsoni (L—20 W—50)
Brown above; reddish-brown breast;
buffy belly with sparse brown streak-

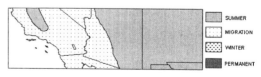

ing on flanks; whitish chin and cere; yellowish legs; in flight note dark flight feathers, whitish wing linings; barred tail with broad, dark subterminal band. *Dark Phase:* Entirely dark brown; tail as in light phase, usually paler toward base. *Immature Light Phase:* Dark above; mottled white and brown below; often with white forehead and dark patches on breast. *Habits:* Soars with wings slightly angled above the horizontal. *Voice:* A shrill, descending "keeeeeeee." *Similar Species:* Voice is distinctive. See Red-shouldered Hawk. *Habitat:* Prairies, savanna, thorn forest, desert scrub. *Abundance and Distribution:* Common to uncommon transient and uncommon to rare summer resident* (Mar.–Oct.) in New Mexico, eastern Arizona (scarce or absent in highlands as breeder) and southern California's San Joaquin Valley; uncommon to rare transient (Mar.–May, Aug.–Oct.) and rare to casual summer resident* in southern California, Nevada, and western Arizona. *Where to Find:* Isleta Lakes and Recreation Area, New Mexico; Buenos Aires National Wildlife Refuge, Arizona; Angeles Crest Highway—From I-210 north of Burbank take Hwy 2 (Angeles Crest Hwy) north into the San Gabriel Mts. Highlands providing views of the San Fernando Valley also can be excellent for viewing migrating raptors in April. *Range:* Breeds in deserts and Great Plains of western North America from Alaska and Canada south to northwestern Mexico; winters in southern South America.

83. Zone-tailed Hawk

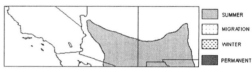

Buteo albonotatus (L—20 W—52)

Black; white lores; yellow cere and legs; black tail with two broad white bands; in flight note Turkey Vulture-like wing pattern of dark wing linings and whitish flight feathers. *Immature:* Flecked with white below. *Habits:* Soars like a Turkey Vulture with wings slightly angled. *Voice:* A "slurred, two-noted, high-pitched whistle" (Edwards 1972:32). *Similar Species:* This species can be distinguished from other dark raptors in flight by its pattern of dark wing linings, light flight feathers, and banded tail. *Habitat:* Arid scrub, pine-oak woodland. *Abundance and Distribution:* Uncommon summer resident* (Mar.–Oct.) of northwestern, central, and southeastern Arizona and southern and central New Mexico; rare to casual straggler and occasional breeder elsewhere in region; has wintered. *Where to Find:* Aravaipa Canyon, Arizona; Redrock Wildlife Area, New Mexico; Bandelier National Monument, New Mexico; Madera Canyon, Arizona. *Range:* Southwestern United States to southern Brazil.

84. Red-tailed Hawk

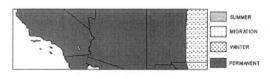

Buteo jamaicensis (L—22 W—53)

A large hawk, extremely variable in plumage; most common adult plumage is mottled brown and white above; white below with speckling across belly;

rusty tail (appears whitish from below); in flight, dark forewing lining contrasts with generally light underwing. *Immature:* Mottled brown and white above; streaked brown and white below; brown tail finely barred with grayish-white. *Light Phase (Krider's):* Much paler; pale orange tail. *Dark Phase (Harlan's):* Dark throughout with some white speckling; dark tail, whitish at base, darker at tip with rusty wash. *Voice:* A hoarse, drawn out, screech, "ke-aaaaaaaah." *Similar Species:* Rusty tail is distinctive for adults. See Red-shouldered Hawk. *Habitat:* Open woodlands, thorn forest, savanna. *Abundance and Distribution:* Uncommon to rare summer resident* except plains of eastern New Mexico where absent as a breeder; common to uncommon winter resident throughout. *Where to Find:* Malibu Creek State Park, California; Bright Angel Trail (Grand Canyon), Arizona; Red Rock Canyon National Conservation Area, Nevada; Fort Sumner State Monument, New Mexico. *Range:* Breeds from subarctic of Alaska and Canada to Panama; winters northern United States south through breeding range; resident in West Indies.

85. Ferruginous Hawk

Buteo regalis (L—23 W—55)

A large, pale buteo; rusty above; dark wings; whitish head streaked with ru-

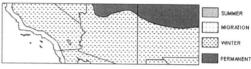

fous; breast and belly speckled with rust; rusty thighs; yellow cere and feet (legs feathered to toes); whitish tail with pale orange terminal band; in flight note entirely white underparts except black wing tips and rusty thighs. *Dark Phase:* Entirely dark brown except for whitish tail and flight feathers. *Immature:* Like adult but thighs whitish. *Voice:* A dry scream. *Similar Species:* The whitish tail, lacking a dark band separates this from other buteos. Dark thighs of adults contrasting with light underparts also are distinctive. *Habitat:* Prairies, savanna, desert. *Abundance and Distribution:* Uncommon to rare permanent resident* in grassy plains of New Mexico and northern Arizona, more numerous in winter; uncommon to rare winter resident (Oct.–Mar.) elsewhere in region at lower and mid-elevations. *Where to Find:* Petrified Forest National Park, Arizona; El Malpais National Monument, New Mexico; Bonanza Trailhead, Nevada; Palomar Mountain State Park, California. *Range:* Breeds from southwestern Canada south to southwestern United States; winters from central and southern portions of breeding range south to central Mexico.

86. Rough-legged Hawk

Buteo lagopus (L—22 W—51)

A large hawk with legs feathered all the way to the toes; mottled brown

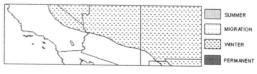

and white above; buffy with brown streaks on breast; dark brown belly; white tail with dark sub-terminal band. *Dark Phase:* Entirely dark except whitish flight feathers and tail with broad, dark, subterminal band. *Immature:* Similar to adult—whitish or finely barred tail with broad, dark, sub-terminal band; base of primaries show white from above in flight. *Habits:* Flies low over open areas, often hovering. *Voice:* A cat-like "keeeeew," dropping in pitch. *Similar Species:* Northern Harrier forages in similar fashion, but has a white rump (not tail), is much slimmer, and lacks dark band contrasting with buffy breast. *Habitat:* Open areas. *Abundance and Distribution:* Uncommon to rare transient and winter resident (Oct.–Apr.) at low to mid-elevations in open, grassy areas of southern Nevada, northern Arizona, and New Mexico; casual in southern California. *Where to Find:* Bright Angel Trail, Grand Canyon, Arizona; Bonanza Trailhead, Nevada; Las Vegas National Wildlife Refuge, New Mexico; Lake Crowley, California. *Range:* Breeds in arctic and subarctic regions of Old and New World; winters mainly in temperate zone.

87. Golden Eagle

SUMMER
MIGRATION
WINTER
PERMANENT

Aquila chrysaetos (L—34 W—71)
Huge; dark brown with golden wash on head and shaggy neck; legs feathered to feet; appears entirely dark in flight. *Immature:* Dark brown with white patch at base of primaries and basal half of tail white. *Voice:* A rapid series of nasal chips. *Similar Species:* See Bald Eagle. *Habitat:* Open areas. *Abundance and Distribution:* Uncommon to rare resident* in open areas of low to mid-elevations. *Where to Find:* Red Rock Canyon National Conservation Area, Nevada; Aubrey Cliffs, Arizona; El Malpais National Monument, New Mexico; Joshua Tree National Monument, California. *Range:* Breeds primarily in open and mountainous regions of boreal and temperate zones in Northern Hemisphere; winters in central and southern portions of breeding range.

Family Falconidae
Caracaras and Falcons
With the exception of the caracara, falcons are sleek birds with pointed wings and long, square tails.

88. Crested Caracara

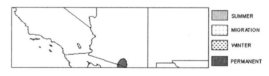

SUMMER
MIGRATION
WINTER
PERMANENT

Caracara plancus (L—23 W—50)
Black body; black, crested crown; white face and neck; white breast barred with black; red cere and eyering; bluish bill; long, yellow legs; in flight note

white patches on basal half of primaries and white (actually finely barred) tail with dark terminal band. *Immature:* Buffy neck and breast. *Habits:* Often feeds on carrion along the road. *Voice:* A low croak. *Similar Species:* The whitish neck, breast, primaries and tail with black bar are distinctive. *Habitat:* Thorn forest, savanna, prairie, arid scrub. *Abundance and Distribution:* Rare resident* of Tohono O'odham Indian lands southwest of Tucson, Arizona. *Where to Find:* Sells Highway; San Bernardino National Wildlife Refuge; Buenos Aires National Wildlife Refuge. *Range:* Southwestern United States to southern Argentina, south Florida; Cuba.

89. American Kestrel

Falco sparverius (L—10 W—22)
A small falcon; gray crown; black and white facial pattern; orange buff back and underparts spotted with brown; blue-gray wings; orange tail with black subterminal bar edged in white. *Female:* Rusty back and wings barred with brown. *Habits:* Perches or hovers a few feet off the ground while foraging; often seen on telephone wires along the road. *Voice:* A rapid, high-pitched "kle-kle-kle-kle-kle." *Similar Species:* Merlin shows a distinctly dark tail barred with white; lacks facial pattern of American Kestrel. *Habitat:* Open areas. *Abundance and Distribution:* Common to uncommon resident* throughout; rare or absent in winter in highlands, and in summer in desert regions of western Arizona and southeastern California. *Where to Find:* Santa Rosa Plateau Preserve, California; Red Rock Canyon National Conservation Area, Nevada; Buenos Aires National Wildlife Refuge, Arizona; Lower Mimbres Valley, New Mexico. *Range:* Breeds nearly throughout Western Hemisphere from subarctic Alaska and Canada to southern Argentina; West Indies; winters from north temperate regions south through breeding range.

90. Merlin

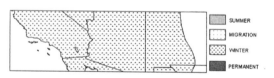

Falco columbarius (L—11 W—25)
A small falcon; slate above, buffy below with dark brown spots and streaks; white throat; brown eyes, yellow cere and legs; black tail, white at base, with two white bars and white terminal edging. *Female:* Dark brown above. *Habits:* A bird hunter; sallies from low perches, using surprise and speed to capture prey. *Voice:* "kwe kwe kwe kwe kwe." *Similar Species:* Merlin shows a distinctly dark tail barred with white; lacks facial pattern of American Kestrel. *Habitat:* Open woodlands, hedgerows, second growth, savanna; often hunts small birds in trees or shrubs bordering water in winter. *Abundance and Distribution:* Uncommon to rare transient and winter resident (Oct.–Mar.) at low to mid-elevations throughout except in plains of eastern New Mexico where scarce or absent. *Where to Find:*

Figure 20. Numerous dams and impoundments along the Colorado River have created waterbird habitat where little or none existed previously. Imperial Valley National Wildlife Refuge on the California/Arizona border is an example. Waterbirds found here include Black Rail, Least Bittern, Fulvous Whistling-Duck, and Tundra Swan.

Figure 21. In 1916, an engineering mistake caused the Colorado River to empty into a desert basin for several months, creating the Salton Sea, thirty-two miles long and fourteen miles wide. More saline than the ocean, the Salton Sea likely has changed the migration patterns of waterbirds. Many species that formerly avoided California's southeastern desert region now migrate through regularly, or remain as residents, including plovers, sandpipers, gulls, bitterns, herons, and waterfowl.

Bitter Lake National Wildlife Refuge, New Mexico; Patagonia Lake State Park, Arizona; Cuyamaca State Park, California; Corn Creek, Desert National Wildlife Range, Nevada. *Range:* Breeds across boreal and north temperate regions of Old and New World; winters in south temperate and tropical zones.

91. Aplomado Falcon
Falco femoralis (L—16 W—37) **Endangered**
A medium-sized falcon; gray above; gray crown; black facial pattern against white face; white throat and breast; black, finely barred belly; rusty thighs; black tail barred with white. *Immature:* Buffy face and breast streaked with brown. *Similar Species:* Merlin lacks facial pattern and dark belly contrasting with light breast. *Habitat:* Savanna, open woodlands, grasslands. *Abundance and Distribution:* Formerly uncommon resident* in southern Arizona and New Mexico; declined sharply in early 1900s, now accidental in Arizona and casual in New Mexico. *Where to Find:* Animas, New Mexico—formerly. Not recorded in recent years. *Range:* Resident from southwestern United States (at least formerly) to southern South America.

92. Peregrine Falcon
Falco peregrinus (L—18 W—40)
A large falcon; dark gray above; white below with spotting and barring on

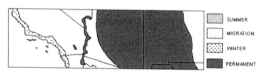

belly and thighs; black crown and cheek with white neck patch; brown eye; yellow eyering, cere, and legs; in flight note large size, long pointed wings, long tail, whitish underparts finely barred and spotted; black and white facial pattern. *Immature:* Dark brown above; buffy below spotted and streaked with brown; has facial pattern of adult. *Habits:* Forages by flying with swift, powerful wing beats, well up in the air, then stooping on prey. *Voice:* A rapid "kee kee kee kee." *Similar Species:* Prairie Falcon is much paler, and shows black axillaries in flight. *Habitat:* Open areas, usually near water. *Abundance and Distribution:* Rare to casual and local resident* in Arizona, Colorado River Valley, and New Mexico at sites with cliffs for nesting; in southern California, rare to casual fall transient and winter resident, particularly along coast. *Where to Find:* Bonanza Trail Head, Nevada; Gila Cliff Dwellings National Monument, New Mexico; Mormon Lake, Arizona; Morro Bay, California. *Range:* Breeds (at least formerly) in boreal and temperate regions of Northern Hemisphere; winters mainly in the tropics.

93. Prairie Falcon
Falco mexicanus (L—18 W—40)
Pale, sandy brown above mottled with brown and white; white below with

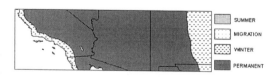

brown spotting; sandy crown with white face; two dark commas extend down from crown, one through the eye, the other through the ear; tail brownish barred with white; in flight note black axillaries against otherwise pale underparts. *Habits:* A bird hunter, stooping on prey from well up in the air. *Voice:* "Kee kee kee kee." *Similar Species:* The Prairie Falcon is much paler than the Peregrine, and shows black axillaries in flight (light axillaries in Peregrine Falcon). *Habitat:* Desert, thorn forest, arid scrub, prairie. Cliffs, crags, canyons or similar situation required for nesting. *Abundance and Distribution:* Uncommon to rare resident* in lower to mid-elevations in southeastern California, southern Nevada, Arizona, and New Mexico east to Great Plains; more numerous in winter when it occurs throughout the region. *Where to Find:* Red Rock Canyon National Conservation Area, Nevada; El Malpais National Monument, New Mexico; Aubrey Cliffs, Arizona; Joshua Tree National Monument, California. *Range:* Breeds in western North America from southwestern Canada to northwestern Mexico; winters from northwestern United States through breeding range to central Mexico.

Order Galliformes
Family Phasianidae
Pheasants, Turkeys, and Grouse
Terrestrial, heavy-bodied, mostly seed and fruit-eating birds with short, curved wings for quick take off.

94. Ring-necked Pheasant
Phasianus colchicus
(Male, L—33 W—31)
A chicken-sized bird with long legs

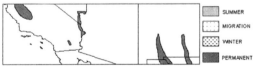

and extremely long, pointed tail; green head with naked red skin on face; white collar; body rich chestnuts, grays, golds and bronzes, spotted with white and brown; grayish-brown, long, pointed tail barred with brown; has spurs on tarsi. *Female:* Pale grayish-brown spotted with dark brown; long, pointed tail. *Voice:* A loud, hoarse "keow-kuk." *Similar Species:* Female could be mistaken for a prairie-chicken, but note long, pointed tail (short and square in prairie-chicken). *Habitat:* Pastures, agricultural fields. *Abundance and Distribution:* Introduced repeatedly throughout the region but self-sustaining populations have been difficult to establish. *Where to Find:* Salton Sea National Wildlife Refuge, California; Lake Mead National Recreation Area, Nevada. *Range:* Native of central Asia. Introduced throughout North America. Self-sustaining populations exist in cool, temperate regions with extensive grain crops and moderate hunting.

95. Sage Grouse

Centrocercus urophasianus (L—28 W—30)

A large, long-tailed, chicken-like bird; mottled black, brown and white above; dark throat; white breast; black belly; buffy-feathered legs to feet; yellow comb over eye. *Female:* Much smaller than the male; mottled brown and white body; dark belly; buff-feathered legs to toes. *Voice:* Various gurgling pops by the male during courtship display; a series of clucks when flushed. *Habits:* Males display on communal courting grounds where they fluff neck and breast feathers and strut with tail fanned upright. *Habitat:* Sagebrush. *Abundance and Distribution:* Sagebrush hills of the White Mountains in eastern California (a bit north of our defined region); formerly in northern New Mexico but extirpated. *Where to Find:* Lake Crowley, California (Childs 1993:76). *Range:* High sagebrush plains of western North America from southern Alberta and Saskatchewan south to southeastern California and northern New Mexico.

96. White-tailed Ptarmigan

Lagopus leucurus (L—13 W—24)
Mottled brown, buff, and white head, neck, breast, and back; white belly,

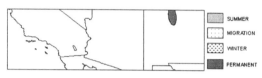

wings, tail, flanks and white-feathered legs and toes; red comb over eye; eyes, bill, and claws black. *Winter:* All white. *Voice:* Soft, chicken-like clucks and hoots. *Habitat:* Mountain meadows, lichen-covered rocks, alpine tundra, and stunted growth at treeline and above. *Abundance and Distribution:* Possible rare and local resident* on high peaks in the Sangre de Cristo Mountains of New Mexico although status uncertain; formerly more widespread in the state, but extirpated. *Where to Find:* Santa Fe Baldy; Valle Vidal. *Range:* High mountains of western North America from Alaska south to New Mexico.

97. Blue Grouse

Dendrapagus obscurus (L—20 W—28)
A charcoal-gray bird the size of a small chicken; white flanks and under-tail

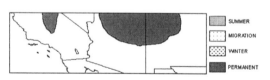

coverts; legs feathered to toes; black tail with gray terminal band; orange eyebrow comb; naked inflated purple skin patch on neck set off by a circle of white feathers with black tips visible during breeding displays. *Female:* Mottled gray and brown with gray belly; dark tail with terminal gray band. *Voice:* A series of booming hoots. *Habits:* During courtship, the male performs an extraordinary display, fluttering close to and around the female, then landing and walking in front of her in a bowed position with tail fanned and wings outstretched. *Habitat:* Mixed boreal forests of oak, pine, aspen, and fir. *Abundance and Distribution:* Rare and local resident* in high mountains. *Where to Find:* Kaibab National Forest, Arizona; Hyde

State Park, New Mexico; Generals Highway, Sequoia National Park, California; Pajarito Ski Area, Bandelier National Monument, New Mexico. *Range:* Mountains of western North America from Yukon and southeastern Alaska south to southern California in the Sierras and to northern Arizona and southern New Mexico in the Rockies.

98. Lesser Prairie-Chicken
Tympanuchus pallidicinctus
(L—16 W—27)

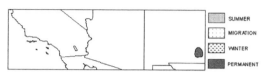

Mottled brown and white above; barred tan and white below; dark tail; during displays long feathers from the nape of the neck are extended upward, and naked golden skin at eyebrows is engorged— the male then puts his head down, stamps his feet and expands throat sacks of naked reddish-orange. *Female:* Lacks throat sacks and has barred tail. *Voice:* A loud, series of moaned *"wooo"*s, alternating with bouts of head-down foot stamping. *Habits:* Courtship displays are given at communal arenas called "leks" or "booming grounds" where several males display at the same time in an open space. *Similar Species:* Lesser Prairie-Chicken is smaller and paler than Greater Prairie-Chicken, and male has red-orange throat sacks (not yellow). *Habitat:* Short-grass prairie; shinnery oak. *Abundance and Distribution:* Rare and local resident* of the eastern plains of New Mexico. *Where to Find:* U.S. 380 Roadside Rest, New Mexico (Zimmerman et al. 1992:166). *Range:* Formerly throughout western shortgrass prairie regions, now reduced to local populations in Colorado, Texas, New Mexico, Oklahoma, and Kansas.

99. Wild Turkey
Meleagris gallopavo
(Male, L—47 W—63)

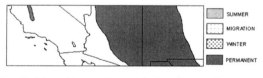

Dark brown body with iridescent bronze highlights; naked red head and neck; blue skin on face with dangling red wattles; hairy beard hanging from breast; tail dark barred with buff; tarsi with spurs. *Female:* Naked facial skin is grayish; lacks beard and wattles. *Habits:* Males associate in groups of two to three, females in larger flocks. *Voice:* A rapid, high-pitched gobble. *Habitat:* Deciduous forest, oak woodlands, thorn forest. *Abundance and Distribution:* Uncommon to rare resident* in coniferous, pine-oak, and riparian woodlands of New Mexico and Arizona. Has been re-introduced on the west slope of the Sierra Nevada. Formerly abundant and widespread in forested areas throughout the region. Virtually extirpated in the 1920s, and re-introduced widely since. *Where to Find:* Mount Charleston Loop, Nevada; Bandelier National Monument, New Mexico; El Malpais National Monument, New Mexico; Mount Trumbull,

Arizona; Ramsey Canyon Preserve, Arizona. *Range:* Formerly from southern Canada to central Mexico, now extirpated from many areas but being re-introduced.

Family Odontophoridae
Quail
Small, plump, terrestrial birds with relatively short, rounded wings and stubby tail.

100. Mountain Quail

Oreortyx pictus (L—11 W—16)
Gray head with two long, black
plumes from forehead; chestnut

throat bordered in black and white; brown back, rump, and tail; gray breast; chestnut flanks with black and white bars; dark brown or black under-tail coverts. *Female:* Similar to male, but with shorter plumes. *Habits:* Mountain Quail have the unquail-like habit of occasionally perching in trees or shrubs when flushed. Dawson (1923; 1575) states that they migrate downslope from highlands in fall on foot. *Voice:* "Tew wok"—accent on first syllable; a single, sharp "kweelk." *Habitat:* Montane chaparral; brushy thickets in highland conifer forests; pinyon-juniper associations; coastal chaparral. *Abundance and Distribution:* Uncommon resident* in highlands of southwestern California. *Where to Find:* Silverwood Lake State Recreation Area; McGill Campground; Black Mountain Campground. *Range:* Pacific coast states from Washington to southern California and northern Baja California; east to Idaho and Nevada.

101. Scaled Quail

Callipepla squamata (L—11 W—15)
Grayish-brown above; scaled gray
and black on neck and nape; brown

head with erect brown crest tipped in buff (hence the name "cotton-top"); spotted and scalloped brown and buff on flanks and belly. *Habits:* Coveys scatter by running along the ground when approached. *Voice:* A nasal "chip CHURP." *Similar Species:* Scaled breast and white-tufted crest are distinctive. *Habitat:* Dry thorn forest, arid scrub, desert. *Abundance and Distribution:* Uncommon to rare and local resident* in central and western New Mexico and southeastern Arizona. *Where to Find:* Tesuque River Bottom, New Mexico; Embudito Canyon, New Mexico; Petrified Forest National Monument, Arizona; Hereford Bridge, Arizona. *Range:* Resident from southwest United States to central Mexico.

102. California Quail

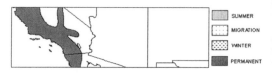

Callipepla californica (L—10 W—15)
Black face and throat outlined in
white; black topknot; brown fore-
head; chestnut cap; scaly black and gray neck and nape; brown back, wings, and
rump; gray breast; scaly chestnut belly; brown flanks streaked with white; gray tail.
Female: Gray above; face and neck mottled brown and buff with dark topknot;
gray breast; scaly buff and brown belly; brown wings; brown flanks streaked with
white. *Habits:* Can occur in very large flocks in winter. *Voice:* A loud, whistled "ka-
ker-ko" three-syllable call with accent on second syllable; also various chuckling
and clucking notes. *Similar Species:* The California Quail has brown flanks streaked
with white, not chestnut streaked with white as in Gambel's; also, belly has scaly
appearance that Gambel's lacks. Call of the California Quail has three syllables
(usually four in Gambel's). *Habitat:* Dry chaparral; brushy hillsides and ravines.
Abundance and Distribution: Common resident* in southwestern California. *Where
to Find:* Santa Barbara Museum of Natural History; Santiago Oaks Regional Park;
Silverwood Audubon Sanctuary; Burnt Rancheria Campground. *Range:* Western
North America from British Columbia south in coastal states of the U.S. and Mexico
to southern Baja California and east to Idaho and Utah.

103. Gambel's Quail

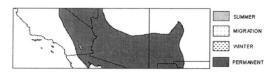

Callipepla gambelii (L—11 W—15)
Pale gray above and on breast; gray
nape streaked with black; chestnut
cap with long, black, curling topknot; black face and throat; beige lower breast and
belly with black central spot; chestnut flanks spotted with white. *Female:* Head is
brownish with buffy throat; shorter topknot. *Habits:* Coveys escape by scattering
on foot. *Voice:* "Chi-ca-co-coo." Also, a hoarse, whistled "coo CUT." *Habitat:* Desert
thickets and mesquite scrub. *Abundance and Distribution:* Common resident* in
deserts of southeastern California and southern Nevada; throughout Arizona except in northeast highlands and extreme deserts of Southwest; western and central
New Mexico. *Where to Find:* Mount Charleston Loop, Nevada; Red Butte, Arizona;
Old Refuge, Las Cruces, New Mexico; Joshua Tree National Monument, California. *Range:* Resident southwestern United States and northwest Mexico.

104. Northern Bobwhite

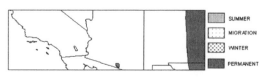

Colinus virginianus (L—10 W—15)
Brown and gray above mottled with
dark brown and white; chestnut sides
spotted with white; white breast and belly scalloped with black; chestnut crown

with short, ragged crest; white eyebrow and throat. *Female:* Tawny eyebrow and throat. *Habits:* Coveys fly and scatter in a burst when approached. *Voice:* Familiar, whistled "hoo WHIT" (bob white), several other calls including a whistled "perdeek." *Similar Species:* Female Northern Bobwhite has tawny rather than whitish throat and flies when approached instead of freezing in place like the Montezuma Quail. *Habitat:* Savanna, prairie, brushy fields, pastures, agricultural areas. *Abundance and Distribution:* Uncommon to rare, local resident* in eastern New Mexico plains; the "Masked Bobwhite" (*Colinus virginianus ridgwayi*) has been re-introduced into southeastern Arizona. *Where to Find:* Buenos Aires National Wildlife Refuge, Arizona. *Range:* Eastern and central United States south to Guatemala; isolated populations in Arizona and Sonora.

105. Montezuma Quail

Cyrtonyx montezumae (L—9 W—17)
Chestnut and brown with white
streakings on back; spectacular black

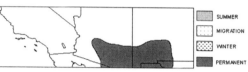

and white facial pattern (like a hockey goalie mask) and chestnut crest; chestnut breast and belly spotted with white on sides; brown wings spotted with dark brown. *Female:* Chestnut and brown above; buffy below with brown flecks; whitish throat; faint facial pattern in brown and white reminiscent of male's. *Habits:* "Freezes" when approached rather than fly (hence the name "fool's quail"). *Voice:* A softly trilled whistle. *Similar Species:* Female Northern Bobwhite has tawny rather than whitish throat, and flies when approached. *Habitat:* Pine-oak and juniper-oak woodlands. *Abundance and Distribution:* Uncommon to rare and local resident* in southwestern and south central New Mexico and southeastern Arizona. *Where to Find:* Water Canyon, New Mexico; Fort Stanton, New Mexico; Appleton-Whittell Research Ranch Sanctuary, Arizona; Canelo Hills Cienega, Arizona. *Range:* Southern Arizona, New Mexico, and west Texas south to central Mexico.

Order Gruiformes

Family Rallidae
Rails, Coots, and Gallinules
Except for the ubiquitous, duck-like coot, these are secretive marsh birds, heard more often than seen. They have cone-shaped or long, narrow bills, short, rounded wings, short tails, and extremely long toes for support in walking on floating vegetation.

106. Black Rail

Laterallus jamaicensis (L—6 W—10)
A tiny (sparrow-sized) rail; dark gray
with chestnut nape and black barring

on flanks; short, black bill. *Habits:* Secretive. *Voice:* "Tic-ee-toonk." *Habitat:* Wet
prairies, marshes. *Abundance and Distribution:* Uncommon to rare resident* at
Salton Sea and lower Colorado River valley. *Where to Find:* West Pond, Imperial
Dam, California; Mittry Lake, Arizona. *Range:* Breeds locally in California, Kansas
and along east coast from New York to Texas, also West Indies; Central and South
America; winters along Gulf coast and in tropical breeding range.

107. Clapper Rail

Rallus longirostris (L—13 W—20)
A large rail; streaked brown and tan
above; buffy below with gray and

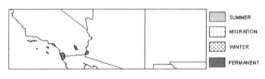

white barring on flanks; head and neck buffy with dark crown; long, pinkish or
yellowish bill; pale greenish legs. *Voice:* "Chik chik chik chik chik," like hitting a
rock with a metal rod. *Similar Species:* King Rail inhabits fresh water (occasionally
brackish) marshes—not salt marshes, and is rustier overall, darker barred on flanks,
has black lores. However, plumage in both species is variable, and they are known
to interbreed. *Habitat:* Salt marshes; cattail marshes along the lower Colorado River.
Abundance and Distribution: Uncommon to rare and local resident* along the
California coast, where the Light-footed Clapper Rail (*Rallus longirostris levipes*),
an endemic subspecies, is found. An endangered freshwater race, the Yuma Clap-
per Rail (*Rallus longirostris yumanensis*) is an uncommon to rare resident* (Apr.–
Sep.) in cattail marshes of the lower Colorado River valley and tributaries, and in
the Salton Sea. *Where to Find:* Upper Newport Bay, California; Tijuana Estuary
National Wildlife Refuge, California (Light-footed race); Mittry Lake Wildlife Area,
Arizona; Salton Sea National Wildlife Refuge, California (Yuma race). *Range:*
Coastal resident from Connecticut to Belize; California to southern Mexico; West
Indies; and much of coastal South America to southeastern Brazil and Peru.

108. Virginia Rail

Rallus limicola (L—10 W—14)
Similar to the King Rail but about
half the size; streaked brown and

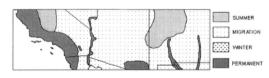

rusty above; tawny below with black and white barring on flanks; gray head with
rusty crown; white throat; long reddish bill; pale legs. *Voice:* "Kik kik kik ki-deek
ki-deek ki-deek." *Similar Species:* The smaller Virginia Rail has gray face (tawny in
larger King Rail) and tawny throat (white in King Rail). *Habitat:* Freshwater and

brackish marshes. *Abundance and Distribution:* The seasonal distribution of this species is not well understood. The bird is an uncommon to rare and local resident* in coastal lowlands and foothills of southern California, Salton Sea, the Colorado, Rio Grande, and Pecos River valleys, and in southeastern Arizona. It occurs as a summer resident* (Apr.–Sep.) at highland marshes and as a transient (Mar.–Apr., Sep.–Oct.) throughout. *Where to Find:* Malibu Lagoon State Beach, California; Mittry Lake, Arizona; Corn Creek, Desert National Wildlife Range, Nevada; Bosque del Apache National Wildlife Refuge, New Mexico. *Range:* Breeds locally from southern Canada to southern South America; winters along coast and in subtropical and tropical portions of breeding range.

109. Sora

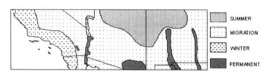

Porzana carolina (L—9 W—14)
A medium-sized rail; streaked brown and rusty above; grayish below with gray and white barring on flanks; gray head with rusty crown; black at base of bill; black throat and upper breast; short, yellow bill; greenish legs. *Female:* Amount of black on throat and breast reduced. *Immature:* Browner overall, lacks black on throat and breast. *Voice:* "Ku-week," also a long descending series of whistles. *Similar Species:* Same size and habitat preferences as Virginia Rail but note short, yellowish, cone-shaped bill in Sora (reddish and long in Virginia Rail). *Habitat:* Fresh and brackish water marshes. *Abundance and Distribution:* The seasonal distribution of this species is not well understood. The bird is an uncommon to rare and local winter resident (Aug.–Apr.) in coastal lowlands and foothills of southern California, and resident* at Salton Sea, the Colorado, Rio Grande, and Pecos River valleys, and in southeastern Arizona. It occurs as a summer resident* (Apr.–Sep.) at highland marshes and as a transient (Mar.–Apr., Sep.–Oct.) throughout. *Where to Find:* Alamo Lake State Park, Arizona; Corn Creek, Desert National Wildlife Range, Nevada; Dulce Lake, New Mexico; Upper Newport Bay, California. *Range:* Breeds from central Canada to southern United States; winters along coast and from southern United States to northern South America and West Indies.

110. Common Moorhen

Gallinula chloropus (L—14 W—23)
A large rail with short, cone-shaped bill and extremely long toes; entirely sooty gray with white edging along wing and white under-tail coverts; red frontal shield of naked skin on forehead; red bill with yellow tip; greenish legs. *Winter:* Similar to Summer but with olive bill, frontal shield, and legs. *Habits:* The extremely long toes enable this rail to walk on lily pads and other floating vegetation

without sinking; swims more than most other rails. *Voice:* Low croaks and whiny, high-pitched squeaks. *Similar Species:* Winter and juvenile Common Moorhen show white edging along folded wing, which American Coot lacks. *Habitat:* Freshwater marshes. *Abundance and Distribution:* Common to uncommon or rare and local resident* at Salton Sea, the Rio Grande and Colorado River valleys, and southeastern Arizona. Winter resident (Aug.–Apr.) in southern California coast and lowlands. *Where to Find:* Huntington Central Park (Lake Talbot), California; Corn Creek, Desert National Wildlife Range, Nevada; Mittry Lake, Arizona/California; Kino Springs, Arizona; Bosque del Apache, New Mexico. *Range:* Breeds locally in temperate and tropical regions of the world; winters mainly in subtropical and tropical zones.

111. American Coot

Fulica americana (L—16 W—26)
A large, black rail, more duck-like
than rail-like in appearance and be-

havior; white bill dark tip; red eye; greenish legs and lobed toes. *Immature:* Paler; pale gray bill. *Habits:* Swims in open water, tipping and diving for food instead of skulking through reeds like most rails; pumps head forward while swimming. *Voice:* Various croaks and cat-like mews. *Similar Species:* Juvenile coot lacks white wing edging of Common Moorhen. *Habitat:* Ponds, lakes, marshes, bays. *Abundance and Distribution:* Locally common to rare summer resident* throughout; common winter resident at lower to mid-elevations wherever there is open water. *Where to Find:* Upper Newport Bay, California; Mittry Lake, Arizona/California; Corn Creek, Desert National Wildlife Range, Nevada; Bosque del Apache National Wildlife Refuge, New Mexico. *Range:* Breeds from central Canada to Nicaragua and West Indies; winters along coast and from central United States to northern Colombia; West Indies.

Figure 22. One of the most productive sites for waterbirds on the California coast is Upper Newport Bay. Birds to be found here include both species of golden plover, Common Tern, both dowitchers, Pacific Loon, Common Loon, Gadwall, and Clark's Grebe.

Figure 23. The lakes, Rio Grande, and bordering riparian areas at Isleta Pueblo, New Mexico, provide excellent stopover habitat for migrating shorebirds, ducks, Green Herons, Black-crowned Night-Herons, Swainson's Hawks, Yellow-breasted Chats, Gray Catbirds, Townsend's Warblers, and Brewer's Blackbirds.

Family Gruidae
Cranes
Long-legged, long-necked birds of marsh and grasslands. Unlike herons, cranes fly with legs and neck extended. Unlike ducks and geese, they often glide in flight.

112. Sandhill Crane

Grus canadensis (L—42 W—74)

A tall, long-necked, long-legged, gray-bodied bird with bustle-like tail;

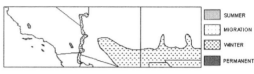

SUMMER
MIGRATION
WINTER
PERMANENT

black legs; red crown. *Immature:* Rusty tinge to gray body; lacks red crown. *Habits:* Normally in family groups of two adults and one or two young. *Voice:* A loud croaking bugle "crrrrahh." *Similar Species:* The larger Whooping Crane is white (tinged with rust in immature), not gray as in Sandhill Crane. *Habitat:* Prairie, savanna, grasslands, pasture, croplands, estuaries, lakes, ponds. *Abundance and Distribution:* Common to uncommon and local winter resident (Oct.–Mar.) in southern Arizona, southern New Mexico, and at Carrizo Plain, Salton Sea, and the lower Colorado River in southern California; common transient (Oct., Mar.) in southern Nevada, and northeastern New Mexico. *Where to Find:* Soda Lake, California; Pharanagat National Wildlife Refuge, Nevada; Willcox Lake, Arizona; Bosque del Apache, New Mexico. *Range:* Formerly bred over much of North America; now breeds in Alaska and northern Canada, south locally in northwestern and northcentral United States and Florida; winters southern United States to southern Mexico.

Order Charadriiformes
Family Charadriidae
Plovers
Plovers are rather compact shorebirds with relatively long legs, short necks, and short, thick bills.

113. Black-bellied Plover

Pluvialis squatarola (L—12 W—25)

A Killdeer-sized plover; checked black and white on back; white

SUMMER
MIGRATION
WINTER
PERMANENT

crown, nape and shoulder; black face, throat and breast; white belly and under-tail coverts. *Winter:* Heavy black bill contrasts with whitish at base of bill; pale eyebrow; crown and back brownish mottled with white; breast is mottled with brown;

belly white; black legs. *Voice:* A gull-like "keee keee kee-a-wee keee." *Similar Species:* The Black-bellied Plover has black axillaries (visible only in flight), which golden-plover species lack. *Habitat:* Beaches, bays, mud flats, estuaries. *Abundance and Distribution:* Common winter resident (Aug.–Apr.), uncommon in summer, along the coast of southern California; uncommon to rare transient (Aug.–Oct., Apr.–May) elsewhere. *Where to Find:* South Bay Marine Biological Study Area, California; Lake Mead, Nevada; San Jacinto Wildlife Area, California; Morgan Lake, New Mexico. *Range:* Breeds in the high arctic of Old and New World; winters along temperate and tropical coasts of the world.

114. American Golden-Plover
Pluvialis dominica (L—11 W—23)
A Killdeer-sized plover; checked black, white, and gold on back and

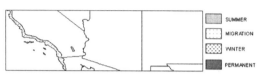

crown; white "headband" running from forehead, over eye and down side of neck; black face, and underparts. *Winter:* Heavy black bill contrasts with white at base of bill; pale eyebrow; crown and back brown and white often flecked with gold; underparts white, speckled with brown on breast; gray legs. *Voice:* A whistled "kew-wee." *Similar Species:* The American Golden-Plover lacks the black axillaries that show clearly on the Black-bellied Plover. American Golden-Plover is larger than the Pacific Golden-Plover; toes do not extend beyond tail tip in flight in American Golden-Plover as they do in Pacific. The two golden-plover species can be difficult to separate, even in the hand; however, the American Golden-Plover occurs in the region as a transient (Apr.–May, Sep.–Oct.), while the Pacific Golden-Plover winters (Aug.–Apr.). *Habitat:* Intertidal mud flats and beaches. *Abundance and Distribution:* Uncommon fall transient (Sep.–Oct.) and rare spring transient (Apr.–May) along the southern California coast. *Where to Find:* Ocean Beach County Park; Upper Newport Bay; Cabrillo National Monument. *Range:* Breeds in high arctic of New World; winters in South America.

115. Pacific Golden-Plover
Pluvialis fulva (L—11 W—23)
A Killdeer-sized plover; checked black, white, and gold on back and

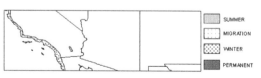

crown; white "headband" running from forehead, over eye and down side of neck; black face, and underparts. *Winter:* Heavy black bill contrasts with white at base of bill; pale eyebrow; crown and back brown and white often flecked with gold; underparts white, speckled with brown on breast; gray legs. *Voice:* A whistled "kew-wee." *Similar Species:* See American Golden-Plover. *Habitat:* Intertidal mud flats and beaches. *Abundance and Distribution:* Rare winter resident (Aug.–Apr.) along southern California coast. *Where to Find:* Ocean Beach County Park; Upper Newport Bay; Cabrillo National Monument. *Range:* Breeds in high arctic of Old World and Alaska; winters along tropical coasts of the Indian and western Pacific Ocean regions; at sea in western Pacific; and along the southern California and northern Baja California coasts.

116. Snowy Plover
Charadrius alexandrinus
(L—7 W—14)

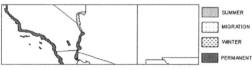

A small plover; grayish-brown crown, back and wings; white forehead, face, collar, and underparts; broad, dark line behind eye; partial dark band across breast, broken in the middle; black bill; black legs. *Immature:* Similar to adult but paler with dark gray legs. *Voice:* A low, whistled "pew-weet." *Similar Species:* The only other small plover that occurs regularly in this region is the Semipalmated Plover. The Snowy has gray legs, gray bill, pale gray back, and black or gray shoulder patch (not complete breast ring); the Semipalmated has orange legs, two-tone bill, orange at base, dark at tip; brown back; complete breast ring. *Habitat:* Sandy beaches, mud flats, salt flats, estuaries, bayshores. *Abundance and Distribution:* Uncommon resident* along the coast, Salton Sea area of southern California, and lower Colorado River valley; more numerous along coast in winter but scarcer inland; rare transient (Apr.–May, Aug.–Sep.) elsewhere. Rare, local summer resident* in southeastern Arizona (Willcox Sewage Lagoon) and southeastern New Mexico (Laguna Grande). *Where to Find:* Point Mugu State Park, California; Devereux Slough, California; Laguna Grande, New Mexico. *Range:* Breeds locally in temperate and tropical regions of the world; winters mainly in subtropical and tropical areas.

117. Semipalmated Plover
Charadrius semipalmatus
(L—7 W—15)

A small plover; brown back and head; white forehead; white post-orbital stripe; orange eyering; orange bill, black at tip; black lores; white chin and collar; black band across throat; white underparts; orange or yellow legs. *Winter:* Brown breast band; dull, dark bill (may show some orange at base). *Immature:* Similar to adult but eyering yellow, bill black at tip, brown at base, legs brown anteriorly, yellow posteriorly. *Voice:* A whistled "tew-wee." *Similar Species:* The other small plovers occurring here are paler and have incomplete breast bands. The Wilson's Plover (a casual or accidental visitor to the area) is larger, heavy-billed, and has flesh-colored legs (orange legs in adult Semipalmated Plover, grayish in juvenile). Fresh footprints in fine sand or mud will reveal the partial toe webbing that is characteristic for this species. Other plovers in this region lack webbing. *Habitat:* Estuarine mud flats, salt flats, beaches, bayshores. *Abundance and Distribution:* Common to uncommon transient (Apr.–May, Aug.–Sep.) throughout; common to uncommon winter resident in California along coast, scarce or absent in summer (late May–early July). *Where to Find:* Upper Newport Bay, California; Pahranagat Refuge, Nevada; Imperial National Wildlife Refuge, Arizona/California; Morgan Lake, New Mexico. *Range:* Breeds in high arctic of North America; winters mainly along temperate and tropical coasts from Georgia and California to southern South America; West Indies.

118. Killdeer

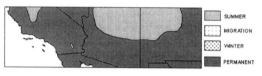

Charadrius vociferus (L—10 W—20) A medium-sized plover; brown back and head; orange rump; white forehead; white post-orbital stripe; orange eyering; dark bill; black lores; white chin and collar; two black bands across throat and upper breast; white underparts; pale legs. *Habits:* Feigns broken wing when young or nest are approached. *Voice:* "Kill de-er," also various peeps. *Similar Species:* The Killdeer is the only plover in this region with two black bars across breast; others have one or none. *Habitat:* Open areas. *Abundance and Distribution:* Common summer resident* throughout; withdraws from highlands in winter. *Where to Find:* Bosque del Apache, New Mexico; Kino Springs, Arizona; San Jacinto Wildlife Area, California; Corn Creek, Desert National Wildlife Range, Nevada. *Range:* Breeds from subarctic Canada and Alaska south to central Mexico, Greater Antilles, western South America; winters along coast from Washington and Massachusetts, and inland from southern United States, south to northern and western South America; West Indies.

119. Mountain Plover

Charadrius montanus (L—9 W—19) Nondescript, medium-sized plover; brown back, nape, and crown; white forehead and eyebrow; brown cheek; whitish below washed with buff on sides of breast; bill black; legs tan. *Habits:* Forages in typical plover fashion—quick runs followed by brief stops. *Voice:* A soft whistle. *Similar Species:* Winter golden-plovers have mottled back with some gold flecks, not plain brown back as in Mountain Plover. *Habitat:* Short-grass prairie, overgrazed pasture, plowed fields, deserts. *Abundance and Distribution:* Uncommon to rare and local summer resident* in plains of northeastern New Mexico (Mar.–Oct.); uncommon to rare winter resident (Nov.–Feb.) on the grasslands of the Carrizo Plain, Salton Sea, and irregularly along coast and at inland desert regions of southern California; transient in grasslands southwest of Albuquerque. *Where to Find:* Stubble fields along Highway 191 from Elfrida to Pearce, Arizona (winter); Capulin Volcano National Monument, New Mexico (breeding); Salton Sea National Wildlife Refuge, California (winter). *Range:* Breeds in dry, western Great Plains from southern Canada to northeastern New Mexico and west Texas; winters California, Arizona, Texas, and northern Mexico.

Family Haematopodidae
Oystercatchers
Stout, gull-like birds; black or black and white with a long, brilliant orange bill.

120. American Black Oystercatcher
Haematopus bachmani
(L—16 W—34)
Gull-sized bird; entirely black body;

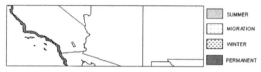

long, bright orange bill; red eyering; pinkish legs. *Immature:* Brownish body; dull orange or dusky bill. *Habits:* Feeds on oysters and other mussels by prying open the shells. *Voice:* A strident "weeep." *Habitat:* Rocky shores, jetties, breakwaters. *Abundance and Distribution:* Uncommon resident on Channel Islands; rare to casual along immediate coast. *Where to Find:* Channel Islands off the coast of southern California. *Range:* Resident along the North American Pacific coast from the Aleutians south to southern California.

Family Recurvirostridae
Avocets and Stilts
A small family of medium-sized, long-legged, long-billed, long-necked shorebirds.

121. Black-necked Stilt
Himantopus mexicanus
(L—14 W—27)
Spindly shorebird with long neck,

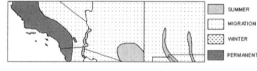

needle-like bill, and long legs; black head, nape, and back; white at base of bill, throat and underparts; white patch behind eye; pink legs. *Female:* Similar to male but paler. *Immature:* Brown rather than black. *Voice:* A rapid, buzzy "keer-keer-keer." *Habitat:* Mud flats, marshes, estuaries, ponds. *Abundance and Distribution:* Common permanent resident* in marshes at lower elevations in southern California; uncommon to rare and local summer resident* (Apr.–Oct.) in southeastern Arizona and in New Mexico impoundments along the Rio Grande and in the eastern plains; common to uncommon transient throughout (Apr.–May, Aug.–Sep.). *Where to Find:* Bosque del Apache, New Mexico; Salton Sea National Wildlife Refuge, California; Willcox Lake, Arizona. *Range:* Breeds locally in western United States and along coast in east from Massachusetts south locally along coasts of Middle and South America to northern Argentina, West Indies; winters from North Carolina south through breeding range.

122. American Avocet
Recurvirostra americana
(L—18 W—32)

Long-legged, long-necked shorebird with long, upturned bill; black and white back and wings; white belly; rusty-orange head; whitish at base of bill; gray legs. *Winter:* Head and neck mostly whitish with little rusty tinge. *Habits:* Forages by swinging submerged bill from side to side as it walks along. *Voice:* "Kleet kleet kleet." *Habitat:* Estuaries, ponds, lakes, mud flats, flooded pastures, bays. *Abundance and Distribution:* Common to uncommon resident* in southern California at Salton Sea, the lower Colorado River impoundments, and at western lowland and foothill marshes; uncommon to rare and local summer resident* (Apr.–Oct.) in southeastern Arizona and in New Mexico at Rio Grande and Pecos River impoundments; common transient throughout (Apr.–May, Aug.–Oct.). *Where to Find:* Salton Sea National Wildlife Refuge, California; Willcox Lake, Arizona; Bosque del Apache, New Mexico; Pharanagat National Wildlife Refuge, Nevada. *Range:* Breeds western and central Canada south through western United States to northern Mexico; winters southern United States to southern Mexico.

Family Scolopacidae
Sandpipers
Scolopacids constitute a diverse assemblage of shorebirds. Breeding plumage for most sandpipers is worn for only a short time, most of which is spent on arctic breeding grounds. As a result it is the winter plumage that is most often critical for identification of shorebirds in the Southwest. Many second-year birds and other non-breeders remain on the wintering ground or migration route through the summer. Hayman et al. (1986) provide a useful identification guide for this difficult group.

123. Greater Yellowlegs

Tringa melanoleuca

(L—14 W—25)

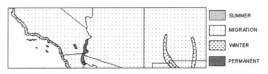

SUMMER
MIGRATION
WINTER
PERMANENT

Mottled grayish-brown above; head, breast and flanks white heavily streaked with grayish-brown; white belly and rump; long, yellow legs; bill long, often slightly up-turned and darker at tip than at base. *Winter:* Paler overall; streaking on breast and head is reduced. *Voice:* Rapid sequence of three, descending notes, "tew tew tew." *Similar Species:* The Greater Yellowlegs is twice the size of the Lesser Yellowlegs; the descending three-note call of the Greater is quite different from the Lesser's "pew" call, which generally is given as a single note or series of notes on the same pitch; Greater's bill is longer, thicker, slightly upturned and dusky (rather than dark) for basal third of lower mandible. *Habitat:* Mud flats, estuaries, marshes, prairies, flooded agricultural fields. *Abundance and Distribution:* Common to uncommon transient (Mar.–Apr., Aug.–Sep.) throughout; uncommon to rare winter resident (Oct.–Feb.) and rare to casual in summer (May–July) along the coast, at Salton Sea, and along the Colorado, Rio Grande, and Pecos River valleys. *Where to Find:* Bosque del Apache, New Mexico; Willcox Lake, Arizona; Upper Newport Bay, California. *Range:* Breeds in muskeg bogs and tundra of northern Canada and Alaska; winters coastal United States south to southern South America; West Indies.

124. Lesser Yellowlegs

Tringa flavipes

(L—11 W—20)

SUMMER
MIGRATION
WINTER
PERMANENT

Mottled grayish-brown above; head, breast and flanks white heavily streaked with grayish-brown; white belly and rump; yellow legs. *Winter:* Paler overall; streaking on breast and head is reduced. *Voice:* Single "pew" alarm note, repeated. *Similar Species:* See Greater Yellowlegs. *Habitat:* Mud flats, pond borders, flooded prairies, swales, estuaries. *Abundance and Distribution:* Common to uncommon transient (Apr.–May, Aug.–Sep.) throughout, more numerous in fall; uncommon to rare winter resident (Oct.–Mar.) in coastal southern California, Salton Sea, and the lower Colorado River valley; a few also summer (June–July) along the coast. *Where to Find:* Pharanagat Refuge, Nevada; San Jacinto Wildlife Area, California; Willcox Lake, Arizona; Morgan Lake, New Mexico. *Range:* Breeds northern Canada and Alaska; winters from Atlantic (South Carolina) and Pacific (southern California) coasts of United States south to southern South America; West Indies.

125. Solitary Sandpiper

Tringa solitaria

(L—9 W—17)

Dark gray back and wings with white spotting; heavily streaked with grayish-brown on head and breast; white eyering; long, greenish legs; tail dark in center, barred white on outer portions. *Winter:* Streaking on head and breast reduced or faint. *Habits:* Often bobs while foraging. *Voice:* A high-pitched "tseet-eet." *Similar Species:* Spotted Sandpiper is found in similar habitats; however, it bobs almost continuously, shows white on wings in flight (no white on wings in Solitary), has a pale eyebrow (Solitary has eyering), and no white spotting on folded wings; tail barring is much more prominent in the Solitary. Stilt Sandpiper and yellowlegs show white rump in flight (dark in Solitary). *Habitat:* Ponds, rivers, lakes. *Abundance and Distribution:* A uncommon to rare transient (Apr.–May, Aug.–Oct.), more numerous in fall. *Where to Find:* San Jacinto Wildlife Area, California; Bill Evans Lake, New Mexico; Buenos Aires National Wildlife Refuge, Arizona; Corn Creek, Desert National Wildlife Range, Nevada. *Range:* Breeds across arctic and boreal North America; winters in southern Atlantic (Georgia, Florida) and Gulf coasts of United States south to southern South America; West Indies.

126. Willet

Catoptrophorus semipalmatus

(L—15 W—27)

Large, heavy-bodied, long-billed shorebird; mottled grayish-brown above and below; whitish belly; broad white stripe on wing is conspicuous in flight. *Winter:* Gray above, whitish below. *Voice:* Shrill "will will-it," repeated. *Similar Species:* Large size, white wing stripes and flight call separate this from other shorebirds. *Habitat:* Estuaries, beaches, coastal ponds, marshes, mud flats. *Abundance and Distribution:* Common resident in southern California, has bred; common to uncommon transient (Apr.–May, July–Aug.) elsewhere. *Where to Find:* Mittry Lake, Arizona/California; Salton Sea National Wildlife Refuge, California; Pharanagat National Wildlife Refuge, Nevada; Dulce Lake, New Mexico. *Range:* Breeds southwestern and south central Canada and northwestern and north central United States, along Atlantic and Gulf coasts (Nova Scotia to Texas); West Indies; winters coastal North America (California and Virginia) south to northern half of South America; West Indies.

127. Wandering Tattler
Heteroscelus incanus
(L—11 W—21)
Gray above; scalloped dark gray and

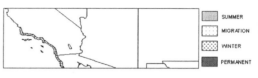

SUMMER
MIGRATION
WINTER
PERMANENT

white below; white forehead, eyeline, and chin; white crissum; yellowish legs and feet; gray bill. *Winter:* Gray above; white forehead; dark lores; gray face, throat, breast and flanks; white belly and under-tail coverts; yellowish legs and feet. *Habits:* Continually bobs while feeding. Also, the Tattler is quite tame, allowing close approach, and often crouching rather than flying. Often feeds alone or in small flocks. *Voice:* Flight call is a distinctive six- to ten-note trill given at the same pitch but with decreasing volume, "tew tu tu tu tu tu." *Similar Species:* The solid gray body (no mottling) contrasting with the white belly and yellowish legs are distinctive. *Habitat:* Rocky shores, jetties, breakwaters. *Abundance and Distribution:* Uncommon to rare winter resident (July–May) and rare to casual summer resident (June–July) along the coast from San Luis Obispo south; casual inland. *Where to Find:* Shell Beach; Point Vicente Park, Palos Verde Peninsula; La Jolla Beach. *Range:* Breeds in the southern half of Alaska, the Yukon, and western British Columbia; also Eurasia and northeastern Siberia. Winters on islands and coasts of the tropical Pacific Ocean, north to southern California.

128. Spotted Sandpiper
Actitis macularia
(L—8 W—13)
Grayish-brown above, white with

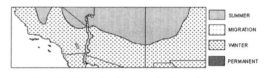

SUMMER
MIGRATION
WINTER
PERMANENT

dark spots below; white eyebrow; bill pinkish with dark tip; legs pinkish. *Winter:* Lacks spots; white below extending toward back at shoulder; grayish smear on side of breast; legs yellowish. *Habits:* Teeters almost continually while foraging; flight peculiar, with stiff-winged bursts and brief glides. *Voice:* "Peet weet." *Similar Species:* See Solitary Sandpiper. *Habitat:* Streams, ponds, rivers, lakes, beaches. *Abundance and Distribution:* Uncommon summer resident* (May–Aug.) in highlands of southern California, southern Nevada, northern Arizona, and northern New Mexico; common to uncommon transient (Apr.–May, Aug.–Oct.) and uncommon to rare winter resident (Nov.–Mar.) elsewhere. *Where to Find:* Rutherford Tract, San Juan River, New Mexico; Martinez Lake, Arizona (transient and winter); Louis Rubidoux Nature Center, California. *Range:* Breeds throughout temperate and boreal North America; winters from the southern United States south to northern Argentina; West Indies.

129. Upland Sandpiper

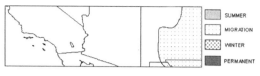

Bartramia longicauda (L—12 W—22)
Large, heavy body, long legs, long
neck, small head and short bill. Plum-
age is light brown with dark brown streaks on back and wings; buff head, neck and
breast mottled with brown; large brown eye. *Voice:* Call—"kip-ip", repeated. *Similar Species:* The Buff-breasted Sandpiper is found in similar habitats; however, it
has clear, unstreaked, buffy underparts contrasting with white wing linings in flight.
Habitat: Prairie, pastures, plowed fields. *Abundance and Distribution:* Formerly a
summer resident of the short grass prairie of northeastern New Mexico; now occurs as a rare transient (Aug.–Sep., Apr.–May, more numerous in fall) in the eastern plains and Rio Grande and Pecos River valleys of New Mexico. *Where to Find:*
Grasslands Turf Ranch, Valencia County; Bosque del Apache National Wildlife
Refuge, New Mexico. *Range:* Breeds across northeast and north central United
States and in Great Plains of Canada; winters South America.

130. Whimbrel

Numenius phaeopus (L—18 W—33)
Mottled gray and brown above; grayish below with dark flecks; crown
striped with dark brown and gray. *Voice:* Call—"kee kee kee kee." *Similar Species:*
Long-billed Curlew is larger, buffy, has a very long, decurved bill, and is not striped
prominently on crown. *Habitat:* Tall grass prairies, estuaries, oyster reefs. *Abundance and Distribution:* Common spring transient (Mar.–Apr.) in coastal southern California, rare to casual inland; uncommon fall transient and winter resident
along coast (July–Feb.), and rare summer straggler (May–June). *Where to Find:*
Tijuana Estuary National Wildlife Refuge, California; Pharanagat National Wildlife Refuge, Nevada; Bosque del Apache, New Mexico; Mittry Lake Wildlife Area,
Arizona/California. *Range:* Breeds in high arctic of Old and New World; winters in
subtropical and tropical regions.

131. Long-billed Curlew

Numenius americanus (L—23 W—38)
A large, heavy-bodied bird with very
long, decurved bill; mottled brown
and buff above; uniformly buffy below; rusty wing linings visible in flight. *Voice:* A
strident "per-leee," repeated. *Similar Species:* See Whimbrel. *Habitat:* Prairies, pastures, lawns, golf courses. *Abundance and Distribution:* Uncommon to rare transient throughout (Mar.–Apr., Aug.–Oct.); rare and local summer resident (may
breed) in plains of northeastern New Mexico; uncommon to rare winter resident

along the coast and resident at Salton Sea and the lower Colorado River valley. *Where to Find:* Fort Sumner State Monument, New Mexico; Salton Sea, California; Pahranagat National Wildlife Refuge, Nevada; Mittry Lake Wildlife Area, Arizona/California. *Range:* Breeds in prairie regions of western United States and southwestern Canada; winters from central California and southern portions of California, Arizona, Texas, and Louisiana south through southern Mexico.

132. Marbled Godwit
Limosa fedoa (L—18 W—31)
Mottled buff and dark brown above; buffy below barred with brown; long,

SUMMER
MIGRATION
WINTER
PERMANENT

upturned bill pink at base, dark at tip; rusty wing linings. *Winter:* Ventral barring faint or lacking. *Voice:* Call—"koo-wik" repeated. *Similar Species:* The Marbled Godwit is mottled buff and brown at all seasons (not gray and white as in the extremely rare Hudsonian Godwit); Marbled Godwit rump is mottled buff (not white as in Hudsonian), and underwing is cinnamon (not dark gray as in Hudsonian). *Habitat:* Bay shores, mud flats, estuaries, flooded prairies. *Abundance and Distribution:* Common transient and winter resident (July–May) with a few non-breeders remaining through the summer along the southern California coast and at Salton Sea. Uncommon to rare fall (Aug.–Sep.) and rare spring (Apr.–May) transient elsewhere in the region. *Where to Find:* Shell Beach, California; Willcox Lake, Arizona; Pahranagat National Wildlife Refuge, Nevada; Maxwell National Wildlife Refuge, New Mexico. *Range:* Breeds northern Great Plains of Canada and extreme northern United States; winters coastal United States from California and South Carolina south to northern South America.

133. Ruddy Turnstone
Arenaria interpres (L—10 W—19)
A plump bird with slightly upturned bill; rufous above, white below with

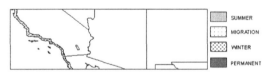

SUMMER
MIGRATION
WINTER
PERMANENT

black breast; black and white facial pattern; two white stripes on wings; white band across tail; orange legs. *Winter:* Grayish above; white below with varying amounts of black on breast and face. *Voice:* A single, whistled "tew," also a low chatter. *Similar Species:* Both turnstone species show a distinctive dorsal pattern in flight of white stripe on the wing, white back stripe, and white rump set off against otherwise dark wings, back and tail. The winter plumage Ruddy Turnstone has orange legs (not dull reddish as in the darker, chunkier Black Turnstone). *Habitat:* Beaches, mud flats. *Abundance and Distribution:* Uncommon transient (July–Sep., Apr.–May) and uncommon to rare winter resident in coastal southern California; rare to casual transient elsewhere in the region. *Where to Find:* Upper Newport Bay;

Figure 24. Perhaps because the old name of "Tijuana Slough" has some pejorative connotations, this site on the California/Mexico border is formally titled the Tijuana Estuary National Wildlife Refuge. Regardless of what they are called, the broad and beautiful marshes are rich with bird life including Heermann's Gull, Whimbrel, Least Tern, and Clapper Rail.

Figure 25. Water in the desert can attract birds not normally found in a region. Such is the case with Many Farms Lake, Arizona, which attracts waterbird species found at few other sites in northeastern Arizona, including Ring-billed Gull, Common Snipe, American Coot, Eared Grebe, and Mallard.

South Bay Marine Biological Area, San Diego; Goleta Point, Santa Barbara. *Range:* Breeds in high arctic of Old and New World; winters in south temperate and tropical regions.

134. Black Turnstone
Arenaria melanocephala
(L—10 W—19)

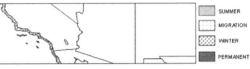

A plump bird with slightly upturned bill; slate gray above; slate gray head and breast; white malar blotch; white belly and under-tail coverts; legs dusky red; bill black; two white stripes on wings; white band across tail. *Winter:* Gray back, head, and breast; white belly and under-tail coverts; reddish legs. *Voice:* A chatter, higher pitched than Ruddy Turnstone. *Similar Species:* See Ruddy Turnstone. *Habitat:* Rocky shores, jetties, breakwaters. *Abundance and Distribution:* Uncommon transient and winter resident (July–May) and rare summer resident in coastal southern California. *Where to Find:* Point Vicente Park, Palos Verde Peninsula; Cabrillo National Monument, San Diego; Goleta Point, Santa Barbara. *Range:* Breeds in coastal Alaska; winters from southeastern Alaska south along the Pacific coast to Sinaloa on the Mexican Pacific coast.

135. Surfbird
Aphriza virgata
(L—10 W—17)

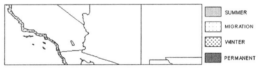

Mottled black, brown and white above; white below with black checks; rump white; tail white with black terminal wedge; white wing stripe on dark wings; bill dark with yellowish basal half of lower mandible. *Winter:* As in breeding but slate gray above and below with white belly; white eyebrow and throat. *Voice:* Call—"tew tew tew." *Similar Species:* The winter turnstones are similar chunky gray birds, but the winter Surfbird has a whitish throat, (dark in turnstones), yellowish legs (reddish or orange in turnstones), and bill yellowish at base (dark in turnstones). *Habitat:* Rocky shores, jetties, breakwaters. *Abundance and Distribution:* Uncommon transient and winter resident (Aug.–Apr.), scarce in summer, along the coast of southern California. *Where to Find:* Point Vicente Park, Palos Verde Peninsula; Cabrillo National Monument, San Diego; Goleta Point, Santa Barbara. *Range:* Breeds in mountain tundra of central Alaska; winters along Pacific Coast of North America and both coasts of Middle and South America.

136. Red Knot

Calidris canutus (L—11 W—21)

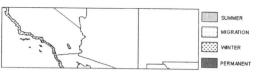

A plump bird, mottled brown and russet above and on crown; rusty below. *Winter:* Pale gray above; grayish breast; whitish belly; white eyebrow; white, finely barred rump. *Voice:* A hoarse "kew kew." *Similar Species:* Dowitchers are white up the back; Sanderling is smaller and lacks white rump; other sandpipers of similar plumage are sparrow-sized. *Habitat:* Beaches, bay shorelines, mud flats. *Abundance and Distribution:* Uncommon transient (Aug.–Sep., Apr.–May) and rare winter resident along southern California coast and Salton Sea; rare to casual in summer. *Where to Find:* Bolsa Chica State Ecological Reserve; South Bay Marine Biological Study Area, San Diego; Salton Sea. *Range:* Breeds in Old and New World high arctic; winters in temperate and tropical coastal regions.

137. Sanderling

Calidris alba

(L—8 W—16)

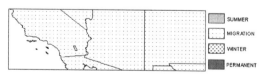

A chunky, feisty peep of the beaches; dappled brown, white and black on back and crown; rusty flecked with white on face and breast; short black legs and bill; lacks hind toe (hallux); white wing stripe. *Winter:* As in breeding but mottled gray and white above; white below; white eyebrow; grayish shoulder patch extends to side of breast. *Habits:* Spends considerable time in chases and fights with other Sanderlings. *Voice:* Call—"kwit." *Similar Species:* Other winter peeps are more or less streaked with grayish on throat and breast (throat and breast are white on winter Sanderling); also Sanderling has palest back. *Habitat:* Beaches. *Abundance and Distribution:* Common winter resident (Aug.–May) and uncommon to rare summer resident (June–July) along southern California coast; uncommon to rare fall transient (Aug.–Sep.) inland. *Where to Find:* Santa Clara River Estuary; Shell Beach; Imperial Beach, San Diego; Pahranagat National Wildlife Refuge, Nevada; Morgan Lake, New Mexico. *Range:* Breeds in high arctic of Old and New World; winters on temperate and tropical beaches.

138. Semipalmated Sandpiper

Calidris pusilla (L—6 W—12)

Dark brown, russet and white above; finely streaked brown and white on head and breast; pale eyebrow with some rusty on crown and cheek; white belly; partial webbing between toes (hence "semipalmated"). *Winter:* Grayish above with grayish wash on head and breast; white belly. *Voice:* Call—"chit" or "chek." *Similar Species:* Winter plumaged Western Sandpiper essentially is identical to winter Semipalmated. They can be separated by voice ("chek" in Semipalmated, "zheet" in Western). The bill of the Western averages longer than that of Semipalmated, and in longer-billed birds there is a noticeable droop at the tip. However, there is considerable overlap in this and all other characters used to separate the winter-plumaged birds in the field, except voice. (Phillips 1975). *Habitat:* Mud flats, ponds, lakes. *Abundance and Distribution:* Rare transient (Aug., Apr.–May). *Where to Find:* Salton Sea, California; Bosque del Apache National Wildlife Refuge, New Mexico. *Range:* Breeds in high arctic of North America; winters along both coasts of Middle and South America to Paraguay (east) and northern Chile (west); West Indies.

139. Western Sandpiper

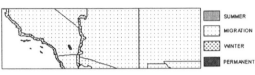

Calidris mauri (L—6 W—12)

Dark brown, russet and white above; finely streaked brown and white on head and breast; pale eyebrow; partial webbing on toes; similar to Semipalmated Sandpiper but whiter on back, and with distinct rusty cheek and supraorbital patches. *Winter:* Grayish above with grayish wash on head and breast; white belly. *Voice:* Call—"zheet." *Similar Species:* See Semipalmated Sandpiper. *Habitat:* Beaches, mud flats, ponds, lakes, estuaries, swales. *Abundance and Distribution:* Common transient and winter resident (July–May) and rare in summer (June–July) in coastal southern California, Salton Sea, and Colorado River valley; common to uncommon transient (Aug.–Sep., Apr.–May) elsewhere. *Where to Find:* Morro Bay, California; Morgan Lake, New Mexico; Davis Dam, Nevada; Avra Valley Sewage Ponds, Arizona. *Range:* Breeds in high arctic of northern Alaska and northeastern Siberia; winters along both coasts of United States from California and North Carolina south to northern South America; West Indies.

140. Least Sandpiper

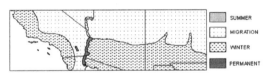

Calidris minutilla (L—6 W—12)

Dark brown and buff on back and wings; head and breast streaked with brown and white; relatively short, thin bill; white belly; yellowish legs (sometimes brown with caked mud). *Winter:* Brownish-gray above; buffy wash on breast. *Voice:* Call—"preep." *Similar Species:* Yellow legs are distinctive (other small peeps have dark legs), as is call note. *Habitat:* Ponds, lakes, swales, mud flats. *Abundance and Distribution:* Common transient and winter resident (July–May) and rare in summer (June–July) in southern California; common to uncommon transient (Aug.–May) throughout and uncommon winter resident except in highlands. *Where to Find:* Salton Sea, California; Davis Dam, Nevada; Buenos Aires National Wildlife Refuge, Arizona; Las Vegas National Wildlife Refuge, New Mexico. *Range:* Breeds across northern North America; winters from coastal (Oregon, North Carolina) and southern United States south to northern half of South America; West Indies.

141. Baird's Sandpiper
Calidris bairdii (L—8 W—15)

A medium-sized sandpiper, dark brown and buff on back and wings;

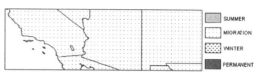

buffy head and breast flecked with brown; wings extend beyond tail. *Voice:* Call— "chureep." *Similar Species:* Brownish (rather than grayish) winter plumage makes this bird look like a large Least Sandpiper. Long wings, black bill and legs, and dark rump separate it from the Least and other peeps. *Habitat:* Ponds, lakes, swales. *Abundance and Distribution:* Uncommon fall transient (Aug.–Sep.), rare or casual in spring (Apr.–May), throughout. *Where to Find:* San Jacinto Wildlife Area, California; Sierra Vista Wastewater Ponds, Arizona; Las Vegas National Wildlife Refuge, New Mexico. *Range:* Breeds in high arctic of North America and northeastern Siberia; winters in western and southern South America.

142. Pectoral Sandpiper
Calidris melanotos (L—9 W—17)

Dark brown, tan, and white on back and wings; head and breast whitish,

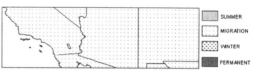

densely flecked with brown; belly white, the dividing line between mottled brown breast and white belly distinct; dark bill; yellow legs. *Voice:* Call—"prip." *Similar Species:* No other sandpiper shows sharp contrast of breast and belly coloration. *Habitat:* Wet prairies, ponds, lakes, swales, agricultural fields. *Abundance and Distribution:* Uncommon fall transient (Sep.–Oct.), rare or casual in spring (Mar.–Apr.), throughout. *Where to Find:* Las Vegas Wash, New Mexico; San Jacinto Wildlife Area, California; Willcox Lake, Arizona; Bosque del Apache National Wildlife Refuge, New Mexico. *Range:* Breeds in the high arctic of northern North America; winters in southern half of South America.

143. Dunlin
Calidris alpina (L—9 W—16)

Rusty and dark brown on back and wings; white streaked with black on

neck and breast; crown streaked with russet and black; large black smudge on belly; long bill droops at tip. *Winter:* As in breeding but with dark gray back; head and breast pale gray with some streaking; white eyebrow; white belly. *Voice:* A hoarse "zheet." *Similar Species:* Dark gray back and long, drooping bill distinguish the winter Dunlin from other gray-breasted peeps. *Habitat:* Ponds, lakes, beaches, mud flats. *Abundance and Distribution:* Uncommon to rare transient (Apr., Oct.) throughout, scarcer eastward in New Mexico; uncommon winter resident (Nov.–Mar.) along coast. *Where to Find:* Upper Newport Bay, California; Overton Wildlife Management Area, Nevada; Bosque del Apache National Wildlife Refuge, New Mexico; Willcox Lake, Arizona. *Range:* Breeds in arctic of Old and New World; winters in temperate and northern tropical regions.

144. Stilt Sandpiper
Calidris himantopus
(L—9 W—17)
A trim, long-necked, long-legged

sandpiper, dark brown and buff on back and wings; crown streaked with dark brown and white; white eyebrow; chestnut pre- and postorbital stripe; white streaked with brown on neck; white barred with brown on breast and belly; long, yellow-green legs; white rump; long, straight bill (twice length of head). *Winter:* Gray and white mottling on back; gray head with prominent eyebrow; gray throat and breast; whitish belly with gray flecks. *Habits:* Often feeds with rapid up-and-down motion in breast-deep water. *Voice:* A low "whurp." *Similar Species:* Winter Lesser Yellowlegs has barred (not gray) tail; winter dowitchers have longer bill (three times length of head), flanks with dark bars or spots, and show white on lower back in flight. *Habitat:* Mud flats, flooded pastures, lakes, ponds. *Abundance and Distribution:* Rare transient (Aug.–Sep., Mar.–Apr.), mainly in fall, throughout; rare winter resident at Salton Sea, California. *Where to Find:* Salton Sea, California; Willcox Lake, Arizona; Bosque del Apache National Wildlife Refuge, New Mexico. *Range:* Breeds in arctic of north-central Canada; winters in central South America.

145. Short-billed Dowitcher
Limnodromus griseus (L—11 W—19)
A rather squat, long-billed sandpiper
(bill is three times length of head);

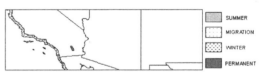

mottled black, white, and buff on back, wings, and crown; cinnamon buff on neck and underparts barred and spotted with dark brown; belly white; white line above eye with dark line through eye; white tail barred with black; white on rump extending in a wedge up back; bill dark; legs greenish. *Winter:* Grayish crown, nape, and back; white line above eye and dark line through eye; grayish neck and breast fading to whitish on belly; flanks and under-tail coverts spotted and barred with dark brown. *Juvenile:* Patterned like adult but paler brown above and on head, and with buffy neck and breast. *Habits:* Often feeds with rapid up-and-down motion, breast-deep in water, usually in small flocks. *Voice:* Repeated "tu tu" or "tu tu tu." *Similar Species:* Short-billed has a two- or three-note whistle, "tu tu tu," while the

Long-billed has a thin "eek." *Habitat:* Mud flats, flooded pastures, ponds, lakes, estuaries. *Abundance and Distribution:* Common transient (Mar.–May, July–Sep.), uncommon winter resident (Oct.–Feb.) and rare summer resident (June) in coastal southern California; common fall and uncommon spring transient at Salton Sea, California; rare fall transient (Aug.–Sep.) elsewhere west of New Mexico, where casual or accidental. *Where to Find:* Montaña de Oro State Park, California; Upper Newport Bay, California; Salton Sea, California. *Range:* Breeds across central Canada and southern Alaska; winters coastal United States (California, South Carolina) south to northern South America; West Indies.

146. Long-billed Dowitcher
Limnodromus scolopaceus
(L—11 W—19)
A squat, long-billed sandpiper (bill is

three times length of head); mottled black, white, and buff on back, wings, and crown; cinnamon buff on neck and underparts barred and spotted with dark brown; belly white; white line above eye with dark line through eye; white tail barred with black; white on rump extending in a wedge up back; bill dark; legs greenish. *Winter:* Grayish crown, nape, and back; white line above eye and dark line through eye; grayish neck and breast fading to whitish on belly; flanks and under-tail coverts spotted and barred with dark brown. *Juvenile:* Patterned like adult in winter. *Voice:* A thin "eek," often repeated. *Similar Species:* See Short-billed Dowitcher. *Habitat:* Mud flats, flooded pastures. *Abundance and Distribution:* Common transient and winter resident (Aug.–May), rare in summer (June–July) at wetlands in coastal, lowland, and foothill regions of southern California; common summer and scarce winter resident at Salton Sea and lower Colorado River valley; uncommon to rare transient (Sep.–Oct., Apr.–May) and rare and local winter resident elsewhere. *Where to Find:* Montaña de Oro State Park, California; Upper Newport Bay, California; Salton Sea, California; Buenos Aires National Wildlife Refuge, Arizona; Las Vegas National Wildlife Refuge, New Mexico. *Range:* Breeds in coastal Alaska, northwestern Canada, and northeastern Siberia; winters southern United States to Guatemala.

147. Common Snipe
Gallinago gallinago (L—11 W—17)
Dark brown back with white stripes; crown striped with dark brown and

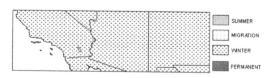

gray; neck and breast streaked grayish-brown and white; whitish belly; tan rump; tail banded with rust and black; very long bill (three times length of head). *Habits:* Normally solitary, retiring, and wary; gives an explosive "zhrrt" when flushed and flies in erratic swoops and dips. *Voice:* Song—given on wing from high in the air, "cheek cheek cheek cheek," plus a winnowing sound made by air passing through the tail feathers. *Habitat:* Marshes, bogs, flooded pastures, wet ditches. *Abundance and Distribution:* Uncommon transient and winter resident (Oct.–Apr.) at low to mid-elevations throughout; uncommon transient in highlands (Sep.–Oct., Mar.–Apr.); summers occasionally in highlands. *Where to Find:* Bosque del Apache, New Mexico; Sierra Vista Sewage Treatment Plant, Arizona; Lake Hemet, San Jacinto Mountains, California. *Range:* Breeds in north temperate and boreal regions of Old and New World; winters in south temperate and tropical regions.

148. Wilson's Phalarope

Phalaropus tricolor

(L—9 W—17)

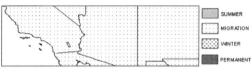

Female: A trim, thin-billed, long-necked bird; chestnut and gray on the back; gray crown and nape; black extending from eye down side of neck; white chin; chestnut throat; white breast and belly. *Male:* Similar but paler. *Winter:* Grayish brown above, white below; gray head with white eyebrow; white chin; rusty throat. *Habits:* Unlike other shorebirds, phalaropes often swim, whirling in tight circles, while foraging. *Voice:* Call—a nasal "wak," repeated. *Similar Species:* Other phalaropes have white foreheads and black and white facial pattern in winter. *Habitat:* Ponds, lakes, mud flats, flooded pastures. *Abundance and Distribution:* Common transient (Aug., May) throughout. *Where to Find:* Overton Wildlife Management Area, Nevada; Bolsa Chica State Ecological Reserve, California; Bosque del Apache, New Mexico; Buenos Aires National Wildlife Refuge, Arizona. *Range:* Breeds western United States, southwestern Canada and in Great Lakes region; winters western and southern South America.

149. Red-necked Phalarope

Phalaropus lobatus (L—8 W—14)

Female: Black with rusty striping on back and flanks; white below; neck

and nape orange; head black; chin white. *Male:* Similar in pattern but paler. *Winter:* Black back with white striping; white below; white forehead; gray-black crown; white eyebrow; black postorbital stripe. *Habits:* Unlike other shorebirds, phalaropes often swim while foraging, whirling in tight circles. *Voice:* Call—a hoarse "chik" or "ker-chik." *Similar Species:* Winter Red Phalarope has a pearl-gray, unstreaked back; Red-necked is almost black on back, striped with white. *Habitat:* Marshes, ponds, lakes; but mainly pelagic. *Abundance and Distribution:* Uncommon to rare fall transient (late July–Sep.) throughout, scarcer and local eastward in New Mexico; uncommon spring transient (Apr.–May) along coast; rare to casual elsewhere in spring. *Where to Find:* Overton Wildlife Management Area, Nevada; Bolsa Chica State Ecological Reserve, California; Sierra Vista Wastewater Ponds, Arizona; Morgan Lake, New Mexico. *Range:* Breeds in northern tundra bogs of Old and New World; winters at sea in southern Pacific and Indian oceans.

150. Red Phalarope
Phalaropus fulicaria (L—9 W—17)
Female: Black back striped with buff;
neck and underparts rusty orange;

SUMMER
MIGRATION
WINTER
PERMANENT

black cap; white cheek; relatively short, heavy bill is yellow at base, black at tip. *Male:* Similar in pattern but paler. *Winter:* Uniform pearl-gray on back; white below; white forehead and front half of crown; gray rear half of crown and nape line; dark postorbital stripe; bill blackish. *Habits:* Unlike other shorebirds, phalaropes often swim while foraging, whirling in tight circles. *Similar Species:* See Red-necked Phalarope. *Habitat:* Beaches, mud flats; but mainly pelagic in winter. *Abundance and Distribution:* Common transient offshore (July–Dec., Apr.–May), uncommon along coast; uncommon to rare and local fall transient inland (July–Dec.); casual in New Mexico. *Where to Find:* Channel Islands boat trip, California. *Range:* Breeds in Old and New World arctic; winters in southern Pacific and Atlantic oceans.

Family Laridae
This family is sub-divided into four distinct groupings: (1) jaegers and skuas, (2) gulls, (3) terns, and (4) skimmers. The jaegers and skuas are dark, heavy-bodied, Herring Gull-sized birds with hooked, predatory beaks and protruding central tail feathers. The wings are long, pointed, and sharply angled at the wrist. Three to four years are spent in subadult and immature plumages before full adult plumage is achieved with the characteristic central tail feathers. Until that time, the central tail feathers are only slightly or moderately protruding. These are the hawks of the oceans. They feed on stolen fish and the eggs and young of other seabirds. Characteristic behavior is chasing gulls and terns in attempts to rob them of captured fish. They are pelagic except during the breeding season. The most probable locality for locating a jaeger is along the immediate coast, offshore islands, or at sea.

Gulls vary in size; most are various patterns of gray and white as adults, although several species are black-headed. Like jaegers, they have several intermediate plumages between hatching and attainment of full adult plumage at two to four years of age. We do not attempt to describe all of these plumages. In most cases, we describe an adult breeding plumage, a winter plumage (where applicable), and a "typical" immature plumage.

Terns are thin-billed, trim-bodied seabirds. Most species forage by plummeting into the water from a height of ten to thirty feet to catch fish.

The skimmers are long-winged birds with long bills shaped like a straight razor in which the lower mandible protrudes beyond the upper. They feed by flying above the water with the lower mandible dipped just below the surface to capture fish.

Field identification of the immature species for some groups within the Laridae can be difficult or impossible. Harrison (1983) and Grant (1982) provide detailed descriptions and keys for advanced students of these birds.

151. Pomarine Jaeger
Stercorarius pomarinus
(L—22 W—48)

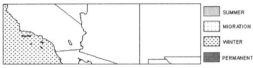

Protruding central tail feathers are twisted; dark brown above; white collar tinged with yellow; whitish below with dark breast band and under-tail coverts. *Dark Phase:* Completely dark brown with white at base of primaries; cheeks tinged with yellow; dark cap. *Immature:* Barred brown or brown and white below. *Similar Species:* The Pomarine Jaeger has twisted tail feathers; Parasitic Jaeger has pointed tail feathers; Long-tailed Jaeger has very long central tail feathers (half of body length). *Habitat:* Pelagic; beaches. *Abundance and Distribution:* Uncommon transient and winter visitor (Aug.–May), mainly offshore; uncommon transient along coast (Aug.–Oct., Apr.–May), rare in winter. *Where to Find:* Channel Islands boat trip; Montaña de Oro State Park cliffs, scanning offshore; Lifeguard Station at Point La Jolla, San Diego, scanning offshore. *Range:* Breeds in Old and New World arctic; winters in temperate and tropical oceans.

152. Parasitic Jaeger
Stercorarius parasiticus
(L—19 W—42)

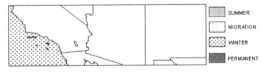

Dark brown above; white collar and white below with faint brown breast band; pointed, protruding central tail feathers; wings dark but whitish at base of primaries. *Dark Phase:* Completely dark brown. *Immature:* Dark brown above; barred reddish brown or brown and white below. *Similar Species:* See Pomarine Jaeger. *Habitat:* Pelagic; beaches. *Abundance and Distribution:* Uncommon transient (Aug.–Dec., May), mainly offshore; uncommon transient along coast (Aug.–Oct., Apr.–May), rare in winter. *Where to Find:* Channel Islands boat trip; Montaña de Oro State Park cliffs, scanning offshore; Lifeguard Station at Point La Jolla, San Diego, scanning offshore. *Range:* Breeds in Old and New World arctic; winters in temperate and tropical oceans.

153. Laughing Gull

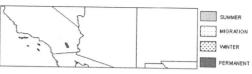

Larus atricilla (L—17 W—40)

Black head; gray back and wings with black wingtips; white collar, underparts, and tail; scarlet bill and black legs; partial white eyering. *Winter:* As in breeding but head whitish with dark-gray ear patch; black bill. *Immature:* Brownish
above and on breast; white belly and tail with black terminal bar. *Voice:* A raucous,
derisive "kaah kah-kah-kah-kah kaah kaah," also a single "keeyah." *Similar Species:*
Laughing Gull has black wingtips and whitish head with dark ear patches in winter; Franklin's Gull shows white tips on black primaries and a darkish hood in
winter. *Habitat:* Beaches, bays, lakes, agricultural areas. *Abundance and Distribution:* Common to uncommon fall transient (July–Oct.) and rare resident at other
times at Salton Sea, California. *Where to Find:* Salton Sea, California. *Range:* Breeds
along both coasts in North America from New Brunswick on the east and northern Mexico on the west, south to northern South America; West Indies.

154. Franklin's Gull

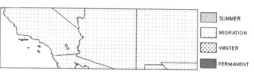

Larus pipixcan (L—15 W—36)

Black head; gray back and wings;
white bar bordering black wingtips
spotted terminally with white; white collar, underparts, and tail; underparts variously tinged with rose; scarlet bill and legs; partial white eyering. *Winter:* As in
breeding but head with a partial, dark hood; black bill. *Immature:* Similar to winter adult but with black terminal tail band. *Voice:* "Ayah." *Similar Species:* See Laughing Gull. *Habitat:* Tall grass prairie, pastures, flooded fields, bays. *Abundance and
Distribution:* Rare fall transient (Oct.–Nov.) along coast; uncommon to rare transient (Oct.–Nov., Apr.–May), more numerous in spring in southern Nevada, Arizona, New Mexico. *Where to Find:* Lake Mead, Nevada; Willcox Lake, Arizona; Las
Vegas National Wildlife Refuge, New Mexico. *Range:* Breeds north-central United
States and south-central Canada; winters along Pacific coast of Middle and South
America.

155. Bonaparte's Gull

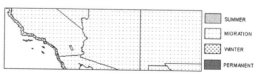

Larus philadelphia (L—14 W—32)

A small gull; black head; gray back;
wings gray with white outer prima-
ries tipped in black; white collar, underparts, and tail; black bill; red legs. *Winter:*
White head with black ear patch. *Immature:* Like winter adult but with black tail
band and brown stripe running diagonally across gray wing; flesh-colored legs;
black bill. *Voice:* A high-pitched, screechy "aaaanhh." *Similar Species:* There are two

Figure 26. Deep water comes close to the shore at La Jolla Point in San Diego. Pelagic species that can be seen occasionally from this vantage point include Pomarine Jaeger, Black-legged Kittiwake, Short-tailed Shearwater, and Sabine's Gull.

Figure 27. The scrub-covered hills, rocky cliffs, and sandy beaches of Montaña de Oro State Park offer a wide range of characteristic California coastal environments that attract a number of interesting bird species. Cormorants, gulls, shorebirds, and pelagic species like the Common Murre and Sooty Shearwater can be seen at times using a spotting scope from the bluffs. Also typical California scrub species such as Chestnut-backed Chickadee and Pacific-slope Flycatcher can be found in the chaparral.

other black-headed gull species that occur regularly in the Southwest: the Laughing Gull and Franklin's Gull. Both are much larger than the Bonaparte's Gull. Also, Bonaparte's Gull has red or flesh-colored legs and feet (not dark as in Laughing and Franklin's). Also, Bonaparte's has white outer primaries tipped with black (Laughing has black outer primaries and Franklin's has black outer primaries tipped with white). *Habitat:* Marine, bays, estuaries, lakes. *Abundance and Distribution:* Common winter resident (Oct.–Apr.) along coast; uncommon to rare transient (Oct.–Nov., Apr.–May) inland. *Where to Find:* Andree Clark Bird Refuge, California; Willcox Lake, Arizona; Morgan Lake, New Mexico; Overton Wildlife Management Area, Nevada. *Range:* Breeds across north-central and northwestern North America in Canada and Alaska; winters south along both coasts, from Washington on the west and Nova Scotia on the east, to central Mexico; also the Great Lakes, Bahamas; and Greater Antilles.

156. Heermann's Gull

Larus heermanni (L—19 W—51)

Dark gray above, pearl below with white head; red bill with black tip;

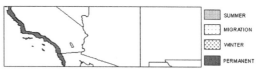

rump pale gray; tail black with narrow white terminal band; wings dark with white tips; legs dark. *Winter:* Head streaked with gray. *Immature:* Dark brown throughout; bill pale at base, black at tip. *Voice:* A "whistled whine, and a co-wak, sometimes repeated." (Edwards 1972:65). *Habitat:* Marine, beaches. *Abundance and Distribution:* Common resident along southern California coast for most of the year (June–Mar.), uncommon to rare in spring (Apr.–May). *Where to Find:* Tijuana Estuary National Wildlife Refuge; Guadalupe County Park; Little Corona City Beach. *Range:* Breeds from central California to southern Mexico, mainly (exclusively?) on coastal islands; Pacific Coast from southern British Columbia to Guatemala during non-breeding period.

157. Mew Gull

Larus canus (L—16 W—43)

White body and tail; dark gray back; gray wings, primaries tipped in black

and white; short, yellow bill; greenish legs; dark eye. *Winter:* Like summer, but mottled with brown on head and breast. *Immature:* First Year—Grayish-brown back; white head mottled with brown; brown below; dark wings and tail; pale legs; two-tone bill, pale at base, dark at tip; Second Year—Gray back; white body, mottled with brown on head and breast; pale legs; two-tone bill. *Voice:* "A low mewing . . . , quee'u or mee'u. Also hiyah-hiyah-hiyah, etc., higher than other gulls." (Peterson 1961:132). *Similar Species:* Solid yellow bill and dark eye separate adults of this species from Ring-billed Gulls; most first-year Mew Gulls have a dark tail, first-year Ring-billed Gulls have a distinct, dark, subterminal band on light tail. *Habitat:* Marshes, lakes, bays. *Abundance and Distribution:* Uncommon to rare winter visitor along southern California coast (Nov.–Feb.), rare to casual inland. *Where to Find:* Santa Maria Municipal Dump; South Bay Marine Biological Area, San Diego; Guadalupe County Park; Little Corona City Beach. *Range:* Breeds western North America (Alaska to Washington) and northern Eurasia; winters along Pacific Coast of North America (southeastern Alaska to southern California); Mediterranean Sea; Middle East and southern Asia.

158. Ring-billed Gull

Larus delawarensis (L—16 W—48)
White body; gray back; gray wings
with black outer primaries tipped

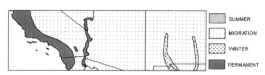

with white; bill orange-yellow with black, subterminal ring; legs pale yellow. *Immature:* Like adult but mottled with brown or gray; bill pale with black tip; whitish tail with black terminal band. *Voice:* A strident "ayah." *Similar Species:* Immature Herring Gulls are much larger; tail is mostly dark in Herring Gull, lacking a sub-terminal band as in immature Ring-billed Gull, and lacks white terminal band. *Habitat:* Lakes, bays, beaches, estuaries. *Abundance and Distribution:* Common to uncommon winter resident (Sep.–May) and uncommon to rare summer resident in wetlands of coastal, lowland, and foothill areas of southern California, Salton Sea, and Colorado River valley; uncommon to rare winter resident at Rio Grande and Pecos River valleys; uncommon to rare transient elsewhere. *Where to Find:* Cochiti Reservoir, New Mexico; Lake Mead, Nevada; Little Corona City Beach, California; Willcox Lake, Arizona. *Range:* Breeds in Great Plains region of central Canada, scattered areas in northern United States; winters across most of United States except northern plains and mountains south to Panama.

159. California Gull

Larus californicus (L—21 W—40)
White body; gray back; gray wings
with black outer primaries tipped

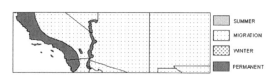

with white; bill yellow with red spot on lower mandible; feet pale yellow. *Winter:* Head and breast smudged with brown. *Immature:* Mottled dark brown in first winter; bill pale with black tip; legs pinkish; tail dark; grayish above, whitish below in second winter; legs pale greenish. *Habits:* This species forages inland locally over agricultural areas of the west. It is much venerated by the Mormons for saving their crops from destruction by locusts during the early settlement years. *Voice:* "Call a soft 'kow kow kow' or 'kuk kuk kuk.'" (Harrison 1983:341). *Similar Species:*

Immature Herring Gull has all black (not two-tone) bill in first winter and pinkish (not greenish) legs in second winter. *Habitat:* Lakes, bays, beaches, estuaries, marine, agricultural fields. *Abundance and Distribution:* Common to uncommon in summer (June–Aug.—non-breeders) at lakes and along the coast throughout much of southern California, Salton Sea, and the Colorado River valley, less common in winter inland (Sep.–May); rare to casual transient (mainly fall—Sep.–Nov.) elsewhere in the region. *Where to Find:* Davis Dam, Nevada/Arizona; Little Corona City Beach, California; Upper Newport Bay, California. *Range:* Breeds west-central Canada and northwestern United States; winters along Pacific Coast from Vancouver to central Mexico.

160. Herring Gull

Larus argentatus (L—24 W—57)
White body; gray back; gray wings with black outer primaries tipped

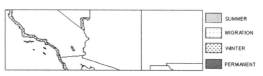

with white; bill yellow with red spot on lower mandible; feet pinkish; yellow eye. *Winter:* Head and breast smudged with brown. *Immature:* Mottled dark brown in first winter; bill black; feet pinkish; tail dark; in second and third winter, grayish above, whitish below variously mottled with brown; tail with broad, dark, terminal band; bill pinkish with black tip; legs pinkish. *Voice:* The familiar, rusty gate squawking "Qeeyah kwa kwa kwa kwa" of all Hollywood shows that include an ocean scene. *Similar Species:* See California Gull. Adult Thayer's Gull can be distinguished (with difficulty) from Herring Gull, with which it used to be considered conspecific, by dark eye, darker pink legs, and outer primary black at base, white at tip (entirely black in adult Herring Gull). *Habitat:* Beaches, bays, marine, lakes, rivers. *Abundance and Distribution:* Common winter resident (Nov.–Mar.) along southern California coast and at Salton Sea; uncommon to rare in winter at Lake Mead; rare to casual in winter elsewhere in region. *Where to Find:* Salton Sea, California; South Bay Marine Biological Area, California; Davis Dam, Nevada/Arizona; Conchas Lake, New Mexico. *Range:* Breeds in boreal and north temperate regions of both Old and New World; winters along coasts of far north, southward into temperate and north tropical regions.

161. Thayer's Gull

Larus thayeri (L—23 W—55)
White body; gray back; gray wings with outer primaries dark gray tipped

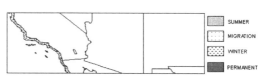

with white; bill yellow with red spot on lower mandible; brown eye (sometimes yellow shot with brown); legs pinkish. *Winter:* Head and breast smudged with brown. *Immature:* Mottled dark brown in first winter; bill black; feet pinkish; tail dark; grayish above, whitish below mottled with brown in second and third winters; bill pinkish with black tip; legs pinkish. *Similar Species:* See Herring Gull. *Habitat:* Beaches, bays, estuaries. *Abundance and Distribution:* Uncommon to rare winter resident (Oct.–Mar.) mainly along southern California coast. *Where to Find:* Santa Maria Municipal Dump; Andree Clark Bird Refuge; Santa Clara River Mouth, Ventura. *Range:* Breeds on polar islands of northern Canada; winters along Pacific Coast from southwestern Canada to Baja California.

162. Yellow-footed Gull

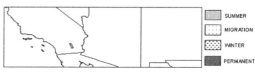

Larus livens (L—27 W—60)

White body; dark gray back and wings; white tail; yellow legs; large, heavy yellow bill with red mark on tip of lower mandible. *Winter:* Similar to breeding plumage, but with dusky wash on back of head and neck. *Immature:* First winter has white body mottled with brown above, white below; dark gray back; mottled brown and white wings; black tail; two-tone bill, black at tip, pale at base; pinkish legs; Second winter similar to adult but with black tail and two-tone bill. *Similar Species:* Yellow legs separate the adult and second-year Yellow-footed Gull from the Western Gull (pinkish legs), with which it was once considered conspecific. *Habitat:* Marine, beaches, jetties, docks, estuaries. *Abundance and Distribution:* Uncommon to rare post-breeding wanderer (June–Sep.) at Salton Sea. *Where to Find:* Salton Sea, California. *Range:* Resident in Gulf of California, breeding on islands; wanders in post-breeding period to Salton Sea and the Sonora coast.

163. Western Gull

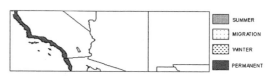

Larus occidentalis (L—25 W—58)

White body; dark gray back and wings; outer primaries black above sparsely tipped with white, gray below; bill very large, yellow with red spot on lower mandible; legs and eyes yellow. *Winter:* Head and breast streaked with brown. *First Winter:* White heavily marked with brown; rump paler; bill black; feet pale pinkish. *Second and Third Winter:* Body white streaked with brown; dark gray mottled with brown on back and wings; tail mostly dark; bill yellowish with black tip; legs pale pink. *Voice:* "Call a deep 'kuk kuk kuk'" (Harrison 1983:342). *Similar Species:* See Yellow-footed Gull. Second- and third-winter birds, and adults are darker backed than Herring Gulls of comparable age. *Habitat:* Marine, beaches, wharves, estuaries; breeds on rocky cliffs. *Abundance and Distribution:* Common resident* along the immediate coast of southern California. *Where to Find:* Santa Maria Municipal Dump; Andree Clark Bird Refuge; Santa Clara River Mouth,

Ventura. *Range:* Breeds along Pacific Coast from southwestern Canada to Baja California; winters in breeding range south to central Pacific coast of Mexico.

164. Glaucous-winged Gull

Larus glaucescens (L—26 W—58)

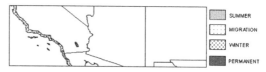

White body and tail with pearly gray back; wings pearly gray with white tips; bill yellow with red spot on tip of lower mandible; legs pinkish. *Winter:* Like breeding but with some brownish mottling on head. *Immature:* First-winter bird is a pale brownish-gray throughout with dark eye; flesh-colored legs; dark bill. Second-winter bird is similar to first winter but with white at tip of bill. Third winter is like adult but with a brownish wash on body. *Similar Species:* The Glaucous-winged Gull has white eyering and dark eye (not yellow eyering and yellow eye as in the larger, rarer Glaucous Gull), and shows gray primary tips (not white as in Glaucous, or black as in most other gulls of the region). This species interbreeds with Western and Herring gulls, so individuals in confusing, intermediate plumage can occur. *Habitat:* Mainly marine or along immediate coast, garbage dumps, trawlers; nests on rocky cliffs. *Abundance and Distribution:* Uncommon winter resident (Nov.–Mar.) along immediate coast; uncommon to rare at Salton Sea. *Where to Find:* Santa Maria Municipal Dump; Andree Clark Bird Refuge; Santa Clara River Mouth, Ventura. *Range:* Breeds from islands in the southern Bering Sea along southern and southeastern Alaska south to Oregon. Winters from breeding range south to southern Baja California and the Gulf of California.

165. Glaucous Gull

Larus hyperboreus (L—27 W—60)

A very large gull; white body; pale gray back; yellow eyering and eye; wings pale gray with outer primaries broadly tipped with white above, mostly white from below; bill yellow with red spot on lower mandible; feet pinkish; wingtips barely extend beyond tail in sitting bird. *Winter:* Head and breast smudged with brown. *First Winter:* Mostly white or with light brown markings; bill pinkish with black tip; legs pinkish; tail white marked with brown. *Second and Third Winter:* Back grayish; bill yellowish with dark tip. *Voice:* "Usually silent, occasionally utters hoarse, deep, Herring Gull-like scream" (Harrison 1983:347). *Similar Species:* See Glaucous-winged Gull. *Habitat:* Coastal regions. *Abundance and Distribution:* Rare winter resident (Dec.–Mar.) along immediate coast. *Where to Find:* Fairmount Park, Riverside; Santa Maria Municipal Dump; Andree Clark Bird Refuge. *Range:* Breeds in circumpolar regions of Old and New World; winters coastal regions of northern Eurasia and North America.

166. Sabine's Gull

Xema sabini (L—14 W—33)

Dark hood; white collar, underparts,

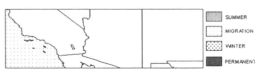

and forked tail; gray back; distinctive pattern of white wing with black primaries and gray shoulder; black bill tipped with yellow; black legs. *Winter:* Similar to breeding but head is white with gray on crown and nape. *Immature:* Mottled brown and white above; white below; forked tail white with black terminal band; bill black; legs gray. *Habitat:* Pelagic; coasts. *Abundance and Distribution:* Uncommon transient offshore (Aug.–Sep., Apr.–May); rarely sighted from coast. *Where to Find:* Channel Islands boat trip; waters off La Jolla beach. *Range:* Breeds circumpolar in Old and New World; winters in tropical seas.

167. Black-legged Kittiwake

Rissa tridactyla

(L—17 W—36)

A small gull; white body; gray back;

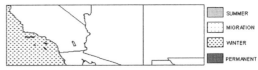

white, slightly forked tail; dark eye; wings gray above, white below tipped with black; bill yellow; legs dark. *Winter:* nape and back of crown gray with dark ear patch. *First Winter:* White marked with black half "collar" on nape; gray back; dark diagonal stripe on upper wing; black ear patch; tail white with black terminal band; bill and legs black. *Voice:* "Kitt-ee-waak." *Similar Species:* Immature Bonaparte's Gull lacks dark "half-collar" at base of neck. *Habitat:* Pelagic; coasts. *Abundance and Distribution:* Uncommon to rare and irregular winter visitor (Nov.–Mar.), mainly offshore. *Where to Find:* Channel Island boat trips; Upper Newport Bay; La Jolla Beach. *Range:* Breeds circumpolar in Old and New World; winters in northern and temperate seas of the Northern Hemisphere.

168. Gull-billed Tern

Sterna nilotica

(L—15 W—36)

A medium-sized tern with a heavy,

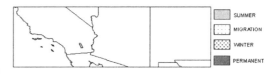

black bill; black cap and nape; white face, neck, and underparts; gray back and wings; tail with shallow fork; black legs. *Winter:* Crown white finely streaked with black. *Habits:* This bird does not dive like most terns. It swoops and sails over marshland for insects. *Voice:* A harsh, nasal "kee-yeek" or "ka-wup." *Similar Species:* Heavy, black, gull-like bill and shallow tail fork are distinctive. *Habitat:* Marshes, wet fields, prairies, bays. *Abundance and Distribution:* Uncommon to rare summer resident (Apr.–Aug.) at Salton Sea, California. *Where to Find:* Southeast corner of the Salton Sea, California. *Range:* Breeds locally in temperate and tropical regions of the world; winters in subtropics and tropics.

169. Caspian Tern

Sterna caspia (L—21 W—52)

A large tern with large, heavy, blood-orange bill; black cap and nape; white

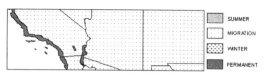

face, neck, and underparts; gray back and wings; tail moderately forked; black legs. *Winter:* black cap streaked with white. *Voice:* A low squawk—"aaaak," repeated. *Similar Species:* Caspian Tern primaries appear dark from below, Royal Tern primaries appear whitish; Royal has white forehead (not black flecked with white) most of the year; Royal's call is a screechy "kee-eer," not a squawk like the Caspian. *Habitat:* Beaches, bays, marine, estuaries, lakes. *Abundance and Distribution:* Common to uncommon transient along coast and at Salton Sea (July–Nov., Apr.–May), uncommon to rare at other times of the year, has bred* in San Diego County; uncommon to rare transient (Apr.–May, Aug.–Sep.) inland at large impoundments along the lower Colorado River and rare to casual transient at large lakes elsewhere in the region. Breeding colony at Bolsa Chica. *Where to Find:* Salton Sea, California; Davis Dam, Nevada/Arizona; Bolsa Chica State Ecological Reserve, California. *Range:* Breeds locally inland and along the coast in temperate, tropical and boreal areas of the world; winters in south temperate and tropical regions.

170. Royal Tern

Sterna maxima (L—20 W—45)

A large tern with yellow or yellow-orange bill; black cap with short,

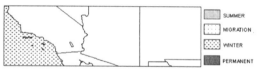

ragged crest; black nape; white face, neck, and underparts; gray back and wings; tail forked; black legs. *Winter:* white forehead and crown; black nape. *Voice:* A screechy "keee-eer." *Similar Species:* See Caspian Tern. *Habitat:* Beaches, bays. *Abundance and Distribution:* Uncommon to rare winter resident (July–Jan.) along the California coast (e.g., San Diego County), offshore, and at Channel Islands; formerly more common. A few breed at Bolsa Chica. *Where to Find:* Channel Islands boat trip; Cabrillo National Monument; Bolsa Chica State Ecological Reserve. *Range:* Breeds locally in temperate and tropical regions of Western Hemisphere and west Africa; winters in warmer portions of breeding range.

171. Elegant Tern

Sterna elegans

(L—17 W—42)

A large tern with long, pointed or-

ange-yellow bill; black cap often with a ragged crest; black nape; white face, neck, and underparts (often tinged with rose); gray back and wings; tail deeply forked; black legs. *Winter:* white forehead and crown; black nape. *Voice:* A screechy "kerr-eek." *Similar Species:* Bill relatively long, thin, and down-turned compared with Royal Tern; call ends in an upward "eek," Royal ends in a downward "err"; in winter plumage, black of crest extends to eye in Elegant Tern, but usually not in Royal Tern. *Habitat:* Sea coasts. *Abundance and Distribution:* Common to uncommon summer resident* (Mar.–Nov.) along the southern California coast, most numerous Aug.–Sep. Breeding colony at Bolsa Chica. *Where to Find:* Santa Clara River Estuary; South Bay Marine Biological Study Area, San Diego; Bolsa Chica State Ecological Reserve. *Range:* Breeds along Pacific Coast from southern California to central Mexico; winters along Pacific Coast from Guatemala to Chile.

172. Common Tern
Sterna hirundo
(L—14 W—31)
A medium-sized tern; red bill, black

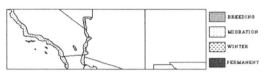

at tip; black cap and nape; white face, neck, and underparts; gray back and wings; entire outer primary, tips, and basal portions of other primaries are black (gray from below); forked tail with gray outer edgings, white inner edgings; red legs. *Winter:* White forehead and crown; back of crown and nape black; bill black; sitting bird shows a dark bar at the shoulder (actually upper wing coverts). *First Breeding:* Similar to adult winter. *Voice:* A harsh "keeeyaak," also "keyew keyew keyew." *Similar Species:* Winter Arctic Tern has white (not dark) basal portions of primaries from below; also see Roseate Tern. *Habitat:* Beaches, bays, marshes, lakes, rivers. *Abundance and Distribution:* Uncommon transient (Apr.–May, Aug.–Oct.) along coast and at Salton Sea, rare at other times of the year; uncommon to rare and irregular fall transient along the Colorado River valley of Nevada, California, and Arizona; casual mainly in fall elsewhere in region. *Where to Find:* Upper Newport Bay; Cabrillo National Monument; Salton Sea. *Range:* Breeds locally in boreal and temperate regions of Old and New World (mostly Canada, northeastern United States, and West Indies); winters in south temperate and tropical regions.

173. Arctic Tern
Sterna paradisaea
(L—16 W—31)
A medium-sized tern; red bill; black

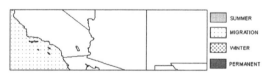

cap and nape; white face; grayish neck, breast, and belly; white under-tail coverts; gray back; wings gray above with dark outer edge of outer primary, white below with primaries narrowly tipped in black; tail deeply forked; red legs. *Winter:* white forehead and crown; back of crown and nape black; bill black. *Voice:* A high, nasal "ki-kee-yah"; also "kaaah." *Similar Species:* See Common Tern. *Habitat:* Mostly marine, beaches. *Abundance and Distribution:* Uncommon offshore transient

(Aug.–Oct.), rare to casual along coast. *Where to Find:* Channel Islands boat trip. *Range:* Breeds in the Arctic; winters in the Antarctic.

174. Forster's Tern

Sterna forsteri

(L—15 W—31)

A medium-sized tern; orange or yel-
low bill with black tip; black cap and nape; white face and underparts; gray back and wings; forked tail, white on outer edgings, gray on inner; orange legs. *Winter:* White head with blackish ear patch; bill black. *Voice:* "Chew-ik." *Similar Species:* Winter Common and Arctic terns have back of crown and nape black (crown and nape are usually white in Forster's Tern). *Habitat:* Marshes, bays, beaches, marine. *Abundance and Distribution:* Common resident* along the coast and at Salton Sea; scarcer along the Colorado River valley. Breeding colony at Bolsa Chica. Uncommon to rare transient (Apr.–May, Aug.–Oct.) elsewhere in the region. *Where to Find:* Bolsa Chica State Ecological Reserve, California; Salton Sea, California, Lake Mead, Nevada/Arizona. *Range:* Breeds locally across northern United States, south-central and southwestern Canada, and Atlantic and Gulf coasts; winters coastally from southern United States to Guatemala; also Greater Antilles.

175. Least Tern

Sterna antillarum

(L—9 W—20) **Endangered**

A small tern; yellow bill with black tip;
black cap and nape with white forehead; white face and underparts; gray back and wings; tail deeply forked; yellow legs. *Winter:* White head with blackish postorbital stripe and nape; bill brown; legs dull yellow. *Voice:* A high pitched "ki-teek ki-teek ki-teek." *Similar Species:* Least Tern has black nape not white as in winter Forster's Tern; also Forster's Tern is much larger. *Habitat:* Bays, beaches, rivers, lakes, ponds. *Abundance and Distribution:* Uncommon summer resident* (Apr.–Sep.) along southern California coast. *Where to Find:* Tijuana Estuary National Wildlife Refuge; Cabrillo National Monument; Bolsa Chica State Ecological Reserve (breeding colony). *Range:* Breeds along both coasts from central California (west) and Maine (east) south to southern Mexico; rare inland population bred along rivers of Mississippi drainage; West Indies; winters along coast of northern South America.

176. Black Tern
Chlidonias niger
(L—10 W—24)
A small tern; dark gray throughout

except white under-tail coverts; slightly forked tail. *Winter:* Dark gray above, white below with dark smudge at shoulder; white forehead; white crown streaked with gray; gray nape; white collar. *Voice:* A high-pitched "kik kik kik." *Habits:* Note swallow-like flight in pursuit of insects. *Habitat:* Marshes, bays, estuaries, lakes, ponds. *Abundance and Distribution:* Common transient and summer resident (May–Sep.) at Salton Sea and along the lower Colorado River valley; uncommon to rare transient (Apr.–May, July–Sep.) elsewhere. *Where to Find:* Salton Sea, California; Las Vegas National Wildlife Refuge, New Mexico; Sierra Vista Wastewater Ponds, Arizona; Pahranagat National Wildlife Refuge, Nevada. *Range:* Breeds in temperate and boreal regions of Northern Hemisphere; winters in tropics.

177. Black Skimmer
Rynchops niger
(L—18 W—45)
Black above; white below; extremely

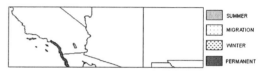

long, straight, razor-shaped bill, red with black tip; lower mandible is longer than the upper. *Immature:* Like adult but mottled brown and white above. *Habits:* Flies above the water with the lower mandible dipped below the surface to capture fish. *Voice:* A mellow "kip," "kee-yip," or "kee-kee-yup." *Habitat:* Beaches, bays, estuaries. *Abundance and Distribution:* Common summer resident* (May–Sep.) at Salton Sea; uncommon to rare and local resident* along the coast. *Where to Find:* Salton Sea; Bolsa Chica State Ecological Reserve (breeding colony); South Bay Marine Biological Area, San Diego. *Range:* Breeds from southern California (west) and New York (east) south to southern South America along coasts and on major river systems; winters in south temperate and tropical portions of breeding range; West Indies.

Figure 29. (right) Crystal Cove State Park's sandy beaches and open scrub provide habitat for Common Barn Owls, Sanderlings, Cassin's Kingbirds, and Northern Harriers.

Figure 28. One of the beauties of Organ Pipe Cactus National Monument, Arizona, is that it is not on the main road to anywhere. Characteristic desert species, such as Greater Roadrunner, Common Poorwill, and Ferruginous Pygmy-Owl, can be found here at any time of the year. March and April are prime visiting times when the desert is blooming (depending on rainfall) and breeding birds are singing, including Cactus Wren and Green-tailed Towhee.

Family Alcidae
Auks, Guillemots, Murres, and Puffins
Aquatic, penguin-like birds streamlined for swimming and diving in pursuit of fish.

178. Common Murre

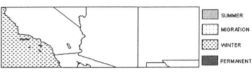

Uria aalge (L—17 W—29)
Dark head, neck, back, and wing upper surface; white breast and belly;
thin, black bill; black webbed feet. *Winter:* Dark above; white below; dark line below eye extends across cheek and down neck. *Immature:* Like adult in winter except bill is smaller; neck and cheek are dark with white line extending behind eye.
Voice: A hoarse moan. *Habitat:* Pelagic, bays; nests on cliffs. *Abundance and Distribution:* Rare and irregular winter resident (Oct.–Mar.), mainly offshore. *Where to
Find:* Channel Islands boat trip; coastal waters off Montaña de Oro State Park and
La Jolla Beach. *Range:* Breeds in northern Atlantic and Pacific oceans; winters at
sea in breeding range south in North America to southern California on the west
and New York on the east; to Portugal in Europe; and to Korea in Asia.

179. Xantus's Murrelet

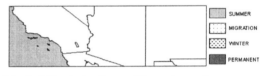

Synthliboramphus hypoleucus
(L—10 W—17)
Black above; white below; broken
white eyering; white wing linings; black bill. *Baja Form:* The subspecies,
Synthliboramphus hypoleucus hypoleucus, which breeds in western Baja California,
has a white line above eye, and extensive white from cheek extending to ear. *Voice:*
"Twittering, finchlike whistles heard after dark" (Peterson 1961:144). *Habitat:* Pelagic; nests on cliffs and in rocky crevices. *Abundance and Distribution:* Uncommon summer resident* (Apr.–June) nesting on Channel Islands and foraging at
sea offshore. *Where to Find:* Channel Islands boat trip. *Range:* Breeds on islands
off the coast of southern California and western Baja California; winters at sea
from waters off northern California to southern Baja California.

180. Craveri's Murrelet

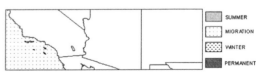

Synthliboramphus craveri
(L—8 W—14)
Dark above; white below; broken
white eyering; black of shoulder extends onto breast; dark underwing linings. *Similar Species:* Craveri's Murrelet has dark underwing linings; underwing linings are

white in Xantus's Murrelet; Craveri's has black shoulder patch (white in Xantus's). *Habitat:* Pelagic; breeds on islands. *Abundance and Distribution:* Rare to casual offshore (Aug.–Sep.). *Where to Find:* Channel Islands boat trip. *Range:* Breeds on islands in the Gulf of California; winters in breeding range and in waters off Baja California and southern California.

181. Ancient Murrelet
Synthliboramphus antiquus
(L—10 W—17)

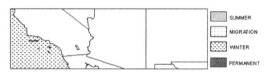

Slate gray back and wings; white below; black head; white shading over and behind eye; white, partial eyering; black throat and breast; yellow bill; white underwing linings contrasting with black axillary region in flight. *Winter:* As in summer, but lacks most of white shading over and behind eye. *Immature:* Like winter adult, but breast is white. *Similar Species:* The Ancient Murrelet differs from the other small alcids by its yellow bill and black throat; black head contrasts with gray back. *Voice:* Twitters, whistles, chirps, heard at night in breeding colonies. *Habitat:* Pelagic, bays; breeds on rocky islands. *Abundance and Distribution:* Uncommon to rare winter visitor (Nov.–Mar.), offshore. *Where to Find:* Channel Islands boat trips. *Range:* Breeds from islands off from British Columbia, southeastern Alaska, southern Alaska, Aleutians and other islands of the northern Pacific south to Korea. Winters in waters of the northern Pacific, south to Korea and southern California.

182. Cassin's Auklet
Ptychoramphus aleuticus (L—9 W—15)
Slate gray nearly throughout; pale gray belly and white under-tail coverts;

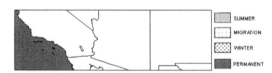

gray underwing linings; darker cap; partial white eyering; stubby, dark bill with pale spot at base. *Immature:* Paler overall than adult; whitish throat. *Voice:* Various croaks heard at night in colonies. *Habitat:* Pelagic; nests in rocky crags and cliffs. *Abundance and Distribution:* Uncommon to rare fall and winter visitor offshore (Oct.–Feb.); breeds* on northern Channel Islands. *Where to Find:* Channel Islands boat trips. *Range:* Breeds from Aleutian Islands south on islands off the North American coast to Guadalupe Island off from northern Baja California.

183. Rhinoceros Auklet
Cerorhinca monocerata (L—14 W—24)
Dusky gray throughout, paler on flanks; feathery white line from be-

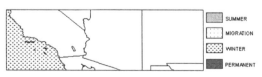

hind eye and from corner of mouth; white eye; heavy orange bill with protuberance from base of upper mandible; red legs. *Winter:* Lacks protuberance from bill; white lines faint. *Immature:* Like winter adult but with dusky eye and bill. *Similar Species:* The heavy, orange bill and solid, smoky gray body are distinctive. *Voice:* Croaks and cries given at night in colonies. *Habitat:* Pelagic; breeds in burrows on islands. *Abundance and Distribution:* Uncommon to rare winter visitor (Nov.–Mar.) offshore. *Where to Find:* Channel Islands boat trips. *Range:* Islands and coasts of the northern Pacific from Japan and Korea; the Kuril Islands; and Aleutians south along western North America to northern Baja California.

184. Tufted Puffin

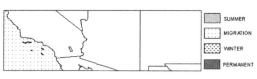

SUMMER
MIGRATION
WINTER
PERMANENT

Fratercula cirrhata (L—15 W—25)
Dark body; white face somewhat darkened around eye with dark line extending behind eye; dark crown; beige plumes trail behind eye down back of neck; huge, orange and horn-colored bill sheath; orange legs. *Winter:* Bill sheath and plumes are lost; face grayish with paler area around eye. *Immature:* Dark above; pale gray below; dark crown; whitish eyeline; dark lores; gray cheek; orange legs and feet; heavy, thick yellowish bill. *Similar Species:* The immature Tufted Puffin has a thick, heavy, rectangular bill; the immature Rhinoceros Auklet has a thinner, more pointed bill. *Voice:* Low growls in colony. *Habitat:* Pelagic; breeds in burrows on islands or along coast. *Abundance and Distribution:* Rare transient (May) offshore; formerly bred* on Channel Islands (until 1940s). *Where to Find:* Channel Islands boat trips. *Range:* Breeds on islands and coastal regions of the northern Pacific, Bering Sea, and Arctic Ocean in eastern Siberia and Western Alaska, south to Korea and central California; winters mainly at sea in the northern Pacific.

Order Columbiformes
Family Columbidae
Doves and Pigeons
These are small to medium-sized, chunky birds with relatively small heads. Larger species generally are referred to as "pigeons" while smaller ones are "doves." They feed on fruits and seeds, and produce "crop milk" (specialized cells sloughed from the esophagus) to feed their young. Clutch size is normally two throughout the group.

185. Rock Dove
Columba livia
(L—13 W—23)

The domestic pigeon is highly vari-
able in color, including various mixtures of brown, white, gray, and dark blue; the
"average" bird shows gray above and below with head and neck iridescent pur-
plish-green; white rump; dark terminal band on tail. *Voice:* A series of low "coo"s.
Habitat: Cities, towns, agricultural areas. *Abundance and Distribution:* Common,
permanent resident* throughout. *Range:* Resident of Eurasia and North Africa; introduced into Western Hemisphere where resident nearly throughout near cities.

186. Band-tailed Pigeon
Columba fasciata (L—15 W—25)
Gray above and below with purplish
cast on head and breast; bronze ter-

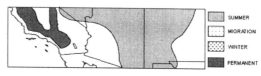

minal band on tail bordered by a dark brown subterminal band; white half-collar
on nape; iridescent bronze upper back; yellow legs and bill with black tip. *Voice:* A
low "hoo-ooo." *Habitat:* Ponderosa pine, montane oak, pine-oak, and pinyon-
juniper forest. *Abundance and Distribution:* Uncommon resident* in the mountains and foothills of southern California; uncommon summer resident* (Apr.–
Oct.) in mountains of Arizona, southern Nevada, and New Mexico; abundance
varies sharply with mast availability (acorns, pinyon nuts, etc.). *Where to Find:*
Hearst Tanks (birds come to drink), Grandview Point on the South Rim of the
Grand Canyon, Arizona; Kyle Canyon, Nevada; American Canyon Spring, Mount
Taylor, New Mexico; Dorothy May Tucker Wildlife Sanctuary, California. *Range:*
Breeds locally in mountains from southwestern Canada south through western
United States and Mexico to northern Argentina; winters in breeding range from
southwestern United States southward.

187. White-winged Dove
Zenaida asiatica (L—12 W—20)
Grayish brown above, grayish below;
gray wings with broad white band on

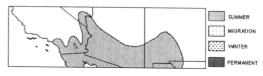

secondaries (visible as a broad white stripe along front edge of folded wing); light
blue skin around red-orange eye; black whisker; red legs; broad white corners
on square tail. *Voice:* A hoarse "caroo-co-coo" ("who cooks for you") or "carroo
coo-ooo coo-wik coo-ooo coo-wik." *Habitat:* Thorn forest, riparian salt cedar, residential areas, agricultural areas. *Abundance and Distribution:* Common to uncommon summer resident* (Apr.–Sep.) in southern deserts throughout; some remain
in winter, especially in residential areas and in southeastern Arizona. *Where to*

Find: Las Vegas, Nevada; Old Refuge, Las Cruces, New Mexico; Organ Pipe Cactus National Monument, Arizona; Anza-Borego Desert State Park, California. *Range:* Breeds from southwestern United States through Middle and western South America to Chile; also in Bahamas and Greater Antilles; winters from northern Mexico south through breeding range.

188. Mourning Dove

Zenaida macroura (L—12 W—18)
Tan above, orange-buff below; brownish wings spotted with dark brown; tail long, pointed, and edged in white; gray cap; black whisker; purplish-bronze iridescence on side of neck; blue eyering; brown eye and bill; pink feet. *Voice:* A low, hoarse "hoo-wooo hooo ho hooo." *Similar Species:* The long, pointed tail separates this from all other doves except the tiny Inca Dove, which has rusty wings and body feathers that appear scale-like. *Habitat:* Prairie, thorn forest, woodlands. *Abundance and Distribution:* Common summer resident* (Apr.–Oct.) throughout; common winter resident in lowlands and foothills; uncommon to rare or absent in highlands. *Where to Find:* Hearst Tanks (birds come to drink), Grandview Point on the South Rim of the Grand Canyon, Arizona; Corn Creek, Desert National Wildlife Range, Nevada; Dorothy May Tucker Wildlife Sanctuary, California; Fort Sumner State Monument, New Mexico. *Range:* Breeds from southern Canada south through United States to highlands of central Mexico, Costa Rica, Panama, Bahamas, Greater Antilles; winters in south temperate and tropical portions of breeding range.

189. Inca Dove

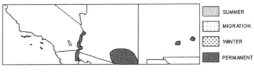

Columbina inca
(L—9 W—11)
A small dove; light brown above with dark brown markings giving the bird a scaly appearance; buffy below with brown barring; long, rounded tail with white outer tail feathers; rusty wing patches show in flight; red eye; brown bill; pink legs. *Habits:* Roosting individuals have the curious habit of sitting atop one another, forming little pyramids. *Voice:* A plaintive "hoo hoo" ("no hope"). *Similar Species:* Inca Doves have long, pointed tail and scaly breast and back; ground doves have short, square tail, and lack "scaly" appearance on back. *Habitat:* Residential areas, thorn forest, savanna. *Abundance and Distribution:* Common but extremely local permanent resident*, mainly along the lower Colorado River valley and in towns of southeastern Arizona and southern New Mexico. Inca Doves probably were not a regular part of the avifauna of the southwest prior to European settlement. *Where to Find:* City parks in

Alamogordo and Roswell, New Mexico; Tucson, Arizona; Imperial Dam, California. *Range:* Resident from southwestern United States to Costa Rica.

190. Common Ground-Dove

Columbina passerina (L—7 W—11)
A very small dove; grayish-brown above with dark brown spotting on wing; gray tinged with pink below with scaly brown markings on breast; gray pileum; red eye; pink bill; flesh-colored legs; rusty wing patches show in flight; black outer tail feathers with white edgings. *Female:* Like male but grayish below (not pinkish), and gray crown is less distinct. *Habits:* Thrusts head forward while walking. *Voice:* "Hoo-wih," repeated. *Similar Species:* See Inca Dove. *Habitat:* Thorn forest, savanna. *Abundance and Distribution:* Common permanent resident* at Salton Sea, California, along lower Colorado River valley of southern California and Arizona, and southwestern Arizona; uncommon summer resident* (Apr.–Sep.) in southern Arizona (west to Organ Pipe National Monument), rare in winter; rare to casual resident* in southwestern New Mexico. *Where to Find:* Salton Sea, California; Organ Pipe National Monument, Arizona; Bosque del Apache National Wildlife Refuge, New Mexico. *Range:* Southern United States south to northern half of South America; West Indies.

Order Cuculiformes

Family Cuculidae
Cuckoos and Roadrunners
Cuckoos are a family of trim, long-tailed birds found in both the Old and New worlds; several species lay their eggs in other birds' nests. Like parrots, woodpeckers, and some other avian groups, cuckoos perch with two toes forward and two toes backward (most birds have three toes forward and one toe backward).

191. Yellow-billed Cuckoo

Coccyzus americanus (L—12 W—17)
A thin, streamlined bird with long, graduated tail; dark bill with yellow lower mandible and eyering; brown above; white below; dark brown tail with white tips; rusty wing patches visible in flight. *Habits:* Slow, deliberate, reptilian foraging movements. *Voice:* A metallic "ka-ka-ka-ka-ka-ka cow cow cow", also a low, hoarse "cow" similar to that of roadrunner. *Similar Species:* Yellow-billed Cuckoo has yellow eyering and lower mandible and rusty wing patches visible in flight (lacking

in the extremely rare Black-billed Cuckoo). *Habitat:* Riparian cottonwood groves and orchards, deciduous and thorn forest, scrub, second growth, savanna. *Abundance and Distribution:* Uncommon to rare summer resident* (Apr.–Sep.) along the Colorado River valley and riparian areas of central and southern Arizona and lowlands and mid-elevation areas of New Mexico west of the Great Plains. *Where to Find:* Corn Creek, Desert National Wildlife Range, Nevada; Aravaipa Canyon Preserve, Arizona; South Kern Reserve, California; Caballo Lake State Park, New Mexico. *Range:* Breeds southeastern Canada and nearly throughout United States into northern Mexico and West Indies; winters north and central South America.

192. Greater Roadrunner
Geococcyx californianus
(L—22 W—22)
Olive above with white feather

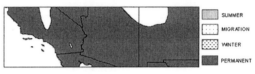

edgings; buffy streaked with brown below; dark brown, ragged crest; extremely long, graduated tail with white tips, held cocked; bare skin behind eye is white anteriorly, pink posteriorly. *Female:* Skin behind eye is blue anteriorly (Folse and Arnold 1976). *Habits:* Almost entirely terrestrial, seldom flies; feeds on lizards, grasshoppers, snakes, small birds and rodents. *Voice:* A descending series of soft, low "coo"s; also a rattle made by vibrating upper and lower mandibles together. *Habitat:* Desert, thorn forest below seven thousand feet. *Abundance and Distribution:* Common permanent resident* in lowland desert and scrub; rare or absent in highlands. *Where to Find:* Organ Pipe Cactus National Monument, Arizona; El Malpais National Monument, New Mexico; Crystal Cove State Park, California; Corn Creek, Desert National Wildlife Range, Nevada. *Range:* Southwestern United States to central Mexico.

Order Strigiformes
Family Tytonidae
Barn Owls
This small, cosmopolitan family is comprised of twelve species, of which only one, the Barn Owl, occurs regularly in North America.

193. Barn Owl
Tyto alba
(L—16 W—45)
Tawny and gray above; white sparsely

spotted with brown below; white, monkey-like face, and large, dark eyes; long legs. *Habits:* Almost strictly nocturnal. *Voice:* Eerie screeches and hisses. *Habitat:*

Savanna, prairie, farmland, thorn forest, desert scrub; roosts in barns, abandoned mine shafts. *Abundance and Distribution:* Uncommon to rare permanent resident* in lowlands and mid-elevations. Easily overlooked because of nocturnal habits. *Where to Find:* Crystal Cove State Park, California; Fort Sumner State Monument, New Mexico; Marana Pecan Grove, Arizona; Lake Mojave, Nevada (abandoned mine shafts). *Range:* Resident in temperate and tropical regions nearly throughout the world.

Family Strigidae
Typical Owls
Owls comprise a large family of fluffy-plumaged, mainly nocturnal raptors. Plumage coloration is mostly muted browns and grays; two toes forward and two backward when perched. Ear structures are asymmetrical for ranging distance to prey.

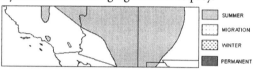

194. Flammulated Owl
Otus flammeolus (L—7 W—16)
A small owl with dark brown eyes,
tawny facial disk, and relatively short ear tufts; mottled dark brown, gray, tawny, and white above; gray and white below streaked with dark brown. *Habits:* Almost strictly nocturnal. *Voice:* A whistled "poot" or "poo-poot." *Similar Species:* Flammulated Owl has dark brown eyes; screech-owls have yellow eyes; screech-owl calls are trills or quavering whistles. *Habitat:* Montane pine, pine-oak, and juniper woodlands; in wooded riparian areas as a transient. *Abundance and Distribution:* Uncommon summer resident* (Apr.–Sep.) in highlands; uncommon to rare transient (Mar.–Apr., Aug.–Sep.) at mid- and lowland riparian woodlands, difficult to find in migration. *Where to Find:* Mount Charleston, Nevada; Hualapai Mountain Park, Arizona; McGill Campground, Mount Pinos, California; Ponderosa Campground, Bandelier National Monument, New Mexico. *Range:* Breeds in western North America from southwestern Canada through mountains of western United States to southern Mexico; winters central Mexico to Guatemala.

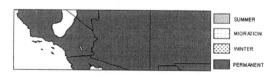

195. Western Screech-Owl
Otus kennicottii (L—9 W—22)
A small, long-eared, yellow-eyed owl with a dark bill; mottled gray, dark
brown, and white above; streaked with gray, brown and white below; gray facial disk with whitish eyebrows. *Voice:* A sequence of increasingly rapid whistles; also a set of two trills, the second longer than the first. *Similar Species:* Screech-owls have

yellow eyes; screech-owl calls are trills or quavering whistles. Flammulated Owl has dark brown eyes and a "poot" or "poo-poot" call. Whiskered Screech-Owl is very similar. Best separated by call. Whiskered Screech-Owl call is a series of whistles at same pitch, and at fairly even tempo (Western Screech-Owl call is a series of accelerating whistles). *Habitat:* Riparian and oak woodland, desert scrub, pinyon-juniper, residential areas. *Abundance and Distribution:* Common to uncommon resident* throughout. *Where to Find:* Hassayampa River Preserve, Arizona; Mount Charleston, Nevada; Irvine Regional Park, California; Guadalupe Canyon, New Mexico. *Range:* Western North America from southeastern Arkansas to central Mexico.

196. Whiskered Screech-Owl
Otus trichopsis (L—8 W—21)
A small, long-eared, yellow-eyed owl
with a dark bill; mottled gray, dark

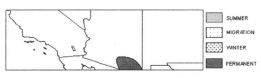

brown, and white above; streaked with gray, brown and white below; gray facial disk with whitish eyebrows. *Voice:* Call is a series of whistles at same pitch, and at fairly even tempo; also a code-like "poo poo poo—poo" with variations, sometimes in duet with mate. *Similar Species:* See Western Screech-Owl. *Habitat:* Montane pine-oak and oak woodlands. *Abundance and Distribution:* Common resident* in canyons of extreme southeastern Arizona. *Where to Find:* Carr Canyon; Cave Creek Canyon; Miller Canyon; Scotia Canyon. *Range:* Resident from southeastern Arizona south through northwestern and central Mexico, Guatemala, El Salvador, Honduras, to northern Nicaragua.

197. Great Horned Owl
Bubo virginianus (L—22 W—52)
A large owl; mottled brown, gray, buff
and white above; grayish-white below

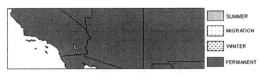

barred with brown; yellow eyes; rusty facial disc; white throat (not always visible); long ear tufts. *Habits:* Eats skunks as well as many other small to medium-sized vertebrates. *Voice:* A series of low hoots, "ho-hoo hooo hoo"; female's call is higher-pitched than male's. *Similar Species:* The smaller Long-eared Owl is streaked rather than barred below and ear tufts are placed more centrally; other large owls lack long ear tufts. *Habitat:* Woodlands. *Abundance and Distribution:* Uncommon permanent resident* throughout. *Where to Find:* Irvine Regional Park, California; Frijoles Canyon, Bandelier National Monument, New Mexico; Hualapai Mountain Park, Arizona; Red Rock Canyon National Conservation Area, New Mexico. *Range:* New World except polar regions.

198. Northern Pygmy-Owl
Glaucidium gnoma
(L—7 W—13)
A small, long-tailed owl; rufous above

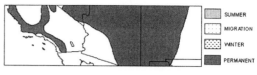

with black "eyespots" on the nape; rufous, white-spotted breast; white belly, heavily streaked with brown; crown spotted with white; yellow eyes; tail brown barred with white. *Gray Phase:* Brownish-gray rather than rufous. *Habits:* Crepuscular hunter of large insects and small birds; mobbed by small birds when found at roost. *Voice:* Monotonously repeated whistles at two- to three-second intervals; dawn or shortly after is a good time to listen for the bird. *Similar Species:* The Northern Pygmy-Owl has white spots on rufous breast and white bars on tail; Ferruginous Pygmy-Owl has white streaks (not spots) on breast and a barred brown and rusty tail; lacks crown spotting; Northern Pygmy-Owl call is faster than that of Ferruginous Pygmy-Owl. *Habitat:* Highland forests of pine, pine-oak, and juniper. *Abundance and Distribution:* Uncommon to rare resident* in highlands; moves downslope and elsewhere to lower elevations in some areas in winter. *Where to Find:* Scheelite Canyon, Arizona; Frijoles Canyon, Bandelier National Monument, New Mexico; Mount Charleston, Nevada; McGill Campground, Mount Pinos, California. *Range:* Resident in western North America from southwestern Canada through western United States and Mexico to Honduras.

199. Ferruginous Pygmy-Owl
Glaucidium brasilianum
(L—7 W—14)
A small, long-tailed owl; rufous above

with black "eyespots" on the nape; white below, heavily streaked with rufous; rufous breast and crown; yellow eyes; tail brown barred with rust. *Habits:* Crepuscular. *Voice:* A whistled "whit whit whit whit whit whit." *Similar Species:* See Northern Pygmy-Owl. *Habitat:* Saguaro cactus desert, riparian forest, savanna, second growth, brushy pastures. *Abundance and Distribution:* Rare to casual permanent resident* in southern Arizona. *Where to Find:* Organ Pipe Cactus National Monument; Patagonia Roadside Rest Area; San Pedro River. *Range:* Southern Arizona and Texas to central Argentina.

200. Elf Owl
Micrathene whitneyi (L—6 W—15)
A small, short-tailed, yellow-eyed
owl; mottled brownish-gray and

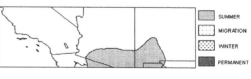

white above; rusty brown and gray on head and breast barred with dark brown; brownish streaks on belly; white stripe on wing. *Habits:* Nocturnal. *Voice:* A series

Figure 30. The aptly named Red Rock Canyon National Conservation Area, outside Las Vegas, Nevada, provides breath-taking scenery and pristine high Sonoran desert habitats. Birds expected of such sites include White-throated Swift, Gambel's Quail, Sage Sparrow, and Lesser Goldfinch.

Figure 31. Cave Creek Canyon in Arizona's Chiricahua Mountains is a place most birders have on their "must see before dropping off the twig" list, as much for the scenery as the birds. Species to be seen in spring and summer include Blue-throated Hummingbird, Hutton's Vireo, Hepatic Tanager, Dusky-capped Flycatcher, and Black-throated Gray Warbler. At other times of the year Mexican Chickadee, Yellow-eyed Junco, Brown Creeper, and Mexican Jay can be found.

of rapid, high-pitched whistles, "whit-whit-whit." *Similar Species:* Short tail and lack of ear tufts separates this species from other small owls found in the region. *Habitat:* Desert scrub, thorn forest, pinyon-juniper. *Abundance and Distribution:* Uncommon to rare summer resident* (Apr.–July) in desert portion of southern Arizona and southwestern New Mexico. *Where to Find:* Madera Canyon, Arizona; Catalina State Park, Arizona; NM 464 to Redrock, New Mexico. *Range:* Breeds from southwestern United States to central Mexico; winters in southern portion of breeding range to southern Mexico.

201. Burrowing Owl

Athene cunicularia (L—9 W—24)

A long-legged, terrestrial owl; brown spotted with white above; white collar, eyebrows and forehead; white below with brown barring. *Habits:* Often associated with prairie dog towns, this owl spends most of its time on the ground or perched on fence posts. *Voice:* A whistled "coo-hoo"; various other squeaks and whistles. *Similar Species:* The long legs and terrestrial habits are distinctive. *Habitat:* Prairies, pastures, agricultural areas. *Abundance and Distribution:* Common to uncommon resident* in lowland and mid-elevation open areas of southern California, southern Arizona, and southern New Mexico; uncommon to rare transient and summer resident* (Apr.–Sep.) in southern Nevada, northern Arizona and northern New Mexico, occasional in winter. *Where to Find:* Maxwell National Wildlife Refuge, New Mexico; San Jacinto Wildlife Area, California; Marana Pecan Grove, Arizona. *Range:* Breeds southwestern Canada and western United States south to central Mexico, Florida, West Indies, and locally in South America.

202. Spotted Owl

Strix occidentalis (L—18 W—42)

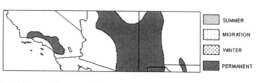

A large, dark-eyed owl; brown spotted with white above and below. *Voice:* A series of three to four hoarse, high-pitched "haaw"s. *Similar Species:* Barred Owl belly is white streaked with brown (not brown spotted with white), and is not spotted with white on crown. *Habitat:* Dense, heavily wooded areas of montane coniferous forest, pine-oak, and riparian forest of canyons. This species prefers thicker vegetation where Great Horned Owls (which eat them) are absent. *Abundance and Distribution:* Uncommon to rare permanent resident* in highlands of region. *Where to Find:* Scheelite Canyon, Arizona; Pine Flat Road, Williams, Arizona; Red Box Ranger Station, San Gabriel Mountains, California; Signal Peak Road, New Mexico. *Range:* Local resident of western montane regions from southwestern Canada to central Mexico.

203. Long-eared Owl

Asio otus (L—14 W—39)

Medium-sized, trim, yellow-eyed owl with long ear tufts; mottled brown

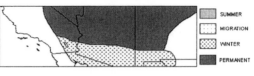

and white above; whitish streaked with brown below; rusty facial disks. *Habits:* Nocturnal. *Voice:* "Haaaaaa"—like a baby's cry; also three to four quick, high-pitched "hoh"s. *Similar Species:* See Great Horned Owl. *Habitat:* Pinyon-juniper, oak, and pine-oak woodland; riparian groves (salt cedar, cottonwood), desert scrub and thorn forest in winter. *Abundance and Distribution:* Rare and irregular resident* in northern portions of region (Apr.–Oct.); rare winter resident in southern portions (Nov.–Mar.). *Where to Find:* Mount Charleston; Nevada; Big Morongo Canyon Preserve, California; Las Vegas National Wildlife Refuge, New Mexico; Catalina State Park, Arizona. *Range:* Breeds in temperate and boreal regions of the Northern Hemisphere; winters in temperate areas and mountains of northern tropical regions.

204. Short-eared Owl

Asio flammeus (L—15 W—42)

A medium-sized owl; brown streaked with buff above; buff streaked with

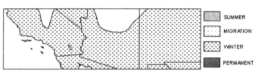

brown below; round facial disk with short ear tufts and yellow eyes; buffy patch shows on upper wing in flight; black patch at wrist visible on wing lining. *Habits:* Crepuscular. Forages by coursing low over open areas, reminiscent of Northern Harrier. *Voice:* A sharp "chik-chik" and various squeaks. *Similar Species:* Tawny color and lack of ear tufts separate this from other owl species. *Habitat:* Savanna, prairie, marshes, estuaries, agricultural fields. *Abundance and Distribution:* Rare winter resident (Nov.–Mar.) throughout except highlands. *Where to Find:* Navajo Indian Irrigation Project, New Mexico; San Jacinto Wildlife Area, California; Las Vegas Wash, Nevada; Spitler Land and Cattle Company alfalfa fields, Elfrida, Arizona. *Range:* Breeds in tundra, boreal, and north temperate areas of Northern Hemisphere, also in Hawaiian Islands; winters in southern portions of breeding range south to northern tropical regions.

205. Northern Saw-whet Owl

Aegolius Acadicus (L—8 W—20)

A small owl; dark brown above with white spotting; white below with

broad chestnut stripes; facial disk with gray at base of beak, gray eyebrows, the rest finely streaked brown and white; yellow eyes. *Immature:* Dark brown back spotted with white; solid chestnut below; chestnut facial disk with white forehead and eyebrows. *Habits:* A tame owl, easily approached. *Voice:* A whistled monotone "hoo hoo hoo hoo"; also a raspy note, given in series of three "saw whetting noises." *Similar Species:* Chestnut underparts are distinctive among small owls. *Habitat:* Pinyon-juniper woodlands, ponderosa pine. *Abundance and Distribution:* Rare resident* in highlands of region; in winter, occasional irruptions bring concentrations of birds to particular parts of the region, but normally the bird remains sparsely distributed in montane breeding habitat. *Where to Find:* Mount Charleston, Nevada; McGill Campground, Sequoia National Forest, California; Forest Loop Road 302, Grand Canyon, Arizona; Valle Vidal, Canjilon Mountain, New Mexico. *Range:* From central Canada south to northern United States and in western mountains south to southern Mexico; winters in breeding range south and east to southern United States.

Order Caprimulgiformes
Family Caprimulgidae
Goatsuckers
Most of the species in this family have soft, fluffy plumage of browns, grays, and buff. Long, pointed wings and extremely large, bristle-lined mouth also are distinctive characteristics of the group. Usually crepuscular or nocturnal, they forage for insects in bat-like fashion with characteristic swoops and dives.

206. Lesser Nighthawk
Chordeiles acutipennis
(L—9 W—22)
Mottled dark brown, gray and white

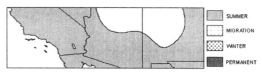

above; whitish below with black bars; white throat; white band across primaries and tail; tail slightly forked. *Female:* Buffy rather than white on throat and wing, lacks white tail bar. *Habits:* Normally forages with a fluttering flight low over the ground, not high above as in Common Nighthawk. *Voice:* A quavering trill. *Similar Species:* Lesser Nighthawk call is a trill; Common Nighthawk call is a sharp, nasal "bezzzt"; Common Nighthawk forages higher above ground, and white on primaries is closer to wrist than in Lesser Nighthawk. *Habitat:* Thorn forest, desert scrub. *Abundance and Distribution:* Common summer resident* (Apr.–Sep.) of lowlands. *Where to Find:* Ballinger Canyon Road, Ventucopa, California; Desert National Wildlife Range, Nevada; Bosque del Apache National Wildlife Refuge, New Mexico; Bill Williams Delta National Wildlife Refuge, Arizona. *Range:* Breeds from southwestern United States south to southern Brazil; winters in southern Mexico south through breeding range.

207. Common Nighthawk

Chordeiles minor (L—9 W—23)
Mottled dark brown, gray and white
above; whitish below with black bars;
white throat; white band across primaries and tail; tail slightly forked. *Female:* Buffy rather than white on throat. *Habits:* Crepuscular. Normally forages high above the ground; has a dive display in which the bird plummets toward the ground, swerving up at the last moment and making a whirring sound with the wings. *Voice:* "Bezzzt." *Similar Species:* See Lesser Nighthawk. *Habitat:* Savannas, grasslands, thorn forest, and a variety of other open and semi-open areas. *Abundance and Distribution:* Common to uncommon summer resident* (Apr.–Sep.) mainly in highlands of southern California, southern Nevada, Arizona, and throughout New Mexico. *Where to Find:* Bandelier National Monument, New Mexico; Mormon Lake, Arizona; Bluff Lake, San Bernardino Mountains, California. *Range:* Breeds locally from central and southern Canada south through United States south to Panama; winters in South America.

208. Common Poorwill

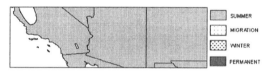

Phalaenoptilus nuttallii (L—8 W—17)
A small nightjar; grayish-brown
above with dark brown markings;
white throat; breast whitish closely barred with gray; wings and tail rounded; outer tail feathers broadly tipped in white. *Habits:* Nocturnal. Hibernates in cold weather. *Voice:* A whistled "poor-will" or "poor-will-ip." *Similar Species:* Nighthawks and Pauraques have white bar on wing; Whip-poor-will is dark brown, not grayish, and has much more white on tail. *Habitat:* Deserts, dry thorn forest. *Abundance and Distribution:* Common summer resident* (Mar.–Oct.) at low to mid-elevations throughout except in California's San Joaquin Valley where rare or absent; rare to casual in winter in southern California and southern Arizona. *Where to Find:* Bonanza Trailhead, Nevada; Canjilon Mountain, New Mexico; Switzer Picnic Area, San Gabriel Mountains, California; Organ Pipe Cactus National Monument, Arizona. *Range:* Breeds from extreme southwestern Canada south through western United States to central Mexico; winters in southern parts of breeding range.

209. Buff-collared Nightjar

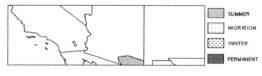

Caprimulgus ridgwayi (L—10 W—19)
Grayish-brown above with dark
brown markings; white breast band
and buffy band across nape; remainder of underparts closely mottled with gray

and tawny; outer tail feathers tipped in white. *Female:* Tail tipped in buff. *Habits:* Nocturnal. *Voice:* An accelerating series of "chuk"s ending with a "chukacheea" (hence the Mexican name for this bird). *Similar Species:* Nighthawks and Common Pauraques have white bar on wing; Whip-poor-will lacks buff collar around nape, and has more white on tail (male). Best located and identified by its distinctive song. *Habitat:* Desert canyons. *Abundance and Distribution:* Rare to casual summer resident* (May–Aug.) in the rugged canyons of southeastern Arizona. *Where to Find:* Aravaipa Canyon; Florida Wash; Guadalupe Canyon. *Range:* Breeds from southeastern Arizona through western Mexico and Guatemala to Honduras. Withdraws from northern portions of the breeding range in winter.

210. Whip-poor-will
Caprimulgus vociferus
(L—10 W—19)
Dark brown mottled with buff above;

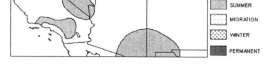

grayish barred with dark brown below; dark throat and breast with white patch; rounded tail with white outer three feathers; rounded wings. *Female:* Has buffy tips rather than white on outer tail feathers. *Habits:* Nocturnal. *Voice:* A rapid, whistled "whip-poor-will" monotonously repeated. *Habitat:* Montane ponderosa pine, pine-oak, pinyon-juniper, and pinyon-fir woodlands; seems to prefer rocky hillsides and canyons. *Abundance and Distribution:* Uncommon to rare summer resident* (Mar.–Oct.), mainly in highlands of southern Nevada, southeastern Arizona, and southwestern New Mexico. *Where to Find:* Mount Charleston, Nevada; Madera Canyon, Arizona; Water Canyon Campground, New Mexico. *Range:* Breeds across southeastern and south central Canada and eastern United States, also in southwestern United States through the highlands of Mexico and Central America to Honduras; winters from northern Mexico to Panama; Cuba; also rarely along Gulf and Atlantic coasts of southeastern United States.

Order Apodiformes
Family Apodidae
Swifts
Swifts are small to medium-sized, stubby-tailed birds with long, pointed wings. In flight, an extremely rapid, shallow wing beat is characteristic.

211. Black Swift

Cypseloides niger (L—7 W—15)
Uniformly black with slightly forked
tail. *Habits:* Crepuscular. Tail is often

fanned in flight. *Voice:* "Plik plik plik." *Similar Species:* The Black Swift has the
long, slim, pointed, swept-back wings and rapid wing beat of swifts. The male
Purple Martin has wider, shorter wing and typical swallow-like flight. *Habitat:*
Mainly montane, especially near cliffs, and crags. *Abundance and Distribution:* Rare
summer resident* (May–Sep.) in mountains of southern California; rare to casual
transient and very local summer resident elsewhere in region. *Where to Find:* Mill
Creek Canyon, San Bernardino Mountains, California; Santa Anita Canyon, Los
Angeles, California. *Range:* Breeds in western Canada and western United States;
also in scattered localities of Mexico, Central America and West Indies; winters
from southern Mexico to Costa Rica; and West Indies.

212. Chimney Swift

Chaetura pelagica (L—5 W—12)
Dark throughout; stubby, square tail;
long narrow wing. *Voice:* Rapid series

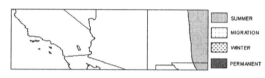

of "chip"s. *Similar Species:* Vaux's Swift insect-like chatter is distinct from the more
musical sequence of the Chimney Swift. *Habitat:* Widely distributed over most
habitat types wherever appropriate nesting and roosting sites are available (chimneys, cliffs, caves, crevices, hollow trees). Often seen over towns and cities where
chimneys are available for roosting. *Abundance and Distribution:* Uncommon to
rare spring transient (Apr.–May) and rare and local summer resident (June–Aug.)
in eastern third of New Mexico, mainly in towns. Casual in summer (Tucson) in
Arizona. *Where to Find:* Clayton; Roswell Spring River Golf Course; Carlsbad.
Range: Breeds throughout eastern North America; winters mainly in Peru.

213. Vaux's Swift

Chaetura vauxi (L—5 W—12)
Dark throughout; somewhat paler
below and on rump; stubby tail and

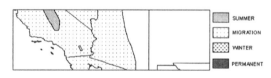

long, narrow wings. *Voice:* A high-pitched, dry rattle. *Similar Species:* The insect-
like chatter of Vaux's Swift is distinct from the more musical sequence of the Chimney Swift. *Habitat:* Widely distributed over most habitat types during migration,
especially fields, marshes, cliffs. *Abundance and Distribution:* Rare to casual
summer resident* in the Sierra Nevada; uncommon to rare transient (Apr.–May,
Sep.–Oct.) in southern California, southern Nevada, and western Arizona; rare to
casual in winter. *Where to Find:* Desert National Wildlife Range, Nevada; Tucson,

Arizona; Upper Newport Bay, California. *Range:* Breeds in coastal California, northwestern United States, Alaska, and southwestern Canada; Mexico, Central and northern South America; winters in tropical portions of breeding range.

214. White-throated Swift

Aeronautes saxatalis (L—6 W—13)
Patterned black and white above and below; notched tail; long, narrow

wings. *Voice:* Rapid series of "chee"s. *Similar Species:* Violet-green swallow lacks black sides, rapid wing beat, and narrow, pointed wings of the swift. *Habitat:* Cliffs, crags, rocky canyons, freeway bridges, cloverleaves. *Abundance and Distribution:* Common transient and local summer resident* in southern California, southern Nevada, Arizona, and western New Mexico; common to uncommon winter resident in southern California, southern Nevada, southern Arizona, and southwestern New Mexico. *Where to Find:* Los Angeles freeway overpasses, California; Upper Carr Canyon, Arizona; Red Rock Canyon National Conservation Area, Nevada; Navajo Dam, New Mexico. *Range:* Breeds in mountains of western United States and southwestern Canada south though Mexico and Central America to Honduras; winters in southern portions of breeding range.

Family Trochilidae
Hummingbirds
Many of the species discussed below have spectacular flight displays that are as characteristic of a species as its plumage. Distribution of western hummingbirds apparently has been affected by the proliferation of nectar feeders. Several of the species recorded below occur regularly during migration and in winter, hundreds of miles from their normal wintering range.

215. Broad-billed Hummingbird

Cynanthus latirostris (L—4 W—5)
Iridescent green above; blue throat, green breast and belly; white under-

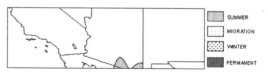

tail coverts; bill red with black tip; tail notched. *Female:* Green above; grayish below with narrow, grayish postorbital stripe; square tail; bill brown with reddish base. *Voice:* Call is a loud chatter. Male's song is a plaintive "tsing." given during arcing flight display. *Similar Species:* White-eared Hummingbird has dark rather than grayish-white cheek of female and immature Broad-billed. *Habitat:* Arid scrub, mesquite-sycamore riparian areas. *Abundance and Distribution:* Common summer resident* (Mar.–Sep.) in southeastern Arizona (from the Huachucas in the east to the Baboquivaris in the west) and Guadalupe Canyon in extreme southwestern New Mexico; rare to casual in winter, mainly at feeders. *Where to Find:* Guadalupe Canyon, New Mexico; Sabino Canyon, Arizona; Madera Canyon, Arizona. *Range:* Breeds from southeastern Arizona, New Mexico, and Big Bend area of Texas south through arid highlands to southern Mexico; winters mainly in southern portion of breeding range.

216. White-eared Hummingbird

Hylocharis leucotis (L—4 W—5)
Iridescent purple crown and chin; white postorbital stripe; green back and breast; whitish belly; orange bill with black tip; dark, square-tipped tail. *Female:* Greenish crown and chin. *Voice:* Metallic chatter. *Similar Species:* See Broad-billed Hummingbird. *Habitat:* Highland pine and pine-oak forests and edges. *Abundance and Distribution:* Rare summer resident* (Apr.–Sep.) in the mountains of southeastern Arizona (Huachucas, Santa Ritas, Chiricahuas); casual in winter at feeders. *Where to Find:* Ramsey Canyon; Madera Canyon; Cave Creek Canyon. *Range:* Highlands of southeastern Arizona and Mexico south to Nicaragua.

217. Violet-crowned Hummingbird

Amazilia violiceps (L—5 W—8)
Bronze green above; white below; green tail; violet crown; pink bill with black tip. Relatively large for a hummingbird. *Female and Immature:* Crown a somewhat greenish-blue. *Voice:* Call a loud chatter similar to that of the Broad-billed Hummingbird; male's song is a high-pitched, insect-like trill of "tis" notes. *Similar Species:* This is the only white-bellied, pink-billed hummer in the region. *Habitat:* Mountain canyons lined with oak, sycamore, mesquite, and cottonwoods; feeders in winter. *Abundance and Distribution:* Uncommon and local summer resident* in mountains of extreme southwestern New Mexico (Guadalupe Canyon) and southeastern Arizona (west to the Santa Ritas). Rare to casual in winter at feeders. *Where to Find:* Guadalupe Canyon, New Mexico; Cave Creek Canyon, Arizona; Madera Canyon, Arizona; Ramsey Canyon, Arizona. *Range:* Breeds from southeastern Arizona and southwestern New Mexico south through mountains of western Mexico to Oaxaca; winters mainly in breeding range though northern populations evidently withdraw somewhat southward.

218. Blue-throated Hummingbird

Lampornis clemenciae (L—5 W—8)

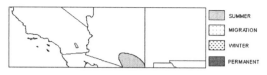

This is a large hummingbird, green above, grayish below with blue throat; black and white face pattern; dark blue tail tipped with white. *Female:* Lacks blue throat. *Voice:* Calls—"tsip," "tseet." *Similar Species:* Female Magnificent Hummingbird has square, dark green tail with grayish tips (not rounded, dark blue tail with extensive white tips of female Blue-throated). *Habitat:* Arid scrub, desert riparian scrub, pine and pine-oak woodlands; mainly sycamore, mesquite, and oak lining canyons in our region. *Abundance and Distribution:* Uncommon to rare summer resident* in mountain canyons of southeastern Arizona (Apr.–Sep.); rare to casual at feeders in winter. *Where to Find:* Madera Canyon; Ramsey Canyon; Cave Creek Canyon. *Range:* Southeastern Arizona and Big Bend of Texas south in central highlands to southern Mexico.

219. Magnificent Hummingbird

Eugenes fulgens (L—6 W—7)

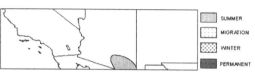

A large hummingbird, green above and dark below with brilliant green gorget and purple crown; white postorbital spot; white at base of tail; notched, green tail. *Female:* Green above, grayish below; white postorbital stripe; square, greenish tail tipped with gray. *Voice:* Call—"chip." *Similar Species:* See Blue-throated Hummingbird. *Habitat:* Montane coniferous forest, pine-oak, and oak woodlands; mainly in sycamore and oak lining mountain canyons in this region. *Abundance and Distribution:* Uncommon summer resident* (Apr.–Sep.) in mountain canyons and highland pine and pine-oak forests of southeastern Arizona; rare in winter at feeders. *Where to Find:* Shannon Campground, Mount Graham; Rucker Canyon, Chiricahua Mountains. *Range:* Breeds locally in southeastern Arizona, western Colorado, and western Texas south through highlands of Mexico and Central America to Nicaragua; winters from northern Mexico south through breeding range.

220. Lucifer Hummingbird

Calothrax lucifer (L—4 W—5)

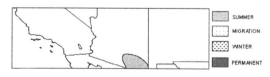

Green above; purple gorget; buff below with greenish flanks; black, scimitar-shaped bill; forked tail. *Female and Immature Male:* Green above, buff below with white post-orbital stripe; rounded, white-tipped tail. *Voice:* Call—a series of high-pitched squeaks. *Similar Species:* White, postorbital stripe in female and immature is distinctive. *Habitat:* Desert scrub, especially agave flowers in dry canyons and at feeders. *Abundance and Distribution:* Rare to casual summer resident* (May–Sep.) in southeastern Arizona. *Where to Find:* Madera Canyon; Ramsey Canyon; Cave Creek Canyon. *Range:* Breeds southeastern Arizona and Big Bend area of Texas south through highlands to southern Mexico; winters central and southern Mexico.

221. Black-chinned Hummingbird
Archilochus alexandri (L—4 W—4)
Green above; whitish below; black
throat. *Female and Immature:* Green

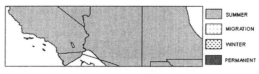

above, whitish below. *Voice:* Song—a series of high-pitched "tsip" notes. *Habitat:* Thorn forest, arid scrub, desert riparian scrub. *Abundance and Distribution:* Common to uncommon summer resident* (Apr.–Aug.) in lowlands and mid-elevations throughout. *Where to Find:* Santiago Oaks Regional Park, California; Red Rock Canyon National Conservation Area, Nevada; Tonto Natural Bridges State Park, Arizona; Bandelier National Monument, New Mexico. *Range:* Breeds in arid portions of southwestern Canada and western United States south to northern Mexico; winters central and southern Mexico.

222. Anna's Hummingbird
Calypte anna (L—4 W—5)
Green above, whitish below with brilliant rose crown and throat. *Female*

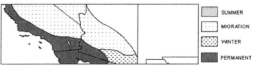

and Immature Male: Green above; grayish below; whitish postorbital stripe; brownish tinge on crown; varying amounts of dark or rose spotting on throat. *Voice:* Song—a series of squeaky chips and buzzes. *Similar Species:* Rose-spotted female Anna's has square tail; females lacking rose spotting are indistinguishable from female Blackchin; female Costa's generally is whitish, not gray, below. *Habitat:* Oak chaparral, thorn forest, second growth, brushy pastures. *Abundance and Distribution:* Common to uncommon resident* in lowlands and mid-elevations of southern California and southwestern Arizona; rare, mainly fall transient (May, Sep.) in southern Nevada; uncommon winter resident (Aug.–Mar.) in southeastern Arizona. *Where to Find:* San Elijo Lagoon Sanctuary, Solana Beach, California; Hassayampa River Preserve, Arizona; Arizona Sonora Desert Museum, Tucson, Arizona. *Range:* Breeds in coastal regions from southwestern Canada to northern Baja California; winters in breeding range and eastward in northern Mexico and southwestern United States border lands.

Figure 32. On a nice summer day, Valley of Fire State Park, Nevada, can be like high noon on Mars. Nevertheless, its desert scrub is a welcome respite from the urban sprawl of Las Vegas, and productive for such typical desert species as Anna's Hummingbird, Ladder-backed Woodpecker, Bushtit, and Western Scrub-Jay.

Figure 33. Driving up from the hot concrete and creosote desert of Las Vegas into the cool of Mount Charleston, Nevada, can be balm in Gilead for the cooked southwestern traveler, even providing some snowy days in winter. The birds are different as well. You can drive all the way up to nine thousand feet, at least in summer when the road is not blocked by snow, and find typical denizens of montane habitat including Williamson's Sapsucker, Northern Goshawk, Pine Siskin, and Steller's Jay.

223. Costa's Hummingbird

Calypte costae (L—4 W—5)

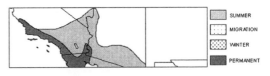

Green above, whitish below with purple head and gorget. *Female:* Green above, whitish below. *Immature Male:* Like female but with purple spotting on throat and head. *Habits:* Spectacular, U-shaped aerial display by male during courtship (Mar.) *Voice:* Call—a nasal "tsink." *Similar Species:* See Anna's Hummingbird. *Habitat:* Desert scrub, oak chaparral, riparian areas. *Abundance and Distribution:* Uncommon to rare summer resident* in lowlands and mid-elevations of southern California, southern Nevada, southern Arizona, and extreme southwestern New Mexico (Guadalupe Canyon); uncommon to rare winter resident along the lower Colorado River valley and coastal southern California. Breeds in deserts (Mar.–May) when most numerous; scarce or absent from these areas at other times of the year. *Where to Find:* Big Morongo Canyon Preserve, California; Saguaro National Park, Arizona; Arizona Sonora Desert Museum, Tucson, Arizona; Guadalupe Canyon, New Mexico. *Range:* Breeds central California, southern Nevada and Utah to southwestern New Mexico, southern Arizona, and northwestern Mexico; winters southern California, Arizona, and northwestern Mexico.

224. Calliope Hummingbird

Stellula calliope (L—3 W—4)

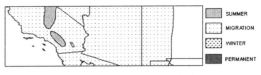

A tiny bird, green above and white below with streaked white and purple gorget. *Female:* Green above buff below with orange buff on flanks; dark throat spotting; tail green with white terminal spots. *Immature Male:* Like female but with some purple spotting on throat. *Voice:* Song—"tsee-ree." *Habits:* Remarkable, cup-shaped, aerial display given by the male during courtship. *Similar Species:* Lack of rufous in tail separates females from Rufous, Broad-tailed, and Allen's hummingbirds. *Habitat:* Open montane coniferous forests and meadows, oak chaparral, desert scrub. *Abundance and Distribution:* Uncommon summer resident* in mountains of southern California; uncommon to rare transient (Mar.–Apr., Aug.–Sep.) elsewhere in southern California (mainly spring), southern Nevada, Arizona (mainly fall), and western New Mexico. *Where to Find:* Mount Pinos Road, California; Lake Fulmor San Jacinto Mountains, California; Ski Run Road, Santa Catalina Mountains, Arizona. *Range:* Breeds in mountains of southwestern Canada and western United States south to southern California and northern Baja California; winters northwestern and central Mexico.

225. Broad-tailed Hummingbird

Selasphorus platycercus (L—4 W—5)
Bronzy-green above; whitish below;
red gorget; rounded green tail; wings

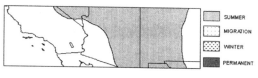

make an insect-like whine in flight. *Female:* Green above; buffy below with dark or purplish-red throat spots; tail a complex pattern of rufous (base), green, black, and white (tips). *Voice:* A high "tsip." The male's wings make a trilling whistle sound in courtship flight display. *Similar Species:* The sound made by male Broad-tailed wings is diagnostic; female Broad-tailed differs from female Rufous and Allen's by buffy (not rusty) flanks, relatively limited rufous on tail, and (when present) purplish-red rather than orange-red throat spots. *Habitat:* Montane coniferous forest, pinyon-juniper and pine-oak woodlands, desert scrub. *Abundance and Distribution:* Common to uncommon transient and summer resident* (May–Aug.) in White, Panamint, and Clark mountains of southern California, Spring Mountains of southern Nevada, also in mountains of Arizona and New Mexico. *Where to Find:* Wyman Canyon, White Mountains, California; Mount Charleston, Nevada; Roosevelt Lake Wildlife Area, Arizona; Capulin Mountain National Monument, New Mexico. *Range:* Breeds in mountains of western United States south through the highlands of Mexico to Guatemala; winters in breeding range from northern Mexico south.

226. Rufous Hummingbird

Selasphorus rufus (L—4 W—4)
Rufous above; whitish below with
rufous flanks and tail; orange-red

gorget; green crown and wings; wings whistle as in Broad-tailed. *Female:* Green above; white below with contrasting rufous flanks; throat often flecked with orange-red; tail rufous at base with white tips. *Voice:* Wings make a whistling noise during flight display. Call—"tsup." *Habits:* Male flies an oval-shaped pattern during courtship display. *Similar Species:* Male Allen's has green (not rufous) back; female is inseparable from female Allen's in the field. The sound made by male Broad-tailed wings is diagnostic; female broadtail differs from female Rufous and Allen's by buffy (not rusty) flanks, relatively limited rufous on tail, and (when present) purplish-red rather than orange-red throat spots. *Habitat:* Mountain meadows, coniferous forest, desert scrub, flowering plants and feeders during migration. *Abundance and Distribution:* Common to rare transient (Mar.–May, July–Sep.) throughout; more numerous spring transient in California, and southwestern Arizona; more numerous fall transient in southern Nevada, northern and eastern Arizona, and New Mexico; rare to casual in winter at feeders. *Where to Find:* Los Alamos Canyon, Bandelier National Monument, New Mexico; Canyon Creek Recreation

Area, Heber, Arizona; Mount Charleston, Nevada. *Range:* Breeds western Canada and northwestern United States; winters southern California and south Texas to southern Mexico.

227. Allen's Hummingbird

Selasphorus sasin (L—4 W—4)
Green crown and back; red gorget; rufous flanks and tail; wings whine in flight as in Rufous and Broad-tailed. *Female:* Green above; white below with contrasting rufous flanks; throat often flecked with orange-red; tail rufous at base with white tips. *Voice:* Call—"chup"; wings whistle during courtship display. *Habits:* Allen's Hummingbird courtship display starts with the male high in the air; it then drops almost to the ground, makes several back-and-forth semi circles, then rises up to begin again. *Similar Species:* See Rufous Hummingbird. Female Rufous and Allen's are inseparable in the field. *Habitat:* Oak chaparral, brushy fields, thickets. *Abundance and Distribution:* Common resident* on Channel Islands and Palos Verdes Peninsula, California; uncommon summer resident* (Mar.–June) in coastal lowlands of southern California; rare to casual fall transient (July–Sep.) in south-central Arizona. *Where to Find:* Channel Islands boat trip; Nojoqui Falls County Park, Santa Barbara, California; South Coast Botanic Garden, Palos Verdes Peninsula, California. *Range:* Breeds along coastal regions of southern Oregon and California; winters from southern California and northwestern Mexico to central Mexico.

Order Trogoniformes
Family Trogonidae
Trogons
Kestrel-sized tropical birds, often brilliantly colored with metallic greens, reds, and blues.

228. Elegant Trogon

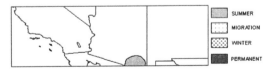

Trogon elegans (L—13 W—16)
Bright green above and below to breast; white breast band; belly red; tail is bronze above, white below with dark tip; yellow bill. *Female:* Like male but brown rather than green; white ear spot. *Immature:* Like female but barred below; spotted wing coverts. *Voice:* A croaking "coah" repeated. *Habitat:* Riparian woodlands (cottonwoods, sycamores) lining mountain canyons. *Abundance and Distri-*

bution: Uncommon to rare summer resident* (Apr.–Sep.) of southeastern Arizona (Huachuca Mountains; Santa Rita Mountains; Chiricahua Mountains). *Where to Find:* Sycamore Canyon; Madera Canyon; Cave Creek Canyon. *Range:* Southern Arizona south through Mexico and Pacific slopes of Central America to Costa Rica.

Order Coraciiformes

Family Alcedinidae
Kingfishers
Stocky, vocal birds; predominantly slate blue or green with long, chisel-shaped bills and shaggy crests; generally found near water where they dive from a perch or from the air for fish.

229. Belted Kingfisher

Ceryle alcyon (L—13 W—22)
Blue-gray above with ragged crest;
white collar, throat, and belly; blue-

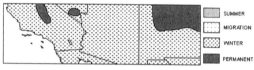

gray breast band. *Female:* Like male but with chestnut band across belly in addition to blue-gray breast band. *Voice:* A loud rattle. *Habitat:* Rivers, lakes, ponds, bays. *Abundance and Distribution:* Uncommon winter resident (Sep.–Apr.) throughout except in higher mountains in northern part of region; uncommon (New Mexico) to rare (southern California, southern Nevada, northern Arizona) summer resident* in highlands. *Where to Find:* Fairmount Park, Riverside, California; Coleman Lake, Arizona; Pahranagat National Wildlife Refuge, Nevada; Bluewater Canyon, Zuni Mountains, New Mexico. *Range:* Breeds throughout most of temperate and boreal North America excluding arid Southwest; winters from southern portion of breeding range south through Mexico and Central America to northern South America; West Indies; Bermuda.

230. Green Kingfisher

Chloroceryle americana (L—9 W—12)
Green above; white collar and belly;
chestnut breast band. *Female:* Green-

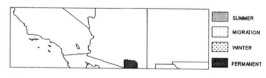

ish breast band. *Voice:* Series of sharp "tic"s. *Habitat:* Streams, rivers, ponds. *Abundance and Distribution:* Uncommon and extremely local resident* of southeastern Arizona. *Where to Find:* San Pedro Riparian National Conservation Area; Arivaca Creek; Sonoita Creek. *Range:* From southern Arizona and central Texas south through Mexico, Central and South America south to central Argentina.

Order Piciformes
Family Picidae
Woodpeckers

A distinctive family of birds with plumages of mainly black and white. Long claws, stubby, strong feet, and stiff tail feathers enable woodpeckers to forage by clambering over tree trunks. The long, heavy, pointed bill is used for chiseling, probing, flicking, or hammering for arthropods. Most species fly in a distinct, undulating manner.

231. Lewis's Woodpecker

Melanerpes lewis (L—11 W—21)
Black with greenish sheen above, reddish below; grayish throat and collar streaked with black on chin; reddish face. Robin size, crow-like flight, and flycatching habits are distinctive. *Immature:* Similar to adult but head, neck, and underparts are brownish. *Voice:* "Churr," "cheeurr," harsh rattle. *Habitat:* Open pine-oak and ponderosa pine woodlands, burned-over forest, cottonwood belts along streams and rivers. *Abundance and Distribution:* Uncommon to rare summer resident* in mountain valleys of northern Arizona and northwestern New Mexico; uncommon transient in southern Nevada; irregular as a transient and occasional winter resident elsewhere in the region except eastern New Mexico where absent. *Where to Find:* Lamar Haines Memorial Wildlife Area, Arizona; Bandelier National Monument, New Mexico. *Range:* Western North America from British Columbia and Alberta south to northern Baja California, Sonora and Chihuahua.

232. Red-headed Woodpecker

Melanerpes erythrocephalus
(L—10 W—18)
Black above, white below with scarlet head. *Immature:* Head brownish. *Voice:* A loud "keeeer." *Habitat:* Deciduous forest, oak woodlands, riparian cottonwood stands, savanna. *Abundance and Distribution:* Summer resident* (Apr.–Oct.) in northeastern New Mexico. *Where to Find:* Maxwell National Wildlife Refuge; Fort Sumner State Monument. *Range:* Eastern North America from central plains and southern Canada to Texas and Florida.

233. Acorn Woodpecker

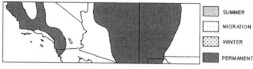

Melanerpes formicivorus (L—9 W—17)
Black back, wings, breast, and tail;
white rump, belly; throat tinged with
yellow; black and white face pattern; crown red. *Female:* Like male but front portion of crown black. *Voice:* A loud, jeering "ja-cob," repeated. *Habitat:* Open oak
and pine-oak woodlands. *Abundance and Distribution:* Common resident* in foothills and mid-elevations where oaks are prevalent. *Where to Find:* Nojoqui Falls
County Park, California; Canyon Creek Recreation Area, Arizona; Canjilon Mountain, Carson National Forest, New Mexico. *Range:* Northwestern Oregon, California, Baja California; Arizona; and New Mexico south through central and western
Mexico, Central America, to the northern Andes of Colombia.

234. Gila Woodpecker

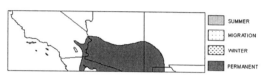

Melanerpes uropygialis
(L—9 W—16)
Black and white on back, and wings;
tail is black with two black-and-white barred central feathers; buff head and underparts; red cap; white patches visible on black primaries in flight. *Female:* Like
male but lacking red cap. *Voice:* A harsh "cheerrrrrr"; also a strident "kyimp." *Similar
Species:* The Golden-fronted Woodpecker has yellow nape (buff in Gila Woodpecker); Ladder-backed Woodpecker has black and white face pattern, which Gila
lacks. Neither the Ladder-backed nor the Golden-fronted show white wing patch
of the Gila. *Habitat:* Dry savanna, desert scrub, saguaro cactus stands, cottonwood
groves. *Abundance and Distribution:* Desert regions of southeastern California,
southern Arizona, and extreme southwestern New Mexico. *Where to Find:*
Guadalupe Canyon, New Mexico; Organ Pipe Cactus National Monument, Arizona; Saguaro National Park, Arizona; Cibola National Wildlife Refuge, California. *Range:* Southern California, Arizona, and New Mexico south through Baja
California and western Mexico to Zacatecas and Aguascalientes.

235. Williamson's Sapsucker

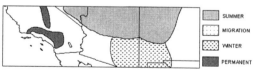

Sphyrapicus thyroideus
(L—9 W—16)
Black above; black breast and yellow
belly; throat red; white rump and wing patch; white postorbital and suborbital
stripes. *Female:* Barred brown and white; black patch on breast; head brownish.
Voice: A nasal "queeer." *Similar Species:* Black patch on breast, brown head, and
lack of white wing patch separates female from immature Red-naped Sapsucker.
Habitat: Subalpine pine (lodgepole, mountain white, mountain hemlock, and

jeffrey) and fir forest, aspen groves, burns; winters in ponderosa pine forest, riparian woodlands, orchards. *Abundance and Distribution:* Uncommon to rare resident* in highlands of southern California; summer resident* of southern Nevada, northern Arizona, and northwestern New Mexico; uncommon to rare transient (Apr., Sep.) and rare winter resident (Oct.–Mar.) at lower elevations in coniferous and mixed forest, riparian groves, and orchards of southeastern Arizona and southwestern New Mexico. Absent from deserts, grasslands, and prairies. *Where to Find:* Mount Charleston, Nevada (breeding); McGill Campground, Mount Pinos, California (breeding); Kaibab Plateau Parkway, Arizona (breeding); Pajarito Mountain Ski Area, New Mexico. *Range:* Breeds in western North America from southern British Columbia and Alberta south to southern California, Nevada, Arizona, and western Colorado; winters in southern portion of breeding range south to Baja California and western Mexico south to Jalisco and Michoacan.

236. Red-naped Sapsucker

Sphyrapicus nuchalis (L—8 W—15)
Black and white above; creamy yellow below with dark flecks on sides;

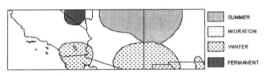

breast black; throat, forehead and crown red with black line separating red in front from red in back of crown; black and white facial pattern. *Female:* White chin. *Immature:* Black wings with white patch, white rump, and checked black and white tail of adults; but barred brownish and cream on head, back, breast, and belly. This is the western form of the Yellow-bellied Sapsucker, formerly considered conspecific. *Voice:* A nasal, whining, descending "cheerrr"; also a distinctive tap sequence on logs during the breeding season—a set of rapid taps followed by two or three taps at greater intervals. *Habitat:* Breeds in montane coniferous and deciduous forest (e.g., aspen, cottonwood, and willow); winters in riparian woodlands, orchards, mesquite thickets. *Abundance and Distribution:* Common resident* in southern Nevada mountains; uncommon to rare summer resident* (Apr.–Sep.) in mountains of northern Arizona, and northwestern New Mexico; uncommon transient and winter resident (Oct.–Mar.) in southern California deserts, southeastern Arizona, southwestern New Mexico, and the Guadalupe Mountains of southeastern New Mexico. *Where to Find:* Mount Charleston, Nevada (breeding); Pajarito Mountain Ski Area, New Mexico (breeding); Arizona Sonora Desert Museum, Tucson, Arizona (winter); San Juan Forestry Station, California (winter). *Range:* Breeds from the Yukon and Northwest Territories to Alberta and eastern British Columbia south through the Rocky Mountain states to Nevada, Arizona, and New Mexico; winters from southwestern United States into Baja California and western Mexico south to Jalisco.

237. Red-breasted Sapsucker

Sphyrapicus ruber (L—9 W—16)

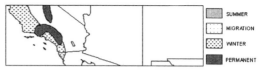

Black and white above; creamy yellow below with dark flecks on sides; head and breast red. *Juvenile:* Like adult but brownish and cream on head, breast and belly—no red. Formerly considered a subspecies of the Yellow-bellied Sapsucker. *Similar Species:* Red-breasted Sapsucker has red breast and creamy yellow underparts flecked with black; Red-headed Woodpecker has white breast and underparts. *Habitat:* Breeds in montane coniferous and mixed forest; winters at lower elevations in groves and woodlands. *Abundance and Distribution:* Uncommon resident* in the Sierra Nevada and elsewhere in highlands of southern California; uncommon to rare winter resident in foothills and lowlands of southwestern California. *Where to Find:* McGill Campground, Mount Pinos (breeding); Santiago Oaks Regional Park (winter). *Range:* Breeds in Pacific coast ranges of the west from the Yukon to southern California; Winters in breeding range from southern British Columbia southward, and in coastal lowlands to northern Baja California.

238. Ladder-backed Woodpecker

Picoides scalaris (L—7 W—13)

Barred black and white above; dirty white below, flecked with black on sides; black triangle framing white cheek is distinctive; red crown and forehead. *Female:* Black crown and forehead. *Voice:* A sharp "peek"; a rapid, descending series of "pik"s. *Similar Species:* Only barred-backed woodpecker with black facial triangle framing white cheek. *Habitat:* Desert scrub, pinyon-juniper, thorn forest, oak woodland, riparian forest, fence rows. *Abundance and Distribution:* Common to uncommon resident* in foothill and wooded desert regions of southeastern California, southern Nevada, Arizona (except northeast), and New Mexico (except northwest). *Where to Find:* Valley of Fire State Park, Nevada; Percha Dam State Park, New Mexico; Joshua Tree National Monument, California; Hualapai Mountain Park, Arizona. *Range:* Southwestern United States south through Mexico to Nicaragua.

239. Nuttall's Woodpecker

Picoides nuttallii (L—7 W—13)

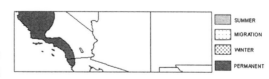

Barred black and white above; white below, flecked with black on sides; black cheek patch with white mustache; red crown. *Female:* Black crown. *Voice:* "Prreeek"; also a high-pitched rattle. *Similar Species:* Only barred-backed woodpecker with black cheek and white mustache. *Habitat:* Oak and riparian woodlands, canyons, orchards, groves. *Abundance and Distribution:* Common to uncommon resident* in foothills and lowlands of southwestern California (west of Sierra Nevada and deserts). *Where to Find:* Tapia County Park, Santa Monica Mountains; Dorothy May Tucker Wildlife Sanctuary, Santa Ana Mountains; Silverwood Audubon Sanctuary, San Diego County. *Range:* Northern California to northern Baja California.

240. Downy Woodpecker

Picoides pubescens (L—7 W—12)
Black and white above; white below;
red cap on back portion of crown.

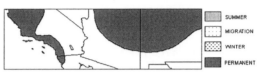

Female: Black cap. *Voice:* A sharp "peek"; a rapid, descending series of "pik"s. *Similar Species:* The white back separates this sparrow-sized woodpecker from all others except the thrush-sized Hairy Woodpecker, which is much larger and has a lower, usually single, call note. Ladder-backed Woodpecker has ladder back. *Habitat:* Forests, second growth, park lands. *Abundance and Distribution:* Uncommon resident* in foothills and lower elevations of southwestern California, northern Arizona, and northern New Mexico. *Where to Find:* Capulin National Monument, New Mexico; Tonto Natural Bridge State Park, Arizona; Louis Rubidoux Nature Center, California. *Range:* Temperate and boreal North America south to southern California, Arizona, New Mexico, and Texas.

241. Hairy Woodpecker

Picoides villosus (L—9 W—15)
Black and white above; white below;
red cap on back portion of crown.

Female: Black cap. *Voice:* A sharp "pick"; a descending series of "pick"s. *Similar Species:* The white back separates this thrush-sized woodpecker from all others except the sparrow-sized Downy Woodpecker, which is much smaller and has a higher-pitched call note and rattle. Ladder-backed Woodpecker has ladder back. *Habitat:* Coniferous, mixed, deciduous and riparian woodlands. *Abundance and Distribution:* Common to uncommon resident* except in deserts, grasslands, and prairies. *Where to Find:* Burnt Rancheria Campground, Mount Laguna, California; Canjilon Mountain Carson National Forest, New Mexico; Red Rock Canyon National Conservation Area, Nevada; Lamar Haines Memorial Wildlife Area, Arizona. *Range:* Temperate and boreal North America south through the mountains of western Mexico and Central America to Panama; Bahamas.

242. Strickland's Woodpecker

Picoides stricklandi (L—8 W—13)
Black back; black tail with black and
white outer tail feathers; white under-

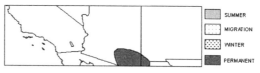

SUMMER
MIGRATION
WINTER
PERMANENT

parts with black spots; black forehead and crown; red at back of crown; black
cheek; white mustache. *Female:* Crown and nape entirely black (lacks red of male).
Voice: "Peeeek"; also a high-pitched rattle. *Similar Species:* The combination of
black back and spotted breast is distinctive. *Habitat:* Montane pine, pine-oak and
fir forest, canyon groves; often forages in dense thickets in upper portions of tree
trunks and branches. *Abundance and Distribution:* Uncommon to rare resident*
in mountains of southeastern Arizona and extreme southwestern New Mexico
(Guadalupe Canyon). *Where to Find:* Madera Canyon, Arizona; Ramsey Canyon,
Arizona; Cave Creek Canyon, Arizona; Guadalupe Canyon, New Mexico. *Range:*
Southeastern Arizona and southwestern New Mexico south in highlands of western Mexico to Michoacan.

243. White-headed Woodpecker

Picoides albolarvatus (L—9 W—14)
Black body; white head and throat;
red on back of crown; black nape;

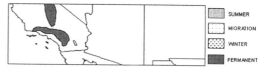

SUMMER
MIGRATION
WINTER
PERMANENT

white middle portion of outer primaries. *Female:* Black on back of crown in place
of red. *Voice:* A hoarse "chik" or "chik-ik." *Similar Species:* White head is distinctive. *Habitat:* Montane pine, pine-oak, and fir forests. *Abundance and Distribution:* Uncommon resident* in mountains of southern California. *Where to Find:*
Piute Mountain Road, Kern County; Palomar Mountain State Park; Charlton Flat
Picnic Area, San Gabriel Mountains. *Range:* Pacific coast mountains from southern British Columbia to southern California.

244. Three-toed Woodpecker

Picoides tridactylus (L—9 W—14)
Back barred black and white or
mostly white; black wings; central tail

SUMMER
MIGRATION
WINTER
PERMANENT

feathers black, outer tail feathers white; black head with white stripe up neck and
white mustache; yellow crown; white below with black barring on flanks. *Female:*
Crown is black flecked with white. *Voice:* A sharp "pik." *Similar Species:* The Three-
toed Woodpecker has black-and-white barring on back (black back in the similar
Black-backed Woodpecker). *Habitat:* Boreal coniferous forest (spruce-fir). *Abundance and Distribution:* Uncommon to rare resident* in boreal regions of White
and San Francisco Mountains and Kaibab Plateau of Arizona and north-central,
and Mogollon mountains of New Mexico. *Where to Find:* Lamar Haines Memorial

Figure 34. Sycamore Canyon, Arizona, is justly famous both for the remote beauty of its cliffs and crags and its rich Neotropical birdlife, including Northern Beardless-Tyrannulet, Sulphur-bellied Flycatcher, Rose-throated Becard, Elegant Trogon, and Painted Redstart.

Figure 35. The combination of dramatic canyon vistas, Anasazi Indian cliff dwellings, and a variety of desert habitats make Arizona's Canyon de Chelly (pronounced, "canyon de shay") a major attraction. This photo of the canyon was taken at White House overlook. Note the cliff dwelling at the lower right, called the "white house" by Navajos. Birds found here include most of the Southwest's corvids—Steller's Jay, Gray Jay, Western Scrub-Jay, Pinyon Jay, Clark's Nutcracker, American Crow, and Common Raven.

Wildlife Area, Arizona; Santa Fe Baldy, New Mexico; Valle Vidal, New Mexico. *Range:* Boreal North America south in the Rockies to northern Arizona and northern New Mexico.

245. Black-backed Woodpecker

Picoides arcticus (L—9 W—14)
Black back and wings; central tail feathers black, outer tail feathers white; black head with white stripe from mustache to neck; yellow crown; white below with black barring on flanks. *Female:* Crown is black. *Voice:* A sharp "pik." *Habits:* Peels bark from dead conifers. Often found in burned areas. *Similar Species:* See Three-toed Woodpecker. *Habitat:* Lodgepole pine, mountain white pine, mountain hemlock, red fir, burned over pine forests. *Abundance and Distribution:* Rare resident* in the Sierra Nevada mountains of southern California. *Where to Find:* High Sierras of southern California. *Range:* Boreal forests of North America south in Rockies to Idaho and Montana, and in Sierras to southern California.

246. Northern Flicker

Colaptes auratus
(L—12 W—20)
Barred brown and black above; tan with black spots below; black breast; white rump. Eastern forms (e.g. *C. a. auratus, C. a. luteus, C. a. borealis*) have yellow underwings and tail linings, gray cap and nape with red occiput, tan face and throat with black mustache. The western "Red-shafted" form (*C. a. colaris*) has red underwings and tail linings, brown cap and nape, gray cheek and throat with red mustache. *Female:* Lacks mustache. *Voice:* A long series of "kek"s first rising, then falling; a "kleer" followed by several "wika"s. *Habitat:* Coniferous forest, pinyon-juniper, pine-oak, oak, and riparian woodland (winter). *Abundance and Distribution:* Common to uncommon resident* nearly throughout. The Red-shafted Flicker is an uncommon resident in mountains, foothills, and neighboring lowlands of southern California, southern Nevada, Arizona, and western New Mexico, moving downslope in winter; Yellow-shafted Flicker is an uncommon winter resident (Nov.–Mar.) in eastern New Mexico. *Where to Find:* San Juan Forestry Station, California (Red-shafted); Grand View Point, South Rim of Grand Canyon, Arizona (Red-shafted); Clayton Lake State Park, New Mexico (Red-shafted); Carlsbad, New Mexico (Yellow-shafted). *Range:* Nearly throughout temperate and boreal North America south in highlands of Mexico to Oaxaca. Leaves northern portion of breeding range in winter.

247. Gilded Flicker

Colaptes nanus (L—10 W—18)

Barred brown and black above; whitish with black spots below; cinnamon
cap; black breast; white rump; bright yellow wing linings; red mustache. *Female:*
Lacks mustache. *Voice:* "Its calls include the familiar *clee-o,* and *kuk-kuk-kuk-kuk,*
and *wicky-wicky-wicky* notes like those of other flickers, on a higher pitch." (Edwards
1972:124). *Habitat:* Desert woodlands, bosques (saguaro, joshua tree, mesquite,
willow, cottonwood), residential areas. *Abundance and Distribution:* Uncommon
resident* in desert riparian areas of southeastern California (principally the Colorado River valley) and Arizona. *Where to Find:* Cedar Canyon Road, Cima, California; Organ Pipe Cactus National Monument, Arizona. *Range:* Southeastern
California and Arizona south through northwestern Mexico to southern Baja California and northern Sinaloa.

248. Pileated Woodpecker

Dryocopus pileatus (L—17 W—27)

Black, crow-sized bird; black and
white facial pattern; red mustache
and crest; white wing lining. *Female:* Has black mustache. *Voice:* Loud "kuk kuk
kuk kuk kuk kuk"—stops abruptly, does not trail off like flicker. The drum is a
loud rattle on a large log, first increasing, then decreasing in pace—lasting two to
three seconds. *Habitat:* Old growth forest—sugar pine, red, white, and douglas
firs, sequoias; also in oaks and cottonwoods. *Abundance and Distribution:* Uncommon resident* in Sierra Nevada Mountains of southern California. *Where to Find:*
Sequoia National Park. *Range:* Much of temperate and boreal North America excluding Great Plains and Rocky Mountain regions.

Order Passeriformes
Family Tyrannidae
Flycatchers and Kingbirds
A large group of mostly tropical songbirds, robin-sized or smaller. They are characterized by erect posture, muted plumage coloration (olives, browns, and grays),
a broad bill, hooked at the tip, and bristles around the mouth. Flycatchers are
mostly insectivorous, often capturing their prey on the wing.

Subfamily Elaeninae
Tyrannulets and Elaenias

249. Northern Beardless-Tyrannulet *Camptostoma imberbe* (L—5 W—7)

Olive above; whitish below with olive wash on breast; buffy wing bars. *Voice:* High-pitched, descending "peeer peeer peeer." *Habits:* This species is quite unobtrusive, and best found by voice. *Similar Species: Empidonax* flycatchers have erect posture and thicker bill; kinglets have eyering; Verdin has straight, pointed bill, tyrannulet has down-curve upper mandible. *Habitat:* Thorn forest (mesquite) and riparian (cottonwood, hackberry) woodlands. *Abundance and Distribution:* Uncommon to rare summer resident* (Apr.–Sep.) in southeastern Arizona and extreme southwestern New Mexico (Guadalupe Canyon); rare to casual in winter. *Where to Find:* Aravaipa Canyon, Arizona; Catalina State Park, Arizona; Sycamore Canyon, Arizona; Guadalupe Canyon, New Mexico. *Range:* Southern Texas, New Mexico, and Arizona south to northern Costa Rica; winters from northern Mexico south through breeding range.

Subfamily Fluvicolinae
Pewees, Phoebes, and Empidonax Flycatchers

250. Olive-sided Flycatcher *Contopus cooperi* (L—8 W—13)

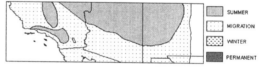

Olive above; white below with olive on sides of breast and belly; white tufts on lower back sometimes difficult to see. *Voice:* "Whit whew whew" (Quick, three beers!). *Similar Species:* Eastern Wood-Pewee is smaller, has wing bars, and lacks dark olive along sides of breast and belly. *Habitat:* Lone, tall, dead snags in ponderosa and sugar pines; white, douglas, and red firs; jeffrey pine and juniper; thorn forest and riparian woodlands during migration. *Abundance and Distribution:* Uncommon summer resident* (Apr.–Sep.) in mountains of southern California, southern Nevada, northern Arizona, and western New Mexico; uncommon to rare transient (Apr.–May, Aug.–Sep.) in lowlands and mid-elevations throughout except eastern plains of New Mexico. *Where to Find:* Mount Charleston, Nevada; Lamar Haines Wildlife Area, Arizona; Sandia Crest, New Mexico; Burnt Rancheria Campground, Mount Laguna, California. *Range:* Breeds in boreal forest across the northern tier of North America and through mountains in west, south to Texas and northern Baja California; winters in mountains of South America from Colombia to Peru.

251. Greater Pewee

Contopus pertinax (L—8 W—13)

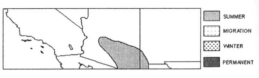

Brownish olive above; similar but lighter below; slight crest; no wing bars; yellowish lower mandible. *Voice:* A plaintive "wheway wheweeaa" (jose maria); also, a regularly-given "pip" call note. *Habits:* Often calls, sings, and forages from an exposed perch. *Similar Species:* Similar in size to Olive-sided Flycatcher but entire underparts are darkish (not just sides), and lower mandible is noticeably lighter in color than upper. *Habitat:* Pine-oak. *Abundance and Distribution:* Uncommon summer resident* (Apr.–Sep.) in central and southeastern Arizona and southwestern New Mexico. *Where to Find:* Sawmill Canyon, Arizona; Mount Lemmon, Arizona; Madera Canyon, Arizona; Willow Creek Campground, New Mexico. *Range:* Breeds from central Arizona and southwestern New Mexico south in highlands of Central America to northern Nicaragua; winters from northern Mexico through Central American breeding range.

252. Western Wood-Pewee

Contopus sordidulus (L—6 W—10)

Dark olive above; olive wash on breast; belly whitish; white wing bars. *Voice:* Nasal "peeaar" song, raspy "peezer" call. *Similar Species:* Cannot be safely separated in the field from Eastern Wood-Pewee except by its raspy "peezer" call note, which is harsher than the "peeyer" of the Eastern Wood-Pewee. Pewees lack eyering of *Empidonax* species. *Habitat:* Pine, pine-oak, and riparian (cottonwoods, willows) woodlands. *Abundance and Distribution:* Common summer resident* (Apr.–Oct.) in middle elevations; absent as a breeder from low deserts, high mountains, and plains of eastern New Mexico; common transient (Apr.–May, Aug.–Sep.) throughout. *Where to Find:* Quatal Canyon, Ventucopa, California; Cox Ranch Visitor's Center, Las Cruces, New Mexico; Canyon Creek Recreation Area, Arizona; Mount Charleston, Nevada. *Range:* Breeds throughout western United States. and Canada south to the highlands of Honduras; winters northern South America.

253. Willow Flycatcher

Empidonax traillii (L—6 W—9)

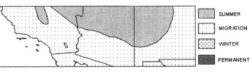

Brownish olive above; whitish below turning to a creamy yellow on belly; greenish on flanks; white wing bars and eyering. *Voice:* A buzzy, slurred "fitz-bew" song; also "wit" call note. *Similar Species:* A combination of behavior, voice, habitat, and minute details of appearance often are needed to separate one species of *Empidonax* flycatcher from another. The song of the Willow Flycatcher is distinctive, and it is the characteristic *Empidonax* species of mountain meadows. On migration, it is very difficult to separate from other members of the group. *Habitat:* Mountain meadows at mid-elevations, willow thickets, riparian forest, chaparral, oak woodlands. *Abundance and Distribution:* Uncommon to rare and irregular summer resident* (Apr.–Aug.) at mid-elevations in the Sierra Nevada of southern California, and valleys, canyons, and mountains (to seven thousand feet) of southern Nevada, northern Arizona, and northwestern New Mexico; uncommon transient (Apr.–June, Aug.–Sep.) throughout. *Where to Find:* Middle Rio Grande Conservancy District south of Albuquerque, New Mexico (brushy thickets); Old Refuge, Las Cruces, New Mexico; South Kern River Reserve, California; Bright Angel Trail to Colorado River, Grand Canyon, Arizona. *Range:* Breeds through much of north and central United States; winters in northern South America.

254. Least Flycatcher

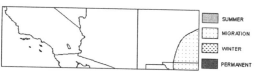

Empidonax minimus (L—5 W—8) Brownish above; white below; wing bars and eyering white. *Habits:* Bobs tail. *Voice:* Song "che bec," given by both sexes during migration and on wintering grounds; call is a brief "wit." *Similar Species:* The Least Flycatcher has a restricted distribution in this region, occurring only in southeastern New Mexico, and only as a transient. Due to the extreme rarity of the species outside this area or at other times of the year, positive identification would require the bird in the hand. The constant tail bobbing of the Least can be used to separate it from the Willow Flycatcher. *Habitat:* Open woodlands. *Abundance and Distribution:* Rare transient (Apr.–May, Aug.–Sep.) in southeastern New Mexico. *Where to Find:* Artesia Cemetery, New Mexico. *Range:* Breeds in northern United States and southern and central Canada west to British Columbia, south in Appalachians to north Georgia; winters from central Mexico to Panama.

255. Hammond's Flycatcher

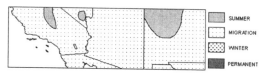

Empidonax hammondii (L—6 W—9) Olive gray above; grayish below with white throat and yellow wash on belly; wing bars and eyering white. *Habits:* Hammond's Flycatchers often forage high in the crowns of tall conifers, so they generally are easier to hear than see. *Voice:* "Tseeput" song is similar to, but huskier than that of Dusky Flycatcher. *Similar Species:* Hammond's Flycatcher bobs tail and flicks wings. The similar Dusky Flycatcher usually only flicks tail; also the Dusky seems to prefer more open habitats than the Hammond's. *Habitat:* Highland coniferous forest (sugar pine; white, red, and douglas firs; sequoia); riparian forest (migration). *Abundance and Distri-*

bution: Common to uncommon summer resident* (May–Aug.) in the highlands of southern California, southern Nevada and northwestern New Mexico; common to uncommon transient (Apr.–May, Sep.–Oct.) elsewhere in the region. The Hammond's migrates south somewhat later than other *Empidonax* because it molts on the breeding ground (most other *Empidonax* molt on the wintering ground). *Where to Find:* Sierra Nevada, California; Bandelier National Monument, New Mexico; Valle Vidal, New Mexico. *Range:* Breeds in western mountains from Alaska to central California and northern New Mexico; winters from southeastern Arizona and northern Mexico through the highlands of Central America to Nicaragua.

256. Gray Flycatcher

Empidonax wrightii (L—6 W—9)
Gray above; grayish white below;
eyering and wing bars white. *Voice:*

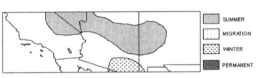

Song—"chi bit," call—"wit." *Similar Species:* Gray Flycatcher dips tail smoothly down instead of jerking it up and down like Hammond's, Dusky, and Least. *Habitat:* Montane arid scrub (pinyon-juniper) and desert scrub. *Abundance and Distribution:* Uncommon to rare summer resident* (May–Aug.) in highland deserts of southern California, southern Nevada, northern Arizona, and western New Mexico; uncommon transient (Apr.–May, Aug.–Sep.) throughout; rare to casual winter resident in lowland mesquite woodlands in southern California, southern Arizona, and southwestern New Mexico. *Where to Find:* Joshua Tree National Monument, California; Water Canyon, Magdalena Mountains, New Mexico; Red Mountain, Arizona; Kyle Canyon, Nevada. *Range:* Breeds in Great Basin from southern Washington, Idaho, and Wyoming south to southern California, Arizona, and New Mexico; winters from southern Arizona through arid regions of Mexico.

257. Dusky Flycatcher

Empidonax oberholseri (L—6 W—9)
Gray tinged with olive above; grayish below; white throat; tinge of yel-

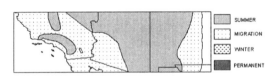

low on belly; eyering and wing bars white. *Voice:* Song a series of "tseeup"s, "seet"s, and "chupit"s in no particular sequence. Very similar to, but more varied and mellow than that of Hammond's Flycatcher. *Similar Species:* See Hammond's Flycatcher. *Habitat:* Montane mixed woodlands (pine-oak) and open pine stands with dense undergrowth of ceanothus, manzanita, chinquapin, and other shrubs; thickets; scrub; edge. *Abundance and Distribution:* Uncommon summer resident* (May–Aug.) in highlands throughout; common to rare transient (Apr.–May, Aug.–Sep.) elsewhere in the region except eastern New Mexico where absent. *Where to Find:* Mount Pinos, California; Mount Charleston, Nevada; Lamar Haines Wildlife Area,

Arizona; Bandelier National Monument, New Mexico. *Range:* Breeds in mountains of western North America from southern Alaska to southern California, Arizona, and New Mexico; winters in highlands from southern Arizona and northeastern Mexico south to Guatemala.

258. Pacific-Slope Flycatcher

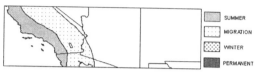

Empidonax difficilis (L—6 W—9)
Olive brown above; yellowish below;
wing bars and eyering whitish. *Voice:*
Song "su weet." Call note, "pik." *Similar Species:* This form formerly was considered a subspecies of the Western Flycatcher, which now has been split into two species, the coastal Pacific-slope Flycatcher and the inland Cordilleran Flycatcher. Though very similar in appearance, their songs are different ("su weet" in Pacific-slope, "wheeseet" in Cordilleran); also, the Pacific-slope Flycatcher has a one-note call ("tseet") as opposed to the Cordilleran, which has a two-note call. Both species differ from other western *Empidonax* in their yellow throat and underparts (juvenile Pacific-Slope birds can be whitish). *Habitat:* Oak savanna, canyon, and riparian woodlands, often near cliffs and stream banks. *Abundance and Distribution:* Uncommon summer resident* (Apr.–Aug.) and rare to casual winter resident in lowlands and foothills of southern California; uncommon to rare transient (Apr.–May, Aug.–Sep.) in desert regions of southern California, southwestern Arizona, and perhaps elsewhere in region, but status unknown. *Where to Find:* Santiago Oaks Regional Park; Montaña de Oro State Park; Hi Mountain Road, Arroyo Grande. *Range:* Breeds from southeastern Alaska and northwestern British Columbia south to southwestern California; winters in Baja California, and from northwestern Mexico south to Oaxaca.

259. Cordilleran Flycatcher

Empidonax occidentalis (L—6 W—9)
Olive green above; yellowish below;
wing bars and eyering creamy. *Voice:*
Song "ter chip." Also, a two-note call. *Similar Species:* See Pacific-Slope Flycatcher. *Habitat:* Riparian woodlands, shady canyons, and stream borders; often near cliffs and houses that provide suitable sites for nest placement (crags, eaves). *Abundance and Distribution:* Common summer resident* (May–Sep.) in mid-elevations of southern Nevada, Arizona, and western New Mexico. Absent from open desert areas of southwestern Arizona and plains of eastern New Mexico. *Where to Find:* Kyle Canyon, Nevada; Madera Canyon, Arizona; Water Canyon Campground, New Mexico. *Range:* Breeds from southern Alberta, Idaho, and Montana south through the western and southwestern United States and western Mexico to Oaxaca; winters in Baja California, and from northwestern Mexico to Oaxaca.

260. Buff-breasted Flycatcher

Empidonax fulvifrons (L—5 W—8)
Olive-brown above; rich buff on
breast; yellowish throat, belly, and

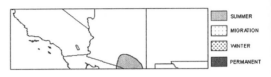

crissum; buffy wingbars; white eyering. *Voice:* Song-"tsik-ee-whew"; call—a low
"pwit." *Habitat:* Open Chihuahuan pine, pine-oak, and sycamore groves of steep
canyons. *Abundance and Distribution:* Uncommon summer resident* (Apr.–Sep.)
in the Huachuca Mountains of southern Arizona; rare to casual in summer in the
Chiricahuas, Santa Ritas, and Santa Catalinas. *Where to Find:* Carr Canyon, Sawmill Canyon Campground, and Scotia Canyon in the Huachucas; Saulsbury Canyon in the Chiricahuas. *Range:* Breeds from southern Arizona through the mountains of west-central Mexico and Guatemala to southern Honduras; winters from
northwestern Mexico south through breeding range and adjacent valleys.

261. Black Phoebe

Sayornis nigricans (L—7 W—11)
All black except for white belly and
crissum. *Immature:* Like adult but

with rusty wingbars and rump. *Habits:* Flicks and fans tail while perched; often
uses mid-stream boulders as perches from which to sally for flies. *Voice:* Rising
"fibee" followed by descending "fibee," repeated. *Habitat:* Sparse vegetation of
shoals, banks, and bars along rivers and streams; woodlands, parks, residential
areas. *Abundance and Distribution:* Common to uncommon resident* in lowland,
foothill, and desert regions of southern California, southern Nevada, western and
southern Arizona, and western and southern New Mexico (east to Guadalupe
Mountains). *Where to Find:* Sitting Bull Falls, Guadalupe Mountains, New Mexico;
Oceano Campground, California; Sabino Canyon Recreation Area, Arizona; Corn
Creek, Desert National Wildlife Range, Nevada. *Range:* Western United States (California, southern Nevada, Arizona, New Mexico, and west Texas) south through
Middle and South America to Argentina. Winters somewhat south of breeding
range in Arizona and New Mexico, and at lower elevations.

262. Eastern Phoebe

Sayornis phoebe (L—7 W—11)
Dark brown above; whitish or yellowish below. Dark cap often has crest-

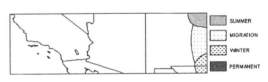

like appearance. Bobs tail. *Voice:* "Febezzt feebezzt," repeated; call a clear "tship."
Similar Species: Eastern Wood-Pewee has distinct wing bars; *Empidonax* have wing
bars and eyering. *Habitat:* Riparian forest; good nest site localities seem to determine
breeding habitat—cliffs, eaves, bridges. *Abundance and Distribution:* Rare to casual

and irregular summer resident* (Mar.–Oct.) in northeast corner of New Mexico; rare fall transient (Oct.–Nov.) in eastern New Mexico; rare to casual winter resident in extreme southeastern New Mexico. *Where to Find:* Percha Dam State Park (fall migration). *Range:* Breeds from eastern British Columbia across southern Canada south through eastern United States (except southern coastal plain); winters southeastern United States south through eastern Mexico to Oaxaca and Veracruz.

263. Say's Phoebe

Sayornis saya (L—8 W—13)
Entirely grayish-brown except for cinnamon buff belly; crissum. *Voice:* "Pitseeeurr," often given in flight; mournful "peeeurr." *Habitat:* Desert scrub, pastures, agricultural areas. *Abundance and Distribution:* Common to uncommon summer resident* (Apr.–Oct.) in northern Arizona and New Mexico, rare to casual in winter; permanent resident in southern Nevada, southeastern California, southern Arizona, and southern New Mexico; winter resident (Nov.–Mar.) in southwestern California. *Where to Find:* Grout Bay Campground, California; Saguaro National Park, Arizona; Desert National Wildlife Range, Nevada; Embudito Canyon, Sandia Mountains, New Mexico. *Range:* Breeds in western North America from Alaska to western Mexico; winters southwestern United States to southern Mexico.

264. Vermilion Flycatcher

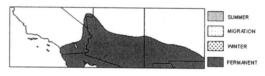

Pyrocephalus rubinus (L—6 W—10)
Black above; scarlet below with scarlet cap. *Female:* Brownish above with whitish throat and chest and orangish or yellowish belly, faintly streaked. *Immature:* Young male is like female with increasing amounts of black above and red below in successive molts, achieving full male plumage in third winter. *Voice:* "Pit-a-see," repeated, often given in flight. *Habitat:* Mesquite thorn forest; desert scrub, often near water; riparian woodlands (cottonwood, sycamore, ash), especially in winter. *Abundance and Distribution:* Uncommon to rare summer resident* (Apr.–Oct.) in lowland desert regions and mid-elevation canyons of southeastern California, southern Nevada, Arizona (except northeast highlands), and southern New Mexico; withdraws southward and to lowland riparian areas in breeding range in winter. *Where to Find:* Patagonia Sonoita Creek Preserve, Arizona; Corn Creek, Desert National Wildlife Range, Nevada; Big Morongo Canyon Preserve, California; Rattlesnake Springs, New Mexico. *Range:* From the southwestern United States south in drier parts of Middle and South America to northern Argentina and Chile.

Subfamily Tyranninae
Kingbirds and *Myiarchus* Flycatchers

265. Dusky-capped Flycatcher

Myiarchus tuberculifer (L—8 W—11)
Olive brown above with dark crest;
throat and chest gray; belly yellow.

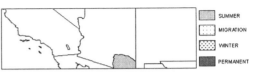

SUMMER
MIGRATION
WINTER
PERMANENT

Voice: A plaintive "wheeeurrr," often given from the highest available perch. *Similar Species:* The Dusky-capped Flycatcher (formerly called the Olivaceous Flycatcher) is the smallest of the Southwest's *Myiarchus* flycatchers. The darker, more pointed crest, brighter yellow underparts, rusty wing bars, and lack of rufous in tail help to distinguish this species from the much paler Ash-throated Flycatcher. The Brown-crested Flycatcher is larger, darker brown above, brighter yellow below, and shows rufous in tail. The regular, plaintive call of the Dusky-capped is the best field mark. *Habitat:* Pine-oak forest and riparian woodland (cottonwood, sycamore). *Abundance and Distribution:* Common summer resident* (May–Aug.) in southeastern Arizona and extreme southwestern New Mexico. *Where to Find:* Patagonia Sonoita Creek Preserve, Arizona; Cave Creek Canyon, Arizona; Sycamore Canyon, Arizona; Guadalupe Canyon, New Mexico. *Range:* Breeds from southeastern Arizona and southwestern New Mexico south through Middle and South America to northern Argentina; winters from southern Mexico south through breeding range.

266. Ash-throated Flycatcher

Myiarchus cinerascens (L—9 W—13)
Brown above; grayish-white throat
and breast; pale yellow belly. *Voice:* A

SUMMER
MIGRATION
WINTER
PERMANENT

harsh "zheep" or "zhrt" often preceded by a sharp "quip." *Similar Species:* The Ash-throated Flycatcher is the palest of the *Myiarchus* flycatchers of the Southwest—whitish throat and pale yellow wash on the belly. The harsh call of the Ash-throated is the best field mark. See Dusky-capped Flycatcher. *Habitat:* Thorn forest, oak savanna, desert scrub, oak-juniper woodlands. *Abundance and Distribution:* Common to uncommon summer resident* (Mar.–Sep.) throughout except in highlands (above four thousand feet); rare winter resident (Oct.–Mar.) in the lower Colorado River valley and southwestern Arizona. *Where to Find:* Lost Palms Oasis, Joshua Tree National Monument, California; Desert National Wildlife Range, Nevada; Coronado National Memorial, Arizona; McMillan Campground, Pinos Altos Mountains, New Mexico. *Range:* Breeds in western United States from Washington, Idaho, and Colorado south to southern Mexico; winters from southeastern California, Arizona and northern Mexico to Honduras on Pacific slope.

Figure 36. The little trading post town of Teec Nos Pos (pronounced "tes nos pos") is located in the rugged Four Corners region of extreme northeastern Arizona. Pinyon-juniper is the predominant habitat type, home to Black-billed Magpie, Band-tailed Pigeon, Gray Flycatcher, and Plumbeous Vireo.

Figure 37. The San Gabriel Mountains loom high above the smog-swamped San Fernando Basin. Here, at places like Switzer Picnic Area, cool montane fir forests provide habitat for Mountain Chickadee, Common Poorwill, Warbling Vireo, and Black-headed Grosbeak.

267. Brown-crested Flycatcher

Myiarchus tyrannulus (L—9 W—13)
Brown above; gray throat and breast;
belly yellow. Formerly called Wied's
Crested Flycatcher. *Voice:* A series of sharp "quip" notes, also a three-note "quip-quit-too." *Similar Species:* The Brown-crested Flycatcher is the largest and darkest of the three southwestern *Myiarchus* flycatchers—with dark back and crest, gray throat, yellow underparts, and some rufous showing in tail. The mellow, "quip" call notes, often given in a series, are the best field mark. See Dusky-capped Flycatcher. *Habitat:* Mesquite thorn forest, oak, and riparian (cottonwood, sycamore) woodlands. *Abundance and Distribution:* Common to uncommon summer resident* (Apr.–Sep.) in the Colorado River Valley, central and southern Arizona, and southwestern New Mexico. *Where to Find:* Saguaro National Park, Arizona; Patagonia Sonoita Creek Preserve, Arizona; Big Morongo Canyon Preserve, California; Guadalupe Canyon, New Mexico. *Range:* Breeds from the southwestern United States south along both slopes in Mexico through Middle and South America to Argentina; winters from southern Mexico south through breeding range.

268. Sulphur-bellied Flycatcher

Myiodynastes luteiventris
(L—8 W—12)
Brown streaked with dark brown
above; yellow with dark streaks below; white eyebrow and dark face patch; rufous tail. *Voice:* "Peee cheee"; also a "kip kip kip" rattle. *Habitat:* Riparian forest (sycamore, cottonwood), canyons, scrub, open woodlands. *Abundance and Distribution:* Common summer resident* (May–Sep.) in southeastern Arizona. *Where to Find:* Sycamore Canyon; Cave Creek Canyon; Garden Canyon. *Range:* Breeds from southern Arizona and northeastern Mexico south through Central America to Costa Rica; winters in northern South America.

269. Tropical Kingbird *Tyrannus*

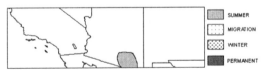

melancholicus (L—9 W—16)
Pearl gray head; dark ear patch; yellowish back, breast and belly; wings
and tail dark brown. *Voice:* Song—a rapid "kip kip kip." *Similar Species:* Couch's Kingbird is indistinguishable from the Tropical in the field except by voice—a harsh "breezeer" accompanies the rapid "kip kip kip" rattle in Couch's; Cassin's Kingbird has buff edgings to wing coverts and tail feather tips; Western Kingbird has white outer tail feathers. The Tropical Kingbird has a slightly forked tail; Cassin's and Western kingbirds have squared-off tail. *Habitat:* Riparian woodlands (cot-

tonwood, willow), tropical savanna. *Abundance and Distribution:* Rare summer resident* (May–Sep.) in the San Pedro, Santa Cruz, and other river valleys and wooded wetland borders of extreme southeastern Arizona. *Where to Find:* Arivaca Cienaga; Buenos Aires National Wildlife Refuge; San Pedro House. *Range:* Breeds from southeastern Arizona and northeastern Mexico south through Central and South America to central Argentina; winters south from central Mexico.

270. Cassin's Kingbird

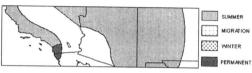

Tyrannus vociferans (L—9 W—16)
Pearl gray head and breast; whitish throat; back and belly yellowish; wings and tail dark brown with buff feather edgings; male's red crown patch usually not visible. *Voice:* A clear "tshi peew." *Similar Species:* The call is distinctive. See Tropical Kingbird. *Habitat:* Pinyon-juniper, riparian woodlands (cottonwood, oak); pine-oak, oak woodlands, savanna. *Abundance and Distribution:* Common to uncommon summer resident* (Apr.–Oct.) in foothills and mid-elevations of southern California (rare or absent from the Sierras and southeastern deserts), southern Nevada, Arizona (except southwest), and New Mexico (except eastern plains); uncommon to rare winter resident in extreme southwestern California. *Where to Find:* Patagonia-Sonoita Creek Preserve, Arizona; Bandelier National Monument, New Mexico; Crystal Cove State Park, California. *Range:* Breeds at mid-elevations of the Rocky Mountains from southern Montana, Wyoming, and Utah through the southwestern United States and Mexican highlands to Oaxaca; winters from northern Mexico to Guatemala.

271. Thick-billed Kingbird

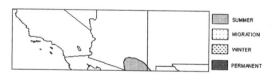

Tyrannus crassirostris (L—10 W—16)
Dark brown above; grayish breast; yellowish belly and under-tail coverts; heavy bill; yellow crest usually is invisible. *Voice:* A loud "wheear." *Habitat:* Riparian woodlands (sycamore, cottonwood), tropical savanna. *Abundance and Distribution:* Uncommon to rare summer resident* (May–Aug.) in extreme southeastern Arizona and southwestern New Mexico (Guadalupe Canyon). *Where to Find:* Guadalupe Canyon, Arizona/New Mexico; Patagonia-Sonoita Creek Preserve, Arizona; Sycamore Canyon, Arizona. *Range:* Breeds from southeastern Arizona, southwestern New Mexico, north-central and western Mexico south to southern Mexico; winters from southern portion of breeding range to northwestern Guatemala.

272. Western Kingbird

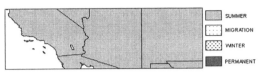

Tyrannus verticalis (L—9 W—15)
Pearl gray head and breast; back and
belly yellowish; wings dark brown;
tail brown with white outer tail feathers; male's red crown patch usually concealed.
Voice: Various harsh twitters; call a sharp "whit." *Similar Species:* See Tropical Kingbird. *Habitat:* Savanna, grasslands. *Abundance and Distribution:* Common transient and summer resident* (Apr.–Oct.) throughout. *Where to Find:* San Xavier
Mission, Arizona; El Malpais National Monument and Conservation Area, New
Mexico; Lopez Lake County Park, California; Desert National Wildlife Range,
Nevada. *Range:* Breeds in western North America from southern British Colum-
bia, Manitoba to northern Mexico; winters from southern Mexico to Costa Rica.

273. Eastern Kingbird

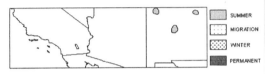

Tyrannus tyrannus (L—9 W—15)
Blackish above; white below; terminal white band on tail; red crest usu-
ally is invisible. *Voice:* A harsh, high-pitched rattle—"kit kit kitty kitty," or "tshee"
repeated. *Habitat:* Savanna, wood margins, open farmland. *Abundance and Distribution:* Uncommon to rare summer resident* (Mar.–Oct.) in central (Rio Grande
near Albuquerque), northeastern (Maxwell National Wildlife Refuge), and
Farmington area of northwestern New Mexico. *Where to Find:* Maxwell National
Wildlife Refuge; Lion's Park, San Juan River. *Range:* Breeds from central Canada
south through eastern and central United States to eastern Texas and Florida; winters in central and northern South America.

274. Scissor-tailed Flycatcher

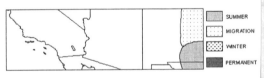

Tyrannus forficatus (L—14 W—14)
Tail black and white, extremely long,
forked. Pearl gray head, back, and
breast, washed with rose on belly, crissum, wing lining; bright rose axillaries; wings
black. *Immature:* Short-tailed; lacks rose color of adult. *Voice:* Series of "kip," "kyeck,"
and "keee" notes. *Habitat:* Savanna, prairie, agricultural lands with scattered trees.
Abundance and Distribution: Uncommon transient (Mar.–Apr., Oct.–Nov.) in eastern New Mexico; uncommon summer resident* (Mar.–Nov.) in southeastern New
Mexico. *Where to Find:* U.S. 380, Roadside Rest Area, forty-two miles east of Roswell.
Range: Breeds in central and southern Great Plains from Nebraska south to northern Mexico; winters from southern Mexico south to Panama.

275. Rose-throated Becard

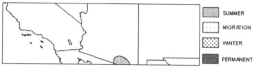

Pachyramphus aglaiae (L—7 W—14)
Grayish black above; white below;
throat red. *Female and Immature:*
Brown above; tawny below; crown dark brown. *Voice:* Plaintive "tseeoo." *Habitat:* Riparian forest. *Abundance and Distribution:* Rare summer resident* (May–Sep.) in southeastern Arizona. *Where to Find:* Patagonia Roadside Rest Area; Patagonia-Sonoita Creek Preserve; Sycamore Canyon. *Range:* Southmost Texas and southeastern Arizona to Costa Rica.

Family Laniidae
Shrikes
The New World species in this group are medium-sized, stocky, predominantly gray and white birds with hooked beaks and strong feet for grasping and killing insects, small mammals, birds, reptiles, and amphibians.

276. Loggerhead Shrike

Lanius ludovicianus (L—9 W—13)
Gray above, paler below; black mask,
wings, and tail; white outer tail feath-
ers and wing patch. *Habits:* Hunts from exposed perches; wary, flees observer with rapid wing beats; larders prey on thorns and barbs. *Voice:* Song a series of weak warbles and squeaks; call is a harsh "chaaa," often repeated three to four times. *Similar Species:* Mockingbird is slighter, lacks heavy, hooked bill, has longer tail, and has no black mask. Unlike the Northern Shrike, the Loggerhead doesn't hover or pump tail, is smaller and grayer with black rather than whitish forehead, grayish rather than whitish rump, and black rather than whitish lower mandible. *Habitat:* Savanna, open desert scrub, pinyon-juniper, farmlands; prefers open, barren areas where perches (such as fence posts or telephone poles) are available for sallying. *Abundance and Distribution:* Common to uncommon resident* nearly throughout except in highlands (up to seven thousand feet) where a summer resident* (Apr.–Aug.). *Where to Find:* Tesuque River Bottom, New Mexico; Big Canyon Trail, Upper Newport Bay, California; Palominas Pond, San Pedro Valley, Arizona; Overton Wildlife Management Area, Nevada. *Range:* Breeds locally over most of the United States and southern Canada south through highlands of Mexico to Oaxaca; winters in all but north portions of breeding range.

277. Northern Shrike
Lanius excubitor (L—10 W—14)

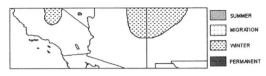

Pearly gray above, faintly barred below; black mask, primaries and tail;
white wing patch and outer tail feathers; heavy, hooked bill. *Habits:* Sits on high,
exposed perches; pumps tail; sometimes hovers while hunting. *Voice:* Song of trills
and buzzes; harsh chatter call is given infrequently. *Similar Species:* See Loggerhead Shrike. *Habitat:* Open woodlands, savanna, farmland. *Abundance and Distribution:* Rare and local winter resident (Nov.–Feb.) in the highlands of the Sierra
Nevada of southern California, southern Nevada (Mount Charleston), northern
Arizona, and northern New Mexico. *Range:* Breeds across boreal regions of Old
and New World; winters in north temperate and southern boreal regions.

Family Vireonidae
Vireos

A predominantly tropical family of small, feisty birds, most of which are patterned
in greens, yellows, grays, and browns. The relatively thick bill has a small, terminal
hook. Most are woodland species that deliberately glean twigs, leaves, and branches
for insect larvae.

278. Bell's Vireo
Vireo bellii

(L—5 W—7)

Grayish green above, whitish with yel-
lowish flanks below; white "spectacles" (lores, eyering, forehead); two faint whitish wing bars. *Habits:* Normally forages in dense thickets. *Voice:* Song a mixture of
"tsitl tsitl tsee" and "tsitl tsitl tsoo" with pauses between phrases; call a raspy "tsoo
weea tsi." *Similar Species:* Hutton's Vireo, Gray Vireo, and Ruby-crowned Kinglet
lack yellow on flanks. Hutton's Vireo has grayish (not white) throat; Gray Vireo
and kinglet lack spectacles. *Habitat:* Thorn forest, riparian thickets. *Abundance and
Distribution:* Rare and local summer resident* (Mar.–Sep.) in the lowlands west of
the desert and along the Colorado River valley in southern California, southern
Nevada, Arizona (except northeast highlands), and southern New Mexico. *Where
to Find:* Big Morongo, California; Tonto Natural Bridge State Park, Arizona; Rattlesnake Springs, New Mexico. *Range:* Breeds in central and southwestern United States
and northern Mexico; winters from southern Mexico to Honduras.

279. Gray Vireo

Vireo vicinior (L—6 W—8)

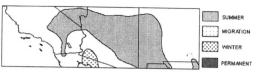

Gray above, whitish below with narrow white eyering and single, faint wingbar. *Habits:* Active for a vireo; bobs tail; females sing. *Voice:* Song a series of varied, musical phrases—"che wee, che wit, chi wur, chi wit," similar to that of Plumbeous Vireo but more rapid. Call—a harsh chatter. *Similar Species:* See Bell's Vireo; Plumbeous Vireo has two prominent, white wing bars and white spectacles. *Habitat:* Desert thorn scrub, oak-pinyon-juniper woodlands. *Abundance and Distribution:* Uncommon to rare summer resident* (Apr.–Sep.) in the eastern foothills of southern California, southern Nevada, southeastern to northern Arizona (upper Sonoran zone), and northwestern and southern New Mexico; winters in southwestern Arizona. *Where to Find:* NM 511, Reese Canyon, New Mexico; Bob's Gap, San Gabriel Mountains, California; Canyon de Chelly, Arizona; Reddington Pass, Santa Catalina Mountains, Arizona; Potosi Mountain, Nevada. *Range:* Breeds southwestern United States and northwestern Mexico; winters in western Mexico.

280. Plumbeous Vireo

Vireo plumbeus

(L—6 W—10)

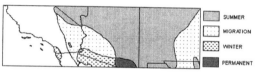

Gray above; white below; gray head with white "spectacles" (lores, forehead, eyering); two white wing bars. *Habits:* A deliberate forager like most vireos, but in contrast to warblers. *Voice:* Song a rich series of "chu wit, . . . chu wee, . . . cheerio," similar to Red-eyed Vireo but with longer pauses between phrases. Call is a whiney "cheeer." *Similar Species:* Cassin's Vireo has yellowish flanks and olive upperparts. *Habitat:* Arid pinyon-juniper and pine-oak woodlands. *Abundance and Distribution:* Common to uncommon summer resident* (Apr.–Sep.) in foothills and mountains (to seven thousand feet) of southern Nevada, Arizona (except southwest), and New Mexico (except eastern plains). Rare to casual in winter in extreme southern California and southern Arizona. *Where to Find:* Santa Rita Lodge, Madera Creek Canyon, Arizona; Bandelier National Monument, New Mexico; Mount Charleston, Nevada. *Range:* Breeds in the Rocky Mountain and Great Basin region of the western United States from southern Idaho, eastern Montana, and the Black Hills of South Dakota south to northwestern Mexico and west Texas; winters from southeastern Arizona south to Colima in western Mexico.

281. Cassin's Vireo

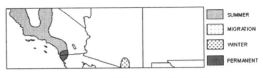

Vireo cassinii (L—6 W—10)

Olive above; whitish below with yellowish flanks; white eyering and lores;
two prominent white wing bars. *Habits:* A deliberate forager like most vireos, but
in contrast to warblers. *Voice:* Song a rich series of "chu wit, . . . chu wee, . . . cheerio,"
similar to Red-eyed Vireo but with longer pauses between phrases. Call is a whiney
"cheeer." *Similar Species:* Plumbeous Vireo is gray above (not olive) and lacks yellow on flanks. *Habitat:* Highland pine and pine-oak woodlands. *Abundance and
Distribution:* Common to uncommon summer resident* (Apr.–Sep.) in foothills
and mountains (to seven thousand feet) of southern California. Rare to casual in
winter in coastal southern California and southeastern Arizona. *Where to Find:*
Palomar Mountain State Park; Black Mountain Campground. *Range:* Breeds from
British Columbia south to northern Baja California; winters from southeastern
Arizona and northwestern New Mexico south to western Guatemala.

282. Hutton's Vireo

Vireo huttoni (L—5 W—8)

Grayish-green above, buff below;
white lores, incomplete eyering, and
wing bars. *Habits:* A rather tame, deliberate forager. *Voice:* Song—"chew wit," often repeated. Call—raspy "za zee zee." *Similar Species:* Ruby-crowned Kinglet has
thin bill, complete eyering, lacks white loral spot, forages nervously (not deliberately) often flitting wings. *Habitat:* Oak, pine-oak, and juniper woodlands, riparian woodlands in winter. *Abundance and Distribution:* Uncommon resident* of
southwestern California; uncommon summer resident* (Apr.–Sep.) and rare winter
resident in southeastern Arizona; rare summer resident* (Apr.–Sep.) and casual in
winter in southwestern New Mexico. *Where to Find:* Placerita Canyon State Park,
California; Santa Barbara Museum of Natural History, California; Herb Martyr
Campground, Arizona; Cherry Creek Campground, Pinos Altos Mountains, New
Mexico. *Range:* Resident along west coast of North America from southern British
Columbia to northern Baja California; southern Arizona, southwestern New
Mexico, and west Texas through western and central Mexico to Guatemala.

283. Warbling Vireo

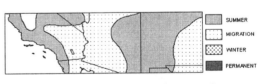

Vireo gilvus (L—6 W—9)

Grayish-green above, whitish washed
with yellow below; white eye stripe;
no wing bars. *Voice:* Song—a long, wandering series of warbles almost always ending with an upward inflection. Call—a hoarse "tswee." *Similar Species:* Can be dif-

ficult to separate from some pale Philadelphia Vireos, most of which are yellower below and have a dark loral spot. *Habitat:* Riparian woodland (cottonwood, aspen, alder), montane pine and fir forest. *Abundance and Distribution:* Common summer resident* (Apr.–Sep.) in mid-elevations and highlands (two thousand to seven thousand feet) of southern California, southern Nevada, Upper Sonoran and Transition zones of Arizona (southeast to northwest), and mountains of New Mexico; common transient (Apr.–May, Sep.–Oct.) throughout. *Where to Find:* Mount Charleston, Nevada; Ceremonial Cave Trail, Bandelier National Monument, New Mexico; Brown Canyon Trail, Ramsey Canyon Preserve, Arizona; Switzer Picnic Area, San Gabriel Mountains, California. *Range:* Breeds across North America south of the arctic region to central Mexico; winters from Guatemala to Panama.

284. Red-eyed Vireo
Vireo olivaceus (L—6 W—10)
Olive above, whitish below; gray cap;
white eyeline; red eye (brown in ju-

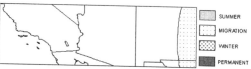

venile). *Voice:* Song—a leisurely, seemingly endless series of phrases, "cheerup, cherio, chewit, chewee," through the middle of long summer days. Male occasionally sings from nest while incubating; call—a harsh "cheear." *Similar Species:* The Red-eyed Vireo is the only gray-capped vireo without wing bars. *Habitat:* Riparian and oak woodland. *Abundance and Distribution:* Rare fall transient (Sep.–Oct.) in eastern New Mexico. *Where to Find:* Artesia Cemetery, New Mexico. *Range:* Breeds over much of North America (not in western United States, Alaska, or northern Canada). Subspecies breed in Central and South America. United States race winters in northern South America.

Family Corvidae
Crows, Jays, and Magpies
Medium-sized to large songbirds; crows and ravens generally have dark plumages, jays are blues, greens, and grays. Most members are social, aggressive, and highly vocal.

285. Gray Jay
Perisoreus canadensis (L—12 W—18)
Gray back and wings; white head with
gray nape; white throat shading to

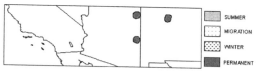

gray on belly and flanks; gray tail with white tip. *Juvenile:* Dark gray throughout.

Voice: A whistled "wheeooo"; also jay-like chucks. *Habitat:* Spruce-fir forests; common at campgrounds in appropriate habitat where they beg and steal food. *Abundance and Distribution:* Common resident* in Rocky Mountain highlands (Hudsonian or boreal zone above eighty-five hundred feet) of east-central Arizona (White Mountains) and northern New Mexico (San Juan, Jemez, and Sangre de Cristo Mountains). *Where to Find:* White Mountains and Canyon de Chelly, Arizona; Santa Fe Baldy, New Mexico. *Range:* Boreal regions of North America from Alaska across Canada to Labrador and south in mountains of the west to east-central Arizona and northern New Mexico.

286. Steller's Jay
Cyanocitta stelleri (L—12 W—18)
Blackish head; crest, and back with
bluish belly; wings and tail blue

barred with black; throat, forehead and supraocular region streaked with white. *Voice:* A loud, harsh "shook shook shook," various other harsh calls; song a softer series of warbles; imitates hawks. *Habitat:* Pine-oak and spruce-fir woodlands. *Abundance and Distribution:* Common resident* of mountains throughout. *Where to Find:* Burnt Rancheria Campground, Mount Laguna, California; J.D. Lake, Kaibab National Forest, Arizona; Mount Charleston, Nevada; McMillan Campground, Pinos Altos Mountains, New Mexico. *Range:* Mountains of western North America from Alaska south through the highlands of Middle America to Nicaragua.

287. Blue Jay
Cyanocitta cristata (L—11 W—16)
Blue above; a dirty white below; blue
crest; white wing bars and tip of tail;

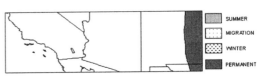

black necklace. *Voice:* A loud, harsh cry "jaaaay," repeated; a liquid gurgle; many other cries and calls; mimics hawks. *Habitat:* Riparian areas (cottonwood), oak woodlands, eastern deciduous forest, residential areas. *Abundance and Distribution:* Uncommon to rare resident* in cottonwoods lining rivers and streams, and residential areas of eastern New Mexico. *Where to Find:* Fort Sumner State Monument; Roswell Zoo; Clayton; Portales. *Range:* Temperate and boreal North America east of the Rockies.

288. Western Scrub-Jay
Aphelocoma californica (L—11 W—13)
Blue above; white throat; gray breast
and belly with dark streaks on throat

and breast; grayish back; black cheek and eye bordered by white above. *Voice:* A harsh "kuweeep"; "kay kay kay kay kay kay"; "keeaah"; other cries. *Similar Species:* Mexican Jay has gray throat, lacks black streaking on throat and breast. *Habitat:* Oak, juniper, pinyon-pine woodlands. *Abundance and Distribution:* Common resident* in lowlands and foothills of region; absent from extreme deserts and higher elevations. *Where to Find:* Bandelier National Monument, New Mexico; Hassayampa River Preserve, Arizona; Oak Canyon Nature Center, Santa Ana Mountains, California; Cold Creek, Spring Mountains, Nevada. *Range:* Western North America from Washington south to southern Mexico; Florida.

289. Mexican Jay
Aphelocoma ultramarina
(L—11 W—13)

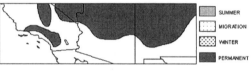

Blue above; grayish below; grayish on back; black cheek and eyeline. Formerly called the Arizona Jay. *Voice:* "Chink," "kek, kek, kek, kek," other calls. *Similar Species:* Mexican Jay has gray throat; lacks black streaking on throat and breast of the Western Scrub-Jay. *Habitat:* Pine-oak-juniper woodlands. *Abundance and Distribution:* Common resident* in southeastern and Arizona southwestern New Mexico. *Where to Find:* Ramsey Canyon, Arizona; Bear Canyon Picnic Area, Mount Lemmon, Arizona; Cave Creek Canyon, Arizona; Cherry Creek Campground, New Mexico. *Range:* Central Arizona, New Mexico, and west Texas south in mountains to south-central Mexico.

290. Pinyon Jay
Gymnorhinus cyanocephalus
(L—11 W—15)

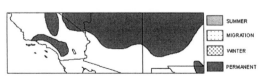

Slaty blue throughout; streaked whitish throat. *Immature:* Grayish below. *Voice:* A high, nasal "kaaaah"; various jay-like chatters. *Habitat:* Pinyon-juniper woodlands, semi-arid scrub. *Abundance and Distribution:* Uncommon to rare resident* in mountains of southern California, southern Nevada, northern Arizona, and northern New Mexico. *Where to Find:* Tsankawi Section, Bandelier National Monument, New Mexico; Baldwin Lake, San Bernardino Mountains, California; Grandview Point, Grand Canyon, Arizona; Mount Charleston, Nevada. *Range:* Rocky Mountain region from Washington to northern Baja California, northern Sonora and western Chihuahua.

291. Clark's Nutcracker
Nucifraga columbiana
(L—16 W—22)

Gray body; wings and central tail feathers black; speculum and outer tail feathers white. *Voice:* A nasal "kaaaaa."

Figure 38. Spectacular cliff dwellings overlook the West Fork of the Gila River at the Gila Cliff Dwelling National Monument, high in New Mexico's Mogollon Mountains. Birds of the site include Canyon Wren, American Dipper, Prairie Falcon, and White-throated Swift. Zimmerman et al. (1992) reported that Common Black-Hawk and Spotted Owl have been found here as well.

Figure 39. A few minutes on the freeway from downtown LA (depending on traffic) brings you to the relative quiet and solitude of Malibu Creek State Park. Here, coastal chaparral, oak woodlands, and grasslands provide habitat for the Wrentit, Nuttall's Woodpecker, Lazuli Bunting, California Quail, and California Thrasher.

Habitat: Lodgepole, whitebark, and jeffrey pines, pinyon-juniper. *Abundance and Distribution:* Common to uncommon (irregular) resident* of high mountains (mostly above eight thousand feet) of southern California, southern Nevada, northern Arizona, and New Mexico; ranges lower in winter. *Where to Find:* Pajarito Mountain Ski Area, New Mexico; Mount Trumbull, Arizona; Mount Charleston, Nevada; McGill Campground, Mount Pinos, California. *Range:* Mountains of western North America from central British Columbia south to southern Arizona and New Mexico.

292. Black-billed Magpie

Pica pica (L—19 W—24)

Striking pattern of black and white body and wings with very long, dark

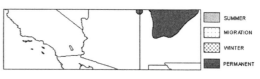

tail. *Voice:* A rapid series of "chek"s; a nasal "aaaah." *Habitat:* Open woodlands, savanna, riparian groves (willows, cottonwoods), grasslands especially near rivers and streams (mud is required for nest construction). *Abundance and Distribution:* Uncommon permanent resident* in extreme northeastern Arizona and northern New Mexico. *Where to Find:* Teec Nos Pos, Navajo Indian Reservation, Arizona; Tesuque River Bottom, New Mexico; Canjilon Mountain, New Mexico. *Range:* Western Canada and United States from Alaska, British Columbia east to western Ontario, south to Oklahoma, New Mexico, Arizona, and California; temperate and boreal Europe and Asia south to northern Africa, Iran, northern India, southeastern Asia, eastern China and Japan.

293. Yellow-billed Magpie

Pica nuttalli (L—17 W—22)

Striking pattern of black and white body and wings with very long, dark

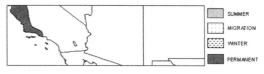

tail; bare, yellow skin around eye; yellow bill. *Voice:* A harsh, "aaaag." *Habitat:* Oak savanna, riparian groves, orchards, residential areas; needs mud or cow dung for nest construction. *Abundance and Distribution:* Common permanent resident* in lowlands of southwestern California. *Where to Find:* Nojoqui Falls County Park; G13, east end, near Bitterwater. *Range:* Resident in Sacramento, San Joaquin, and coast range valleys of California from Shasta County in the north to Santa Barbara County in the south.

294. American Crow

Corvus brachyrhynchos

(L—18 W—36)

Black throughout. *Voice:* A series of

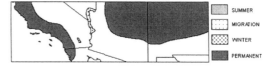

variations on "caw"—fast, slow, high, low, and various combinations; nestlings and fledglings use an incessant, nasal "caah." *Habitat:* Riparian woodlands, oak savanna, grasslands, farmlands, and residential areas in winter. *Similar Species:* Ravens croak and have wedged shaped rather than square tail of crows. *Abundance and Distribution:* Uncommon resident* at lowlands and mid-elevations in southwestern California, northern Arizona, and northern New Mexico; uncommon winter visitor in southern Nevada; uncommon to rare or casual and irregular winter visitor along the Colorado River. Absent from desert regions except in riparian woodlands. *Where to Find:* Oak Canyon Nature Center, California; Randall Davey Audubon Center, Santa Fe, New Mexico; Phon D. Sutton Recreation Area, Arizona; Overton Wildlife Management Area, Nevada. *Range:* Temperate and boreal North America; migratory in northern portion of range.

295. Chihuahuan Raven
Corvus cryptoleucus
(L—19 W—40)
Black throughout; feathers of neck

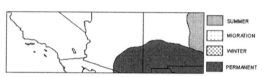

are white basally (only show when ruffled). *Voice:* A croak. *Habitat:* Dry thorn forest desert. *Similar Species:* The Common Raven is larger and has a lower croak. *Abundance and Distribution:* Uncommon to rare resident* in lowlands of eastern and southern New Mexico and southern Arizona; partially migratory, with some individuals moving southward in winter. *Where to Find:* Water Canyon, New Mexico; Willcox Lake Wildlife Area, Arizona. *Range:* Western Kansas and eastern Colorado south through Arizona, New Mexico, and Texas; and the central highlands of Mexico to Guanajuato, San Luis Potosí and southern Tamaulipas. Northern populations are at least partially migratory.

296. Common Raven
Corvus corax (L—24 W—48)
Black throughout; large, heavy bill; shaggy appearance in facial region;

wedge-shaped tail. *Voice:* A harsh, low croak. *Habitat:* Rugged crags, cliffs, canyons as well as a variety of forested and open lands. *Similar Species:* See Chihuahuan Raven and American Crow. *Abundance and Distribution:* Common to uncommon resident* throughout except in Great Plains region of eastern New Mexico. *Where to Find:* Dry Cimarron River, New Mexico; Desert National Wildlife Range, Nevada; Carrizo Plain, California; Red Butte, Arizona. *Range:* Arctic and boreal regions of the Northern Hemisphere south through mountainous regions of the Western Hemisphere to Nicaragua, and in the Eastern Hemisphere to North Africa, Iran, the Himalayas, Manchuria, and Japan.

Family Alaudidae
Larks
Small, terrestrial songbirds with extremely long hind claws. The breeding song of these open country inhabitants is often given in flight.

297. Horned Lark

Eremophila alpestris

(L—7 W—13)

Brown above; white below with black bib; face and throat whitish or yellowish with black forehead and eyeline; black horns raised when singing. *Female:* Similar pattern but paler. *Immature:* Nondescript brownish above; whitish below with light streaking; has dark tail with white edging and long hallux like adult. *Voice:* Series of high-pitched notes, often given in flight; call is a thin "tseet." *Similar Species:* Immature lark is similar to pipits, but is grayish white rather than buffy on face and underparts. *Habitat:* Short-grass prairie, plowed fields, roadsides, sand flats. *Abundance and Distribution:* Locally common resident* throughout. *Where to Find:* Fort Sumner State Monument, New Mexico; Desert National Wildlife Range, Nevada; Willcox Lake, Arizona; Carrizo Plain, California. *Range:* Breeds in North America south to southern Mexico; winters in southern portion of breeding range.

Family Hirundinidae
Swallows and Martins
Mostly small, sleek birds with pointed wings. Swallows forage on flying insects, which they take on the wing.

298. Purple Martin

Progne subis (L—8 W—16)

Iridescent midnight blue throughout. *Female and Immature:* Dark blue

above; dirty white, occasionally mottled with blue below; grayish collar. *Voice:* Various squeaky "quik"s and "querks"s repeated in a short harsh series. *Similar Species:* The Black Swift has the long, slim, pointed, swept-back wings and rapid wing beat of swifts. The male Purple Martin has wider, shorter wing, and typical swallow-like flight. *Habitat:* Open areas—limited by nesting sites. Nests in colonies, originally in trees, now often in specially constructed martin houses. *Abundance and Distribution:* Uncommon to rare transient (Mar., Sep.) throughout; uncommon to rare and local summer resident* (Apr.–Aug.) in the lowlands and foothills of southwestern California, Arizona (except high mountains and extreme deserts), and western New Mexico. *Where to Find:* Nojoqui Falls County Park, California; Arizona Sonora Desert Museum, Arizona; Lake Roberts, New Mexico. *Range:* Breeds in open areas over most of temperate North America south to the highlands of southern Mexico; winters in Amazon Basin of South America south to northern Argentina and southeastern Brazil.

299. Tree Swallow
Tachycineta bicolor (L—6 W—13)
Iridescent blue above; pure white be-
low with slightly forked tail. *Female:*

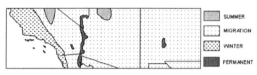

Similar in pattern to male, but duller. *Immature:* Grayish brown above; whitish below. *Voice:* Series of "weet tuwit tuweet" with twitters. *Similar Species:* Violet Green Swallow is greener above, has white on sides of rump and around eye (post-loral and supraloral areas on Tree Swallow are dark). *Habitat:* Lakes, ponds, marshes—any open area during migration. *Abundance and Distribution:* Uncom-mon to rare transient (Mar.–Apr., Aug.–Sep.) throughout; rare and local summer resident* (May–Aug.) in northern Arizona; uncommon winter resident (Aug.–Apr.) in southwestern California; resident* at Salton Sea and Colorado River val-ley of California, Arizona and southern Nevada. *Where to Find:* Salton Sea, Cali-fornia; Overton Wildlife Management Area, Nevada; Bill Williams Delta National Wildlife Refuge, Arizona. *Range:* Breeds over most of boreal and temperate North America south to the southern United States; winters from southern United States south to Costa Rica and Greater Antilles.

300. Violet-green Swallow
Tachycineta thalassina (L—6 W—13)
Iridescent green above; pure white
below with slightly forked tail; white

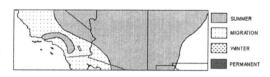

on both sides of rump; white of underparts extends to cheek and above eye. *Fe-male:* Similar in pattern to male, but duller. *Immature:* Grayish brown above; whitish below. *Voice:* "Tsip tseet tsip" with rapid twitter. *Similar Species:* See Tree Swallow. *Habitat:* Mountain forests, canyons, open areas in migration; nests in cliffs, crags, hollow trees. *Abundance and Distribution:* Uncommon summer resident* (Mar.–Oct.) in the mountains, foothills, and along the Colorado River in southern Cali-fornia, southern Nevada, Arizona, and New Mexico; common transient through-out southern California. *Where to Find:* Capulin National Monument, New Mexico; Rose Canyon Lake, Santa Catalina Mountains, Arizona; Mount Charleston, Ne-vada; McGill Campground, Mount Pinos, California. *Range:* Breeds in mountains of western North America from Alaska to southern Mexico; winters from southern California and northwestern Mexico south to Costa Rica.

301. Northern Rough-winged Swallow
Stelgidopteryx serripennis
(L—6 W—12)

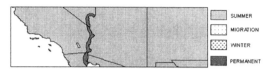

Grayish brown above; grayish throat and breast becoming whitish on belly. *Voice:* A harsh "treet," repeated. *Similar Species:* Bank Swallow has distinct dark breast band set off by white throat and belly. *Habitat:* Lakes, rivers, ponds, streams, most open areas during migration. *Abundance and Distribution:* Common transient (Feb.–May, Aug.–Oct.) throughout region; uncommon to rare and local summer resident* (Apr.–Aug.) throughout where stream banks are available for nesting; uncommon to rare resident* in the Colorado River valley. *Where to Find:* Salton Sea National Wildlife Area, California; Corn Creek, Desert National Wildlife Range, Nevada; Tumacacori National Monument, Arizona; Tesuque River Bottom, New Mexico. *Range:* Breeds locally over most of temperate North America; winters from southern Texas and northern Mexico south to Panama.

302. Bank Swallow
Riparia riparia (L—6 W—12)
Brown above; white below with brown collar. *Voice:* "Bzzt," repeated

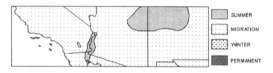

in a harsh rattle. *Similar Species:* See Northern Rough-legged Swallow. *Habitat:* Lakes, rivers, ponds, most open areas during migration. *Abundance and Distribution:* Common to uncommon transient (Apr.–May, Aug.–Sep.) over most of region; uncommon to rare summer resident* (Apr.–Sep.) along the lower Colorado River valley, Salton Sea, northeastern Arizona (Canyon de Chelly), and northwestern and central New Mexico where stream banks are available for nesting. *Where to Find:* Salton Sea National Wildlife Area, California; Corn Creek, Desert National Wildlife Range, Nevada; Tumacacori National Monument, Arizona; Tesuque River Bottom, New Mexico. *Range:* Cosmopolitan, breeding over much of Northern Hemisphere continents, wintering in the tropics of Asia, Africa, and the New World.

303. Cliff Swallow
Petrochelidon pyrrhonota
(L—6 W—12)
Dark above; whitish below with dark

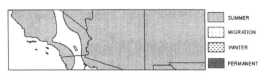

orange or blackish throat; orange cheek; pale forehead; orange rump; square tail.

Immature: Similar to adults but duller. *Voice:* Song—a series of harsh twitters. *Similar Species:* Cave Swallow has buffy (rather than dark) throat. The mud nest of the Cliff Swallow is gourd-like (Cave Swallow's is open-topped). *Habitat:* Most open areas during migration, savanna, agricultural areas, near water. This species seems to be limited by nesting locations during the breeding season (farm buildings, culverts, bridges, cliffs—near potential mud source). This species is the legendary "Swallow of Capistrano" with such famously regular, migratory habits (supposedly returning to nesting sites at the mission of San Juan de Capistrano each spring on March 19th). Unfortunately, the birds have not nested at the mission for several years. *Abundance and Distribution:* Common transient (Mar.–May, Aug.–Oct.) throughout; locally common summer resident* (Apr.–Aug.). *Where to Find:* Grout Bay Campground, San Bernardino Mountains, California; Mormon Lake, Arizona; Overton Wildlife Management Area, Nevada; La Ventana, El Malpais, New Mexico. *Range:* Breeds over most of North America to central Mexico; winters central and southern South America.

304. Cave Swallow

Petrochelidon fulva (L—6 W—12)
Dark above; whitish below with buffy throat; orange cheek; pale forehead;

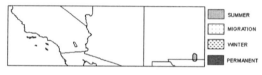

orange rump; square tail. *Immature:* Similar to adults but duller. *Voice:* Song is a rapid series of squeaks. *Similar Species:* See Cliff Swallow. *Habitat:* Open areas, near water; nests in sinkholes, caves, and most recently, culverts. *Abundance and Distribution:* Common summer resident* (Mar.–Sep.) in Carlsbad Caverns National Park, New Mexico, nesting in caves. *Where to Find:* Carlsbad Caverns National Park, New Mexico. *Range:* Breeds from New Mexico and central Texas south through central and southern Mexico; Greater Antilles; northern South America in Ecuador and Peru; winters in southern portion of breeding range.

305. Barn Swallow

Hirundo rustica (L—7 W—13)
Dark blue above; orange below with deeply forked tail. *Immature:* Paler

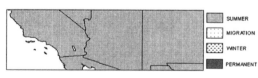

with shorter tail. *Voice:* Song is a series of squeaks and twitters, some harsh, some melodic. *Habitat:* Savanna, prairie, open areas near water; like most swallows, it requires special sites for nesting, such as bridges, culverts, and buildings. *Abundance and Distribution:* Locally common to rare summer resident* (Mar.–Oct.) throughout. *Where to Find:* Bottomless Lakes State Park, New Mexico; Agua Caliente Lake, Tucson, Arizona; Overton Wildlife Management Area, Nevada; Big Canyon, Upper Newport Bay, California. *Range:* Cosmopolitan—breeds over much of

Northern Hemisphere continents; winters in South America; Africa; northern Australia; Micronesia.

Family Paridae
Chickadees and Titmice
Small, perky, active birds with gray and white plumages; generally these birds forage in small groups, feeding on arthropods and seeds.

306. Black-capped Chickadee
Poecile atricapillus (L—5 W—8)
Black cap, throat, and bib contrasting with white cheek; dark gray back,

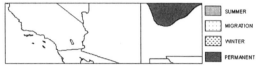

SUMMER
MIGRATION
WINTER
PERMANENT

and grayish-white breast and belly; white edging to gray secondaries. *Voice:* "Fee bee"; "chicka dee dee." *Habitat:* Woodlands. *Similar Species:* Overlaps in the southwest with only the Mountain Chickadee, which has a white line over the eye (lacking in the Black-capped Chickadee). Call notes and songs for all species are distinctive. *Abundance and Distribution:* Common to uncommon resident* in highlands of northern New Mexico. *Where to Find:* Jackson Lake State Game Refuge; Rutherford Tract, San Juan River; Rio Grande Nature Center, Albuquerque. *Range:* Temperate and boreal North America south to California, New Mexico, Oklahoma, and New Jersey; south in Appalachians to North Carolina.

307. Mountain Chickadee
Poecile gambeli (L—5 W—8)
Gray above; lighter gray below; black cap and bib; white eyeline. *Voice:* A

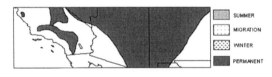

SUMMER
MIGRATION
WINTER
PERMANENT

rough "chick a dee a dee a dee"; "see dee dee" or "see dee see dee." *Habitat:* Montane coniferous forest and pine-oak (above four thousand feet); also in oak groves, orchards, aspen, and cottonwoods at lower elevations in winter. *Similar Species:* See Black-capped Chickadee. *Abundance and Distribution:* Common resident* at high elevations (above three thousand feet) throughout the region. *Where to Find:* Mount Charleston, Nevada; Grandview Point, Grand Canyon, Arizona; Switzer Picnic Area, San Gabriel Mountains, California; Dome Meadow, Jemez Mountains, New Mexico. *Range:* Mountains of western North America from northern British Columbia and Alaska south to southern California, Arizona, New Mexico, and Texas.

308. Mexican Chickadee

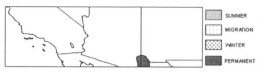

Poecile sclateri (L—5 W—8)

Black cap, throat, and extensive bib (to shoulder) contrasting with white cheek; dark gray back, and grayish-white breast and belly; flanks gray. *Voice:* Call—a low, buzzy "zay zee"; song—a warbled whistle. *Habitat:* Pine-oak and conifer woodlands above five thousand feet. *Abundance and Distribution:* Common to uncommon resident* in the highlands of the Chiricahua Mountains of extreme southeastern Arizona and the Animas Mountains of southwestern New Mexico; some individuals move to lower elevations in winter. *Where to Find:* Rustler Park, Arizona; Pinery Canyon, Arizona; Massai Point, Chiricahua National Monument, Arizona. *Range:* Resident from southeastern Arizona and southwestern New Mexico through the mountains of western Mexico to Oaxaca.

309. Chestnut-backed Chickadee

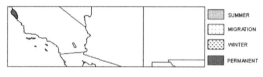

Poecile rufescens (L—5 W—8)

Chestnut back; black cap and bib; white cheek; grayish-white underparts. *Voice:* A hoarse, rapid "tsik a tee tee." *Habitat:* Pine, pine-oak, oak woodlands, willows. *Abundance and Distribution:* Uncommon resident* in coastal lowlands of southern California. *Where to Find:* Santa Maria River Mouth; Montaña de Oro State Park. *Range:* Coastal regions from southern Alaska (Prince William Sound) south to central California.

310. Bridled Titmouse

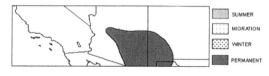

Baeolophus wollweberi

(L—6 W—9)

Gray above; paler below; conspicuous crest; distinctive black and white face pattern. *Voice:* Song—"weeta weeta weeta"; call—a high, clipped "sik-a-dee-dee." *Habitat:* Willow, cottonwood, mesquite, oak, pine-oak, and pinyon-juniper woodlands. *Abundance and Distribution:* Common to uncommon resident* in mid-elevations (four thousand to six thousand feet) of central and southeastern Arizona and southwestern New Mexico. *Where to Find:* Water Canyon Campground, New Mexico; Bill Evans Lake, New Mexico; Madera Canyon, Arizona; Molino Basin Campground, Arizona. *Range:* Central Arizona and southwestern New Mexico south through the highlands of western and central Mexico.

311. Oak Titmouse

Baeolophus inornatus (L—6 W—9)

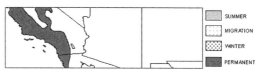

Gray throughout; slight crest. *Voice:*
Song—"weedee weedee weedee";
harsh "chick a dee dee." *Habitat:* Oak woodlands. *Abundance and Distribution:*
Uncommon resident* in lowlands and mid-elevations of southern California.
Where to Find: Dorothy May Tucker Wildlife Sanctuary; Santa Barbara Museum
of Natural History; Malibu Creek State Park. *Range:* Coastal oak woodlands of
California and Baja California.

312. Juniper Titmouse

Baeolophus griseus (L—6 W—9)

Gray throughout; slight crest. *Voice:*
Song—"weedee weedee weedee";
harsh "chick a dee dee." *Habitat:* Pinyon-juniper and pine-oak woodlands. *Abundance and Distribution:* Uncommon resident* in lowlands and mid-elevations of
southern Nevada, northern and eastern Arizona and New Mexico (except eastern
plains). *Where to Find:* Grandview Point, Grand Canyon, Arizona; Juniper Campground, Bandelier National Monument, New Mexico; Valley of Fire State Park,
Nevada. *Range:* Western United States from southern Oregon, Idaho, and Wyoming south to southern Arizona, New Mexico, and west Texas.

Family Remizidae
Verdin
As Phillips (1986:98) notes, this little bird has caused considerable taxonomic consternation, having been placed in Paridae (chickadees), Coerebinae (honeycreepers), and Polioptilinae (gnatcatchers) by different authors. Currently, it is placed
in its own family (American Ornithologists' Union 1998).

313. Verdin

Auriparus flaviceps

(L—5 W—7)

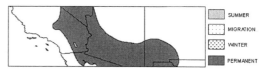

Gray body above and below; yellowish head; chestnut shoulder. Immature is uniformly grayish-brown, somewhat paler
below. *Voice:* Song—a weak "tsee see see" or "tseeip"; call—a series of rapid "tsip"s.
Habitat: Thorn forest, oak-juniper, desert. *Similar Species:* Immature Verdin is similar to Bushtit but lacks brown cheek patch and has tail shorter than body (Bushtit
has tail equal to or longer than body). *Abundance and Distribution:* Common to

Figure 40. Relics of a pre-historic swamp lie like giant flotsam on a sea of sand at Arizona's Petrified Forest National Park. Birds found here are characteristic of the Sonoran Desert and include Bendire's Thrasher, Sage Thrasher, Curve-billed Thrasher, Rock Wren, Cassin's Finch, and Black-throated Sparrow.

Figure 41. It is less than a thirty-minute drive from the bustle of downtown Tucson to the falls, pools, and sycamore-lined shoals of Molino Canyon. Birds to be found here include Virginia's Warbler, Bridled Titmouse, Mexican Jay, Crissal Thrasher, and Scott's Oriole (spring and early summer).

uncommon resident* in low and mid-elevation deserts of southeastern California, southern Nevada, southern Arizona, and southwestern New Mexico. *Where to Find:* Salton Sea National Wildlife Refuge, California; Desert National Wildlife Range, Nevada; Florida Wash, Santa Rita Mountains, Arizona; Percha Dam State Park, New Mexico. *Range:* Southwestern United States and Mexico south to Jalisco, Hidalgo, and Tamaulipas.

Family Aegithalidae
Bushtit
This family is composed of a single species, as described below.

314. Bushtit
Psaltriparus minimus
(L—5 W—6)

Gray above; paler below; brown cheek patch (interior subspecies); black eyes; elongate tail. Immature males, and some adult males have black cheek patch. The subspecies from coastal California (*P. m. minimus*) has a brown cap and grayish cheek. *Female:* Like male but with yellow eyes. *Voice:* Various "tsit"s and "tsee"s. *Habitat:* Oak, oak-juniper, pine-oak, thorn forest, desert scrub. *Similar Species:* See Verdin. *Abundance and Distribution:* Common to uncommon resident* in lowlands and mid-elevations nearly throughout except in desert areas of southeastern California and southwestern Arizona, and the Great Plains of eastern New Mexico where rare or absent. *Where to Find:* Lower San Juan Picnic Ground, California; Molino Basin Campground, Arizona; Echo Amphitheater, Abiquiu, New Mexico; Red Rock Canyon National Conservation Area, Nevada. *Range:* Western North America from southern British Columbia and southern Idaho east to Colorado, New Mexico, and Texas south through central and western Mexico to Guatemala.

Family Sittidae
Nuthatches
Nuthatches are peculiar birds in both appearance and behavior. Long-billed, hunched little beasts, built for probing bark on tree trunks, they creep along the trunks, usually from the top down (not bottom up like Brown Creepers).

315. Red-breasted Nuthatch

Sitta canadensis (L—5 W—8)
Gray above; orange buff below; black
cap with white line over eye. *Female
and Immature:* Paler buff below. *Voice:* A nasal, high-pitched series of "anh"s. *Habitat:* Boreal zone fir and pine forests in summer; coniferous and mixed woodlands, and deciduous woodlands in winter. *Abundance and Distribution:* Uncommon resident* in highlands throughout the region; rare and irregular fall transient and winter resident (Nov.–Mar.) in lowlands. *Where to Find:* Lamar Haines Wildlife Area, Arizona; Capulin Volcano National Monument, New Mexico; Mount Charleston, Nevada; Dawson Saddle, San Gabriel Mountains, California. *Range:* Breeds in boreal, transitional, and montane forests of North America from Alaska across the northern tier of Canada to Labrador south to New Jersey, New York, Ohio, and Michigan; to North Carolina in the Appalachians and to New Mexico, California, and Arizona in the Rockies; winters throughout breeding range and over much of United States south to central Texas, northwestern Mexico, and northern Florida.

316. White-breasted Nuthatch

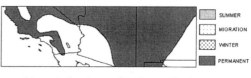

Sitta carolinensis (L—6 W—11)
Gray above; white below with black
cap; buffy flanks. *Female:* Cap is gray
or dull black. *Voice:* A series of "yank"s. *Habitat:* Oak, pine-oak, pinyon-juniper, and pine forest; also in aspen and cottonwood. *Abundance and Distribution:* Uncommon to rare resident* at mid-elevations in mountains throughout; some individuals move into lowlands in winter (Nov.–Mar.); rare or casual in desert regions of southeastern California and southwestern Arizona, and in Great Plains region of eastern New Mexico. *Where to Find:* El Cariso Campground, California; Mount Charleston, Nevada; Lamar Haines Memorial Wildlife Area, Arizona; Jackson Lake Refuge, New Mexico. *Range:* Southern tier of Canada and most of the United States; local in Great Plains region; highlands of Mexico south to Oaxaca.

317. Pygmy Nuthatch

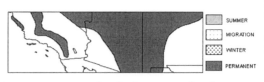

Sitta pygmaea (L—5 W—8)
Gray above, buff below; dark grayish-
brown cap; white cheeks, throat, and
nape. *Habits:* While other nuthatches forage on tree trunks, the Pygmy Nuthatch forages at the tips of branches in needle and cone clusters. *Voice:* A rapid series of "peeep"s; also a two-note "weebee." *Habitat:* Open, park-like, pine woodlands, especially ponderosa pine (jeffrey pine on the east slope of the Sierras). *Abundance and Distribution:* Uncommon resident* at mid- and high elevations in mountains

of the region. *Where to Find:* Ceremonial Cave Trail, Bandelier National Monument, New Mexico; Lamar Haines Memorial Wildlife Area, Arizona; Mount Charleston, Nevada; Black Mountain Campground, San Jacinto Mountains, California. *Range:* Pine forest of western North America from central British Columbia and Montana south through the western United States and highlands of Mexico to Jalisco, Morelos and Veracruz.

Family Certhiidae
Creepers
This is a small family with only five representatives worldwide, one of which, the Brown Creeper, occurs in the New World. Creepers, like nuthatches, are built for probing tree trunks. These no-necked bits of brown and white fluff have long, decurved bills and stiff tails for foraging over tree trunks, picking arthropod larvae from bark. They usually forage beginning from the bottom of a tree trunk and move up, opposite from the way a nuthatch works a trunk.

318. Brown Creeper

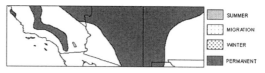

SUMMER
MIGRATION
WINTER
PERMANENT

Certhia americana (L—5 W—8)
Brown streaked and mottled with white above; white below; white eyeline; decurved bill. *Voice:* A high-pitched "tseeee." *Habitat:* Firs, pondersosa, lodgepole, jeffrey, and other pines; most woodland types in winter. *Abundance and Distribution:* Uncommon resident* in the mountains of the region; irregularly at lower elevations in winter (Nov.–Mar.). *Where to Find:* Summit Grove, Palomar Mountain, California; Pajarito Ski Area, Bandelier National Monument, New Mexico; Lamar Haines Memorial Wildlife Area, Arizona; Mount Charleston, Nevada. *Range:* Breeds in boreal, montane, and transitional zones of North America south through the highlands of Mexico and Central America to Nicaragua; winters nearly throughout in temperate, boreal, and montane regions of the continent.

Family Troglodytidae
Wrens
Wrens are a large, mostly Neotropical family of superb songsters. Most species have brown and white plumages, sharp, decurved bills, and short, cocked tails. Nests often are built in a cavity or a completely closed structure of grasses.

319. Cactus Wren

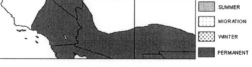

Campylorhynchus brunneicapillus
(L—9 W—11)
Mottled brown and white above; buff
below heavily spotted and streaked with dark brown, especially on the throat; dark brown cap with white eyeline. *Voice:* A rolling series of "chrrr"s; Edward Abbey (1973:22) calls it "a small bird with a big mouth and a song like the sound of a rusty adding machine"; also a series of "tschew"s. *Habitat:* Cholla cactus, thorn forest, desert. *Abundance and Distribution:* Common to uncommon resident* in lowland deserts of southern California (local along coast to Ventura County), southern Nevada, western and southern Arizona, and southern New Mexico. *Where to Find:* Cibola National Wildlife Refuge, California; Oliver Lee Memorial State Park, New Mexico; Organ Pipe Cactus National Monument, Arizona; Red Rock Canyon National Conservation Area, Nevada. *Range:* Southwestern United States south through arid and semi-arid regions of Mexico to Michoacan.

320. Rock Wren

Salpinctes obsoletus (L—6 W—9)
Grayish-brown above; whitish below
with faint streaks; rusty rump and tail
with dark subterminal band. *Voice:* "tik ear"; a mixture of buzzes, trills. *Habitat:* Rocky canyons, talus slopes, arroyos, cliffs, and crags. *Abundance and Distribution:* Common resident* nearly throughout except at high elevations (above nine thousand feet), where a summer resident* (Apr.–Sep.); mostly absent from the eastern plains of New Mexico. *Where to Find:* Buckhorn Flat Campground, San Gabriel Mountains, California; Frijoles Canyon, Bandelier National Monument, New Mexico; cliffs on east side of Mormon Lake, Arizona; Red Rock Canyon National Conservation Area, Nevada. *Range:* Breeds in western North America from southwestern Canada to central Mexico; winters in southern half of breeding range and along Pacific coast.

321. Canyon Wren

Catherpes mexicanus (L—6 W—8)
Brownish above and below with dark
spots; contrasting white throat and
gray cap. *Voice:* A limpid, descending "tuwee tuwee tuwee tuwee," voice of the western canyon lands; also a harsh "cheeeer." *Habitat:* Canyons, crags, cliffs, outcrops of arid and semi-arid regions. *Abundance and Distribution:* Uncommon resident* at mid-elevations nearly throughout; scarce or absent in low, desert regions of southeastern California and southwestern Arizona, and eastern Great Plains area of New

Mexico; moves to lower elevations in winter. *Where to Find:* Gila Cliff Dwellings National Monument, New Mexico; Kofa National Wildlife Refuge, Arizona; Red Rock Canyon, Nevada; Borrego Palm Canyon Campground, California. *Range:* Western North America from southern British Colombia, Idaho, and Montana south to the highlands of southern Mexico.

322. Bewick's Wren

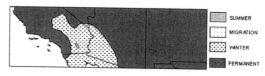

Thryomanes bewickii (L—5 W—7)
Grayish-brown above; white below with prominent white eyeline and long, active tail. *Voice:* A series of buzzy whistles and warbles reminiscent of the Song Sparrow; also a harsh "churr." *Habitat:* Thorn forest, savanna, oak and pine-oak woodland, riparian thickets, shrubby fields, pinyon-juniper. *Abundance and Distribution:* Common to uncommon permanent resident* in lowlands and foothills nearly throughout; uncommon summer resident* (Apr.–Sep.) in highlands (below seven thousand feet) of the Sierras, northeastern Arizona and northern New Mexico; uncommon winter resident (Oct.–Mar.) in shrubby washes of the dry deserts of southeastern California and southwestern Arizona. *Where to Find:* Red Rock Canyon National Conservation Area, Nevada; Bandelier National Monument, New Mexico; Tapia County Park, Santa Monica Mountains, California; Desert View, Grand Canyon, Arizona. *Range:* Breeds in most of temperate North America (except Atlantic coastal and southern portions of Gulf states) south in highlands to southern Mexico; eastern United States populations have become scarce in recent years; winters in southern portion of breeding range.

323. House Wren

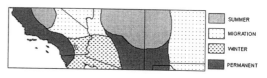

Troglodytes aedon (L—5 W—7)
Brown above, buff below; buff eyeline; barred flanks. *Voice:* A rapid, descending trill, "chipy-chipy-chipy-chipy," with associated buzzes and churrs. *Habitat:* Thickets, undergrowth, and tangles in riparian forest, woodlands and hedgerows; also in pine, oak, and pine-oak undergrowth in summer. *Similar Species:* Winter Wren is a richer brown below, has shorter tail, and more prominent barring on flanks and belly. Songs and calls are very different. *Abundance and Distribution:* Uncommon resident* in foothills, and summer resident* (Apr.–Sep.) in highlands (below eight thousand feet) of southern California, northern and southeastern Arizona, and northern New Mexico; common transient (Oct.–Nov., Mar.–Apr.) throughout; uncommon to rare winter resident in lowlands of southern California, southern Arizona, and southern New Mexico. *Where to Find:* North Rim, Grand Canyon, Arizona; Mount Charleston, Nevada; Dorothy May Tucker

Wildlife Sanctuary, California; Capulin Volcano National Monument, New Mexico. *Range:* Breeds (Northern House Wren group) in temperate North America from southern Canada south to south-central United States; winters in southern United States south to southern Mexico. The Southern House Wren group, now considered to be conspecific with the Northern, is resident over much of Mexico, Central and South America, and the Lesser Antilles.

324. Winter Wren

Troglodytes troglodytes (L—4 W—6)
Brown above; brownish-buff below;
buffy eyeline; barred flanks and belly;

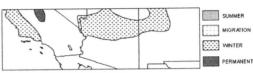

short tail. *Voice:* A rich, cascading series of trills and warbles; calls are staccato "chuck"s, "kip"s, "churr"s. *Habitat:* Thickets, tangles, undergrowth of fens, bogs, and swamps; highland old growth sequoia, red fir, douglas fir, and sugar pine in summer; lowland riparian thickets in winter. *Similar Species:* See House Wren. *Abundance and Distribution:* Uncommon resident* on the west slope of the Sierra Nevada (up to eight thousand feet) in southern California; uncommon to rare winter resident (Oct.–Mar.) in coastal highlands and mid-elevations of southern California (south to Los Angeles County), Lake Mead and the Grand Canyon in northern Arizona, and the mountains and foothills of northern New Mexico. Rare to casual elsewhere in winter in the region. *Where to Find:* Sequoia National Park, California (resident); Nojoqui Falls County Park, California (winter); Bright Angel Trail, Grand Canyon, Arizona (winter); Cottonwood Canyon, Zuni Mountains, New Mexico (winter). *Range:* Most of Palearctic; breeds in boreal regions of North America from Alaska and British Columbia to Labrador, south along the Pacific coast to central California and in the Appalachians to north Georgia; winters from the central and southern United States to northern Mexico.

325. Marsh Wren

Cistothorus palustris (L—5 W—7)
Brown above; black back prominently
streaked with white; white eyeline and

throat; buff underparts. *Voice:* A rapid series of dry "tsik"s, like the sound of an old sewing machine; call is a sharp "tsuk." *Habitat:* Cattail and bulrush marshes, wet prairies. *Abundance and Distribution:* Uncommon resident* in marshes of lowlands in coastal southern California, Salton Sea, and Colorado River valley; rare summer resident* (Apr.–Sep.) in northwestern New Mexico; uncommon to rare winter resident* (Oct.–Mar.) at lowland to mid-elevation marshes throughout. *Where to Find:* Lions Park, Farmington, New Mexico (summer); Picacho Reservoir, Arizona (winter); Salton Sea National Wildlife Refuge, California; Floyd Lamb

State Park, Nevada. *Range:* Breeds across central and southern Canada and northern United States, southward along both coasts to northern Baja California and southeastern Texas; rare and local in inland United States; winters along both coasts, and southern United States to southern Mexico.

Family Cinclidae
Dippers
Dippers constitute a small family (four species) of drab, wren-like birds, highly specialized for foraging for aquatic arthropods on the bottom of mountain streams and rivers.

326. American Dipper

Cinclus mexicanus (L—7 W—12)
Blackish-gray throughout; short,
stubby tail. *Immature:* Dark gray

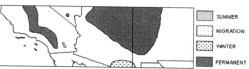

above; paler below; yellowish bill. *Habits:* Distinctive continual bobbing and habit of walking underwater in mountain streams. *Voice:* Boisterous series of trills and warbles; a sharp "zheet" call. *Habitat:* Cataracts, rushing mountain streams, tarns; rocky walls, bridges, or log jams needed for nest sites. *Abundance and Distribution:* Common resident* in high mountains throughout the region wherever rushing streams or glacial lakes are available; irregularly to lower elevations in winter. *Where to Find:* Sequoia National Park, California; Lamar Haines Memorial Wildlife Area, Arizona; Catwalk, Glenwood, New Mexico. *Range:* Breeds in mountains of western North America from Alaska to Panama; winters over most of breeding range except where waters are frozen.

Family Regulidae
Kinglets
A small, New World family of birds containing only two species, as described below.

327. Golden-crowned Kinglet

Regulus satrapa (L—4 W—7)
Greenish above, whitish below; white
wing bars, white eyeline; male has

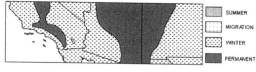

orange crown bordered by yellow and black; female has yellow crown bordered in black. *Habits:* Continually flicks wings while foraging. *Voice:* Call—a high-pitched "tse tse tse"; song—a series of "tsee"s first rising, then descending in pitch. *Similar Species:* Ruby-crowned has broken white eyering that Golden-crowned lacks; Golden-crowned has white eyeline that Ruby-crowned lacks. *Habitat:* Breeds in boreal zone mature spruce-fir and pine forest, especially red and douglas firs, sugar and ponderosa pines; a variety of woodland habitats in winter. *Abundance and Distribution:* Common resident* in boreal zone highlands of southern California, Arizona, and New Mexico; irregularly common to rare or absent in winter (Oct.–Mar.) in forested areas at lower elevations throughout. *Where to Find:* Burnt Rancheria Campground, Laguna Mountains, California (winter); Mount Charleston, Nevada (winter); Pajarito Mountain Ski Area, Bandelier National Monument, New Mexico (breeding); Kaibab Plateau Parkway, Grand Canyon, Arizona (breeding). *Range:* Breeds in boreal North America (except Great Plains); in Appalachians south to North Carolina; south in Rockies to Guatemala; winters from southern Canada and the United States south through highland breeding range in Mexico and Guatemala.

328. Ruby-crowned Kinglet

Regulus calendula (L—4 W—7)

Greenish above, whitish below; white wing bars, broken white eyering.

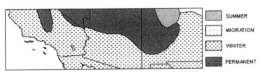

SUMMER
MIGRATION
WINTER
PERMANENT

Adult male has scarlet crown. *Immature and Female:* Lack scarlet crown. *Habits:* Continually flicks wings while foraging. *Voice:* Song begins with a series of "tsee" notes followed by lower pitched "tew" notes and terminated by a series of "teedadee"s. Distinctive "tsi tit" call. *Similar Species:* See Golden-crowned Kinglet. *Habitat:* Mature spruce-fir, lodgepole pine, and mountain hemlock of the highland boreal zone in summer; a variety of woodlands during winter. *Abundance and Distribution:* Common to rare summer resident* (Apr.–Sep.) in boreal highlands of northern New Mexico; uncommon to rare resident* in the Sierra Nevada of southern California, and the highlands of southern Nevada and northern Arizona; common winter resident (Oct.–Mar.) throughout the region. "Every small patch of salt cedar along the (Colorado) river has its winter resident kinglet, as they establish and defend resource territories during that time." (Brown et al. 1987:233). *Where to Find:* Burnt Rancheria Campground, Laguna Mountains, California (winter); Mount Charleston, Nevada (winter); Pajarito Mountain Ski Area, Bandelier National Monument, New Mexico (breeding); Kaibab Plateau Parkway, Grand Canyon, Arizona (breeding). *Range:* Breeds in boreal North America from Alaska to Labrador south to northern New York, Michigan, Minnesota; and in the Rockies south to New Mexico and Arizona; winters over most of the United States, Mexico and Guatemala; resident populations in Guadalupe Island (Baja California), and Chiapas?.

Family Sylviidae
Old World Warblers and Gnatcatchers
The sylviids are a group of mainly Old World species, most of which are slim, arboreal birds, comparable in size to the New World warblers (Parulidae). The family is represented in the southwestern region by only three species of gnatcatchers (Genus *Polioptila*), as described below.

329. Blue-gray Gnatcatcher
Polioptila caerulea (L—5 W—7)
Bluish-gray above, white below; tail
black above with white outer feath-

ers (tail appears white from below); white eyering. Adult male in breeding plumage (Apr.–Aug.) has black forehead and eyeline. Sexes nearly identical in non-breeding plumage. *Voice:* Song is a barely audible string of high-pitched warbles and squeaks; "tsee" call note. *Similar Species:* The tail of both the Black-tailed and California gnatcatchers appear mostly black from below; Black-tailed and California males have black caps in breeding plumage (Apr.–Aug.). *Habitat:* Willow and cottonwood thickets, sagebrush, oak, pine-oak, pinyon-juniper; desert scrub (mesquite) in winter. *Abundance and Distribution:* Uncommon summer resident* (Apr.–Sep.) at mid-elevations (below five thousand feet) in mountains of southern California, northeastern Arizona, and northern and western New Mexico; uncommon permanent resident* in lowlands and foothills of southern California, southern Nevada, and southeastern to northwestern Arizona and southwestern New Mexico; uncommon winter resident (Oct.–Mar.) in lowland scrub and deserts of southeastern California and southwestern Arizona. *Where to Find:* Red Rock Canyon National Conservation Area, Nevada; Lake Perris State Recreation Area, California (winter); Molino Basin Campground, Arizona (breeding); Bandelier National Monument, New Mexico. *Range:* Breeds in the temperate United States south through Mexico to Guatemala; winters in the southern Atlantic (from Virginia south) and Gulf states; and in the west from California, Arizona, New Mexico, and Texas south throughout Mexico and Central America to Honduras; resident in the Bahamas.

330. California Gnatcatcher
Polioptila californica
(L—5 W—7) **Endangered**
Bluish-gray above; dingy gray below;
tail black above with white outer feathers (appears black from below); indistinct white eyering. Adult male in breeding plumage (Apr.–Aug.) has black cap. Sexes

nearly identical in non-breeding plumage. *Voice:* Song a metallic "tsee Dee Dee Dee Dee"; call a repeated, mewing "chee." *Similar Species:* The California Gnatcatcher has grayish underparts (not white, as in Black-tailed). The Black-tailed Gnatcatcher tail shows black feathers broadly tipped with white from below. The California Gnatcatcher tail appears narrowly tipped with white from below. The California Gnatcatcher has a whiney "mew" call note; the Black-tailed call note is a series of "tsee" notes or a harsh "tseer." Also note that these two species (formerly considered races of the same species) overlap only slightly in range. Coastal county birds should be California Gnatcatchers; interior desert birds should be Black-tailed (see Dunn and Garrett [1987] for more extensive discussion of differences). *Habitat:* Thorn forest, coastal sage brush, desert scrub (mesquite, creosote bush, cholla cactus). *Abundance and Distribution:* Uncommon resident* in native desert scrub of coastal California from Los Angeles County to the Mexican border. *Where to Find:* Forrestal Drive, Palos Verdes Peninsula; Border Field State Park; Crystal Cove State Park. *Range:* Coastal California (Los Angeles County) south to northwestern Baja California.

331. Black-tailed Gnatcatcher

Polioptila melanura (L—5 W—7)

Bluish-gray above, white below; tail black above with white outer feath-

SUMMER
MIGRATION
WINTER
PERMANENT

ers; tail appears black from below, broadly tipped with white; indistinct white eyering. Adult male in breeding plumage (Apr.–Aug.) has black cap. Sexes nearly identical in non-breeding plumage. *Voice:* Song a metallic "tsee dee dee dee dee;" call a harsh "tseer," or repeated "tsee." *Similar Species:* See California Gnatcatcher. A Mexican species, the Black-capped Gnatcatcher (*P. nigriceps*) is casual in Chino and Sycamore canyons of extreme southern Arizona. The male of this species is distinguished from the male Blue-gray Gnatcatcher by its black cap (in summer) and from the Black-tailed Gnatcatcher by the tail, which appears white from below (not black). *Habitat:* Desert riparian groves and scrub, dry thorn forest (mesquite and catclaw). *Abundance and Distribution:* Common to rare resident* in the desert regions of southeastern California, southern Nevada, northwestern to southeastern Arizona, and the middle and lower Rio Grande valley of southern New Mexico. *Where to Find:* Dripping Springs Natural Area, Las Cruces, New Mexico; Saguaro National Park, Arizona; Corn Creek Desert National Wildlife Refuge, Nevada; Salton Sea National Wildlife Refuge, California. *Range:* Southeastern California, southern Nevada, northwestern to southeastern Arizona, southern New Mexico, and southern borderlands of Texas south to central Mexico.

Figure 42. Canjilon Mountain in the Carson National Forest is an excellent representative of the high peaks of New Mexico's Sangre de Cristo range. Its mixed conifer-aspen habitats are home to Grace's Warbler, Band-tailed Pigeon, Long-eared Owl, Olive-sided Flycatcher, and the Hermit Thrush.

Figure 43. Long drives on rural roads are rewarded with the serene oak woodlands, cotton-wood groves, and Mediterranean scrub of Pinnacles National Monument, California. Typical birds include Fox Sparrow, Yellow-billed Magpie, Anna's Hummingbird, and Willow Flycatcher.

Family Turdidae
Thrushes, Bluebirds, and Solitaires
A group of medium-sized birds most of which are cryptically colored in browns and grays. The thrush family is considered by many to contain the most beautiful singers in the bird world. Though you may debate whether the Wood Thrush, Hermit Thrush, Slate-colored Solitaire, or Nightingale holds the top position, few would contest their place in the Top Ten.

332. Eastern Bluebird

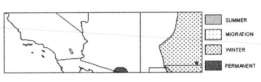

Sialia sialis (L—7 W—12)
Blue above, brick red below with white belly. *Female:* Similar but paler.
Voice: A whistled "cheer cheerful farmer"; "tur lee" call. *Similar Species:* Western Bluebird male has blue (not red) throat; Western Bluebird female has gray (not reddish) throat. *Habitat:* Open woodlands, savanna, oak and pine-oak associations. *Abundance and Distribution:* Uncommon resident* in extreme southeastern Arizona and southeastern New Mexico (Rattlesnake Springs); uncommon to rare or casual winter resident (Oct.–Mar.) in central and southeastern New Mexico. *Where to Find:* Sycamore Canyon, Arizona; Sawmill Canyon, Arizona; Rattlesnake Springs, New Mexico. *Range:* Breeds in eastern North America from southern Saskatchewan to New Brunswick south to Florida and Texas; through highlands of Mexico and Central America to Nicaragua; Bermuda; winters in southern portion of breeding range (central and eastern United States southward).

333. Western Bluebird

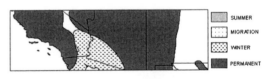

Sialia mexicana (L—7 W—12)
Head, throat, and upper parts deep blue; back and shoulders with some rusty color; breast brick red; belly white. *Female:* Similar but with head and back gray-blue, pale orange breast. *Voice:* A whistled "pew pew pewee"; "pew" call note. *Similar Species:* See Eastern Bluebird. *Habitat:* Open oak, pine-oak, ponderosa pine, and pinyon-juniper with grassy under story; also in chaparral and desert scrub in winter wherever berries (juniper, mistletoe, etc.) are available. *Abundance and Distribution:* Common to uncommon resident* at mid-elevations (below five thousand feet) in mountains and foothills of southern California, southern Nevada, Arizona (except southwest), and New Mexico (except northeast and eastern plains); uncommon to rare and irregular winter resident (Oct.–Mar.) in lowlands and desert areas nearly throughout when and wherever berry crops are available, common in some years, absent in others. *Where to Find:* Grandview Point, Grand Canyon,

Arizona; Cherry Creek Campground, Pinos Altos Mountains, New Mexico; G13 near Bitterwater, California; Mount Charleston, Nevada. *Range:* Breeds in western North America from southern British Columbia, Montana, and Wyoming south to the highlands of central Mexico.

334. Mountain Bluebird
Sialia currucoides (L—7 W—13)
Blue above; paler blue below. *Female:*
Grayish-blue above; bluish wings;

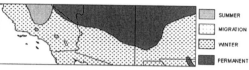

grayish-white below. *Voice:* Song—a whistled "tew lee"; call—"tew." *Similar Species:* Other bluebirds more or less rusty below. *Habitat:* Highland meadows (up to twelve thousand feet); pinyon-juniper; open ponderosa pine, pine-oak and pinyon-juniper woodland, hedgerows, grasslands, agricultural areas in winter. Feeds on juniper, mistletoe, and other desert berry crops in winter. *Abundance and Distribution:* Uncommon summer resident* (Apr.–Sep.) in montane regions of southern California; resident* in mountains of southern Nevada, northern Arizona, and western and northern New Mexico and the Guadalupe Mountains of southeastern New Mexico; uncommon to rare and irregular winter resident (Oct.–Mar.) throughout. *Where to Find:* Terry Flat, Arizona (summer); Carrizo Plain, California (winter); Langmuir Laboratory, Magdalena Mountains, New Mexico; Lee Canyon Ski Area, Mount Charleston, Nevada. *Range:* Breeds in western North America from Alaska, Yukon, and northern Manitoba south to southern California, Arizona, and New Mexico; winters in southern portion of breeding range from southern British Columbia and Montana south through Texas and northern Mexico.

335. Townsend's Solitaire
Myadestes townsendi (L—9 W—14)
Gray body; black, notched tail with
white outer tail feathers; buff wing

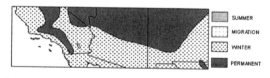

patches; white eyering. *Voice:* Song—a long series of warbles; call—"eek." *Habitat:* Shrubby understory of montane coniferous forest; juniper, arid and semi-arid thorn forest in winter. *Abundance and Distribution:* Uncommon resident* in the highlands (up to nine thousand feet) of southern California, southern Nevada, northeastern quarter of Arizona, and northern New Mexico from tree line down to pine forests. Uncommon to rare and irregular winter resident (Oct.–Apr.) throughout. *Where to Find:* Mount Charleston, Nevada; North Rim, Grand Canyon, Arizona; Vivian Meadows, San Bernardino Mountains, California; Langmuir Laboratory, Magdalena Mountains, New Mexico. *Range:* Breeds in western North America from Alaska and the Yukon south to New Mexico, Arizona, and southern California; winters in southern half of breeding range from southern British Columbia and Alberta to Texas, and in highlands to southern Mexico; resident population in highlands of north and central Mexico.

336. Veery

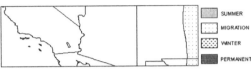

Catharus fuscescens (L—7 W—12)
Russet above (more brownish in western subspecies); throat buff with indistinct spotting; whitish belly. *Voice:* Song—a whistled, wheezy, descending "zheew zheew zhoo zhoo"; call—"zink." *Similar Species:* Breast spotting is more distinct in Swainson's and Gray-cheeked Thrush; Swainson's has distinct eyering; russet tail of Hermit Thrush contrasts with gray-brown back. *Habitat:* Willow thickets in riparian areas. *Abundance and Distribution:* Rare spring transient (Apr.–May) in eastern New Mexico; apparently has bred* in the Springer Mountains of extreme eastern Arizona and perhaps in the Manzano Mountains of central New Mexico. *Where to Find:* Rio Pueblo Valley; Perico Creek (as spring transients). *Range:* Breeds across southern Canada and northern United States, south in mountains to Georgia in the east and Colorado in the west; winters in northern South America.

337. Swainson's Thrush

Catharus ustulatus (L—7 W—12)
Brown or grayish-brown above, buffy below with dark spotting; lores and eyering buffy. *Voice:* Song—"zhoo zhoo zhee zhee" with rising pitch; call—"zheep." *Similar Species:* The whitish or buff eyering of the Swainson's Thrush distinguishes this bird from the Gray-cheeked Thrush and western populations of the Veery. Also, flanks of the Swainson's Thrush are buffy, not grayish as in western Veeries. *Habitat:* Breeding—thickets in coniferous forest, bogs, alder swamps; migration and winter—moist woodlands, riparian thickets. *Abundance and Distribution:* Uncommon spring (May) and rare fall (Sep.) transient throughout; uncommon to rare summer resident* in thick riparian growth of canyons in coastal southern California; rare summer resident* in dense under story of fir forests in the Sierras of southern California, the San Francisco and White Mountains of north-central and eastern Arizona, and the highlands of north-central New Mexico. *Where to Find:* Guadalupe Dunes County Park, Santa Barbara, California (breeding); municipal golf course, Roswell Spring River Golf Course, New Mexico (spring transient); Madera Canyon, Arizona (spring transient); Corn Creek, Desert National Wildlife Range, Nevada (spring transient). *Range:* Breeds in boreal North America from Alaska across Canada to Labrador south to the northern United States; south in mountains and along coast to southern California and in mountains to northern New Mexico; winters in southern Mexico, Central America, and the highlands of South America.

338. Hermit Thrush

Catharus guttatus (L—7 W—12)

Grayish-brown above; whitish below
with dark spotting; whitish eyering;

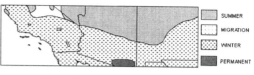

rusty tail, often flicked. *Voice:* Distinct phrases, each beginning with a long, whistled note followed by a trill; trills of different phrases have different inflection; call, "tuk tuk tuk" or a raspy "zhay." *Similar Species:* The rusty tail of the Hermit Thrush distinguishes this bird from the other *Catharus* thrush species (Swainson's, Veery, and Gray-cheeked). *Habitat:* Breeding—boreal and upper transition zone forests of spruce-fir forest, ponderosa pine; sequoia, lodgepole, and whitebark pines; migration and winter—riparian thickets, broad-leaf woodlands, thorn forest. *Abundance and Distribution:* Uncommon summer resident* (Apr.–Sep.) in the spruce-fir forests of montane southern California, southern Nevada, Arizona (except southwest quarter), and New Mexico (except eastern plains); uncommon transient and winter resident (Oct.–Mar.) nearly throughout (except in highlands). *Where to Find:* Nojoqui Falls County Park, California (winter); North Rim, Grand Canyon, Arizona (breeding); Langmuir Laboratory, Magdalena Mountains, New Mexico (breeding); Lee Canyon Ski Area, Spring Mountains, Nevada (breeding). *Range:* Breeds in boreal Canada and northern United States, south in mountains to southern California, Arizona, New Mexico, and west Texas; winters from the southern United States north along coasts to southern British Columbia and New Jersey, and south through Mexico (excluding Yucatan Peninsula) to Guatemala and El Salvador; resident population in Baja California.

339. American Robin

Turdus migratorius (L—10 W—17)

Dark gray above, orange-brown below; white lower belly; white throat

with dark streaks; partial white eyering. *Voice:* Song—a varied series of whistled phrases, "cheerily cheerup cheerio." Call—"tut tut." *Habitat:* A wide variety of forest and parkland will serve as breeding habitat so long as there is rich, moist soil containing earthworms for foraging and mud available for nest construction. Ponderosa pine, pinyon-juniper, broadleaf and mixed forest; scrub, parkland, riparian forest, oak woodlands, and residential areas in winter. *Abundance and Distribution:* Common summer resident* (Apr.–Sep.) from four thousand to ten thousand feet and permanent resident* in foothills below four thousand feet of southern California, southern Nevada, Arizona (except southwest quarter), and New Mexico. Common winter resident (Oct.–Mar.) throughout except in high mountains. *Where to Find:* Grandview Point, Grand Canyon, Arizona (breeding); Water Canyon Campground, Magdalena Mountains, New Mexico (breeding); Mount

Charleston, Nevada (breeding); Palomar Mountain State Park, California (breeding). *Range:* Breeds nearly throughout Canada and United States south through central highlands of Mexico; winters from southern half of breeding range into Guatemala; western Cuba; Bahamas; resident population in Baja California.

340. Varied Thrush

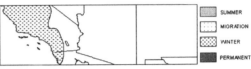

Ixoreus naevius (L—9 W—16)

Slate blue or gray above, brick red below; black breast band; black face patch; brick red eyeline, wing bars. *Female:* Patterned like male but brownish above; brownish breast band and cheek. *Voice:* Song—a series of long, wavering whistles and trills of different pitches; call—"tsook." *Habitat:* Oak-lined canyons, dense thorn scrub, chaparral thickets (winter) feeding on acorns and berries. *Abundance and Distribution:* Uncommon to rare winter resident (Oct.–Mar.) in the lowlands and foothills of southern California (not in deserts of southeast corner); rare to casual and irregular winter visitor elsewhere in the region. *Where to Find:* Nojoqui Falls County Park; El Cariso Campground (rare); Huntington Central Park (rare). *Range:* Breeds in northwestern North America from Alaska through the Yukon and British Columbia to northern California; winters south from British Columbia to southern California.

Family Timaliidae
Babblers and Wrentit
Taxonomists have debated about the familial relationships of the Wrentit since its discovery. Recently, genetic studies have placed the bird in the Old World group Timaliidae, wren and thrasher-like birds called "babblers" because many species in the family associate in noisy flocks. The Wrentit is the only New World representative.

341. Wrentit

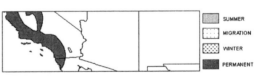

Chamaea fasciata (L—6, W—9)

A drab, brownish bird (grayish in southern populations) with faint streaking below, dark line through the eye, and white eye. The long, rounded tail usually is held at an angle. *Voice:* A rapid series of sharp notes followed by a descending trill. The male sings throughout the year. *Habitat:* California Mediterranean scrub and oak woodland, and mixed pine-oak. *Abundance and Distribution:* Common resident* in coastal lowlands and foothills of southwestern California.

Where to Find: Guadalupe Dunes County Park; Dorothy May Tucker Wildlife Sanctuary; Malibu Creek State Park. *Range:* Resident in the lowlands and foothills of the Pacific coastal region from southern Washington to northern Baja California.

Family Mimidae
Thrashers and Mockingbirds
Long-tailed, medium-sized birds, several of which have a somewhat fierce appearance due to their decurved bills and colored eye (orange, yellow, white). Several of the species include phrases from the songs of other species in their own songs.

342. Gray Catbird
Dumetella carolinensis
(L—9 W—12)

Slate gray throughout, black cap and tail, rusty under-tail coverts. *Voice:* A stream of whistles, mews, squeaks; sometimes mimics other species; call a nasal, catlike mew. *Habitat:* Willow thickets in riparian areas; tangles, heavy undergrowth in coniferous and broadleaf woodlands; second growth, hedgerows. *Abundance and Distribution:* Rare to casual summer resident* (Apr.–Sep.) in mountains of north-central New Mexico and east-central Arizona; uncommon to rare transient in eastern New Mexico. *Where to Find:* Oxbow Lake, Rio Grande Nature Center, Albuquerque, New Mexico (breeding); Dry Cimarron River Valley, New Mexico (breeding); San Rafael Ponds, El Malpais, New Mexico (breeding). *Range:* Breeds throughout eastern, central, and northwestern United States and southern Canada. Winters along central and southern Atlantic and Gulf coasts south through the Gulf and Caribbean lowlands of Mexico and Central America to Panama; Bahamas; Greater Antilles; resident in Bermuda.

343. Northern Mockingbird
Mimus polyglottos (L—10 W—14)

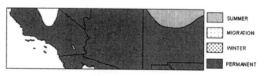

Gray body, paler below; black tail with white outer tail feathers; white wing bars and white patches on wings. *Habits:* Often flies to the ground and spreads wings and tail in a mechanical fashion while foraging. *Voice:* A variety of whistled phrases, repeated several times and including pieces of other bird songs. *Similar Species:* Loggerhead Shrike has heavy, hooked bill, short tail, and black mask. *Habitat:* Arid and semi-arid thorn forest, savanna, old fields, hedgerows, agricultural areas, residential areas. *Abundance and Distribution:* Common permanent resident* in residential areas and elsewhere in arid and semi-arid scrub throughout except in high mountains; common to uncommon summer resident* (Apr.–Sep.) in northern New Mexico. *Where to Find:* Big Canyon, Upper Newport Bay, California; Sabino Canyon Recreation Area, Arizona; Sandstone Bluffs Overlook, El Malpais, New Mexico; Desert National Wildlife Range, Nevada. *Range:* Resident in central and southern United States and Mexico to Oaxaca; Bahamas; Greater Antilles.

344. Sage Thrasher

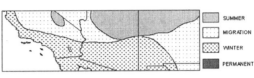

Oreoscoptes montanus (L—9 W—13) Grayish-brown above; whitish below with dark streaking; yellowish eye; white wing bars and tail tips. *Voice:* A continuous series of warbles and trills; call— "chuk." *Habitat:* Sagebrush plains; semi-arid and arid scrub and thorn forest. *Similar Species:* This is the only thrasher species with a gray back and heavily streaked underparts. *Abundance and Distribution:* Common summer resident* (Mar.–Sep.) in sagebrush thickets of montane valleys (four thousand to eight thousand feet) in the highland sage canyons of southeastern California, northern Arizona, and northern New Mexico; uncommon transient and winter resident (Oct.–Mar.) in desert areas of southern California, southern Arizona, and southern New Mexico; transient (Mar.–Apr., Sep.–Oct.) elsewhere in the region. *Where to Find:* Petrified Forest National Monument, Arizona (breeding); Dry Cimarron River Valley, New Mexico (breeding); Joshua Tree National Monument, California (winter). *Range:* Breeds in deserts of western North America from southern British Columbia, Montana, and South Dakota south to northern New Mexico and southern California; winters from southern California, Arizona, New Mexico, and Texas south to north-central Mexico.

345. Brown Thrasher

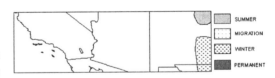

Toxostoma rufum (L—11 W—13) Rufous above, whitish below with dark streaking; yellowish eye. *Voice:* A long sequence of brief phrases of squeaky warbles, each phrase given twice. *Similar Species:* The Brown Thrasher is distinguished from western thrashers by its rufous back (gray in western species). *Habitat:* Tangles, undergrowth, and thickets of forests, old fields, hedgerows, riparian forest, thorn forest. *Abundance and Distribution:* Rare and local summer resident* (Apr.–Sep.) in northeastern New Mexico; rare winter resident (Oct.–Mar.) in lowland river valleys of eastern New Mexico. *Where to Find:* Dry Cimarron Valley (breeding). *Range:* Breeds across eastern and central North America from southern Canada west to Alberta and south to east Texas and southern Florida; winters in southern portion of breeding range.

346. Bendire's Thrasher

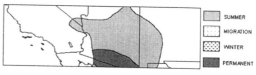

Toxostoma bendirei (L—10 W—12)
Gray above; pale gray below with distinct arrowhead-shaped spotting;
yellow eye; bill only slightly decurved and whitish at base; no wing bars. *Voice:* A
continuous warble of repeated phrases. *Similar Species:* Bendire's Thrasher is smaller
than the Curve-billed Thrasher, has a nearly straight bill that is whitish at the base
of the lower mandible (not deeply curved and dark as in Curve-billed), yellow
rather than orange eye, no wing bars, distinct arrowhead-shaped spots on breast
(in fresh plumage). *Habitat:* Open desert—especially at borders between grassy or
bare areas and cholla cactus, creosote bush, and yucca scrub. *Abundance and Distribution:* Uncommon to rare summer resident* (Mar.–July) in deserts of northern Arizona, western New Mexico, southeastern California, and southern Nevada;
uncommon permanent resident in southern Arizona. *Where to Find:* Petrified Forest
National Park, Arizona; Catalina State Park, Arizona; NM 338 to Animas, New
Mexico. *Range:* Breeds from southern California, southern Nevada, southern Utah,
and New Mexico to west-central Mexico; winters from southeastern Arizona to
southwestern Mexico.

347. Curve-billed Thrasher

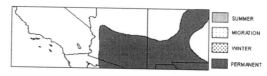

Toxostoma curvirostre (L—11 W—13)
Gray above, pale gray below with indistinct spotting; orange-red eye; bill
solid black, sharply decurved; whitish wing bars and tail corners. *Voice:* A series of
musical warbles with the call notes, "whit" and "whit wheet," interspersed; some
mimicking of other species *Similar Species:* See Bendire's Thrasher. *Habitat:* Cholla
cactus desert, dry thorn forest, arid scrub; also in towns. *Abundance and Distribution:* Common resident* of the Lower Sonoran zone of southern Arizona and New
Mexico (scarce or absent from northern and northwestern mountains and eastern
plains; northern populations may be partially migratory). *Where to Find:* Hualapai
Mountain Park, Arizona (at lower elevations); Arizona Sonora Desert Museum;
Bosque del Apache National Wildlife Refuge, New Mexico. *Range:* Southern Arizona, New Mexico, southern Colorado, western Oklahoma, and Texas south in
arid areas to southern Mexico.

348. California Thrasher

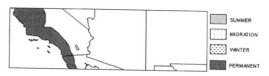

Toxostoma redivivum (L—12 W—14)
Uniform dark gray above; whitish
throat; gray breast; buffy belly and
under-tail coverts; white line above eye; dark mustache; dark eye. *Voice:* Song—a

long series of whistled and raspy phrases, often repeated once or twice. Occasionally imitates other bird species and sounds. Call—a guttural, "tshek." *Similar Species:* The California Thrasher has buffy under-tail coverts (not rusty as in the closely related [conspecific?] Crissal Thrasher); also the California Thrasher has dark eye (not yellowish as in Crissal). The California Thrasher is found west of the California deserts; Crissal is found in these deserts and eastward. *Habitat:* Dense chaparral of canyon slopes; brushy thickets with low, dense overstory and relatively bare ground underneath. *Abundance and Distribution:* Common permanent resident* in the coastal lowlands, foothills, and lower mountains of southwestern California. *Where to Find:* Casper's Wilderness Park; Nojoqui Falls County Park; Torrey Pines State Reserve. *Range:* Resident from northern California (Humboldt and Shasta counties) to northern Baja California, west of Sierra and Cascade ranges, and deserts.

349. Crissal Thrasher

Toxostoma crissale (L—12 W—13)
Gray above; paler below; whitish
throat; black "mustache"; rusty

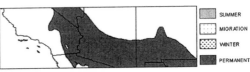

under-tail coverts; bill long, sharply decurved. *Voice:* Song is similar to Curve-billed Thrasher but less hurried; "pitchoree," "tscha," and "tuwit" call notes. *Similar Species:* See California Thrasher. Also, Curve-billed and Bendire's Thrashers lack rusty under-tail coverts and black mustache and have a spotted breast. *Habitat:* Low thorn forest and riparian thickets in desert regions; pinyon-juniper. *Abundance and Distribution:* Uncommon resident* of southeastern California, southern Nevada, Arizona (except highlands of northeast), and southern New Mexico (to north-central region along the Rio Grande valley). *Where to Find:* Red Rock Canyon National Conservation Area, Nevada; Salton Sea National Wildlife Refuge, California; Catalina State Park, Arizona; Old Refuge, Las Cruces, New Mexico. *Range:* Southwestern United States and western Mexico.

350. Le Conte's Thrasher

Toxostoma lecontei (L—11 W—13)
Pearly gray above and below; contrasting dark gray tail; buffy under-

tail coverts; white throat; dark bill and eye. *Habits:* Often runs along on ground with tail cocked. *Voice:* Sings mostly at dawn and dusk; the whistled phrases are given with pauses and occasional repetitions; call—"tew-weep." *Similar Species:* The dark tail contrasting with pearly-gray body is distinctive. *Habitat:* Open desert, sparse arid scrub (creosote bush, scattered mesquite, salt bush), desert washes. *Abundance and Distribution:* Uncommon to rare and local resident* in low desert areas of the San Joaquin Valley Desert, and deserts east of the Sierra Nevada in southeastern California, southern Nevada, and extreme western and southwestern Arizona. *Where to Find:* Desert National Wildlife Range, Nevada; Anza-Borrego Desert State Park, California; Kofa National Wildlife Refuge, Arizona. *Range:* Resident in the deserts of central and southern California, southern Nevada, western Arizona, Baja California, and extreme northwestern Mexico (Sonora).

Family Sturnidae
Starlings
Starlings are an Old World family with no members native to the New World. They are medium-sized, relatively long-billed songbirds, often with iridescent plumage. Several of the species mimic the songs of other birds.

351. European Starling

Sturnus vulgaris (L—9 W—15)
Plump, short-tailed, and glossy black
with purple and green highlights and

long, yellow bill in summer. *Winter:* Dark billed and speckled with white. *Habits:* Erect waddling gait when foraging on ground; forms large roosting flocks during non-breeding season. *Voice:* Various squeaks, harsh "churr"s, whistles and imitations of other bird songs—often with repeated phrases; call—a high pitched, rising "tseee." *Similar Species:* Other black birds are shorter billed, longer tailed; winter bird is speckled with white; summer bird has yellow bill. *Habitat:* Towns, savanna, farmland. *Abundance and Distribution:* Common resident* of cities, towns, and farmlands throughout. *Range:* New World—resident from southern Canada to northern Mexico; Bahamas and Greater Antilles; Old World—Breeds in temperate and boreal regions of Eurasia; winters in southern portions of breeding range into north Africa, Middle East, and southern Asia.

Family Motacillidae
Pipits
Chaff-colored, long-tailed birds of open country. Like larks, they have an extremely long hind claw, and often call and sing on the wing. They pump their tails with each step as they walk along the ground in search of seeds and insects.

352. American Pipit

Anthus rubescens (L—7 W—11)

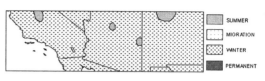

Sparrowlike in size and coloration but sleek and erect in posture, walks rather than hops, and has thin bill; grayish-brown above; buffy below streaked with brown; whitish throat and eyeline; white outer tail feathers; dark legs; wags tail as it walks; undulating flight. *Voice:* Flight song a sibilant "chwee" repeated; call—"tsee-eet." *Similar Species:* American Pipit has unstreaked back and dark legs; Sprague's Pipit has streaked back and flesh-colored legs; Vesper Sparrow has cone-shaped bill (not narrow); hops rather than walks. *Habitat:* Short-grass prairie, plowed fields, swales, mudflats, roadsides, desert washes; pond, stream, and river margins. *Abundance and Distribution:* Uncommon and local summer resident* (May–Sep.) in alpine zone (above ten thousand feet) in the Sierra Nevada of southern California, the San Francisco and White Mountains of north-central and eastern Arizona; the Sangre de Cristo and White Mountains of northern and central New Mexico, and, possibly, on top of Mount Charleston in southern Nevada; common transient (Sep.–Oct., Apr.–May) and uncommon winter resident (Oct.–Apr.) throughout (except open desert and highlands). *Where to Find:* Morgan Lake, New Mexico; Avra Valley Sewage Lagoons, Tucson, Arizona; Overton Wildlife Management Area, Nevada; plowed fields of the Wister Unit, State Imperial Wildlife Area, Salton Sea, California. *Range:* Breeds in arctic regions of the Old and New World, and in mountainous areas and high plateaus of temperate regions; winters in temperate regions and high, arid portions of the tropics.

353. Sprague's Pipit

Anthus spragueii (L—7 W—11)

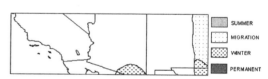

Streaked brown above; whitish below streaked with brown; pale legs; white outer tail feathers; walks rather than hops; bobs tail. *Habits:* Flight on flushing from tall grasses is characteristic with sharp ascent followed by a plummet back into the grasses. *Voice:* Flight song a series of high, sweet notes, descending in pitch; call a hoarse "tseep." *Similar Species:* See American Pipit. *Habitat:* Grasslands, dunes, pastures. *Abundance and Distribution:* Rare transient (Apr., Oct.) in northeastern New Mexico; rare winter resident (Nov.–Mar.) in southeastern Arizona and southeastern New Mexico. *Where to Find:* San Rafael Grassland, Arizona; Buenos Aires National Wildlife Refuge, Arizona; southeast of the US 380 Bridge at the Pecos River, New Mexico. *Range:* Breeds from north-central Alberta east to southern Manitoba and south into Montana, South Dakota, North Dakota, and western Minnesota; winters from southern Arizona, New Mexico, Texas, Arkansas, Louisiana, Mississippi, and Mexico to southern Veracruz, Puebla, and Michoacan.

Figure 44. Patagonia Lake State Park northeast of Nogales can be a little hectic in the summer. But at other times of the year, and especially during migration, its open water and marshes are a good place for shorebirds, waterfowl, marsh birds, and riparian species like the Common Yellowthroat, Yellow-headed Blackbird, White-winged Dove, Green-winged Teal, and Ruddy Duck.

Figure 45. Chinle Wash is a familiar landmark for readers of Tony Hillerman's fascinating novels set on the Navajo "big res." This photo was taken from the Highway 191 bridge, 7.4 miles west of Round Rock, Arizona. Birds found here are typical of desert riparian areas elsewhere in the region including Lesser Goldfinch, Bewick's Wren, and Black-chinned Hummingbird.

Family Bombycillidae
Waxwings

Waxwings are a small family of sleek, brown, crested birds with bright waxy tips on their secondaries. They are highly social during the non-breeding portion of the year, feeding mostly in flocks on tree fruits and berries.

354. Bohemian Waxwing

Bombycilla garrulus (L—8 W—14)
Dapper grayish-brown above and below with a sharp crest; black mask and throat; tail black with yellow tip; rusty under-tail coverts; primaries black with

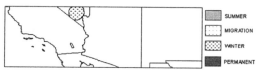

white and yellow markings; secondaries with waxy red tips. *Immature:* Faint streaking below; whitish face and throat. *Voice:* High, thin, wavering "tseeeeet," louder and rougher than Cedar Waxwing. *Similar Species:* Cedar Waxwing has whitish rather than chestnut under-tail coverts and lacks yellow and white markings on wings. *Habitat:* Orchards and fruiting trees; apples, juniper, hawthorn, mountain ash; cemeteries, arboreta, and other places where exotic fruiting trees are present. *Abundance and Distribution:* Rare and irregular winter visitor (Nov.–Apr.) in southern Nevada; casual elsewhere in the region. *Range:* Breeds in North America from Alaska and northwestern Canada to northwestern United States; winters northwestern United States and western Canada irregularly south and east across temperate United States. Eurasian populations breed in boreal regions; winter in south boreal and temperate areas of the Old World.

355. Cedar Waxwing

Bombycilla cedrorum (L—7 W—11)
Natty brown above and below with sharp crest; black face and throat; yel-

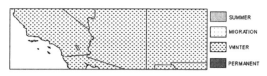

low wash on belly; tail tipped with yellow; red waxy tips to secondaries. *Immature:* Faint streaking below, lacks waxy tips. *Voice:* A thin, gurgling "tseee." *Similar Species:* See Bohemian Waxwing. *Habitat:* Open coniferous and deciduous woodlands, bogs, swamps, and shrubby, overgrown fields; cemeteries, arboreta, residential areas where fruiting trees are found. *Abundance and Distribution:* Uncommon (irregular) transient and winter resident (Sep.–May). *Where to Find:* Cemeteries, arboreta, and botanical gardens with their unusual concentrations of exotic trees fruiting at different times of the year; Santigo Oaks Regional Park; Sandia Park, New Mexico; Bill Williams Delta National Wildlife Refuge, Arizona. Transient and winter flocks frequent fruiting trees (such as mountain ash, mulberry, mistletoe, pyracantha, crabapple, and juniper). *Range:* Breeds across southern Canada and northern United States south to northern California, Kansas, and New York; winters in temperate United States south through Mexico and Central America to Panama and the Greater Antilles.

Family Ptilogonatidae
Silky Flycatchers
This family is a small, Neotropical group of trim, crested birds; mostly frugivorous.

356. Phainopepla

Phainopepla nitens (L—8 W—12)

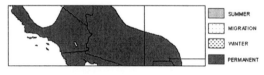

Male black except for white primaries (visible in flight) and red eye; ragged crest; long tail. *Female and Immature:* Brownish-gray; grayish primaries and under-tail coverts. *Habits:* Solitary birds sally for insects from exposed perch; small flocks feed on mistletoe and other berries. *Voice:* Song—a thin warble; call—a low, softly whistled "wirrp." *Habitat:* Desert scrub and riparian thickets, juniper-oak woodland, sites infested with mistletoe. *Abundance and Distribution:* Uncommon to rare or casual resident* in lowlands and foothills at densities that vary seasonally in southern California, southern Nevada, Arizona (except northeast), and southwestern and south-central New Mexico. It breeds in the desert areas in spring (Feb.–May), then moves to coastal (California) or higher elevations (inland) during the hot summer months before returning to desert regions in the fall. *Where to Find:* Old Refuge, Las Cruces, New Mexico; Saguaro National Park, Arizona; Overton Wildlife Management Area, Nevada; Yaqui Well, Anza-Borrego Desert State Park, California. *Range:* Breeds in southwestern United States, western and central Mexico; winters in all but extreme north portions of breeding range.

Family Peucedramidae
Olive Warbler
Like that of the Wrentit and Bushtit, taxonomic status of the Olive Warbler has been debated intensely among taxonomists. Current consensus places the species in its own family separate from the Wood Warblers, Parulidae, with which it is often included.

357. Olive Warbler

Peucedramus taeniatus (L—5 W—7)
Gray above with rusty hood and black
mask; white below with two white

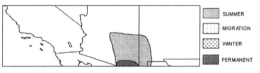

wing bars and white outer tail feathers; *Female and Immature male:* Tawny or yellowish hood but still show dark mask. *Voice:* Song—a whistled "weeta" repeated; call—"tew." *Habitat:* Montane pine and pine-oak woodlands. *Abundance and Distribution:* Uncommon to rare summer resident* (Mar.–Sep.) in southeastern Arizona and southwestern New Mexico; rare to casual in winter. *Where to Find:* Bear Canyon Picnic Area, Mount Lemmon, Arizona; Barfoot Park, Chiricahua Mountains, Arizona; Signal Peak, Pinos Altos Mountains, New Mexico. *Range:* Breeds from southeastern Arizona and southwestern New Mexico through the highlands of Mexico and Central America to Nicaragua; winters throughout all except northern portions of breeding range.

Family Parulidae
Wood Warblers
This is a large group composed mostly of small species, many of which are migratory. Males of several species are brightly colored.

358. Tennessee Warbler

Vermivora peregrina (L—5 W—8)
Olive above, white below with gray
cap, white eye stripe and dark line

through eye. Immatures are tinged with yellow. *Voice:* Song—a series of rapid "tsip"s followed by a series of rapid "tsi"s; call—a strong "tsip". *Similar Species:* The Tennessee Warbler lacks streaking on breast and has white under-tail coverts. The Orange-crowned Warbler has faint streaking on breast and yellow under-tail coverts. Also, the Tennessee is greener above than the Orange-crown, and has a more prominent eye stripe. *Habitat:* Coniferous woodlands; riparian, oak, and thorn forest. *Abundance and Distribution:* Rare transient (Sep.–Oct., Apr.–May) in extreme eastern New Mexico; casual transient elsewhere in the region. *Where to Find:* Artesia Cemetery, New Mexico. *Range:* Breeds across boreal North America; winters from southern Mexico to northern South America.

359. Orange-crowned Warbler

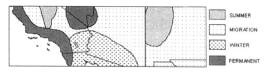

Vermivora celata (L—5 W—8)
Greenish-gray above, dingy yellow
faintly streaked with gray below;
grayish head with faint whitish eye stripe; orange crown visible on some birds at close range. *Voice:* Song—a weak, fading trill; call—a strong "cheet." *Similar Species:* See Tennessee Warbler. Immatures of some Yellow Warblers are similar but have yellow (not gray) under-tail lining. *Habitat:* Riparian thickets, thorn forest. *Abundance and Distribution:* Uncommon resident* in the lowlands and foothills of southern California and Nevada; summer resident* (Apr.–Sep.) in highlands of the Sierras and mountains of western New Mexico and eastern Arizona (White, Chuska, Pinal, and Pinaleno ranges); winter resident (Sep.–Mar.) in desert riparian areas of southeastern California and southern Arizona; transient (Apr., Sep.) throughout. *Where to Find:* Signal Peak Road, Pinos Altos Mountains, New Mexico; Oak Canyon Nature Center, Santa Ana Mountains, California; Mittry Lake, Arizona (winter). *Range:* Breeds in western and northern North America; winters from the southern United States, Mexico, Belize, and Guatemala.

360. Nashville Warbler

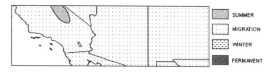

Vermivora ruficapilla (L—4 W—7)
Olive above, yellow below; gray head;
white eyering; rufous cap. *Female:*
Dingier; lacks reddish cap. *Voice:* Song—"Tsepit tsepit tsepit" followed by a trilled "tseeeeeeeeeeee"; call—"tsip." *Habitat:* Deciduous oak and maple forest, ponderosa pine, white fir (breeding); riparian, oak, and thorn forest (migration and winter). *Abundance and Distribution:* Common summer resident* (Apr.–Aug.) on the west slope of the Sierra Nevada of southern California (six thousand to eight thousand feet) south to the Greenhorn Mountains of Kern County; uncommon to rare transient (Apr., Sep.) throughout; rare in winter along the California coastal lowlands. *Where to Find:* Tanque Verde Wash, Santa Catalina Mountains, Arizona; Louis Rubidoux Nature Center, California; Sandia Park Pond, New Mexico. *Range:* Breeds across extreme north-central and northeastern United States, south-central and southeastern Canada, and northwestern United States; winters from south Texas, Mexico, and Central America to Honduras.

361. Virginia's Warbler

Vermivora virginiae (L—5 W—8)

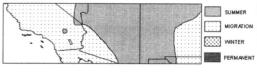

Gray above, white below with yellow breast; greeenish-yellow rump and under-tail coverts; rufous crown patch; white eyering. *Female:* Dingier breast; no rufous crown. *Habits:* Wags tail while foraging. *Voice:* Song—"tsip tsip tsip tsip tsip tsweet tsweet," rising inflection at the end; call—"tsip." *Similar Species:* Yellow on breast and under-tail coverts separate this species from Lucy's Warbler, which has grayish breast and under-tail coverts; also Lucy's Warbler has rufous rump (greenish in Virginia's). *Habitat:* Montane riparian thickets, desert scrub, oak-pinyon-juniper. *Abundance and Distribution:* Common to rare summer resident* (Mar.–Aug.) in transition and Canadian zones of Arizona (east to northwest), southern Nevada, western New Mexico, and Clark Mountain, New York, and northeastern portion of the San Bernardino Mountains of southern California; common to rare transient (Mar., Aug.–Sep.) throughout. *Where to Find:* Mount Lemmon, Arizona; Clark Mountain, California; Mount Charleston, Nevada; Coal Mine Campground, Cibola National Forest, New Mexico. *Range:* Breeds in the southwestern United States; winters in western Mexico.

362. Lucy's Warbler

Vermivora luciae (L—4 W—7)

Gray above, white below; white eyering and cheek; rufous crown patch and rump. *Voice:* Song—"tsweeta tsweeta tsweeta chee chee chee chee" and variations. *Similar Species:* See Virginia's Warbler. *Habitat:* Arid scrub and desert riparian thickets (mesquite, cottonwood, sycamore). *Abundance and Distribution:* Uncommon to rare and local summer resident* (Mar.–Aug.) along the Colorado River and other desert canyons in southern California; common to uncommon summer resident* (Mar.–Aug.) in lower and upper Sonoran zones of Arizona (most of state except northeast quarter), southern Nevada, and southwestern New Mexico. *Where to Find:* Organ Pipe Cactus National Monument, Arizona; Imperial Dam, California; Big Morongo Canyon Preserve, California; Redrock Wildlife Area, Gila River, New Mexico; Sunset Park, Las Vegas, Nevada. *Range:* Breeds in the southwestern United States and northwestern Mexico; winters in western Mexico.

363. Yellow Warbler

Dendroica petechia (L—5 W—8)

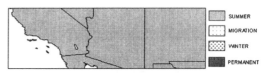

Yellow throughout, somewhat dingier on the back; yellow tail spots. Male variably streaked below with reddish. *Voice:* Song—"tseet tseet tseet tsitsitsi tseet" (Sweet, sweet, sweet, I'm so sweet"); call—"chip." *Similar Species:* Some immature Yellow Warblers are quite greenish, resembling immature Orange-crowned Warblers, but they have yellow (not gray) under-tail lining. *Habitat:* Riparian thickets of cottonwood, sycamore, and willow; hedgerows. *Abundance and Distribution:* Common transient and common to rare summer resident* (Apr.–Sep.) throughout; rare to casual winter resident in southern California. *Where to Find:* Woodlands bordering streams and rivers; Hassayampa River Preserve, Arizona; Redrock Wildlife Area, New Mexico; Santa Maria River mouth, California. *Range:* Breeds across most of North America. Winters from extreme southern United States through Mexico and Central America to northern and central South America. Resident races in mangroves of West Indies, Central and South America.

364. Yellow-rumped Warbler

Dendroica coronata (L—5 W—8)

Blue-gray above; black breast and sides; white belly; yellow cap, rump

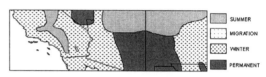

and shoulder patch; white wing patch. Breeding males of the eastern and northern race have white throat; western race has yellow throat. *Female:* Brownish above, dingy below with faint streaking; yellow rump. *Voice:* Song—a weak trill, rising at the end "tsitsitsitsitsitsee." "Chit" call note often given in flight. *Habitat:* Breeds in a variety of montane coniferous forest (four thousand to ten thousand feet); most types of trees and scrub during migration; riparian groves in winter. *Abundance and Distribution:* Common summer resident* (Apr.–Oct.) in highlands of southern California, southern Nevada, Arizona (except southwest), and New Mexico; common transient (Mar.–Apr., Oct.–Nov.) throughout; winter resident (Nov.–Mar.) in lowlands and mid-elevations of southern California, southern Arizona, and southern New Mexico. *Where to Find:* Roosevelt Lake Wildlife Area, Arizona (breeding); Hyde Memorial State Park, New Mexico (breeding); Oak Canyon Nature Center, Santa Ana Mountains, California (winter). *Range:* Breeds across northern boreal North America and in mountains of the west south to southern Mexico; winters from central and southern United States to Panama and the West Indies.

365. Black-throated Gray Warbler

Dendroica nigrescens (L—5 W—8)

Dark gray above, whitish below with white wing bars; distinct facial pat-

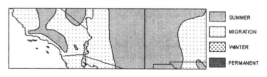

tern of black crown, white eye stripe, black eyeline and ear stripe, white chin stripe, and yellow loral spot. Male has black throat and breast (whitish in female). *Voice:* Song—"tseta tseta tseta tseeet cha" with rising inflection on penultimate syllable. *Similar Species:* Female Cerulean Warbler has bluish cap and buffy (not gray) cheek patch. *Habitat:* Arid pinyon, oak, and juniper scrub. *Abundance and Distribution:* Uncommon summer resident* (Apr.–Aug.) in high upper Sonoran or transition zones (three thousand to seven thousand feet) of southern California, southern Nevada, Arizona (southeast to northwest), and New Mexico; uncommon transient (Mar.–Apr., Aug.–Sep.) throughout; a few individuals winter in the southern portion of the region, especially at Salton Sea, the lower Colorado River valley, and Bosque del Apache. *Where to Find:* Sycamore Canyon, Arizona; High Rolls Country Store, Alamogordo, New Mexico; Greenspot Picnic Ground, San Bernardino Mountains, California; Red Rock Canyon National Conservation Area, Nevada. *Range:* Breeds western United States and northwestern Mexico; winters from southwestern United States to southern Mexico.

366. Black-throated Green Warbler
Dendroica virens (L—5 W—8)
Green above; black bib; green crown; golden face; white belly. *Female:* Usu-

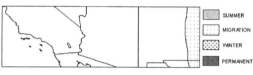

ally has some gray or black across breast. *Voice:* Song—a lazy, insect-like "zee zee zee zoo zee" or "zoo zee zeezee zoo"; call—"chip." *Similar Species:* The female Black-throated Green Warbler has a greenish back, not gray as in Hermit Warbler. *Habitat:* Coniferous and mixed forest; riparian and oak woodland; thorn forest. *Abundance and Distribution:* Rare fall transient (Sep.–Oct.) in eastern New Mexico; casual transient elsewhere in region. *Range:* Breeds across central and southern Canada and north-central and northern United States, also south in the Appalachians and along the coastal plain to Georgia; winters from south Texas and south Florida through Mexico and Central America to Panama; West Indies.

367. Townsend's Warbler
Dendroica townsendi (L—5 W—8)
Greenish above, yellow breast; white wing bars and belly; distinct facial

pattern of black crown, yellow eye stripe, black eyeline and ear stripe, yellow chin stripe. Male has black throat (yellow in female). *Voice:* Song—a high-pitched, buzzy "zee zee zee tseetsee"; call—"tseet." *Similar Species:* Black-throated Green Warbler male lacks black ear patch. Female Black-throated Greens lack the heavy, dark face patch and yellow throat and breast of female Townsend's. *Habitat:* Pine and oak forest. *Abundance and Distribution:* Uncommon to rare transient (Sep.–Oct., Apr.–May) throughout, more numerous in highlands; uncommon to rare winter resident (Oct.–Apr.) in the coastal lowlands of southern California south to Santa Barbara; rare to casual in winter in southeastern Arizona. *Where to Find:* Santa Barbara Museum of Natural History, California; Mount Charleston, Nevada;

Water Canyon Campground, New Mexico; Ramsey Vista Campground, Huachuca Mountains, Arizona. *Range:* Breeds in mountains of northwestern North America from Alaska to Oregon and Wyoming; winters in western coastal regions of the western United States and the highlands of Mexico and Central America south to Costa Rica.

368. Hermit Warbler

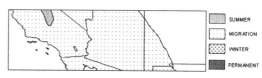

Dendroica occidentalis (L—5 W—8)
Gray above, white below; yellow head
with black throat and nape. *Female:*
Dark green nape and crown; throat grayish or white. *Voice:* Song—a high pitched "tseetl tseetl tseetl tseee"; call—"tseet." *Similar Species:* Female Hermit has gray back (not greenish as in Black-throated Green); lacks yellow in front of female Townsend's. *Habitat:* Fir, pine, pine-oak, juniper. *Abundance and Distribution:* Common summer resident* (May–Aug.) in the highlands (four thousand to eight thousand feet) of the western Sierra Nevada south to Tulare County, California; rare transient (Apr.–May, Aug.–Sep.) in southern California and southern Nevada; uncommon to rare transient in highlands of Arizona; rare transient (fall) in southwestern New Mexico; a few birds winter in southern California. *Where to Find:* Generals Highway, Sequoia National Park, California. *Range:* Breeds in coastal ranges and Sierra Nevada of the western United States; winters in the highlands of Mexico and Central America south to Nicaragua.

369. Grace's Warbler

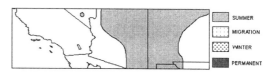

Dendroica graciae (L—5 W—8)
Dark gray above, white below with
yellow bib; black lores; gray cheek;
yellow eye stripe; black streaks on sides. *Habits:* Forages by creeping along branches, occasionally sallying after insects. *Voice:* Song—a weak trill; two or three introductory notes followed by a trill; call—"snip." *Habitat:* Ponderosa and other pines; pine-oak. *Abundance and Distribution:* Common summer resident* (Apr.–Sep.) in transition zone highlands (five thousand to seven thousand feet) of Arizona and New Mexico. *Where to Find:* North Rim, Grand Canyon, Arizona; Cave Creek Canyon, Arizona; Canjilon Mountain, Sangre de Cristo Mountains, New Mexico; Pine Tree Trail, Cox Ranch Visitors' Center, Las Cruces, New Mexico. *Range:* Breeds in mountains of the southwestern United States; also in highlands and lowland pine savanna of Mexico and Central America south to Nicaragua; winters in breeding range from central Mexico southward.

370. Black-and-white Warbler

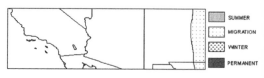

Mniotilta varia (L—5 W—9)
Boldly striped with black and white
above and below. *Female:* Faint gray-
ish streaking below. *Habits:* Clambers up and down tree trunks and branches,
Nuthatch fashion. *Voice:* Song—a weak "wesee wesee wesee"; call—"pit." *Similar
Species:* This is the only species with white median stripe in black cap, and peculiar
trunk-foraging behavior. *Habitat:* Deciduous and mixed forest; riparian and oak
woodlands; thorn forest. *Abundance and Distribution:* Uncommon to rare transient (Apr.–May, Aug.–Sep.) in eastern New Mexico; rare to casual transient elsewhere in the region; few records from northern Arizona; occasional winter records
from southern portions of the area. *Where to Find:* Percha Dam State Park, New
Mexico; Marana Pecan Grove, Arizona. *Range:* Breeds across Canada east of the
mountains and in the eastern half of the United States; winters from extreme southern United States, eastern Mexico and Central America to northern South America;
West Indies.

371. American Redstart

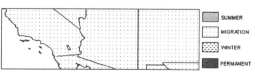

Setophaga ruticilla (L—5 W—9)
Black above and below with brilliant
orange patches on tail, wings, and
sides of breast; white under-tail coverts. *Female:* Grayish brown above, whitish
below with yellow patches on tail, wings and sides of breast. *Immature male:*
Salmon-colored patches on sides of breast. *Habits:* This species catches much of
its prey on the wing in brief sallies. Often fans tail and droops wings while foraging. *Voice:* One individual often will have three or four different songs, even alternating song types from one phrase to the next. Some common phrases are "tsee
tsee tsee tsee tseet," "tsee tsee tsee tsee tsee-o," "teetsa teetsa teeetsa teetsa teet"
(Peterson 1963:227); call—a strong "chip." *Habitat:* Deciduous forest; riparian and
oak woodland; thorn forest. *Abundance and Distribution:* Rare transient (Apr.–
May, Sep.–Oct.) throughout, more numerous in eastern and central New Mexico;
rare to casual in winter in southern portions of the region; casual in summer.
Where to Find: Percha Dam State Park, New Mexico; Marana Pecan Grove, Arizona; Date Palm Grove, Brawley, California. *Range:* Breeds across Canada south of
the arctic region and in the eastern half of the United States except the southeastern coastal plain; winters from central Mexico south to northern South America;
West Indies.

372. Ovenbird

Seiurus aurocapillus (L—6 W—10)
Olive above, white below with heavy,
dark streaks; orange crown stripe

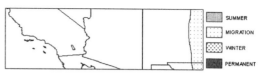

bordered in black; white eyering. *Habits:* Walks on forest floor, flicking leaves and duff while foraging for invertebrates. *Voice:* Song—a loud "teacher teacher teacher teacher." *Similar Species:* Northern and Louisiana Waterthrush have a prominent white or yellowish eye stripe. Also, Ovenbirds do not bob while walking as the waterthrushes do. *Habitat:* Deciduous forest; riparian and oak woodland. *Abundance and Distribution:* Rare transient (Sep., May) in eastern New Mexico, more numerous in fall; rare to casual transient in southern Nevada, and Arizona. *Where to Find:* Artesia Cemetery, New Mexico; Marana Pecan Grove, Arizona. *Range:* Central and eastern Canada and central and eastern United States south to the Atlantic and Gulf coastal plain; winters from southern Florida and southern Mexico south through Central America to northern Venezuela; West Indies.

373. Northern Waterthrush

Seiurus noveboracensis (L—6 W—10)
Brown above, white or yellowish below with dark streaking on throat and

breast; prominent creamy or yellowish eye stripe. *Habits:* Forages on the ground, bobbing as it walks, usually in boggy or wet areas. *Voice:* Song—"chi chi chi chewy chewy will will"; call—"chink". *Similar Species:* Louisiana Waterthrush has clear white throat (not streaked) and buffy flanks. *Habitat:* Swamps, bogs, swales, ponds, rivers, lakes, mangroves, usually near stagnant water. *Abundance and Distribution:* Rare to casual transient (Apr.–May, Aug.–Sep.) in New Mexico, Arizona, south-eastern California (Salton Sea), and southern Nevada. *Where to Find:* Isleta Lakes and Recreation Area, New Mexico; Escapule Wash, San Pedro River, Arizona. *Range:* Breeds in boreal North America south of the Arctic Circle; winters from central Mexico south through Central America to northern South America; Caribbean basin.

374. MacGillivray's Warbler

Oporornis tolmiei (L—5 W—8)
Olive above, yellow below; gray hood
with black on breast; incomplete

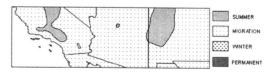

white eyering. *Female:* Brownish-yellow head and partial eyering. *Habits:* Forages low and on the ground. *Voice:* Song—a loud, clear "chewy chewy chewy chewit chewit." *Habitat:* Shrubby undergrowth of spruce-fir, sequoia, and other conifer-ous forests; dense thickets; riparian forest; oak woodlands. *Abundance and Distri-*

bution: Uncommon summer resident* (May–Aug.) in highlands (three thousand to eight thousand feet) of the Sierra Nevada in southern California, White Mountains and San Francisco Mountains of Arizona, and northwestern quarter of New Mexico; uncommon to rare transient (Apr.–May, Aug.–Sep.) throughout. *Where to Find:* Pajarito Mountain Ski Area, New Mexico; Hi Mountain Road, San Luis Obispo, California; Tanque Verde Wash, Santa Catalina Mountains, Arizona. *Range:* Breeds in the western United States and southwestern Canada; winters in the highlands of Mexico and Central America to Panama.

375. Common Yellowthroat

Geothlypis trichas (L—5 W—7)
Olive above, yellow below with black mask. *Female:* Brownish above, bright yellow throat fading to whitish on belly; brownish on sides. *Habits:* Skulks in low, marsh vegetation. *Voice:* Song—"wichity wichity wichit"; call—a harsh "chuk." *Similar Species:* Lack of eyeline, eyering and wing bars plus whitish belly separates female from other warblers. *Habitat:* Marshes, streams, estuaries, wet meadows, riparian areas; reed beds bordering rivers, ponds, and streams. *Abundance and Distribution:* Common but local summer resident* (Mar.–Sep.) throughout except southeastern California and southwestern Arizona; common winter resident in southern California and southern Arizona along the Colorado River valley. *Where to Find:* San Pedro River, Arizona; Sandia Park Pond, New Mexico; Imperial Dam, California. *Range:* Breeds from Canada south throughout the continent to southern United States and in highlands to southern Mexico; winters southern United States to Costa Rica; Bahamas, Greater Antilles.

376. Wilson's Warbler

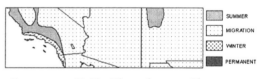

Wilsonia pusilla (L—5 W—7)
Olive above, yellow below with a black cap. *Female:* Often has only a partially black or completely greenish-yellow crown. *Habits:* Flycatches at mid- to upper canopy level, using short, sallying flights. *Voice:* Song—"Chee chee chee chee chipy-chipy-chipy-chipy" (almost a trill); call—a hoarse "ship." *Similar Species:* Female differs from female Yellow Warbler by brownish tail lacking yellow spots. *Habitat:* Montane riparian thickets (willow, alder, aspen, dogwood), thorn forest, oak woodlands. *Abundance and Distribution:* Uncommon summer resident* (May–Aug.) in highlands (four thousand to eight thousand feet) of the Sierra Nevada, rare to casual summer resident* in foothills of southern California; uncommon summer resident in the San Juan and Sangre de Cristo Mountains of northern New Mexico; common to uncommon transient (Apr.–May, Aug.–Sep.)

throughout; rare to casual in winter in the lowland coastal region of southern California (north to Ventura County). *Where to Find:* Hyde Memorial State Park, New Mexico (breeding); Louis Rubidoux Nature Center, California (transient); Bear Canyon Picnic Area, Mount Lemmon, Arizona (transient). *Range:* Breeds in boreal regions of northern and western North America; winters from southern California and Texas south through low to mid-elevations of Mexico and Central America to Panama.

377. Red-faced Warbler
Cardellina rubrifrons (L—5 W—8)
Gray above; red face and breast; black crown and ear; white nape, rump,

and belly. *Immature:* Similar but paler. *Habits:* Often feeds by hanging at the tips of branches, in chickadee fashion. *Voice:* A high, thin series of "tseeit"s. *Habitat:* Montane fir, spruce, pine, and oak forests. *Abundance and Distribution:* Common to uncommon summer resident* of the transition and boreal zones of southeastern to central Arizona and the southwestern quarter of New Mexico. *Where to Find:* Pinery Canyon, Arizona; Rustler Park, Arizona; Langmuir Laboratory, New Mexico. *Range:* Breeds from Arizona south to west-central Mexico; winters in highlands from western Mexico to Honduras.

378. Painted Redstart
Myioborus pictus (L—6 W—9)
Black back, head and breast; red belly; white wing patch and outer tail feath-

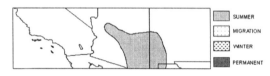

ers. *Immature:* Paler with blackish belly. *Habits:* Flicks wings and fans tail while foraging. *Voice:* Song—a warbled "wetew-wetew-wetew-weet"; call—a clear "peep." *Habitat:* Oak, pine-oak, juniper, pinyon. *Abundance and Distribution:* Common summer resident* (Apr.–Sep.) of the upper Sonoran zone of central and southeastern Arizona, and southwestern quarter of New Mexico; rare to casual in extreme southeastern Arizona in winter. *Where to Find:* Cherry Creek Campground, Pinos Altos Mountains, New Mexico; Mount Lemmon, Arizona; Madera Canyon, Arizona. *Range:* Breeds from southwestern United States and mountains of western Mexico to Nicaragua; winters in southern portion of breeding range.

379. Yellow-breasted Chat
Icteria virens (L—7 W—10)
A nearly thrush-sized warbler; brown above; yellow throat and breast; white

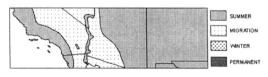

belly and under-tail coverts; white eyering and supraloral stripe; lores black or grayish. *Habits:* Very shy; sings in flight. *Voice:* A varied series of clear whistles and harsh, scolding "chak"s and "jeer"s. *Habitat:* Dense thickets, brushy pastures, riparian and oak forest undergrowth, thorn forest. *Abundance and Distribution:* Uncommon to rare and local summer resident* (Apr.–Aug.) in upper and lower Sonoran zones of northern and southeastern Arizona and New Mexico, Colorado River valley, Salton Sea, and coastal lowlands and foothills of southwestern California; transient (Apr.–May, Sep.–Oct.) throughout. *Where to Find:* Big Morongo Canyon Preserve, California; San Pedro Riparian National Conservation Area, Arizona; Isleta Lakes and Recreation Area, New Mexico. *Range:* Breeds in scattered regions nearly throughout the United States and southern Canada south to central Mexico; winters from central Mexico to Panama.

Family Thraupidae

Tanagers

Most tanagers are Neotropical in distribution. Only four species occur in the United States, three of which are found regularly in the Southwest. Males are predominantly red (Hepatic Tanager, Summer Tanager, Scarlet Tanager) or yellow and red (Western Tanager). Females are brownish or greenish.

380. Hepatic Tanager

Piranga flava (L—8 W—13)

Red with gray cheek patch and grayish tinge on back and flanks. *Female*

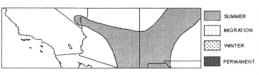

SUMMER
MIGRATION
WINTER
PERMANENT

and Immature male: Grayish-brown above, yellowish below with gray cheek patch and yellowish crown. *Voice:* Song—rough, robin-like phrases; call—"tshup." *Similar Species:* Summer Tanager lacks contrasting cheek patch and usually (during breeding season) has a brownish bill (black in Hepatic). *Habitat:* Montane oak, pine-oak, pine, and pinyon-juniper forest. *Abundance and Distribution:* Uncommon summer resident* (Apr.–Sep.) in southern Nevada, central and southeastern Arizona, western and southeastern New Mexico. *Where to Find:* Little Walnut Picnic Area, Silver City, New Mexico; Madera Canyon, Arizona; South Fork, Cave Creek Canyon, Arizona; Pine Tree Trail, Cox Ranch Visitors' Center, New Mexico. *Range:* Breeds from the southwestern United States through the mountains of Mexico, Central America, and South America to northern Argentina; winters in all but the northernmost parts of its range.

381. Summer Tanager

Piranga rubra (L—8 W—13)

Red. *Female and Immature Male:*
Tawny brown above, more yellowish

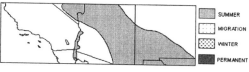

below; second-year males and some females are blotched with red. *Voice:* Song—slurred, robin-like phrases; call—"pit-a-chuk." *Similar Species:* See Hepatic Tanager. *Habitat:* Broadleaf riparian stands (willow, cottonwood, sycamore, walnut) of the lower Sonoran zone. *Abundance and Distribution:* Uncommon to rare summer resident* (Apr.–Sep.) along the Colorado River and locally elsewhere in southern Nevada, Arizona (except southwest and northeast), and central and southern New Mexico. *Where to Find:* Rattlesnake Springs, New Mexico; Bonita Creek, Gila Box Riparian National Conservation Area, Arizona; Big Morongo Canyon Preserve, California. *Range:* Breeds across eastern and southern portions of the United States and northern Mexico; winters from southern Mexico through Central America to northern South America.

382. Western Tanager

Piranga ludoviciana (L—8 W—13)
Red head; yellow below with yellow
rump, neck and shoulder; black back,

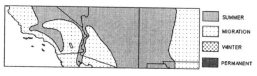

wings and tail with two white wing bars; winter male lacks red on head. *Female and Immature male:* Similar to winter male but duller. *Voice:* Song—hoarse and robin-like with pauses between phrases; call—"chit-it" or "chit-a-chit." *Similar Species:* Female resembles some female orioles but has heavy tanager bill; yellowish rump and nape contrast with olive back. *Habitat:* Open montane fir, pine, and pine-oak forest; arid thorn and riparian forest during migration. *Abundance and Distribution:* Common to uncommon summer resident* in mountains and foothills (three thousand to nine thousand feet) of southern Califonia, along the Colorado River, southern Nevada, northern and eastern Arizona, and western and central New Mexico; common to uncommon transient (Apr.–May, Aug.–Sep.) nearly throughout. *Where to Find:* Pine Cove Road, San Jacinto Mountains, California; Cottonwood Campground, New Mexico; Petrified Forest Drive, Arizona; Mount Charleston, Nevada. *Range:* Breeds in the mountains of western North America from Alaska to northwestern Mexico; winters from central Mexico through Central America to Costa Rica.

Family Emberizidae
Cardinals, Buntings, New World Grosbeaks, and Sparrows
Small to medium-sized birds with conical bills. The buntings, cardinals, and grosbeaks have brightly colored males, while the sparrows generally are cryptically colored in various shades and patterns of browns and grays.

383. Green-tailed Towhee

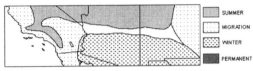

Pipilo chlorurus (L—7 W—10)
Green above, gray below with rufous crown and white throat; long,
rounded tail. *Habits:* Like other towhees, this bird spends most of its time on the ground using backward kick-hops to scatter duff and expose seeds and invertebrate prey. *Voice:* Song—opens with a few melodic whistles followed by a dry trill; calls—"chink," and a nasal "eyew." *Habitat:* Montane thickets, sagebrush, and low deciduous scrub; thorn forest; brushy pastures; hedgerows. *Abundance and Distribution:* Uncommon summer resident* (May–Aug.) in highlands of southern California, southern Nevada, northern Arizona, and northern New Mexico; uncommon transient (Apr.–May, Aug.–Sep.) throughout; uncommon winter resident (Sep.–Apr.) in southern Arizona and New Mexico; rare to casual in southern California. *Where to Find:* Mount Pinos Road, California (breeding); Organ Pipe Cactus National Monument, Arizona (winter); Sabino Canyon Recreation Area, Santa Catalina Mountains, Arizona (winter); Hyde Memorial State Park, New Mexico (breeding). *Range:* Breeds in the western United States, mostly in montane regions; winters from southern California, southern Arizona, southern New Mexico and Texas south to central Mexico.

384. Spotted Towhee

Pipilo maculatus (L—8 W—11)
Red eye; black head, breast and back; rufous sides; white belly; tail black
and rounded with white corners; white spotting on back and white wing bars in both sexes. *Female:* Patterned like male, but with brown or gray head, breast, and back. *Habits:* See Green-tailed Towhee. *Voice:* Song—"tsip tsip tsip tseeee" and variations in western races; call—"chewink," "shrrinnk." *Habitat:* Undergrowth and thickets of deciduous woodlands; riparian, oak and thorn forest. *Abundance and Distribution:* Common permanent resident* in lowlands throughout except in southeastern California, southwestern Arizona, and eastern New Mexico; summer resident* (Apr.–Sep.) at mid-elevations (four thousand to eight thousand feet); winter resident (Sep.–Apr.) in southeastern California, southwestern Arizona, and

eastern New Mexico. *Where to Find:* Santa Barbara Museum of Natural History grounds in California; Mormon Lake, Arizona; Sandia Park, New Mexico; Desert National Wildlife Range, Nevada. *Range:* Breeds from extreme southern Canada across the United States (except most of Texas) and in the highlands of Mexico and Guatemala; winters from central and southern United States to Mexico and Guatemala.

385. Canyon Towhee

Pipilo fuscus (L—9 W—12)

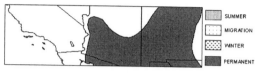

Grayish-brown above, paler below; rusty crown; buffy throat with brown necklace across breast and dark brown central breast spot; rusty under-tail coverts; long, rounded tail. *Voice:* Song—an accelerating series of "chipi"s ending in a dry trill; call—"chap." *Similar Species:* The Canyon Towhee has a rufous cap (not brown as in the California Towhee). Abert's Towhee has a black face. *Habitat:* Arid scrub. *Abundance and Distribution:* Common resident* of Arizona (except northern highlands) and New Mexico (except eastern plains). *Where to Find:* Bandelier National Monument, New Mexico; Bill Evans Lake, New Mexico; Arizona Sonora Desert Museum, Tucson, Arizona. *Range:* Resident from the southwestern United States (Arizona to Texas) south to central Mexico.

386. California Towhee

Pipilo crissalis (L—9 W—12)

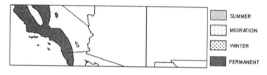

Brown above, paler below with tawny throat and chestnut under-tail coverts; broken brown necklace. Formerly considered to be a subspecies of *P. fuscus*. *Voice:* Call—a metallic "cheek"; song—a series of "tsik" notes of increasing frequency and ending in a trill. *Similar Species:* See Canyon Towhee. *Habitat:* Chaparral, shrubby hillsides, scrub, lawns, gardens. *Abundance and Distribution:* Common resident* in southern California west of the Sierra Nevada and deserts of the southeast; up to four thousand feet in the western foothills of the Sierra Nevada. *Where to Find:* El Dorado Nature Center, Long Beach; Tapia County Park, Santa Monica Mountains; Oak Canyon Nature Center, Santa Ana Mountains. *Range:* Resident from southwestern Oregon through western California south to southern Baja California.

387. Abert's Towhee

Pipilo aberti (L—9 W—11)

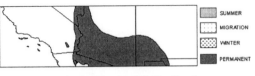

Brown above, paler below with black face; rufous under-tail coverts; long, rounded tail. *Voice:* Song—two trills at different pitches; call—"eek." *Similar Species:* Canyon Towhee is grayer, has central breast spot and lacks black face. *Habitat:* Desert riparian scrub (willow, cottonwood, mesquite). *Abundance and Distribution:* Common resident* of riparian habitats of the lower Sonoran zone of southeastern California (Salton Sea, Colorado River valley), Arizona (except northeast), and southwestern New Mexico. *Where to Find:* Imperial Dam, California; Mittry Lake, Arizona; San Pedro House, Arizona; Redrock Wildlife Area, Gila River, New Mexico. *Range:* Southern California, southern Nevada, Arizona, southwestern New Mexico, and northwestern Mexico.

388. Rufous-winged Sparrow

Aimophila carpalis (L—6 W—8)

Gray crown streaked with reddish-brown; gray face with two black mustache marks and reddish-brown line through eye; dark bill; gray back streaked with black; brown wings with rufous shoulder patch, two white wing bards, and rufous lesser wing coverts; pale gray below; long, brown, rounded tail. *Voice:* Song— A variable series of "tsip"s followed by a trill; call—"tseet." *Habitat:* Mixed bunch grass, thorn scrub, cholla cactus. *Abundance and Distribution:* Common to uncommon resident* of the lower Sonoran zone of extreme south-central Arizona; rare winter resident further west. *Where to Find:* Florida Wash; San Xavier Mission; Saguaro National Park. *Range:* Resident from south-central Arizona to southern Sinaloa, Mexico.

389. Cassin's Sparrow

Aimophila cassinii (L—6 W—8)

Grayish streaked with brown above, dirty white below; white corners on rounded tail. *Voice:* Song—a tinkling trill followed by two notes, "tse-tse-tse-tse-tse chik cheek"—usually given in a flight display. *Similar Species:* Cassin's Sparrow has white corners at tip of tail; also Cassin's Sparrow song starts with trill and ends with lone whistle notes. Botteri's Sparrow lacks white at tips of tail, and song ends in a trill rather than in two lone whistles. *Habitat:* Thorn forest, brushy fields, arid grasslands, and scrub. *Abundance and Distribution:* Uncommon summer resident* (Apr.–Aug.) in eastern New Mexico; uncommon to rare transient (July–Sep.) in southeastern Arizona and southern New Mexico; rare winter resident in extreme southern New Mexico, casual in southeastern Arizona. *Where to Find:* NM 14 at San Marcos, New Mexico (breeding); Clayton Municipal Airport, New Mexico (breeding); Garden Canyon, Fort Huachuca, Arizona. *Range:* Breeds in dry grasslands of the Great Plains from Colorado and Nebraska south to northern and central Mexico; winter distribution is poorly known, but apparently the bird migrates from northern portion of its range.

390. Botteri's Sparrow

Aimophila botterii (L—6 W—9)
Gray streaked with brown above; dirty white below; crown gray, finely streaked with brown. *Voice:* Song—one or two introductory "tsip" notes followed by an accelerating trill; call—a dry "tik." *Similar Species:* Cassin's Sparrow has white corners at tip of tail; also Cassin's Sparrow song starts with trill and ends with lone whistle notes. *Habitat:* Tall sacaton grass, cord grass, savanna, mesquite grasslands, pastures. *Abundance and Distribution:* Uncommon to rare and local resident* in southeastern Arizona. *Where to Find:* San Xavier Mission; Marana Pecan Grove; Patagonia-Sonoita Creek Preserve. *Range:* Southeastern Arizona and south Texas south locally through Mexico and Central America to northwestern Costa Rica; northern populations may be migratory although non-singing birds are extremely difficult to locate and identify. As Phillips et al. (1964:200) state, "Its winter range is almost wholly a matter of conjecture!"

391. Rufous-crowned Sparrow

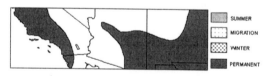

Aimophila ruficeps (L—6 W—8)
Grayish streaked with brown above, dirty white below; rusty crown and dark malar stripe ("whisker"); whitish supraloral stripe. *Habits:* Bold for a sparrow. *Voice:* Song—a trill; call—characteristic "teer teer teer." *Similar Species:* Other rufous-capped sparrows lack black whisker. *Habitat:* Rocky, arid scrub; oak-juniper and pine-oak. *Abundance and Distribution:* Common to uncommon and local resident* of the foothill (to three thousand feet) canyon lands and hillsides of southern California, central and southeastern Arizona, and New Mexico (except northwest and north-central mountains). *Where to Find:* Montaña de Oro State Park, California; Catalina State Park, Arizona; Oliver Lee Memorial State Park, New Mexico. *Range:* Southwestern and south-central United States to southern Mexico, apparently migratory in northeastern portions of range.

392. Five-striped Sparrow
Aimophila quinquestriata
(L—6 W—10)
Dark, reddish-brown above; grayish

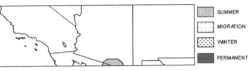

sides with white throat and belly; black malar stripe; gray cheek outlined in white; dark cap; black central breast spot; dark tail. *Habits:* Males sing from prominent shrubs such as ocotillo or mesquite. *Voice:* Song—"tsip tsip tsee tseep," "tsip tsip tsip tsee tsee tsee" or similar variations of a brief introductory series of chips followed by a second series higher or lower in pitch than the first. *Similar Species:* Immature Black-throated Sparrow has a mottled back, white outer tail feathers, and lacks black central breast spot. *Habitat:* Dense desert scrub on rocky canyon slopes. *Abundance and Distribution:* This species is a rare and local summer resident* (May–Sep.) in southeastern Arizona; may be present in winter as well, but difficult to locate because of secretive habits. *Where to Find:* Sycamore Canyon; California Gulch; Sonoita Creek. *Range:* Breeds from southeastern Arizona south through the mountains of western Mexico to Jalisco; withdraws from northern parts of the breeding range in winter.

393. American Tree Sparrow
Spizella arborea (L—6 W—9)
Streaked brownish above; dingy white
below with dark breast spot; rufous

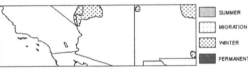

crown; two white wing bars. *Voice:* Song—a rapid, high-pitched series of notes "tse tse tse tsetl tse" and similar variations; call—"tsetl-de." *Similar Species:* This is the only rufous-capped sparrow with a dark spot on an unstreaked breast. *Habitat:* Open, shrubby areas, weedy fields, overgrown pastures, prairies. *Abundance and Distribution:* Uncommon to rare winter resident in the Colorado River valley of Nevada and northern Arizona, north-central Arizona, and locally in northwestern, northeastern, and southeastern New Mexico. *Where to Find:* Maxwell National Wildlife Refuge, New Mexico; Jackson Lake Refuge, New Mexico; Lake Mead National Recreation Area, Nevada/Arizona. *Range:* Breeds in bog, tundra, and willow thickets of northern North America; winters in southern Canada, northern and central United States

394. Chipping Sparrow
Spizella passerina (L—5 W—8)
A small sparrow, streaked rusty
brown above, dingy white below with

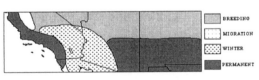

two white wing bars; rufous cap (somewhat streaked in winter); white eyebrow; black eyeline. *Immature:* Streaked crown; gray or buffy eyebrow; brown cheek patch. *Voice:* Song—a rapid, metallic trill; call—"tsip." *Similar Species:* Adult facial pattern is distinctive; immature is similar to Clay-colored Sparrow, but has grayish rather than buffy rump. *Habitat:* Open ponderosa and other pine forests; pine-oak and oak woodlands; orchards, parks, suburbs, and cemeteries with scattered coniferous trees. *Abundance and Distribution:* Uncommon summer resident* (Apr.–Oct.) in the highlands (three thousand to nine thousand feet) of southern California, southern Nevada, northern and eastern Arizona, and New Mexico; transient (Mar.–Apr., Sep.–Oct.) throughout; winters (Oct.–Apr.) in lowlands of southern California, southern Arizona, and southern New Mexico. *Where to Find:* Chilao Recreation Area, San Gabriel Mountains, California (breeding); Petrified Forest Drive, Arizona (breeding); Lake Roberts, New Mexico (breeding); Mount Charleston, Nevada. *Range:* Breeds over most of North America south of the tundra, south though Mexico and Central America to Nicaragua; winters along coast and in southern portions of the breeding range.

395. Clay-colored Sparrow

Spizella pallida (L—5 W—8)
Streaked brown above, buffy below;
streaked crown with central gray
stripe; grayish eyebrow; buffy cheek patch outlined in dark brown; gray nape; two white wing bars. *Voice:* Song—a buzzy "zee zee zee," the number and speed of the zees varies; call—"sip." *Similar Species:* The immature Clay-colored Sparrow has a buffy rump rather than the grayish rump seen in the immature Chipping Sparrow. *Habitat:* Grasslands, savanna, dry thorn forest, brushy pastures. *Abundance and Distribution:* Uncommon to rare transient (Apr., Sep.) in eastern New Mexico. *Where to Find:* Perico Creek, New Mexico; Grasslands Turf Ranch, New Mexico. *Range:* Breeds from central Canada to the north-central United States; winters from Texas south through the highlands of central Mexico to Guatemala.

396. Brewer's Sparrow

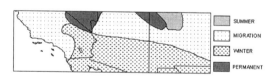

Spizella breweri (L—6 W—8)
Streaked brownish above, buff below;
crown buffy, finely streaked with dark
brown; buffy eyebrow; white eyering; tawny cheek patch; buffy rump; two buffy wing bars. *Voice:* Song—trills at different pitches; call—"chip." *Similar Species:* White eyering and finely streaked crown (no central stripe) separate this desert species from the Clay-colored Sparrow and immature Chipping Sparrow. *Habitat:* Creosote bush (*Larea*) deserts, arid scrub, dry thorn forest, sagebrush (*Artemesia*). *Abundance and Distribution:* Common resident* in dry montane regions (six thousand to nine thousand feet) southeastern California, southern Nevada, northeastern Arizona, and northwestern New Mexico; common to uncommon summer resi-

dent* (Apr.–Oct.) in north-central New Mexico; uncommon to rare winter resident (Sep.–Apr.) in lowland desert regions of southern California, southern Arizona, and southern New Mexico; common to rare or casual transient (Apr.–May, Sep.–Oct.) elsewhere. *Where to Find:* Dulce Lake, New Mexico (breeding); Valle Vista Campground, Mount Pinos, California (breeding); Tanque Verde Wash, Santa Catalina Mountains, Arizona (winter). *Range:* Breeds in desert regions of western North America; winters in the southwestern United States to central Mexico.

397. Field Sparrow

Spizella pusilla (L—6 W—8)

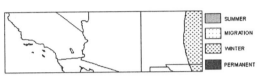

Pink bill; streaked brown above, buff below; crown with gray central stripe bordered by rusty stripes; two white wing bars. *Voice:* Song—a series of "tew"s, beginning slowly and accelerating to a trill; call—"tsee." *Similar Species:* No other plain-breasted sparrow has pink bill. *Habitat:* Savanna, old fields, brushy pastures, thorn scrub. *Abundance and Distribution:* Uncommon to rare transient and winter resident (Oct.–Apr.) in eastern plains of New Mexico. *Where to Find:* Conchas Lake; Clayton. *Range:* Breeds across the eastern half of the United States and southeastern Canada; winters in the southern half of the breeding range and into Florida, south Texas, New Mexico, and northeastern Mexico.

398. Black-chinned Sparrow

Spizella atrogularis (L—6 W—8)

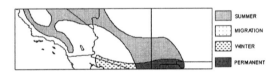

Black face and throat; pink bill; gray head, breast, belly and rump; streaked brown back. *Female and Immature male:* Black face nearly or completely lacking. *Voice:* Song—a series of "tsweet"s accelerating into a trill; call—"sip." *Similar Species:* "Gray-headed" form of the Dark-eyed Junco has white outer tail feathers (dark in Black-chinned Sparrow), unstreaked back and gray (not brown) wings. *Habitat:* Arid slopes covered with tall, dense thorn forest; desert scrub. *Abundance and Distribution:* Uncommon to rare and local summer resident* (May–Aug.) in the foothills of southern California, southern Nevada, southeastern to northwestern Arizona, and southern New Mexico; uncommon winter resident (Sep.–Apr.) in southern Arizona and southern New Mexico. *Where to Find:* Red Rock Canyon National Conservation Area, Nevada; French Joe Canyon, Whetstone Mountains, Arizona; Dorothy May Tucker Wildlife Sanctuary, California; Pine Tree Trail, Cox Ranch Visitors' Center, New Mexico. *Range:* Mountains of the southwestern United States to western and central Mexico; northern populations (California, Arizona, New Mexico, Utah) are migratory.

399. Vesper Sparrow

Pooecetes gramineus (L—6 W—10)
Grayish streaked with brown above;
white with brown streaks below;

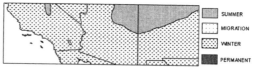

rusty shoulder patch; white outer tail feathers. *Voice:* Song—"chew chew chee chi-chi-chi tititiiti"; call—"chip." *Similar Species:* Savannah Sparrow has yellow lores and brown (not white) outer tail feathers. *Habitat:* Montane sagebrush scrub; short grass prairie; savanna; arid scrub; agricultural fields. *Abundance and Distribution:* Uncommon to rare summer resident* (Apr.–Sep.) in highlands (six thousand to nine thousand feet) of southern California, northeastern Arizona, and northern New Mexico; uncommon transient (Mar.–Apr., Sep.–Oct.) in open areas throughout; uncommon winter resident (Nov.–Mar.) nearly throughout except in highlands. *Where to Find:* Dulce Lake, New Mexico (breeding); Lake Elsinore State Recreation Area, California (winter); San Xavier Mission, Arizona (winter). *Range:* Breeds across much of northern North America to the central United States; winters in the southern United States and Mexico.

400. Lark Sparrow

Chondestes grammacus (L—7 W—11)
Streaked brown above; dingy below;
distinctive chestnut, white and black

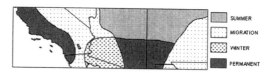

face pattern; white throat; black breast spot; white corners on black, rounded tail. *Voice:* Song—towhee-like "drink-your-teee," often followed by various trills; call—"tseek." *Habitat:* Sagebrush scrub, prairie, savanna, thorn forest, agricultural fields. *Abundance and Distribution:* Uncommon summer resident* (May–Aug.) in upper Sonoran and transition zones of Arizona (except southwest) and New Mexico (except southeast); uncommon to rare and local resident* in southern California (except deserts); uncommon transient (Sep., Apr.) throughout; uncommon winter resident (Oct.–Mar.) in southern Arizona and southwestern New Mexico. *Where to Find:* Otay Lakes, San Diego, California; Ramsey Canyon, Huachuca Mountains, Arizona; Bosque del Apache National Wildlife Refuge, New Mexico (summer). *Range:* Breeds in Canadian prairie states and across most of the United States except eastern, forested regions, south into northern Mexico; winters from the southern United States to southern Mexico.

401. Black-throated Sparrow

Amphispiza bilineata (L—6 W—9)
Dark gray above, whitish below; black
throat and breast; gray and white face

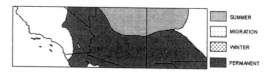

pattern; white outer tail feathers. *Immature:* Similar to adult but breast faintly streaked rather than black. *Voice:* Song—two introductory "weet"s followed by a trill on a different pitch. *Similar Species:* Immatures can resemble Sage Sparrow, but lack black breast spot. *Habitat:* Dry thorn forest, desert scrub, juniper. *Abundance and Distribution:* Common to uncommon resident* in the desert areas of southeastern California, Arizona, Nevada, and southern New Mexico; summer resident* of northeastern Arizona and northern New Mexico (Apr.–Sep.). *Where to Find:* Carlsbad Caverns National Park, New Mexico; Shannon-Broadway Desert, Tucson, Arizona; Cedar Canyon Road, Cima, California; Red Rock Canyon National Conservation Area, Nevada. *Range:* Breeds in the western United States from southern Oregon, Idaho, and Wyoming south to central Mexico; winters in southern half of breeding range.

402. Sage Sparrow

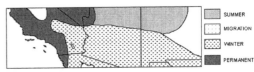

Amphispiza belli (L—6 W—10)
Grayish streaked with brown above; whitish below with black central breast spot; distinctive gray and white face pattern; black tail with white corners. *Habits:* Flicks and cocks tail; often hops to cover with tail cocked rather than fly. *Voice:* Song—a few, clear whistled notes; first ascending, then descending. *Similar Species:* See Black-throated Sparrow. *Habitat:* Desert scrub, thorn forest, sagebrush (*Artemesia*), salt bush, mesquite, creosote bush (*Larea*), arid grasslands. *Abundance and Distribution:* The distribution of this species is complex. Highland populations (five thousand to eight thousand feet) are common to uncommon summer residents* (Apr.–Aug.) in southern California, southern Nevada, northeastern Arizona, and northwestern New Mexico; foothill populations are uncommon to rare and local permanent residents*; highland populations move to lower elevations in the upper Sonoran zone of southern Nevada, Arizona, and New Mexico in winter (Sep.–Apr.); populations from the north winter in the desert regions of southeastern California, southern Arizona, and southern New Mexico. *Where to Find:* Hwy 264, ten miles east of Keams Canyon, Hopi Indian Reservation, Arizona; Red Rock Canyon National Conservation Area, Nevada; Butterbredt Spring Wildlife Sanctuary, California; Dulce Lake, New Mexico. *Range:* Breeds in deserts and arid grasslands of the western United States; winters from the southwestern United States to northwestern Mexico.

403. Lark Bunting

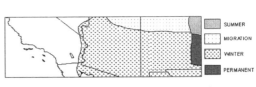

Calamospiza melanocorys
(L—7 W—11)
A stocky, black finch with white wing patches; white undertip of tail. *Female:* Streaked brown and gray above; whitish

below with brown streaks; white or buffy wing patch and under-tail tip. *Winter Male:* Like female but with black chin and heavier breast streaking. *Habits:* Often in flocks. *Voice:* Song—"chik chik chik chik tse-e-e-e-e tik-tik-tik-tik"; variable but usually in this pattern of introductory whistles followed by a trill on a different pitch and a second trill at a third pitch; call—"tsoo wee." *Similar Species:* Immature Harris's Sparrow has pink (not brown) bill and two white wing bars rather than a wing patch. *Habitat:* Shortgrass prairie, desert scrub, agricultural fields. *Abundance and Distribution:* Irregular summer resident* (Apr.–Aug.) in grasslands of eastern New Mexico; winter resident (Oct.–Mar.) in southern New Mexico, southern Arizona, and Colorado River valley; transient (Aug.–Oct., Mar.–Apr.) elsewhere in New Mexico and Arizona. *Where to Find:* NM 26 between Hatch and Deming, New Mexico (winter); Capulin National Monument, New Mexico (breeding); San Pedro House, San Pedro Valley, Arizona (winter); Spitler Cattle Co., Hwy 191, Arizona (winter). *Range:* Breeds in the Great Plains from southern Canada to northern Texas; winters from southern Arizona, New Mexico, and west Texas south to northern Mexico.

404. Savannah Sparrow
Passerculus sandwichensis
(L—6 W—9)

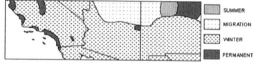

Buff striped with brown above; whitish variously streaked with brown below; yellow or yellowish lores; whitish or yellowish eyebrow; often with dark, central breast spot. Plumage is highly variable in amount of yellow on face and streaking on breast according to subspecies, several of which winter in the region. *Habits:* Often in flocks. *Voice:* Song—a high-pitched, insect-like "tseet tsitit tsee tsoo"; call—"tsee." *Similar Species:* Savannah Sparrow has yellow lores and brown (not white) outer tail feathers; Vesper Sparrow has white outer tail feathers and lacks yellow lores. *Habitat:* Grasslands, savanna, pastures, agricultural fields, coastal marshes. *Abundance and Distribution:* Common to uncommon resident* in the salt marshes of coastal southern California; uncommon and local summer resident* (Apr.–Aug.) in the highland meadows (six thousand to ten thousand feet) on the east slopes of the Sierra Nevada of southern California; also a summer resident (Apr.–Aug.) in central Arizona and northern New Mexico; common to uncommon transient (Apr.–May, Sep.–Oct.) throughout; common to uncommon winter resident nearly throughout except in highlands. *Where to Find:* Carrizo Plain, California (winter); Bosque del Apache National Wildlife Refuge, New Mexico; Arivaca Cienaga, Arizona (winter). *Range:* Breeds throughout northern half of North America south to the central United States; also breeds in the central highlands of Mexico and Guatemala; winters in the coastal and southern United States, Mexico, Guatemala, Belize, and Honduras.

405. Grasshopper Sparrow

Ammodramus savannarum

(L—5 W—8)

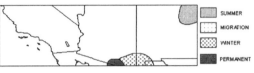

A stubby, short-tailed bird; streaked brown above; creamy-buff below; buffy crown stripe; yellow at bend of wing; yellowish or buffy lores and eyebrow. *Voice:* Song—an insect-like "tsi-pi-ti-zzzzzzzzz"; call—a weak "kitik." *Habitat:* Shortgrass prairie, overgrazed pasture, savanna. *Abundance and Distribution:* Rare resident* in southeastern Arizona; uncommon summer resident* (Apr.–Aug.) in northeastern New Mexico; rare winter resident in southwestern New Mexico. *Where to Find:* Maxwell National Wildlife Refuge, New Mexico; Sonoita Grasslands, Arizona. *Range:* Breeds across the northern and central United States; southern Mexico to northwestern South America; Bahamas, and Cuba; winters in the southern United States, Mexico, and elsewhere within its tropical breeding range.

406. Baird's Sparrow

Ammodramus bairdii

(L—6 W—9)

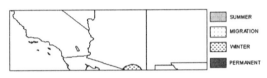

Streaked brownish above; buffy below with brown streaks across the breast forming a necklace; buffy crown and eyebrow stripes; buffy cheek patch; dark malar stripes. *Habits:* Secretive; when flushed, the bird flutters briefly in a zig-zag pattern low over the grass only to dive quickly into the grass again. Difficult to observe. *Voice:* Song—very high pitched "tsit tsitleeeeeeee"; call—"tik." *Similar Species:* The buffy eyeline, crown stripe and narrow black streaks forming a necklace on the breast are distinctive on the rare occasions when a good, clear look can be had of the bird. *Habitat:* Tall, dense grasslands; savanna. *Abundance and Distribution:* Rare winter resident (Nov.–Mar.) in southeastern Arizona. *Where to Find:* Buenos Aires National Wildlife Refuge; Sonoita Grasslands; Palominas Road, upper San Pedro Valley. *Range:* Breeds in the northern Great Plains; winters in Texas, southern Arizona, and northwestern Mexico.

407. Fox Sparrow

Passerella iliaca (L—7 W—11)

Hefty, for a sparrow—nearly thrush-sized; streaked dark or rusty brown above; whitish below with heavy dark or rusty streakings that often coalesce as a blotch on the breast; rusty rump and tail. *Habits:* Forages in towhee fashion, jump-kicking its way through forest duff. *Voice:* Song—whistled, with three- to four-second-long varied phrases; call—"tshek." *Similar Species:* Hermit Thrush has long, thrush bill (not short, conical bill of sparrow), and unstreaked back. *Habitat:* Montane chaparral; thickets and undergrowth of deciduous, mixed, and coniferous wood-lands, and thorn forest. *Abundance and Distribution:* Common summer resident* (Apr.–Aug.) in the highlands (five thousand to nine thousand feet) of southern California; rare transient in southern Nevada, Arizona, and New Mexico; uncom-mon winter resident (Sep.–Apr.) in the lowland and foothill chaparral of south-western California; rare and local winter resident (Sep.–Apr.) in southern Arizona. *Where to Find:* La Cumbre Peak fire lookout, East Camino Cielo Road, California (winter); Dorothy May Tucker Wildlife Sanctuary, California (winter); Arivaca Creek, Arizona (winter). *Range:* Breeds across the northern tier of North America and in the mountains of the west; winters in the coastal and southern United States

408. Song Sparrow

Melospiza melodia (L—6 W—9)
Streaked brown above; whitish below
with heavy brown streaks and central
breast spot; gray eyebrow; dark whisker and post-orbital stripe. *Voice:* Song—"chik sik-i-sik choree k-sik-i-sik," many variations; call—a nasal "chink." *Similar Spe-cies:* Fox Sparrow head is unstriped brownish—lacks light/dark striping of Song Sparrow. *Habitat:* Swamps, inland and coastal marshes, riparian thickets (reeds, sedges), wet meadows, brushy fields. *Abundance and Distribution:* Common but local permanent resident* from sea level to nine thousand feet throughout except southern New Mexico where present only as a winter resident (Oct.–Apr.); high-land populations (six thousand to nine thousand feet) partially migratory sum-mer residents* (Apr.–Oct.). *Where to Find:* Oak Canyon Nature Center, Santa Ana Mountains, California; Rutherford Tract, San Juan River, New Mexico; Patagonia-Sonoita Creek Preserve, Arizona. *Range:* Breeds across temperate and boreal North America; winters in temperate breeding range, southern United States and north-ern Mexico; resident population in central Mexico.

409. Lincoln's Sparrow

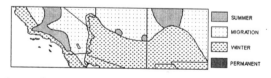

Melospiza lincolnii (L—6 W—8)
Streaked brown above; patterned gray
and brown face; white throat and
belly; distinctive finely streaked, buffy breast band. *Voice:* Song—a series of brief trills at different pitches; call—"shuk." *Similar Species:* Finely streaked, buffy breast band is unique. *Habitat:* Montane, boggy thickets and meadows (willows, sedges) (summer); riparian and oak woodlands, thorn forest, brushy fields, hedgerows (winter). *Abundance and Distribution:* Common to uncommon summer resident* (May–Oct.) in the highlands (four thousand to nine thousand feet) of southern California, central Arizona (White and San Francisco Mountains), and northern

New Mexico; uncommon to rare transient (Apr.–May, Oct.–Nov.) throughout; uncommon to rare winter resident in lowlands, Salton Sea, and Colorado River valley, southern Arizona, and southern New Mexico. *Where to Find:* Big Lake Loop, White Mountains, Arizona (breeding); Louis Rubidoux Nature Center, California (winter); Pajarito Mountain Ski Area, New Mexico (breeding). *Range:* Breeds across the northern tier of North America and in the mountains of the west; winters in the coastal and southern United States south through Mexico and Central America to Honduras.

410. Swamp Sparrow

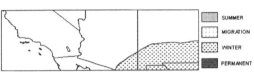

Melospiza georgiana (L—6 W—8)
Rusty crown with central grayish
stripe; gray face; streaked brown
above with rusty wings; whitish throat but otherwise grayish below with tawny flanks—faintly streaked. *Voice:* Song—long "chipy-chipy-chipy" trills at various pitches and speeds; call—"chip." *Similar Species:* Only the Swamp and Rufous-crowned among rusty-crowned sparrows lack white wing bars. Rufous-crowned Sparrow, which lacks rusty wings and faint breast streaking of Swamp Sparrow, lives in desert scrub. *Habitat:* Northern peat bogs (summer); coastal and inland marshes, wet grasslands, brushy pastures (winter). *Abundance and Distribution:* Uncommon winter resident (Nov.–Mar.) in southern New Mexico; rare and local winter resident in southeastern Arizona. *Where to Find:* Bitter Lake National Wildlife Refuge, New Mexico; Carlsbad Caverns National Park, New Mexico; Bosque del Apache Wildlife Refuge, New Mexico. *Range:* Breeds in central and eastern Canada and north-central and northeastern United States; winters in eastern and south-central United States south to eastern and central Mexico.

411. White-throated Sparrow

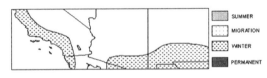

Zonotrichia albicollis (L—7 W—9)
White throat; alternating black and
white (or black and buff) crown sti-
pes; yellow lores; streaked brown above; grayish below. *Voice:* Song—A thin, wavering whistle often heard in March thickets "poor sam peabody peabody"; call—"seet." *Habitat:* Woodland thickets, brushy fields. *Abundance and Distribution:* Uncommon to rare winter resident (Oct.–Apr.) in the coastal lowlands and foothills of southern California, southern Arizona, and southern New Mexico. *Where to Find:* Patagonia-Sonoita Creek Preserve, Arizona; Louis Rubidoux Nature Center, California; Middle Rio Grande Conservancy District, New Mexico. *Range:* Breeds across most of boreal Canada and northeastern and north-central United States; winters eastern and southern United States and northern Mexico.

412. Harris's Sparrow

Zonotrichia querula (L—8 W—11)

SUMMER
MIGRATION
WINTER
PERMANENT

A large sparrow with black breast, throat, and crown (gray cast in winter); gray face with black ear patch; pink bill; streaked brown and gray on back; white belly with black flanks. *Immature:* Crown mottled; throat white with dark malar stripe. *Voice:* Song—a clear, whistled "see see see" repeated at different pitches; also some "chipy" notes; call—"chik." *Similar Species:* Immatures of other *Zonotrichia* sparrows lack black on breast. *Habitat:* Scrub, undergrowth in open woodlands, savanna, thickets, brushy fields, hedgerows. *Abundance and Distribution:* Uncommon to rare transient (Oct., Mar.) in New Mexico; uncommon to rare winter resident (Oct.–Mar.) in central and southern New Mexico, the upper Colorado River valley, and coastal southern California. *Where to Find:* Middle Rio Grande Conservancy District, New Mexico; Bosque del Apache National Wildlife Refuge, New Mexico; Bitter Lake National Wildlife Refuge, New Mexico. *Range:* Breeds in the tundra of north-central Canada; winters in the central and southern Great Plains of the United States.

413. White-crowned Sparrow

Zonotrichia leucophrys

(L—7 W—10)

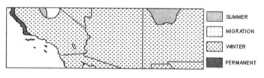

SUMMER
MIGRATION
WINTER
PERMANENT

Black and white striped crown; gray neck, breast, and belly; streaked gray and brown back; pinkish bill. *Immature:* Crown stripes are brown and gray. *Voice:* "Tsee tsee tsee zzeech-i chi-i-i"; call—"chip." *Similar Species:* White-throated Sparrow is also a large, plain-breasted, striped-crowned sparrow, but it has a white throat and yellow lores. *Habitat:* Montane meadows (breeding); thickets in coniferous and deciduous woodlands, brushy fields, thorn forest (winter). *Abundance and Distribution:* Common summer resident* (May–Sep.) in the Sierra Nevada highlands (six thousand to ten thousand feet), along the coast of southern California, and northern New Mexico; may breed at timberline in the White and San Francisco Mountains of Arizona; uncommon transient and winter resident (Oct.–Apr.) nearly throughout except in mountains. *Where to Find:* Hyde Memorial State Park, New Mexico (breeding); Dorothy May Tucker Wildlife Sanctuary, California (winter); Sunset Park, Las Vegas, Nevada (winter); Santa Rita Experimental Range, Santa Rita Mountains, Arizona. *Range:* Breeds in northern and western North America; winters across most of the United States south to central Mexico.

414. Golden-crowned Sparrow

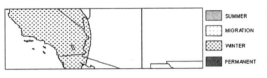

Zonotrichia atricapilla

(L—7 W—10)

Yellow crown bordered by blackish
stripes; streaked gray and brown above; dingy white below; two white wing bars.
Immature: Yellow crown somewhat dingy. *Voice:* Song—a whistled "oh dear" or
"oh dear me"; call—"zink." *Habitat:* Bogs (summer), thickets, scrub, brushy pastures and fields. *Abundance and Distribution:* Uncommon winter resident (Oct.–
Apr.) in the lowlands and foothills (to three thousand feet) of southwestern California; rare to casual winter resident (Oct.–Apr.) in southeastern California and
the Colorado River valley; casual winter resident elsewhere in the region. *Where to
Find:* Tapia County Park, Santa Monica Mountains, California; Burnt Rancheria
Campground, Laguna Mountains, California; Middle Rio Grande Conservancy
District, New Mexico. *Range:* Breeds along the western coastal regions of Alaska
and Canada; winters along the western coastal areas of the United States.

415. Dark-eyed Junco

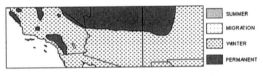

Junco hyemalis (L—6 W—10)

This species consists of three, well-
marked groups, formerly considered
separate species, in which the plumage is quite distinct. *"Slate-colored" group:* Male
is entirely dark gray except for white belly and outer tail feathers, and pinkish bill;
the female is similar but brownish rather than gray. *"Oregon" group:* Male has black
head, brown back and sides, gray rump, and white belly and outer tail feathers;
the female is similar but has a grayish head. *"Gray-headed" group:* Gray head and
underparts; black lores; brown back; white outer tail feathers. *Voice:* Song—A trill,
given at different speeds and pitches; call—"tsik." *Habitat:* Fir, lodgepole, and ponderosa pine forest (breeding); madrone and oak woodlands (summer), open mixed
woodlands, grasslands, agricultural fields. *Abundance and Distribution:* Locally
common resident* in coastal oak woodlands and highlands of southwestern California (to ten thousand feet), southern Nevada, northern and central Arizona,
and northern New Mexico; common transient and winter resident (Oct.–Apr.)
throughout. *Where to Find:* Escudilla Mountain, Arizona (breeding); Palomar
Mountain State Park, California (breeding); Mount Charleston, Nevada (breeding); Pajarito Mountain Ski Area, New Mexico (breeding). *Range:* Breeds across
northern North America and in the mountains of eastern and western United
States; winters from southern Canada south through the United States to northern Mexico.

416. Yellow-eyed Junco

Junco phaeonotus (L—6 W—9)

Yellow eye set off by gray head and black lores; brown back; grayish white below; gray rump; white outer tail feathers. *Voice:* Song—three to four whistled, repeated phrases; call—"tsip." *Similar Species:* "Gray-headed" form of Dark-eyed Junco has a black eye. *Habitat:* Montane fir, pine, and pine-oak forest. *Abundance and Distribution:* Uncommon resident* of southeastern Arizona. *Where to Find:* Bear Canyon Picnic Area, Mount Lemmon; Santa Rita Lodge, Madera Canyon; South Fork, Cave Creek Canyon, Chiricahua Mountains. *Range:* Montane forest from southeastern Arizona south through highlands of Mexico to western Guatemala.

417. McCown's Longspur

Calcarius mccownii (L—6 W—11)

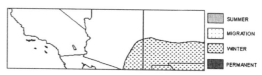

Black cap, whisker, breast; white throat and belly; streaked brown above; chestnut wing patch; tail black in center and at tip, the rest white. *Winter male and female:* Brown rather than black cap, whisker, and breast; bill buffy or pinkish with a dark tip. *Voice:* Song—a long, wandering series of warbles, given in flight; call—a short, metallic "ti-ti-ti- ti." *Similar Species:* Large amount of white on base and sides of tail distinguish winter birds from Lapland and Smith's longspurs; chestnut wing patch of McCown's separates it from the Chestnut-collared Longspur. *Habitat:* Shortgrass prairie, plowed fields. *Abundance and Distribution:* Uncommon to rare winter resident (Oct.–Mar.) in grasslands and pastures of central and southern New Mexico and southeastern Arizona. *Where to Find:* Bitter Lake National Wildlife Refuge, New Mexico. *Range:* Breeds in the northern and central Great Plains from southern Canada to Nebraska; winters in Kansas, Oklahoma, Texas, southern New Mexico, southeastern Arizona and northwestern Mexico.

418. Lapland Longspur

Calcarius lapponicus (L—6 W—11)

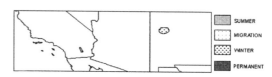

Black head and breast with white or buff face pattern; rusty nape; streaked brown above; white belly; tail is all dark except for outermost tail feathers. *Winter male and female:* Brownish crown; buffy eyebrow, nape, and throat with darker brown mottlings on breast and flanks; buffy cheek outlined by darker brown. *Voice:* Song—short phrases of squeaky, slurred notes, given in flight; call—"tseeu." *Similar Species:* Mostly dark tail with white edgings distinguishes this bird from Chestnut-collared and McCown's longspurs; Smith's Longspur is uniformly buffy below, not white with streaks. *Habitat:* Shortgrass prairie, plowed fields, overgrazed pasture. *Abundance and Distribution:* Rare to casual winter resident (Nov.–Mar.) in grasslands of central New Mexico and Salton Sea, California. *Where to Find:* Grasslands Turf Ranch, New Mexico; Salton Sea National Wildlife Refuge, California. *Range:* Breeds in tundra of extreme northern North America and Eurasia; winters in temperate regions of the Old and New World.

419. Chestnut-collared Longspur

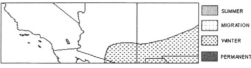

Calcarius ornatus (L—6 W—11)
Black and white face pattern; chestnut nape; yellow throat; black breast and flanks; white belly; base and sides of tail white; center and tip of tail dark. *Winter male and female:* Streaked brown above and on crown; buffy below with various amounts of black on breast; male often has black and white shoulder patch; bill grayish. *Voice:* Song—"tsee tseeoo tseeoo tsee" and similar squeaky phrases, repeated; call—"chi-pi." *Similar Species:* The bill of the Chestnut-collared Longspur is grayish; the bill of McCown's Longspur is pinkish. *Habitat:* Shortgrass prairie, plowed fields, overgrazed pasture. *Abundance and Distribution:* Uncommon to rare winter resident (Nov.–Mar.) in eastern and southern New Mexico, southeastern Arizona, and Salton Sea, California. *Where to Find:* Palominas Pond, Arizona; Salton Sea National Wildlife Refuge, California; Bitter Lake National Wildlife Refuge, New Mexico. *Range:* Breeds in the Great Plains of south-central Canada and the north-central United States; winters in south-central and southwestern United States and northwestern Mexico.

420. Northern Cardinal

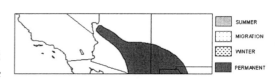

Cardinalis cardinalis (L—9 W—12)
Red with crest; black face patch at base of red bill. *Female and immature male:* Crested like male but greenish-brown, paler below, bill brownish or reddish *Voice:* Song—loud, ringing whistle "whit-chew," repeated; call—a sharp "peak." *Similar Species:* Female and immature cardinal have a sharp, reddish-orange, conical bill as compared with the snubbed, yellowish bill of the grayer female Pyrrhuloxia. *Habitat:* Oak and riparian woodland, thickets, mesquite thorn forest, foothill canyon thorn forest. *Abundance and Distribution:* Common resident* of the lower Sonoran zone of central and southern Arizona (absent from open desert areas) and southwestern New Mexico. *Where to Find:* Organ Pipe Cactus National Monument, Arizona; Sabino Canyon, Arizona; Patagonia-Sonoita Canyon Preserve, Arizona; Picnic Area, State Fish Hatchery at Glenwood, New Mexico. *Range:* Eastern United States and southeastern Canada; southwestern United States, Mexico, Guatemala, and Belize.

421. Pyrrhuloxia

Cardinalis sinuatus (L—9 W—12)

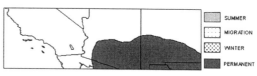

SUMMER
MIGRATION
WINTER
PERMANENT

Dusty gray with red crest, face, belly, wings, and tail. *Female:* Similar but red on face mostly lacking. *Voice:* Similar to Northern Cardinal—"whit whit whit whit." *Similar Species:* See Northern Cardinal. *Habitat:* Dense, arid thorn forest; desert scrub and wash vegetation. *Abundance and Distribution:* Common to uncommon permanent resident* of the lower Sonoran zone of southern Arizona and southern New Mexico; evidence of migration in some populations. *Where to Find:* Bosque del Apache National Wildlife Refuge, New Mexico; Redrock Wildlife Area, New Mexico; Patagonia-Sonoita Creek Preserve, Arizona; Ramsey Canyon Road, Arizona. *Range:* Arid regions of southern Arizona, southern New Mexico, southern Texas south to central Mexico.

422. Rose-breasted Grosbeak

Pheucticus ludovicianus

(L—8 W—13)

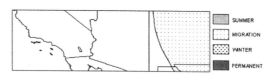

SUMMER
MIGRATION
WINTER
PERMANENT

Black head, back, wings, and tail; brownish in winter; red breast; white belly, rump, wing patches, and tail spots. *Female:* Mottled brown above, buffy below heavily streaked with dark brown; white eyebrow and wing bars. *First-year male:* Like female but shows rose tints on breast and underwing coverts. *Second-year male:* Patterned much like adult male but splotched brown and black on head and back. *Voice:* Song—rapid, robin-like phrases; call—a sharp "keek" or "kik." *Similar Species:* Female Black-headed Grosbeak is only faintly streaked below, and has yellowish rather than pale buff breast. *Habitat:* Deciduous forest, riparian and oak woodlands, thorn forest, savanna. *Abundance and Distribution:* Rare spring transient (Apr.–May) in New Mexico; casual at other seasons and locations. *Where to Find:* Water Canyon Campground, New Mexico; Roswell Zoo, New Mexico. *Range:* Breeds in northeastern United States, central and southeastern Canada; winters from southern Mexico south through Central America to northern South America and western Cuba.

423. Black-headed Grosbeak

Pheucticus melanocephalus

(L—8 W—13)

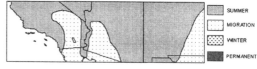

SUMMER
MIGRATION
WINTER
PERMANENT

Black head; body a rich orange buff streaked with black on the back; wings black with two white wing bars. *Female and Immature male:* Brown head with white eyebrow; brown streaked with buff above; buffy below with faint brownish streaks; white wing bars on brown wings. This species is considered by some authors to be a western form of the Rose-breasted

Grosbeak. *Voice:* Song—rapid, robin-like phrases; slightly hoarser and lower pitched than the Rose-breasted Grosbeak; call—"kik." *Similar Species:* See Rose-breasted Grosbeak. *Habitat:* Ponderosa pine and pine-oak woodlands, riparian and thorn forest. *Abundance and Distribution:* Common to uncommon summer resident* (Apr.–Sep.) nearly throughout except deserts of southeastern California and southwestern Arizona; common to uncommon transient (Apr.–May, Sep.–Oct.) throughout. *Where to Find:* North Rim, Grand Canyon, Arizona; Frijoles Canyon, Bandelier National Monument, New Mexico; Red Rock Canyon National Conservation Area, Nevada; Switzer Picnic Area, San Gabriel Mountains, California. *Range:* Breeds from southwestern Canada through the western United States and highlands of northern and central Mexico; winters in central Mexico.

424. Blue Grosbeak

Guiraca caerulea (L—7 W—11)
Dark blue with two rusty wing bars.
Female and Immature male: Brown-

SUMMER
MIGRATION
WINTER
PERMANENT

ish above, paler below with tawny wing bars, often has a blush of blue on shoulder or rump. *Habits:* Flicks and fans tail. *Voice:* Song—a rapid series of up and down warbles, some notes harsh, some slurred; call—"chink." *Similar Species:* Male and female Indigo Bunting resemble corresponding sex of Blue Grosbeak but are smaller and lack tawny wing bars and massive grosbeak bill. *Habitat:* Riparian thickets (willow, cottonwood, mesquite), savanna, scrub, brushy pastures, hedgerows. *Abundance and Distribution:* Uncommon to rare and local summer resident* (May–Aug.) in lowlands throughout except southwestern Arizona and eastern New Mexico. *Where to Find:* South Kern River Preserve, California; Catalina State Park, Arizona; Tesuque River Bottom, New Mexico; Corn Creek, Desert National Wildlife Range, Nevada. *Range:* Breeds from central and southern United States through Mexico and Central America to Costa Rica; winters from northern Mexico to Panama; rarely Cuba.

425. Lazuli Bunting

Passerina amoena (L—6 W—9)
Turquoise head, back and rump; rusty
breast and buffy belly; two white wing

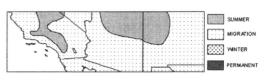

SUMMER
MIGRATION
WINTER
PERMANENT

bars. *Female:* Brown above, paler below with two buffy wing bars; often has blue cast on rump. *Voice:* Song—three- to four-second phrases of rough, slurred warbles; call—"tsik." *Similar Species:* Female Indigo Bunting lacks bluish rump and wing bars are indistinct. However, these two species (subspecies?) interbreed in areas of overlap in central and southwestern United States producing hybrids with mixed plumage characters. *Habitat:* Willow thickets, hedgerows, savanna, thorn forest.

Abundance and Distribution: Uncommon to rare and local summer resident* (Apr.–Sep.) in mountains and foothills of southern California, northern Arizona, and northern New Mexico; uncommon to rare transient (Apr.–May, Aug.–Sep.) elsewhere in the region; rare to casual in winter in southeastern Arizona. *Where to Find:* Valle Vista Campground, Mount Pinos, California; West Fork, San Gabriel River, California; Jackson Lake State Game Refuge, New Mexico; Marana Pecan Grove, Arizona. *Range:* Breeds from southwestern Canada and western United States; winters in western Mexico.

426. Indigo Bunting

Passerina cyanea (L—6 W—9)

Indigo blue. *Female and Immature male:* Brown above, paler below with

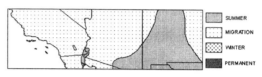

faint streaking on breast. *Winter adult and Second-year males:* Bluish with variable amounts of brown on back and wings. *Voice:* Song—warbled phrases of paired or triplet notes; call—"tsink." *Similar Species:* See Blue Grosbeak and Lazuli Bunting. *Habitat:* Riparian thickets, hedgerows, brushy fields, savanna, thorn forest. *Abundance and Distribution:* Uncommon to rare and local summer resident* (Apr.–Oct.) along the lower Colorado River valley, southeastern Arizona, and New Mexico. Rare transient (Apr.–May, Sep.–Oct.) throughout. Phillips et al. (1964) considered the Indigo and Lazuli buntings to be a single species in which the Indigo represents the more eastern form and the Lazuli the western. Hybrids between the two have been recorded in the Flagstaff, Arizona, area and elsewhere. The Indigo form has become much more evident throughout the region over the past twenty years. *Where to Find:* San Pedro River, Arizona; South Kern River Reserve, California; Middle Rio Grande Conservancy District south of Albuquerque, New Mexico; Corn Creek, Desert National Wildlife Range, Nevada. *Range:* Breeds from extreme southeastern and south—Central Canada south through eastern and southwestern United States; winters from central Mexico to Panama and the West Indies.

427. Varied Bunting

Passerina versicolor (L—6 W—8)

Blue head and rump; rose below and on back; red nape; black face; rose

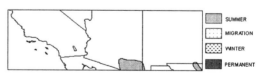

areas are brownish in winter male. *Female and Immature male:* Grayish brown. *Voice:* Song—three to four weakly warbled phrases; call—"tink." *Similar Species:* Female Varied Bunting is the only gray bunting with unstreaked breast in the region. *Habitat:* Riparian thickets (mesquite), thorn forest, hedgerows. *Abundance and Distribution:* Uncommon to rare and local summer resident* (May–Aug.) in southeastern Arizona and Guadalupe Canyon and Carlsbad Caverns National Park in New Mexico. *Where to Find:* Sycamore Canyon, Arizona; Florida Wash, Arizona; Carlsbad Caverns National Park, New Mexico. *Range:* Breeds from United States-Mexico border to Guatemala; winters in southern half of breeding range.

428. Painted Bunting

Passerina ciris (L—6 W—9)

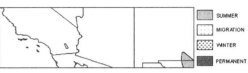

Purple head, red underparts and rump; green back; dark wings and tail. *Female and Immature male:* Bright green above, paler below; dark wings and tail. *Voice:* Song—a prolonged series of rapid warbles; call—"tsip." *Similar Species:* Other female buntings are brownish or grayish, not green. *Habitat:* Riparian and thorn forest, oak woodlands, savanna, brushy pastures, hedgerows. *Abundance and Distribution:* Uncommon to rare and local summer resident* (Apr.–Sep.) in southeastern New Mexico, mainly in salt cedar groves along the Pecos River. *Where to Find:* Pecos River north of Brantley Lake, New Mexico; Rocky Arroyo, Guadalupe Mountains, New Mexico. *Range:* Breeds in coastal Georgia and South Carolina, south-central United States, and northeastern Mexico; winters from northern Mexico south to western Panama; also south Florida, Bahamas, and Cuba.

429. Dickcissel

Spiza americana

(L—6 W—9)

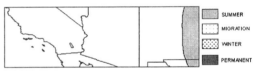

Patterned like a miniature meadowlark—black bib (gray in winter) and yellow breast; streaked brown above; grayish head with creamy eyebrow; rusty red wing patch. *Female and Immature male:* Patterned like male but paler yellow below and without black bib. *Voice:* Song—a dry "chik sizzzle," also a "brrrzeet" given in flight. *Similar Species:* Pale females and immatures resemble female House Sparrow but usually have traces of yellow on pale white (not dirty white) breast, a clear, whitish or yellowish eyebrow, and some chestnut on shoulder. *Habitat:* Prairies, savannas, agricultural fields. *Abundance and Distribution:* Rare summer resident (May–Aug.) and fall transient (Sep.–Oct.) in eastern New Mexico plains. *Where to Find:* Fort Sumner State Monument, New Mexico; Sitting Bull Falls, New Mexico. *Range:* Breeds across the eastern and central United States and south-central Canada; winters mainly in northern South America.

Family Icteridae
Orioles and Blackbirds
Most migratory icterids are dimorphic with large, strikingly colored males, and smaller, more cryptically colored females.

430. Red-winged Blackbird *Agelaius phoeniceus* (L—8 W—14)
Black with red epaulets bordered in orange. *Female and Immature male:*

Dark brown above, whitish below heavily streaked with dark brown; whitish eyebrow and malar stripes. *Second-year male:* Intermediate between female and male—black blotching, some orange on epaulet. *Voice:* Song—"konk-ka-ree"; call—a harsh "shek." *Similar Species:* Blackbird size and bill separate females from female Purple and House finches, which also are heavily streaked. The male redwing is distinguished from the male Tricolored Blackbird (found only in California coastal marshes) by brighter scarlet epaulets bordered in yellow (not white). Female redwings have bellies streaked brown and white; female Tricolored has solid, dark belly. *Habitat:* Inland and coastal marshes (breeding), brushy fields, tallgrass prairie, grain and hay fields, grain storage areas (winter). *Abundance and Distribution:* Common resident* throughout except in highlands (three thousand to nine thousand feet) where a summer resident* (Mar.–Oct.). *Where to Find:* Harbor Regional Park, California; Floyd Lamb State Park, Nevada; Willcox Lake, Arizona; Bosque del Apache National Wildlife Refuge, New Mexico. *Range:* Breeds nearly throughout North America from the Arctic Circle south to Costa Rica; winters from temperate portions of breeding range south; resident populations in Bahamas and Cuba.

431. Tricolored Blackbird
Agelaius tricolor (L—9 W—14)
Black with red epaulets bordered in white. *Female and Immature male:*

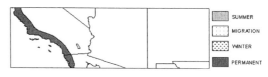

Dark brown above, whitish below heavily streaked with dark brown; whitish eyebrow and malar stripes. *Second-year male:* Intermediate between female and male—black blotching, some orange on epaulet. *Voice:* Song—"kon ke kaaaaan," coarse; lacks high-pitched ending of the Redwing. *Similar Species:* See Red-winged Blackbird. *Habitat:* Marshes, flooded rice fields, ditches, wet meadows, agricultural fields, grain storage areas. *Abundance and Distribution:* Uncommon and local resident* in southwestern California lowlands. *Where to Find:* San Jacinto Wildlife Area; Shipley Nature Center, Huntington Beach; El Dorado Nature Center, Long Beach.

Range: Coastal lowlands and central valley of California from Sonoma County south to the Mexican border, and northwestern Baja California.

432. Eastern Meadowlark

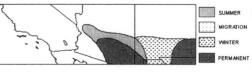

Sturnella magna (L—10 W—15)
Streaked brown and white above; yellow below with a black or brownish "V" on the breast; crown striped with buff and dark brown; tail is dark in center, white on outer edges. *Voice:* Song—a plaintive "see-ur see-ur," the second phrase at a lower pitch than the first; call—a rattling, harsh "ka-kak-kak-kak-kak." *Similar Species:* Western Meadowlark is paler on the back; malar stripe is white in Eastern, yellow in Western. *Habitat:* Tallgrass prairie, savanna, grain and hay fields, overgrown pastures. *Abundance and Distribution:* Common to uncommon and local summer resident* (Mar.–Sep.) in grasslands of central Arizona and southern New Mexico; rare in winter (Oct.–Mar.); common permanent resident* in southeastern Arizona and southeastern New Mexico; winter resident in central New Mexico. *Where to Find:* Bitter Lake National Wildlife Refuge, New Mexico; Sonoita Grassland, Arizona. *Range:* Breeds from southeastern Canada and the eastern and southern United States west to Arizona; Mexico through Central and northern South America; Cuba; winters through most of breeding range except northern portions.

433. Western Meadowlark

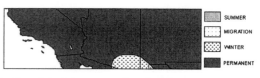

Sturnella neglecta (L—10 W—15)
Streaked brown and white above; yellow below with a black or brownish "V" on the breast; crown striped with buff and dark brown; tail is dark in center, white on outer edges. *Voice:* Song—"tsee chortelee chi chor"; very different from the plaintive Eastern Meadowlark song; rattle given in flight is similar to that of the Eastern Meadowlark. *Similar Species:* See Eastern Meadowlark. *Habitat:* Shortgrass prairie, overgrazed pasture, savanna. *Abundance and Distribution:* Common permanent resident* in lowland and foothill grasslands throughout (except southeastern Arizona); common to uncommon and local winter resident (Oct.–Mar.) in southeastern Arizona and southwestern New Mexico. *Where to Find:* Desert National Wildlife Range, Nevada; San Xavier Mission, Tucson, Arizona (winter); Grasslands Turf Ranch, New Mexico; Sunrise Highway, Laguna Mountains, California. *Range:* Breeds across the prairies of southwestern and south-central Canada, and all except eastern third of the United States, south to central Mexico; winters in southern half of the breeding range.

434. Yellow-headed Blackbird
Xanthocephalus xanthocephalus
(L—10 W—16)
Black body with yellow head and

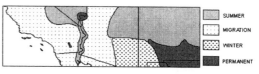

breast; white wing patch. *Female and Immature male:* Brown body; yellowish breast and throat; yellowish eyebrow. *Voice:* Song—"like a buzz saw biting a hard log." (Edwards in Oberholser 1974:808); call—a croak. *Similar Species:* Female could be confused with female Great-tailed Grackle but it has a short, square tail (not long and wedge-shaped), and is usually yellowish, not buff, on breast. *Habitat:* Marshes, brushy pastures, agricultural fields. Favorite sites for these and several other blackbird species are cattle feedlots and grain elevators in winter. *Abundance and Distribution:* Uncommon to rare and local permanent resident*, more common in summer (Mar.–Oct.), in Salton Sea, Lake Mead, and southeastern New Mexico; common to uncommon summer resident* (Mar.–Oct.) in northeastern Arizona, northern New Mexico, southern Nevada, and along the Colorado River valley; uncommon transient (Apr.–May, Sep.–Oct.) throughout; uncommon to rare and local winter resident (Oct.–Mar.) in southeastern Arizona and southwestern New Mexico. *Where to Find:* Mittry Lake Wildlife Area, Arizona; Corn Creek, Desert National Wildlife Range, Nevada; Bosque del Apache National Wildlife Refuge, New Mexico; Salton Sea, California. *Range:* Breeds in south-central and southwestern Canada, north-central and northwestern United States; winters from southern California, Arizona, and New Mexico south to central Mexico.

435. Brewer's Blackbird
Euphagus cyanocephalus (L—9 W—15)
Entirely black with purplish gloss on
head (in proper light); yellow eye;

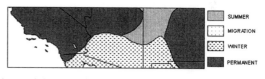

some fall males are tinged rusty. *Female:* Dark brown above with dark brown eye, slightly paler below. *Voice:* Song—"chik-a-chik-a-perzee chik-a-chik-a-perzee"; call—"chik." *Similar Species:* The female Brewer's Blackbird is solid brown below (not buffy with faint gray streaking as in the smaller female Brown-headed Cowbird); the all-black males resemble Bronzed Cowbirds, but the cream-colored eye (not orange-brown) is diagnostic. *Habitat:* Prairies, pastures, agricultural fields, feedlots, grain elevators. *Abundance and Distribution:* Common to uncommon permanent resident* in southern California, southern Nevada, northern Arizona, and eastern New Mexico; uncommon and local summer resident* and transient (Apr.–Oct.) in the highlands (four thousand to ten thousand feet) of the Sierra Nevada of southern California and northern New Mexico; common winter resident (Oct.–Mar.) in southern Arizona and southwestern New Mexico. *Where to Find:* Big Canyon Trail, Upper Newport Bay, California; Desert National Wildlife

Range, Nevada; Willcox Lake, Arizona (winter); Bosque del Apache National Wildlife Refuge, New Mexico. *Range:* Breeds in the western and central United States and Canada; winters in the breeding range from southwestern Canada and the western United States southward into the southern United States to central Mexico.

436. Common Grackle

Quiscalus quiscula (L—12 W—17)
Entirely black with bronze gloss on head in proper light (purple headed

eastern form is casual in the west); tail long and rounded; cream-colored eye. *Female:* Dull black; whitish eye; tail not as long as male's. *Voice:* Song—a repeated squeak, like a rusty hinge, with "chek"s interspersed; call—"chek." *Similar Species:* Cowbirds and blackbirds have short, square tails (not long and rounded as in grackles). Female Common Grackles have a dark head, lacking buffy eyeline, and a dark throat (larger female Great-tailed Grackles have a buffy throat and buffy line over the eye). *Habitat:* Open woodlands, urban areas, agricultural fields, pastures, grain storage areas. *Abundance and Distribution:* Common to uncommon transient and summer resident* (Mar.–Oct.) in northeastern New Mexico; resident in southern and central New Mexico, mainly along water courses, agricultural areas, and urban centers. *Where to Find:* Bosque del Apache National Wildlife Refuge; Middle Rio Grande Conservancy District; Roswell South Park Cemetery, New Mexico. *Range:* Breeds east of the Rockies in Canada and United States; winters in the southern half of the breeding range.

437. Great-tailed Grackle

Quiscalus mexicanus (Male L—18 W—24; Female L—14 W—18)
Entirely black with purplish gloss on

head (in proper light); tail wedge-shaped and longer than body; creamy eye. *Female:* Brown above, paler below; buffy eyebrow; creamy eye; wedge-shaped tail not as long as male's. *Voice:* Song—"kak kak kak kak weeeooo weeeooo kik kik kik" with numerous variations, given while fluffing out and waving wings by males at a display perch; calls—several different ones including a strident "cheak" familiar to those with homes near their large roosts. *Similar Species:* The long tail is distinctive, even for females. *Habitat:* Marshes, riparian areas (salt cedar, willow, false willow), citrus groves (breeding), agricultural areas, roadsides, pastures, grain storage sites, urban and residential areas. *Abundance and Distribution:* Common permanent resident* in southeastern California, southern Nevada, southeastern Arizona, and southern New Mexico; partially migratory, becoming scarce and local in winter (Oct.–Mar.) in New Mexico except in urban areas where common throughout the year. *Where to Find:* Salton Sea National Wildlife Refuge, California; Corn Creek, Desert National Wildlife Range, Nevada; San Xavier Mission, Arizona; Bosque del Apache National Wildlife Refuge, New Mexico. *Range:* Southwestern United States south through Mexico and Central America to northern South America.

438. Bronzed Cowbird

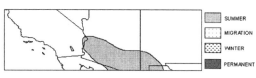

Molothrus aeneus (L—9 W—14)

Entirely black with bronzy sheen in proper light; eye is red during the breeding season, orange-brown in winter; neck ruff gives male a hunch-backed appearance. *Female:* Dull black; orange-brown eye; little or no neck ruff. *Habits:* Male hovers in front of perched female as part of breeding display. Like the Brown-headed Cowbird, this species is a social parasite, laying its eggs in the nests of other species. *Voice:* Song—a squeaky, bubbly "gurgl eeee"; call—"shek." *Similar Species:* Bronzed Cowbirds have red or orange-brown eyes; Brewer's Blackbirds have cream-colored eyes. *Habitat:* Thorn forest, savanna, agricultural fields, urban areas, feedlots, grain elevators. *Abundance and Distribution:* Uncommon to rare and local summer resident* (Apr.–Aug.) in southern Arizona, southeastern California (Salton Sea; Colorado River valley), and southwestern New Mexico; extremely local in winter (at grain storage areas) in southeastern Arizona. *Where to Find:* Organ Pipe National Monument, Arizona; Salton Sea National Wildlife Refuge, California; Bill Evans Lake, New Mexico. *Range:* Borderlands of the southwestern United States (isolated population in Louisiana) south through Mexico and Central America to central Panama.

439. Brown-headed Cowbird

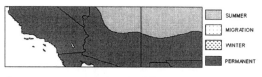

Molothrus ater (L—7 W—13)

Black body; brown head. *Female:* Brown above, paler below with grayish streakings. *Habits:* A social parasite, laying its eggs in other birds' nests. *Voice:* Song—a series of high-pitched whistles (tseee), guttural chatters, and rising squeaks; call—"chek." *Similar Species:* See Brewer's Blackbird. *Habitat:* Prairie, savanna, pastures, agricultural fields, feedlots, grain elevators. *Abundance and Distribution:* Common permanent resident* throughout except in highlands (three thousand to ten thousand feet) of southern California, northern Arizona, and northern New Mexico where a common summer resident* (Apr.–Aug.); numbers increase in winter with northern migrants, and concentrate at roosts and grain storage areas. *Where to Find:* Salton Sea National Wildlife Refuge, California; Sierra Vista Wastewater Ponds, Arizona; Bosque del Apache National Wildlife Refuge, New Mexico;

Desert National Wildlife Range, Nevada. *Range:* Breeds across most of North America from south of the arctic to central Mexico; winters in the southern half of its breeding range.

440. Orchard Oriole

Icterus spurius (L—7 W—10)

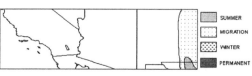

Black hood, wings and tail; bright chestnut belly, wing patch, lower back and rump. *Female:* Greenish-yellow above, yellow below with two white wing bars; blue-gray legs. *Second-year male:* Like female but with black throat and breast. *Voice:* Song—"tsee tso tsee tsoo tewit tewit tewit tseerr" and similar wandering twitters; call—"kuk." *Similar Species:* The female Orchard Oriole has an unstreaked greenish-yellow back; the female Scott's Oriole has dark streaking on crown and back; female Western Tanager has a stubby bill (not long and pointed). *Habitat:* Riparian woodlands, savanna, orchards, brushy pastures, residential areas. *Abundance and Distribution:* Uncommon and local summer resident* in the lower Pecos River valley of southeastern New Mexico; rare spring transient (Apr.–May) in eastern New Mexico. *Where to Find:* Rattlesnake Springs, New Mexico. *Range:* Breeds across the eastern and central United States south into central Mexico; winters from central Mexico south through Central America to northern South America.

441. Hooded Oriole

Icterus cucullatus (L—8 W—11)

Orange head, belly, and rump; black face, throat, and center of breast; black upper back and tail; wings black with white wing bars and primary edgings. *Female:* Brownish-orange above, buffy orange below; white wing bars and primary edgings. *Voice:* Song—a catbird-like series of rapidly warbled notes interspersed with harsher notes and trills; call—"cheek." *Similar Species:* The adult male Hooded Oriole is the only oriole in the region with an orange crown (black in others); the female Hooded Oriole has a yellowish belly (paler in female Bullock's form of the Northern Oriole). The female Orchard Oriole is very similar to the female Hooded—the female Orchard is somewhat greener than the Hooded, has a shorter, more square tail (not rounded), and occurs only in eastern New Mexico regularly in the region. *Habitat:* Thorn forest, oak mottes, riparian forest, palms. *Abundance and Distribution:* Uncommon to rare and local summer resident* (Apr.–Aug.) in the lowlands and foothills of southern California, southern Nevada, western and southern Arizona, and southern New Mexico. *Where to Find:* Santiago Oaks Regional Park, California; Rattlesnake Springs, New Mexico; Hualapai Mountain Park, Arizona; Red Rock Canyon National Conservation Area,

Nevada. *Range:* Breeds in the southwestern United States south to southern Mexico; winters in western, central and southern Mexico.

442. Baltimore Oriole

Icterus galbula (L—8 W—12)

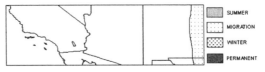

Black hood, back and wings; tail black at base and center but outer terminal portions orange; orange belly, rump and shoulder patch. *Female and Immature male:* Orange-brown above, yellow-orange below with varying amounts of black on face and throat; white wing bars. *Voice:* Slurred rapid series of easily imitated whistles; call—a chatter; also—"wheweee". *Similar Species:* The female Baltimore Oriole is greenish above with dark streaks on the back, and orangish below while the female Bullock's is grayish above (not streaked) and whitish below. The smaller, female Hooded and Orchard orioles are yellowish or greenish-yellow on the belly. Male Baltimore Oriole has a black hood and orange epaulet while male Bullock's has a black cap and throat, with orange cheeks and superciliary stripe, and a white epaulet. *Habitat:* Riparian woodland (sycamore, cottonwood, willow), orchards, oak woodlands, hedgerows, second growth. *Abundance and Distribution:* Rare transient (Apr.–May, Sep.–Oct.) and rare to casual summer resident in eastern New Mexico. *Where to Find:* Rattlesnake Springs, New Mexico. *Range:* Breeds from southeastern and central Canada (west to Alberta and Saskatchewan) south across the eastern half of the United States to east Texas and central Louisiana, Mississippi, Alabama, and north Georgia. Winters from southern Mexico through Middle America to Colombia; also in the Greater Antilles.

443. Bullock's Oriole

Icterus bullockii (L—8 W—12)

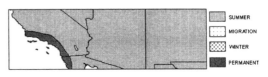

Black above and orange below with orange cheeks and eyebrow; black throat and eyeline, white patch on black wings; tail is orange on the sides, black at the center and tip. *Female and Immature male:* Unstreaked grayish-olive above and yellowish or buff throat and breast; whitish belly. *Voice:* A sibilant "sip-pit ip-pert-seee-per-sip-pit-ip-pert-sip" with many variations; call—"tseeip." *Similar Species:* See Baltimore Oriole. *Habitat:* Riparian woodland (sycamore, cottonwood, willow), orchards, oak woodlands, hedgerows, second growth. *Abundance and Distribution:* Common to uncommon summer resident* (May–Aug.) of southern California and southern Nevada; uncommon summer resident* (May–Aug.) in riparian areas of the upper Sonoran zone of southeastern to northwestern Arizona and New Mexico; common transient (Apr., Sep.–Oct.) throughout. *Where to Find:* Oak Canyon Nature Center, Santa Ana Mountains, California; Marana Pecan Grove,

Arizona; Corn Creek, Desert National Wildlife Range, Nevada. *Range:* Breeds from southwestern and south-central Canada (British Columbia to Saskatchewan) south through the western and central United States to northern Mexico; winters from coastal southern California and Texas south to Guatemala.

444. Scott's Oriole
Icterus parisorum (L—9 W—13)
Body yellow; black hood extending to middle of back; tail and wings black;

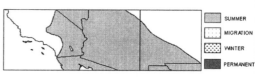

yellow shoulder patch; wedge-shaped tail. *Female and Immature male:* Streaked brownish and yellow on crown and back; yellowish below with various amounts of black on face, throat and breast; white wing bars. *Voice:* Song—a whistled "chi-per-ti chi-per-ti cheep per-ti per-ti"; call—"chek." *Similar Species:* The female Scott's Oriole has dark streaking on crown and back; the female Orchard Oriole has an unstreaked greenish-yellow back. *Habitat:* Montane desert scrub (yucca, Joshua tree associations); oak chaparral, pinyon-juniper. *Abundance and Distribution:* Uncommon to rare and local summer resident* (Apr.–July) in arid montane and desert regions of southeastern California (rarely west to San Diego area), southern Nevada, Arizona, and New Mexico (mainly western and southern portions); some winter at residential bird feeders in southeastern Arizona. *Where to Find:* Kofa National Wildlife Refuge, Arizona; Rattlesnake Springs, New Mexico; Quatal Canyon, California. *Range:* Breeds from the borderlands of the southwestern United States south to west-central Mexico; winters in southern portions of the breeding range.

Family Fringillidae
Old World Finches
Like many of the emberizids, finches are small to medium-sized birds with thick, conical bills for eating seeds and fruits.

445. Gray-crowned Rosy-Finch
Leucosticte tephrocotis (L—6 W—10)
Brown back, breast, and head; crown dark brown anteriorly, gray posteri-

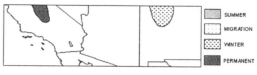

orly; rosy lower back, rump, belly, wings, and shoulder patch; tail dark brown and slightly forked. *Female:* Brown with some rosy tints on wings, rump, and belly. *Voice:* Song—a series of chirps at different pitches like that of the House Sparrow. *Habitat:* Alpine meadows, tundra, cliffs, rock slides, and snowfields. *Abundance* *and Distribution:* Uncommon to rare and local summer resident* (Apr.–Oct.) on peaks above timberline (eighty-five hundred feet) in the Sierra Nevada of southern California; irregularly to lower elevations in winter; also rare to casual in winter in the mountains of northern New Mexico. *Range:* Breeds from western and northern Alaska and northwestern Canada south in the Sierra Nevada to southern California; winters southward, eastward, and at lower elevations in breeding range.

446. Brown-capped Rosy-Finch

Leucosticte australis (L—6 W—10)
Brown back, breast, and head; crown
dark brown; rosy lower back, rump,

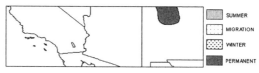

belly, wings, and shoulder patch; tail dark brown and slightly forked. *Female:* Brown with some rosy tints on wings, rump, and belly. *Voice:* Song—a series of chirps at different pitches like that of the House Sparrow. *Habitat:* Alpine meadows, tundra, cliffs, rock slides, and snowfields. *Abundance and Distribution:* Uncommon to rare and local summer resident* (Apr.–Oct.) on peaks above timberline (eighty-five hundred feet) in the Sangre de Cristo Mountains of northern New Mexico; moves to somewhat lower elevations in winter. *Where to Find:* Santa Fe Baldy, New Mexico. *Range:* Breeds in the Rocky Mountains from Wyoming to north-central New Mexico; winters at lower elevations in breeding range.

447. Pine Grosbeak

Pinicola enucleator (L—9 W—14)
Rosy head, breast, and rump; gray
flanks and belly; black back, wings,

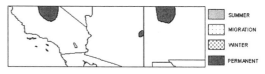

and tail; white wing bars; heavy, black grosbeak bill. *Female:* Gray body; head tinged with yellow; whitish shading below eye; white wing bars. *Voice:* Song—a weak twitter, rising and falling; call—a faint "che chu." *Habitat:* Lodgepole and whitebark pines, mountain hemlock, and red fir, often bordering streams or tarns. *Abundance and Distribution:* Uncommon to rare resident* from seven thousand feet to tree line in the Sierra Nevada of southern California, the White Mountains of eastern Arizona, and in the Sangre de Cristo, San Juan, and Jemez Mountains of northern New Mexico; irregular winter visitor to the highlands of northern Arizona. *Where to Find:* Santa Fe Baldy, New Mexico; Escudilla Mountain, Arizona. *Range:* Breeds in boreal forest of the Old and New Worlds, south to New Mexico in the Rockies; winters in southern portions of the breeding range south into north temperate regions of the Old and New World.

448. Purple Finch

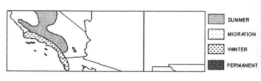

Carpodacus purpureus (L—6 W—10)
Rosy head and breast; whitish belly;
brown above suffused with rose; rose rump; tail is notched; under-tail coverts white.
Female and Immature male: Brown above; white below heavily streaked with brown;
brown head with white eyebrow and malar stripes; under-tail coverts white. *Voice:*
Song—a rapid, tumbling series of slurred notes and trills; call—"chit." *Similar
Species:* The "chit" call note of the Purple Finch is distinct from the three-syllable
"chi-di-lip" of the Cassin's Finch and the nasal "wink" call note of the House Finch.
The male Purple Finch is rosier overall and lacks brown streaking as on the flanks
of the male House Finch; male Cassin's Finch is more a pale pink than rose, and
has a heavier bill than the Purple Finch. The female Purple Finch has a pronounced
dark jaw stripe and white eyeline, which the female House Finch lacks, while that
of the female Cassin's Finch is less distinct. *Habitat:* Ponderosa, sugar, and lodgepole pines; douglas, red, and white firs; sequoia, incense cedar (breeding). Pine-
oak, oak woodlands (winter). *Abundance and Distribution:* Common summer resident* (Apr.–Sep.) in the highlands (three thousand to eight thousand feet) of southern California; lowlands and foothills of southwestern California in winter (Oct.–
Mar.); rare transient (Mar.–Apr., Oct.–Nov.) in southern Nevada; irregular winter
visitor in small numbers to southern Arizona. *Where to Find:* Dorothy May Tucker
Wildlife Refuge, California (winter); McGill Campground, Mount Pinos, California. *Range:* Breeds across Canada, the northern borderlands, and the western mountains of the United States south into Baja California; winters throughout the United
States except in the Great Plains and western deserts.

449. Cassin's Finch

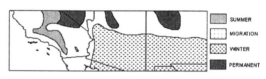

Carpodacus cassinii (L—7 W—11)
Brown above; red cap; rosy throat and
breast; white belly with brown streak-
ing on flanks. *Female and Immature male:* Brown above; buffy below with fine,
brownish streaks; buffy post-ocular stripe. *Voice:* Song—a rapid, series of twitters
and squeaks; call—"chi-di-lip." *Similar Species:* See Purple Finch. *Habitat:* Lodgepole and whitebark pines, mountain hemlock, aspen and cottonwood (breeding),
pine, pine-oak, pinyon-juniper, oak woodlands (winter). *Abundance and Distribution:* Common summer resident* (Apr.–Aug.) in the highlands (five thousand
to ten thousand feet) of southern California, southern Nevada, northeastern Arizona, and northern New Mexico; common to rare and irregular transient and winter
resident (Sep.–Mar.) to lower elevations in breeding range and in the Upper
Sonoran and transition zones of Arizona and New Mexico; rare to casual and

irregular in winter in the lowlands and foothills of southwestern California. *Where to Find:* North Rim, Grand Canyon, Arizona; Mount Charleston, Nevada; Santa Fe Baldy, New Mexico; McGill Campground, Mount Pinos, California. *Range:* Resident in the western mountains of North America from British Columbia to New Mexico and southern California; winters in the southwestern United States and northwestern Mexico.

450. House Finch

Carpodacus mexicanus (L—6 W—10)
Brown above with red brow stripe; brown cheeks; rosy breast; whitish streaked with brown below. *Female and Immature male:* Brown above; buffy head and underparts finely streaked with brown; buffy pre-orbital stripe in some. *Voice:* Song—a long series of squeaks and warbles; call—a nasal "wink." *Similar Species:* See Purple Finch. *Habitat:* Thorn forest, arid scrub, pine-oak, pinyon juniper, sagebrush, agricultural, and urban areas. *Abundance and Distribution:* Common resident* in lowlands and mid-elevations (to six thousand feet) throughout; northern and higher elevation populations may be partially migratory. *Where to Find:* Yaqui Well, Anza-Borrego Desert, California; Red Rock Canyon National Conservation Area; Shannon-Broadway Desert, Tucson, Arizona; Bosque del Apache National Wildlife Refuge, New Mexico. *Range:* Resident from southwestern Canada throughout much of the United States except Great Plains, south to southern Mexico.

451. Red Crossbill

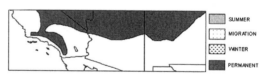

Loxia curvirostra (L—7 W—11)
Red with dark wings and tail; crossed bill. *Female and Immature male:* Yellowish with dark wings and tail. *Voice:* Song—two-note "tsoo tee" repeated three or four times followed by a trill; call—repeated "kip" notes in flight. *Similar Species:* The "chri-chri" call notes of the White-winged Crossbill (which is casual in northern parts of the region) are distinct from the "kip" call note of the Red Crossbill. Also note that the White-winged Crossbill has two white wing bars, which the Red Crossbill lacks. *Habitat:* Lodgepole, whitebark, and jeffrey pines (breeding), ponderosa pine, pinyon pine, and a variety of other coniferous species during nonbreeding periods. *Abundance and Distribution:* Irregularly common to rare resident* in the highlands of southern California, southern Nevada, Arizona, and New Mexico, breeding mainly above eight thousand feet in lodgepole, whitebark, and jeffrey pines. Travels widely during the non-breeding period throughout the region, mainly to transition and boreal zone forests, wherever pine nut crops (such

as ponderosa pine, pinyon pine, etc.) are available. *Where to Find:* Santa Fe Baldy, New Mexico; Mount Charleston, Nevada; North Rim, Grand Canyon, Arizona; Bluff Lake, San Bernardino Mountains, California. *Range:* Resident in boreal regions of the Old and New World, south in the mountains of the west through Mexico and the highlands of Central America to Nicaragua; winters in breeding range and irregularly south in north temperate regions of the world.

452. Pine Siskin
Carduelis pinus
(L—5 W—9)
Streaked brown above; whitish below

with brown streaks; yellow wing patch and at base of tail. *Voice:* Song—A sequence of "chipy chipy" notes interspersed with raspy, rising "zeeeech" calls; call—a nasal "schree." *Similar Species:* The heavily streaked body and yellow patches on wings and base of tail distinguish this bird from other small finches. *Habitat:* A wide variety of coniferous and mixed forests (resident), riparian and oak woodlands, savanna (winter). *Abundance and Distribution:* Common summer resident* (May–Aug.) in the highlands (three thousand to ten thousand feet) of southern California, southern Nevada, Arizona (except western deserts), and New Mexico; irregularly common to rare transient and winter resident (Sep.–Apr.) in breeding range and to lower elevations. *Where to Find:* Black Mountain Campground, California; North Rim, Grand Canyon, Arizona; Mount Charleston, Nevada; Santa Fe Baldy, New Mexico. *Range:* Breeds in boreal regions of northern North America, and in western mountains south through the United States and highlands of Mexico to Veracruz; winters in all except the extreme northern portions of the breeding range and in most of the temperate United States.

453. Lesser Goldfinch
Carduelis psaltria (L—5 W—8)
Black above; yellow below; white
patches on black primaries. *Female*

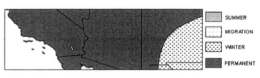

and Immature male: Greenish above, yellow below; dark wings with white patches on primaries. *Voice:* Song—a long sequence of twitters, buzzes, and jeers; calls—a plaintive, whistled "tseoo" given in flight; also "tsoo-doo." *Habits:* Undulating flight is characteristic of both the Lesser and American goldfinches, usually accompanied by characteristic flight calls. *Similar Species:* American Goldfinch female is normally more brownish than green above and more whitish than yellow below; female Lesser normally has yellow under-tail coverts (white in American Goldfinch). *Habitat:* Thorn forest, arid scrub, oak-juniper and pine-oak woodlands, riparian woodlands (cottonwoods, willows). *Abundance and Distribution:* Common to uncommon summer resident* (Apr.–Oct.) in lowlands and mid-eleva-tions throughout except in deserts of southeastern California and southwestern Arizona where rare or casual; less common in winter (Nov.–Mar.) in northern Arizona and northern New Mexico; uncommon to rare winter resident in lower Sonoran zone riparian areas of southeastern Caliornia and southwestern Arizona. *Where to Find:* Sabino Canyon Recreation Area, Arizona; Percha Dam State Park, New Mexico; Red Rock Canyon National Conservation Area, Nevada; Tapia County Park, Malibu, California. *Range:* Breeds in the southwestern United States and Mexico south through Central America to central South America; winters in all but the northern portions of the breeding range.

454. Lawrence's Goldfinch

Carduelis lawrencei (L—5 W—8) Grayish-brown above; black face; yel-low breast and belly; yellow patches on dark wings; yellow lower back and rump. *Female and Winter male:* Grayish-brown above; yellowish breast; belly grayish or buff; yellow patches on dark wings; yellow on rump. *Voice:* Song—a succession of squeaky, high-pitched twitters. *Similar Species:* Other goldfinches lack yellow on wings and rump. *Habitat:* Oak chaparral, pinyon-juniper. *Abundance and Distribution:* Uncommon to rare and local summer resident* (Apr.–Aug.) in the lowlands and foothills of southwestern California to the western edge of the Mojave Desert; rare to casual winter resident (Sep.–Mar.) in breeding range; irregularly common to rare winter resident (Sep.–Mar.) in southeastern California (Colorado River valley), Arizona (except northeast), and extreme southwestern New Mexico. *Where to Find:* S6 Hwy, Summit Grove, Palomar Mountain, California (breeding); Quatal Canyon, California (breeding); Marana Pecan Grove, Arizona (winter); Tanque Verde Wash, Arizona (winter). *Range:* Breeds in coastal central and southern California and northern Baja California; winters in breeding range and eastward to southern Arizona and northwestern Mexico.

455. American Goldfinch

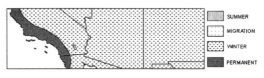

Carduelis tristis (L—5 W—9) Yellow body; black cap, wings and tail; white at base of tail and wing bar; yellow shoulder patch. *Female and Winter male:* Brownish above; yellowish or buff breast; whitish belly; dark wings with white wing bars. *Habits:* Usually in flocks; dipping-soaring flight, like a roller coaster; almost always giving characteristic flight call—"ker-chik ker-chik-chik-chik." *Voice:* Song—a sequence of trills, whiney "tsoowee"s, and "ker-chik"s; flight call—a characteristic and unmistakable "ker-chik ker-chik-chik-chik." *Similar Species:* See Lesser Goldfinch. *Habitat:* Prairie, savanna, thorn forest, brushy pastures, and fields. *Abundance and Distribution:* Uncommon resident* in the lowlands and foothills of southwestern California; uncommon to rare winter resident (Nov.–Mar.) elsewhere throughout. *Where to Find:* Silverwood Audubon Sanctuary, San Diego, California (resident); Bluewater Lake State Park (below dam), New Mexico (winter); Kino Springs, Arizona (winter). *Range:* Breeds across southern Canada, northern and central United States to southern California and northern Baja California in west; winters in the central and southern United States and northern Mexico.

456. Evening Grosbeak
Coccothraustes vespertinus
(L—8 W—13)

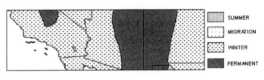

A chubby bird with heavy, yellowish or whitish bill; yellow body; black crown and brownish head with yellow forehead and eyebrow; black tail and wings with white wing patch. *Female:* Grayish above, buffy below; dark malar stripe; white wing patch. *Habits:* Usually in flocks. *Voice:* Calls—a sharp "peak" and a hoarse "peer." *Habitat:* Coniferous and mixed forest; often at bird feeders in winter. *Abundance and Distribution:* Uncommon to rare resident* in the highlands (three thousand to eight thousand feet) of the Sierra Nevada of southern California, north-central to southeastern Arizona, and northwestern and north-central New Mexico; irregularly uncommon to rare winter resident (Nov.–Mar.) in southern Nevada, and southern and eastern New Mexico. *Where to Find:* North Rim, Grand Canyon, Arizona; Dome Meadow, Jemez Mountains, New Mexico; Capulin Volcano National Monument, New Mexico. *Range:* Breeds in boreal portions of central and southern Canada, northern and western United States, south in western mountains to western and central Mexico; winters in breeding range and in temperate and southern United States

---

Family Passeridae
House Sparrows
This family has no native representatives in the New World. House Sparrows were introduced from the Old World, and have spread throughout the hemisphere in agricultural and urban habitats.

457. House Sparrow

Passer domesticus (L—6 W—10)

A chunky, heavy-billed bird; brown above with heavy, dark brown streaks;

SUMMER
MIGRATION
WINTER
PERMANENT

dingy gray below; gray cap; chestnut nape; black lores, chin, and bib. *Female:* Streaked buff and brown above; dingy gray below; pale buff post-orbital stripe. *Voice:* Song—"chip cheap chip chip chi-chi-chi chip"; call—"cheap." *Similar Species:* Pale females and immature Dickcissels resemble House Sparrow female but usually have traces of yellow on pale white (not dirty white) breast, a clear, whitish or yellowish eyebrow, and some chestnut on shoulder. *Habitat:* Urban areas, pastures, agricultural fields, feed lots, farms, grain elevators. *Abundance and Distribution:* Common resident* throughout. *Where to Find:* Date palms, Imperial Dam, California; Portal, Arizona; Roswell Zoo, New Mexico; Las Vegas, Nevada. *Range:* Resident in boreal, temperate, and subtropical regions of the Old and New World; currently expanding into tropical regions. Introduced into the Western Hemisphere in 1850.

Casual and Accidental Species

Yellow-billed Loon

Least Grebe

Red-necked Grebe

Laysan Albatross

Short-tailed Albatross

Northern Fulmar

Murphy's Petrel

Mottled Petrel

Cook's Petrel

Wedge-tailed Shearwater

Buller's Shearwater

Black-vented Shearwater

Wilson's Storm-Petrel

Fork-tailed Storm-Petrel

Band-rumped Storm-Petrel

Wedge-rumped Storm-Petrel

Least Storm-Petrel

White-tailed Tropicbird

Red-tailed Tropicbird

Masked Booby

Blue-footed Booby

Brown Booby

Red-footed Booby

Anhinga

Magnificent Frigatebird

Tricolored Heron

Reddish Egret

Yellow-crowned Night-Heron

White Ibis

Glossy Ibis

Roseate Spoonbill

Emperor Goose

Trumpeter Swan

American Black Duck

Mottled Duck

Garganey

Baikal Teal

Tufted Duck

King Eider

Harlequin Duck

Oldsquaw

Masked Duck

Swallow-tailed Kite

Broad-winged Hawk

White-tailed Hawk

Gyrfalcon

Chukar

Sharp-tailed Grouse

Yellow Rail

Purple Gallinule

Common Crane

Whooping Crane

Mongolian Plover

Wilson's Plover

Piping Plover

American Oystercatcher

Gray-tailed Tattler

Little Curlew

Hudsonian Godwit

Bar-tailed Godwit

Red-necked Stint
White-rumped Sandpiper
Sharp-tailed Sandpiper
Curlew Sandpiper
Buff-breasted Sandpiper
Ruff
American Woodcock
Long-tailed Jaeger
Little Gull
Black-headed Gull
Lesser Black-backed Gull
Sandwich Tern
Sooty Tern
Kittlitz's Murrelet
Parakeet Auklet
Horned Puffin
Ruddy Ground-Dove
Thick-billed Parrot
Black-billed Cuckoo
Groove-billed Ani
Barred Owl
Boreal Owl
Chuck-will's-widow
Xantus's Hummingbird
Berylline Hummingbird
Cinnamon Hummingbird
Plain-capped Starthroat
Ruby-throated Hummingbird
Eared Trogon
Golden-fronted Woodpecker
Red-bellied Woodpecker
Yellow-bellied Sapsucker
Eastern Wood-Pewee
Yellow-bellied Flycatcher
Acadian Flycatcher
Nutting's Flycatcher
Great Crested Flycatcher
Great Kiskadee
Couch's Kingbird
White-eyed Vireo

Black-capped Vireo
Yellow-throated Vireo
Philadelphia Vireo
Yellow-green Vireo
Tufted Titmouse
Carolina Wren
Sedge Wren
Black-capped Gnatcatcher
Gray-cheeked Thrush
Wood Thrush
Rufous-backed Robin
Aztec Thrush
White Wagtail
Black-backed Wagtail
Blue-winged Warbler
Golden-winged Warbler
Northern Parula
Chestnut-sided Warbler
Magnolia Warbler
Cape May Warbler
Black-throated Blue Warbler
Blackburnian Warbler
Yellow-throated Warbler
Pine Warbler
Prairie Warbler
Palm Warbler
Bay-breasted Warbler
Blackpoll Warbler
Cerulean Warbler
Prothonotary Warbler
Worm-eating Warbler
Swainson's Warbler
Louisiana Waterthrush
Kentucky Warbler
Connecticut Warbler
Mourning Warbler
Hooded Warbler
Canada Warbler
Slate-throated Redstart
Scarlet Tanager

White-collared Seedeater

Worthen's Sparrow

Le Conte's Sparrow

Smith's Longspur

Snow Bunting

Yellow Grosbeak

Bobolink

Rusty Blackbird

Streak-backed Oriole

Black Rosy-Finch

White-winged Crossbill

Common Redpoll

APPENDIX 2
Birding Sites in the Southwest —A Locator

Directions are provided below to get to more than four hundred of the Southwest's best birding sites. The sites are listed alphabetically by state. Each is mentioned in one or more of the species accounts as being one of the best or, in some cases, the only place where a particular bird is known to be found in the region. I have tried to provide at least one such site for each species from each of the four states. In compiling the list, I have leaned heavily on existing bird-finding guides and take responsibility for any errors. I have been personally to only about a quarter of the sites. Nevertheless, if you use this list with "an open mind, and a sense of humor" (as my Ph.D. advisor, Dwain Warner used to say), you should have some fun prospecting for birds.

When using the list, keep three important things in mind. (1) Never leave the paved road without a full tank of gas and plenty of water. (2) Routes that go above four thousand feet may be closed between October and May, and those above seven thousand feet almost certainly are closed. (3) Mileages are estimates for the most part—designed to put you in the right vicinity. Consider incorrect mileages to be a challenge to your sense of adventure, and you probably will be happier. It also is helpful to have detailed maps. In addition to the state highway maps, gazeteers for each of the states can be extremely useful. DeLorme (Tel. 207-865-4171) makes gazeteers for Arizona, southern California, and Nevada, and Benchmark Maps (Tel. 510-845-1474) makes them for all of the states in the region.

In most cases, the bird-finding guides have much more detailed information than I provide on the routes to take and what you are likely to find. The guides consulted for many of the sites in this list are as follows: *New Mexico Bird Finding Guide* by Dale Zimmerman et al. (1992); *A Birder's Guide to Southeastern Arizona* by Richard Taylor et al. (1995); *Finding Birds in Southeastern Arizona* by William Davis and Stephen Russell (1995); *A Birder's Guide to Southern California* by Harold Holt (1990); *Where Birders go in Southern California* by Henry Childs (1993); *Birding Arizona* by Bill McMillon (1995); *Southern Nevada: A Seeker's Guide* by C. Titus (1991).

Abbreviations used in the descriptions are as follows:

I = Interstate Highway

NM = New Mexico State Highway

AZ = Arizona State Highway

NV = Nevada State Highway

FS = Forest Service Road

jct. = junction

CA = California State Highway

mi. = miles

hq. = headquarters

IR = Indian Reservation Road

CH = County Highway

ARIZONA (128)

Agua Caliente Lake, Tucson—In Tucson, take Exit 256 from I-10 east onto E. Grant Rd. and continue east about 10.7 mi. to jct. with Tanque Verde Rd. Bear left on Tanque Verde Rd. Continue east on Tanque Verde to jct. with Soldier Trail. Turn left (north) on Soldier Trail and go about 2 mi. to jct. with Roger Rd. Turn right (east) on Roger Rd., and go 0.5 mi. to park entrance.

Alamo Lake State Park—From the jct. of US 60 and Alamo Dam Rd. in the west-central Arizona town of Wenden, go north on Alamo Dam Rd. 38 mi. to Alamo Lake State Park.

Allen Severson Memorial Wildlife Area—From the jct. of US 60 and AZ 77 just east of the eastern Arizona town of Show Low, turn north on AZ 77 and go 3 mi. to enter the area.

Appleton-Whittell Research Ranch Sanctuary—From the jct. of AZ 82 and AZ 83 in Sonoita, head south on AZ 83 4.1 mi. to jct. with Elgin Rd. Turn left (east) on Elgin Rd. and proceed 4.8 mi. to Elgin-Canelo Rd. Turn right on Elgin-Canelo Rd. and go 0.7 mi. to jct. with Babocomeri Ranch Rd. Bear left on Babocameri Ranch Rd. and go 2 mi. to jct. with Research Ranch Rd. Bear right at Research Ranch Rd. Proceed 1.3 mi. to the sanctuary. Bear right where the road splits and go 0.4 mi. to the hq.

Aravaipa Canyon Preserve—From the jct. of I-10 and US 191 at Exit 352, take US 191 north 17 mi. to jct. with AZ 266. Turn left (west) on AZ 266 and proceed west on AZ 266 20 mi. to Bonita. At Bonita, continue northwest on AZ 266 (now Bonita-Klondyke Rd.). Go 31 mi. to Klondyke. Continue beyond Klondyke 3.4 mi. to where the road splits. Bear left, following sign to the preserve.

Arivaca Cienaga—From I-19, 33 mi. south of Tucson, take Exit 48 to Arivaca Rd. Proceed 22 mi. west on Arivaca Rd. to the refuge entrance (on left, marked with sign).

Arivaca Creek—From I-19, 33 mi. south of Tucson, take Exit 48 to Arivaca Rd.

Proceed 23 mi. west to the village of Arivaca. Continue west 2 mi. on Arivaca Rd. to a parking lot and trailhead for the creek on the left.

Arizona Sonora Desert Museum, Tucson—In Tucson, take Exit 263 off from I-10 for West Ajo Way (AZ 86). Go west on Ajo Way 8 mi. to jct. with Kinney Rd. Turn right (northwest) on Kinney Rd. and proceed 8 mi. to the entrance to the museum on the left.

Aubrey Cliffs—At Seligman in northwestern Arizona, take Exit 123 north from I-40 onto US 66 west. Follow US 66 20 mi. northwest to a dirt road that goes off to the right (north) across Aubrey Valley and over a pass through the cliffs to Rose Well. This road passes through Boquillos Ranch. There are two gates to open (and close) at the ranch hq. (2.3 mi. from US 66). The entire area along US 66 from Seligman, and much of the road to Rose Well, is a large prairie dog town. The site has been used for black-footed ferret re-introductions.

Aubrey Valley—See Aubrey Cliffs.

Avra Valley Sewage Ponds—In Tucson, take Exit 263 off I-10 for West Ajo Way (AZ 86). Go west on Ajo Way 11 mi. to jct. with San Joaquin Rd. Turn right (northwest) on San Joaquin Rd. and proceed 0.6 mi. to jct. with Snyder Hill Rd. Turn left (west) on Snyder Hill Rd. and go about 3 mi. to the entrance to the sewage ponds on the right (sign).

Barfoot Park, Chiricahua Mountains—From I-10 at St. Simon, take Exit 382 south onto the Paradise-St. Simon Rd. Follow the Paradise-St. Simon Rd. about 24 mi. to Paradise. At Paradise, the road becomes FS 42B. Continue south another 3 mi. on FS 42B to jct. with FS 42. Turn right on FS 42 and proceed to Onion Saddle and jct. with FS 42D (about 2 mi.). Make a sharp left (south) onto FS 42D. Continue on FS 42D for about 2 mi. to Barfoot Junction. Turn right (north) at Barfoot Junction toward Buena Vista Peak and Barfoot Park (1 mi.).

Bear Canyon Picnic Area, Mount Lemmon—In Tucson, take Exit 256 from I-10 east onto E. Grant Rd. and continue east about 10.7 mi. to jct. with Tanque Verde Rd. Bear left on Tanque Verde Rd. Continue east on Tanque Verde to jct. with Catalina. Bear left (northeast) on Catalina, and follow this road north all the way up into the Mount Lemmon sites. The Bear Canyon site is at milepost 10, about 15 mi. from Tucson.

Big Lake Loop, White Mountains—At the jct. of AZ 260 and AZ 261 just west of the eastern Arizona town of Springerville, go south on AZ 261 about 16 mi. to Big Lake. Where the road splits at Big Lake, bear left on FS 113. Follow FS 113 about 2.5 mi. to jct. with FS 285. Go left (north) on FS 285, which goes back to Springerville. This loop will take you through grasslands, highland conifer forest, and mountain meadows.

Bill Williams Delta National Wildlife Refuge—At the western Arizona border, take Exit 9 off from I-40 and follow AZ 95 south 42 mi. to jct. with Bill Williams

Hwy. (just after crossing Bill Williams River). Turn left (east) on Bill Williams Hwy., which passes through the refuge for the next 10 mi. or so.

Bonita Creek, Gila Box Riparian National Conservation Area—In southeastern Arizona, take Exit 352 off from I-10 and follow US 191 north 34 mi. to the jct. of US 191 and US 70 in Safford. Turn right (east) on combined US 70/191 and proceed about 7 mi. to jct. with San Jose Rd. Bear left (northeast) on San Jose Rd. (becomes Buena Vista Rd.), and continue about 5 mi. to the village of Sanchez. The Gila River bottom is here. Unimproved roads and trails follow the river east from Sanchez about 3 mi. to the conservation area. The confluence of Bonita Creek and the Gila River is about 6 mi. northeast of Sanchez.

Bright Angel Trail, Grand Canyon—From I-40 at Williams, take Exit 165 and go north on US 180/AZ 64 56 mi. to Grand Canyon Village. Where the road splits into East and West Rim Drives, bear left on West Rim Drive. Bright Angel Trail crosses West Rim Drive about 2 mi. west of the split. Follow the trail down into the canyon.

Brown Canyon Trail, Ramsey Canyon Preserve—From the jct. of I-10 and AZ 90 (Exit 302) west of Benson, go south on AZ 90 about 34 mi. to the jct. with AZ 92. Go south on AZ 92 about 6 mi. to jct. with Ramsey Canyon Rd. Turn right (west) on Ramsey Canyon Rd. and go west about 2.3 mi. to the Brown Canyon Trailhead (on the right, about 0.3 mi. after the road makes a bend to the southwest).

Buenos Aires National Wildlife Refuge—From I-19, 33 mi. south of Tucson, take Exit 48 to Arivaca Rd. Proceed 22 mi. west to the town of Arivaca. Continue west on Arivaca Rd. about 12 mi. to jct. with AZ 286 (Tucson-Sasabe Rd.). Turn left (south) on AZ 286 and go 4.4 mi. to the entrance road for the refuge hq. Turn left (east) and follow signs to the hq. for maps and information.

California Gulch—From I-19 about 87 mi. south of Tucson, take Exit 12 onto Ruby Rd. (AZ 289). Go west on Ruby Rd. about 11 mi. (past Peña Blanca Lake) to jct. with FS 39. Turn right (west) on FS 39 and go another 9 mi. or so to a marked turnoff to the left for Sycamore Canyon. From this turnoff, continue west on FS 39 another 5.6 mi. or so to FS 217 (0.7 mi. past the old Ruby town site). Turn to the left (marked with a sign, "Arizona Western Mine"). Proceed 1.3 mi. to a dam. Bear right past the dam and proceed 0.8 mi. beyond the fork to a three-way junction. Turn left at the junction, and then right in 0.1 mi. Go 1.2 mi. to a left turn marked with a sign saying "Keep left for California and Warsaw Canyon." Turn left, and go 0.4 mi. to a parking area (Taylor 1995:202).

Canelo Hills Cienega—From the jct. of AZ 82 and AZ 83 in Sonoita, head south on AZ 83 15 mi. to a sign marked "Two Triangle Ranch Turnoff." Turn left and proceed 0.6 mi. to this Nature Conservancy preserve.

Canyon Creek Recreation Area, Heber—From I-40, take Exit 286 south onto AZ 77. Proceed south on AZ 77 about 3 mi. to jct. with AZ 377. Turn right (southwest) on AZ 377 and proceed 25 mi. to jct. with AZ 277. Turn right (west) on AZ

277 to jct. with AZ 260. Turn right on AZ 260, and go 24 mi. to jct. with the Young-Heber Hwy. (AZ 288). Turn left (south) on the Young-Heber Hwy. and go about 3 mi. to jct. with Fish Hatchery Rd. Turn left (east) on Fish Hatchery Rd. to enter the recreation area. The road splits about 3 mi. ahead into Fish Hatchery Rd. and Canyon Creek Rd.

Canyon de Chelly National Monument—From I-40 at the eastern Arizona town of Chambers, take Exit 333 and go north on US 191 38 mi. to jct. with AZ 264 at Ganado. Turn left (west) on AZ 264 and go 6 mi. until US 191 turns north again. Turn right (north) on US 191 and go 31 mi. to jct. with IR 7. Turn right (east) on IR 7 and proceed 2 mi. to Chinle. Follow signs to monument hq. (maps, information, checklist available).

Carr Canyon, Huachuca Mountains—From the jct. of I-10 and AZ 90 (Exit 302) west of Benson, go south on AZ 90 about 34 mi. to the jct. with AZ 92. Go south on AZ 92 about 7 mi. to jct. with Carr Canyon Rd. Turn right (west) on Carr Canyon Rd. and go about 9 mi. to the Ramsey Vista Campground. The trailhead for Carr Canyon Trail begins here and goes west.

Catalina State Park—Eight mi. north of Tucson on I-10, take Exit 240 onto Tangerine Rd. east. Follow Tangerine Rd. 15 mi. east to jct. with AZ 77. Turn right (south) on AZ 77 and go about 2 mi. to a left (east) turn into the park.

Cave Creek Canyon, Chiricahua Mountains—From I-10 at St. Simon, take Exit 382 south onto the Paradise-St. Simon Rd. Follow the Paradise-St. Simon Rd. about 24 mi. to the jct. with FS 42B just north of Paradise. Take the left fork, toward Portal about 5 mi. to jct. with FS 42. Turn right (southwest) on FS 42. FS 42 goes up Cave Creek Canyon. Ranger station is about 1 mi. ahead.

Chinle Wash—From I-40 at the eastern Arizona town of Chambers, take Exit 333 and go north on US 191 38 mi. to jct. with AZ 264 at Ganado. Turn left (west) on AZ 264 and go 6 mi. until US 191 turns north again. Turn right (north) on US 191 and go 54 mi. to where US 191 makes a sharp bend to the right (east) and crosses Chinle Wash. Park on the east side of the bridge, and explore the wash.

Cholla Lake—Six mi. west of the eastern Arizona town of Holbrook, take Exit 280 south off from I-40. Turn right (west) and go a few hundred yards paralleling the interstate to Cholla Lake.

Coleman Lake—From I-40 at Williams, take Exit 163 south onto the Perkinsville Rd. Go south on Perkinsville Rd. about 7 mi. to jct. with Bill Williams Loop Rd. Turn right (west) on Bill Williams Loop Rd. and go about 2 mi. to jct. with Coleman Lake Rd. Turn right and proceed about 1 mi. to the lake.

Coronado National Memorial—From the jct. of I-10 and AZ 90 (Exit 302) west of Benson, go south on AZ 90 about 34 mi. to the jct. with AZ 92. Go south on AZ 92 about 16 mi. to jct. with Coronado Rd. Turn right (south) onto Coronado Rd. and follow signs to the visitor center (about 5 mi.).

Desert View, Grand Canyon—From I-40 at Williams, take Exit 165 and go north on US 180/AZ 64 56 mi. to Grand Canyon Village. Where the road splits into East and West Rim Drives, bear right on the East Rim Drive (AZ 64) and proceed 22 mi. to Desert View.

Escapule Wash, San Pedro River—From the jct. of I-10 and AZ 90 (Exit 302) west of Benson, go south on AZ 90 about 30 mi. to the town of Sierra Vista. AZ 90 turns left (east) here for about 3 mi., then turns right (south). After this right turn, continue south on AZ 90 about half a mile to jct. with Charleston Rd. Turn left (east) on Charleston Rd. and go 6 mi. to jct. with Escapule Rd. Turn right (south) on Escapule Rd. and proceed 0.3 mi. to parking area.

Escudilla Mountain—From the eastern Arizona town of Springerville, go south on US 180 about 19 mi. to jct. FS 56. Turn left (east) on FS 56. At about 3 mi., FS 56 makes a sharp right turn. Continue on FS 56 past this turn another 3 mi. or so until the road splits to make a loop around Terry Flat. The trailhead for Escudilla Mountain begins about half a mile beyond the split from the left fork of FS 56.

Florida Wash, Santa Rita Mountains—From I-19, 35 mi. south of Tucson, take Exit 63 east onto FS 62 (Continental-White House Canyon Rd.). Go east on FS 62 about 8 mi. to jct. with FS 70 (Madera Canyon Rd.). Turn right (south) on FS 70. Proceed south on FS 70 about 0.6 mi. to the bridge over Florida Wash (third bridge crossed on the route). Park and explore the wash.

Forest Loop Road 302, Grand Canyon—This loop follows a series of Forest Service roads through the Kaibab National Forest. A good map will help a great deal in following these instructions, and for exploring elsewhere in the area. From I-40 at Williams, take Exit 165 and go north on US 180/AZ 64 38 mi. to jct. with Red Butte Rd. (FS 302). Turn right (east) on FS 302 and proceed about 7 mi. to jct. with FS 305A. Turn right (south) on FS 305A. Continue south on FS 305A about 7 mi. to jct. with FS 305. Turn right (west) on FS 305 and return to US 180 (2.5 mi.).

French Joe Canyon, Whetstone Mountains—From the jct. of I-10 and AZ 90 (Exit 302) west of Benson, go south on AZ 90 about 10 mi. to a dirt road and gate with a sign for the canyon on the right. Turn right and go through the gate (be sure to close it), and continue west for about 3 mi. to a parking area and trails up into the canyon.

Garden Canyon, Ft. Huachuca—From the jct. of I-10 and AZ 90 (Exit 302) west of Benson, go south on AZ 90 about 34 mi. to the jct. with AZ 92 and Fry Blvd. Turn right (west) on Fry Blvd., and go 3 mi. to entrance of Ft. Huachuca (driver's license, registration, and proof of insurance required to get permit for entry onto the fort grounds). Continue west for 2 mi. to the marked turnoff for Garden Canyon. Turn left (south) and go 4 mi. or so to the entrance of the canyon where the road bends to the southwest. Proceed another 2.5 mi. to picnic areas and parking.

Goose Lake, Colorado River—From I-40 at the western Arizona border town of Topcock, exit north onto Old Hwy. 65. Watch for signs for Havasu National Wildlife Refuge Hq. for maps and information. Goose Lake is on your left for the next 20 mi. traveling north.

Grand View Point, South Rim, Grand Canyon—From I-40 at Williams, take Exit 165 and go north on US 180/AZ 64 56 mi. to Grand Canyon Village. Where the road splits into East and West Rim Drives, bear right on the East Rim Drive (AZ 64) and proceed about 10 mi. to Grand View Point Trail (on the left).

Guadalupe Canyon—The instructions for this route begin in western New Mexico. From I-10 near the western border of New Mexico, take Exit 11. Go south on NM 338 54 miles to Geronimo Trail (CH C2). Turn right (west) on Geronimo Trail and proceed about 20 mi. to the jct. with Guadalupe Canyon Road. Turn left (east) on Guadalupe Canyon Road (you are now in Arizona) and proceed 9 mi. to the gate across the road. Park off the road beside the gate, and walk up the road to the canyon. The lower half of the canyon is in Arizona. The upper half is in New Mexico.

Hassayampa River Preserve—From the jct. of US 60 and US 93 in the central Arizona town of Wickenburg, go southeast on combined US 60/93 3 mi. to the turnoff (on the right side of the road) for the preserve. Turn right and enter the preserve.

Hearst Tanks, Grandview Point, South Rim, Grand Canyon—From I-40 at Williams, take Exit 165 and go north on US 180/AZ 64 56 mi. to Grand Canyon Village. Where the road splits into East and West Rim Drives, bear right on the East Rim Drive (AZ 64) and proceed about 10 mi. to Grand View Point Trail (on the left).

Herb Martyr Campground—See Cave Creek Canyon entry. Continue on FS 42 about 4 mi. to jct. with FS 42A. Take the left fork (FS 42 A) and go 3 mi. or so to Herb Martyr Campground (well marked).

Hereford Bridge, San Pedro River—From the jct. of I-10 and AZ 90 (Exit 302) west of Benson, go south on AZ 90 about 34 mi. to the jct. with AZ 92. Go south on AZ 92 about 9 mi. to jct. with Hereford Rd. Turn left (east) on Hereford Rd. and proceed about 9 mi. to Hereford Bridge. Park on the east side of the bridge to explore area.

Hualapai Mountain Park, Kingman—At Kingman, Exit 53 from I-40 and go south on US 66 (Andy Devine Ave.) 1.9 m to jct. with Hualapai Mountain Rd. Turn left (east) on Hualapai Mountain Road and go 10 mi. to the park hq. Stop for maps, information, and checklist.

Hwy 191 from Elfrida to Pearce—From I-10, 9 mi. south of Willcox, take Exit 331 onto US 191 south. Follow US 191 about 23 mi. to Pearce. Continue on US 191 east for 9 mi., then south for 13 mi. to Elfrida. This section of the road is good for transients that use plowed fields, e.g., Mountain Plover.

Imperial National Wildlife Refuge—Half of this refuge is in California, while the other half is in Arizona. The hq. is on the Arizona side. To get to the hq. for maps, information, and checklist, take Exit 2 off from I-8 and go north on US 95. Proceed on US 95 north 21 mi. to jct. with Martinez Lake Rd. Turn left (northwest) on Martinez Lake Rd. and follow signs for about 14 mi. to the refuge hq.

J. D. Dam Lake, Williams—From I-40 at Williams, take Exit 163 south onto Perkinsville Rd. Go south on Perkinsville Rd. about 9 mi. to jct. with FS 110 (White Horse Lake Rd.). Turn left (east) on FS 110 and go about 12 mi. to jct. with FS 105. Turn right (west) on FS 105 and go about 1 mi. to the lake.

Kaibab National Forest, Williams—See Coleman Lake and J.D. Dam Lake entries. The roads into these sites traverse representative habitat of the national forest.

Kaibab Plateau Parkway—From I-40 east of Flagstaff, take Exit 201 north onto US 89. Follow US 89 north 104 mi. to Bitter Springs. Bear left at Bitter Springs on US 89 Alt. Continue on US 89 Alt 53 mi. to jct. with AZ 67 at Jacob Lake. Turn left (south) on AZ 67 (Kaibab Plateau Parkway) and go 44 mi. south to North Rim.

Kino Springs—From I-19 north of Nogales, take Exit 8 and continue on Business 19 south 3 mi. to jct. with AZ 82. Take AZ 82 east (toward Patagonia) for about 4.5 mi. to jct. with Kino Springs Dr. Turn right (south) onto Kino Springs Dr. Proceed 1 mi. to ponds. The ponds are private property. Permission for entry can be obtained at the pro shop, another mile down the road.

Kofa National Wildlife Refuge—From I-10 at Quartzite, take Exit 17 onto frontage road going east paralleling I-10. Continue east about 1.6 mi. to jct. with US 95. Turn right (south) on US 95, and go south about 30 mi. to jct. with King Rd. Turn left (east) on King Rd. and proceed to refuge hq. for maps and information.

Lamar Haines Memorial Wildlife Area—In Flagstaff, take Exit 195 north off from I-40 to AZ 89A. Follow AZ 89A about 2 mi. to jct. with US 180. Turn left (north) onto US 180 and go about 8 mi. on US 180 to jct. with FS 516. Turn right (north) on FS 516 and go about 7 mi. to the wildlife area.

Madera Canyon—From I-19, 35 mi. south of Tucson, take Exit 63 east onto FS 62 (Continental-White House Canyon Rd.). Go east on FS 62 about 8 mi. to jct. with FS 70 (Madera Canyon Rd.). Turn right (south) on FS 70. Proceed south on FS 70 about 3.5 mi. to the entrance of Madera Canyon. Continue south on FS 70 for trails, picnic areas, and campgrounds.

Many Farms Lake—From I-40 at the eastern Arizona town of Chambers, take Exit 333 and go north on US 191 38 mi. to jct. with AZ 264 at Ganado. Turn left (west) on AZ 264 and go 6 mi. until US 191 turns north again. Turn right (north) on US 191 and go 45 mi. to Many Farms. Watch for a signed dirt road going off to the right to Many Farms Lake. Turn right on this road and follow it about 1 mi. to the lake.

Marana Pecan Grove (also known as Pinal Airpark Pecan Grove), Tucson—From I-10 north of Tucson, take Exit 232 west onto Pinal Airpark Rd. Go west on

Pinal Airpark Rd. 2.5 mi. to jct. with Trico Rd. Turn left (south) on Trico Rd. and go about 1 mi. to an unmarked dirt road. Turn right (west) on this road and go about 0.7 mi. to the grove.

Martinez Lake, Imperial National Wildlife Refuge—See Imperial National Wildlife Refuge entry. Martinez Lake is located at the refuge hq.

Massai Point, Chiricahua National Monument—At Willcox, take Exit 344 off I-10 onto Haskell Rd. Go southwest on Haskell Rd. 4 mi. to jct. with AZ 186. Turn left (southeast) on AZ 186. Proceed on AZ 186 about 35 mi. to jct. with AZ 181. Turn left (east) on AZ 181 and go about 5 mi. to the hq. and visitor center. Get maps and information here. From the visitor center, continue east on Bonita Canyon Dr. 8 mi. to Massai Point.

Miller Canyon, Huachuca Mountains—From the jct. of I-10 and AZ 90 (Exit 302) west of Benson, go south on AZ 90 about 34 mi. to the jct. with AZ 92. Go south on AZ 92 about 10 mi. to jct. with Miller Canyon Rd. Turn right (west) on Miller Canyon Rd. and go about 3 mi. to the Miller Canyon Trailhead.

Mittry Lake, Colorado River, Yuma—Take Exit 2 off from I-8 and go north on US 95 18 mi. to jct. with Imperial Dam Rd. Turn left (west) on Imperial Dam Rd. and go about 6 mi. to the Mittry Lake Wildlife Area.

Molino Basin Campground—In Tucson, take Exit 256 from I-10 east onto E. Grant Rd. and continue east about 10.7 mi. to jct. with Tanque Verde Rd. Bear left on Tanque Verde Rd. Continue east on Tanque Verde to jct. with Catalina. Bear left (northeast) on Catalina, and follow this road north all the way up into the Mount Lemmon sites. Molino Canyon and campground are about 10 mi. from Tucson.

Mormon Lake, Flagstaff—Immediately south of the jct. of I-40 and I-17 on I-17, take Exit 339 east onto Lake Mary Rd. Follow Lake Mary Rd. southeast for about 22 mi. to the lake.

Mount Lemmon—See Molino Basin Campground entry. From Tucson to the top of Mount Lemmon is about 35 mi.

Mount Trumbull—From I-40 east of Flagstaff, take Exit 201 north onto US 89. Follow US 89 north 104 mi. to Bitter Springs. Bear left at Bitter Springs on US 89 Alt. Continue on US 89 Alt. 53 mi. to jct. with AZ 67 at Jacob Lake. From Jacob Lake, continue west on US 89 Alt. 30 mi. to Fredonia and jct. with AZ 389. Go west on AZ 389 about 10 mi. to jct. with Pipe Spring Rd. Turn left on Pipe Spring Rd., then right in 0.3 mi. on Mount Trumbull Loop Rd. Go southwest on Mount Trumbull Loop Rd. about 60 mi. to Mount Trumbull Wilderness.

Muleshoe Ranch Reserve, Willcox—At Willcox, take Exit 344 off from I-10 onto Haskell Rd. Go southwest on Haskell Rd. 4 mi. to jct. with Airport Rd. and AZ 186. Turn right on Airport Rd. and go west about 15.5 mi. until the road splits. Take the right fork (Muleshoe Rd.) and proceed 14 mi. to the reserve hq. at Hooker's Hot Springs.

Nogales Sewage Ponds—From I-19 about 87 mi. south of Tucson, take Exit 12 and cross to the frontage road on the east side. Turn left (north) about 1 mi. to small sign on the right for "Waste Water Plant." Turn right (east) and proceed to plant.

North Rim, Grand Canyon—See Kaibab Plateau Parkway entry.

Organ Pipe Cactus National Monument—From I-8 at the southwestern Arizona town of Gila Bend, take Exit 115 south on AZ 85. Follow AZ 85 south 74 mi. to the monument visitor center.

Palominas Pond, San Pedro River Valley—From the jct. of I-10 and AZ 90 (Exit 302) west of Benson, go south on AZ 90 about 34 mi. to the jct. with AZ 92. Go south on AZ 92 about 19 mi. to jct. with Palominas Rd. Turn left (north) on Palominas Rd. and proceed about 0.3 mi. The pond is 300 yards off the road to the east.

Palominas Road, San Pedro River Valley—From the jct. of AZ 92 Palominas Rd., turn right (south) on Palominas Rd. and proceed about 4 mi. to the Mexican border. Habitats available along the road include mesquite grassland and riparian.

Parker Dam, Colorado River—At the western Arizona border, take Exit 9 off from I-40 and follow AZ 95 south 45 mi. to Parker Dam.

Patagonia Lake State Park—From I-19 north of Nogales, take Exit 8 and continue on Business 19 south 3 mi. to jct. with AZ 82. Take AZ 82 east (toward Patagonia) about 11 mi. to a turnoff (marked) to the left on Patagonia Lake Rd. and proceed 4 mi. to the hq. (maps, checklist) and lake.

Patagonia Roadside Rest Area—From the Business 19 jct. with AZ 82, take AZ 82 east (toward Patagonia) about 14.8 mi. to the rest stop on the right.

Patagonia Sonoita Creek Preserve—From the rest area, proceed another 0.2 mi. and turn left off AZ 82 onto a dirt road. Cross the creek and make an immediate right turn to enter the preserve. The road continues north along the creek for about 0.6 mi. before making a right turn and re-crossing the creek into Patagonia.

Petrified Forest Drive—From I-40 in eastern Arizona, take Exit 341 and follow signs to the Petrified Forest National Park Hq. and Visitor Center. Get maps, information, and checklist. Petrified Forest Drive goes south from here about 29 mi.

Petrified Forest National Park—See Petrified Forest Drive entry.

Phon D. Sutton Recreation Area—On US 60 (Superstition Freeway) in Tempe, take Exit 188 north onto Bush Hwy. Proceed north on Bush Hwy. about 12 mi. to the entrance to the recreation area (on the left).

Picacho Peak—From I-10, 50 miles north of Tucson, take Exit 319 to Picacho Peak State Park and follow signs to the park hq. for information, maps and checklist.

Picacho Reservoir—From I-10, 57 mi. north of Tucson, take Exit 211 onto AZ 87. Proceed north on AZ 87 9.3 mi. to jct. with Selma Hwy. Turn right on this dirt road, go 0.3 mi., turn right and go 0.1 mi., then turn left and go 1.2 mi. to reservoir embankment. Turn left and drive up on embankment.

Pine Flat Road, Williams—From I-40 at Williams, take Exit 163 south onto Perkinsville Rd. Go south on Perkinsville Rd. about 10 mi. to jct. with FS 354. Proceed south on FS 354 about 7 mi. to jct. with FS 105 (Pine Flat Road). Turn left and go about 8 mi. to jct. with FS 110 (White Horse Lake Rd.). To complete this loop, turn left on FS 110, and follow it back to Perkinsville Rd.

Pinery Canyon, Chiricahua National Monument—See Massai Point entry. Use maps and information from visitor center to locate Pinery Canyon (west from visitor center to jct. with AZ 181, then south on FS 42 [Pinery Canyon Rd.]).

Ramsey Canyon Preserve—From the jct. of I-10 and AZ 90 (Exit 302) west of Benson, go south on AZ 90 about 34 mi. to the jct. with AZ 92. Go south on AZ 92 about 6 mi. to jct. with Ramsey Canyon Rd. Turn right (west) on Ramsey Canyon Rd. and go about 3 mi. to the preserve.

Ramsey Vista Campground, Huachuca Mountains—From the jct. of I-10 and AZ 90 (Exit 302) west of Benson, go south on AZ 90 about 34 mi. to the jct. with AZ 92. Go south on AZ 92 about 7 mi. to jct. with Carr Canyon Rd. Turn right (west) on Carr Canyon Rd. and go about 9 mi. to the campground.

Red Butte—From I-40 in Williams, take Exit 165 north onto AZ 64 and go north 39 mi. to jct. with FS 320 (Red Butte). Turn right on FS 320, and go 1.2 mi. to jct. with FS 340. Proceed about 0.5 mi. to trail going off to the right to Red Butte.

Red Mountain—In Flagstaff, take Exit 195 north off I-40 to AZ 89A. Follow AZ 89A about 2 mi. to jct. with US 180. Turn left (north) onto US 180 and go about 32 mi. on US 180 to a turnoff to the left for Red Mountain. This turnoff is about 0.6 mi. beyond the turnoff to the left for FS 760.

Reddington Pass, Santa Catalina Mountains—In Tucson, take Exit 256 from I-10 east onto E. Grant Rd. and continue east about 10.7 mi. to jct. with Tanque Verde Rd. Bear left on Tanque Verde Rd. Continue east on Tanque Verde 21.1 mi. to Redington Pass (Tanque Verde becomes Redington Rd. east of Tucson).

Roosevelt Lake—From the jct. of US 60 and AZ 79 in Florence Junction east of Phoenix, proceed east on US 60 about 36 mi. to jct. with AZ 88. Turn left (north) on AZ 88 and go 29 mi. to Roosevelt Lake and Tonto National Monument.

Roosevelt Lake Wildlife Area—From the jct. of Roosevelt Lake with AZ 188, turn right (north) on AZ 188 and go about 9 mi. to wildlife area (on right).

Rose Canyon Lake, Mount Lemmon—See Molino Basin and Mount Lemmon entries. The Rose Canyon Lake site is at milepost 17 (left turn), about 22 mi. from Tucson.

Rucker Canyon, Chiricahua Mountains—From I-10 southwest of Willcox, take Exit 331 and follow US 191 south 35 mi. to jct. with Rucker Canyon Rd. Turn left (east) on Rucker Canyon Rd. about 10 mi. until it splits into Kuykendall Cutoff Rd.

(left) and Rucker Canyon Rd. (right). Take the right fork and go about 18 mi. to Rucker Canyon Campgrounds and Recreation Area.

Rustler Park Recreation Area—See Barfoot Park entry. At Barfoot Junction, turn left (south) and go 1 mi. to Rustler Park.

Sabino Canyon Recreation Area—In Tucson, take Exit 256 from I-10 east onto E. Grant Rd. and continue east about 9.3 mi. to jct. with Santiago Canyon Rd. Turn left (north) on Santiago Canyon Rd., and proceed 4.5 mi. to the recreation area.

Saguaro National Park—In Tucson, take Exit 263 off from I-10 for West Ajo Way (AZ 86). Go west on Ajo Way 8 mi. to jct. with Kinney Rd. Turn right (northwest) on Kinney Rd. and proceed 9.2 mi. to jct. with Mile Wide Rd. Continue north another mile or so to the park visitor center. Follow signs to the center (maps, information, and checklist available).

San Bernardino National Wildlife Refuge—The instructions for this route begin in western New Mexico. From I-10 near the western border of New Mexico, take Exit 11. Go south on NM 338 54 miles to Geronimo Trail (CH C2). Turn right (west) on Geronimo Trail and proceed about 27 mi. to a sharp left (marked) for the refuge.

San Pedro House—From the jct. of I-10 and AZ 90 (Exit 302) west of Benson, go south on AZ 90 about 34 mi. to the jct. with AZ 92 and Fry Blvd. in Sierra Vista. Turn left (east) and continue on AZ 90 about 7.6 mi. to the well-marked entrance (on the right) for the San Pedro House. Maps, information, and checklist available for the San Pedro Riparian National Conservation Area.

San Pedro Riparian National Conservation Area—See above entry for San Pedro House.

San Pedro River—See above entry for San Pedro House.

San Rafael Grassland—At the jct. of AZ 82 and Harshaw Rd. in the southeastern Arizona town of Patagonia, bear right onto Harshaw Rd. (FS 58) and proceed about 10 mi. to jct. with FS 765 (Meadow Valley Rd.). Turn left (north) on FS 765 and go 2 mi. to a right turn onto a dirt track that goes 0.5 mi. to Bog Hole Wildlife Area. Explore surrounding grasslands and wetlands.

San Xavier Mission—From I-19 in Tucson, take Exit 99 west onto Ajo Way. Go about 1 mi. west on Ajo Way to jct. with South Mission Rd. Turn left (south) on South Mission Rd., and go 5.6 mi. to jct. with San Xavier Rd. Turn left (east) on San Xavier Rd. and go 0.6 mi. to the mission. The area around the mission has mesquite desert scrub habitat.

Santa Cruz River Valley—From I-19 60 mi. south of Tucson, take Exit 29 onto the East Frontage Rd. Go north on the East Frontage Rd., paralleling the freeway, about 0.7 mi. to the entrance to the Tumacacori National Monument on the right. Enter the monument and park. A footpath goes north from here along the Santa Cruz River.

Santa Rita Experimental Range, Santa Rita Mountains—From I-19, 35 mi. south of Tucson, take Exit 63 east onto FS 62 (Continental-White House Canyon Rd.). Go east on FS 62 about 10 mi. until the road splits into FS 62 (left fork) and FS 62A (right fork). Bear right on FS 62A about 4 mi. to the range.

Santa Rita Lodge, Madera Canyon—From I-19, 35 mi. south of Tucson, take Exit 63 east onto FS 62 (Continental-White House Canyon Rd.). Go east on FS 62 about 8 mi. to jct. with FS 70 (Madera Canyon Rd.). Turn right (south) on FS 70. Proceed south on FS 70 about 4.5 mi. to Santa Rita Lodge.

Saulsbury Canyon, Chiricahua Mountains—See Turkey Creek entry.

Sawmill Canyon, Fort Huachuca—See Garden Canyon entry for directions to the fort and entry requirements. Continue west for 2 mi. to the marked turnoff for Garden Canyon. Turn left (south) and go 4 mi. or so to the entrance of the canyon where the road bends to the southwest. Proceed another 2.5 mi. to picnic areas, parking, and the end of the paved road. Proceed 2.8 mi. to the trailhead for Sawmill Canyon. Take the left fork and walk into the canyon area.

Scheelite Canyon, Fort Huachuca—See Garden Canyon entry for directions to the fort and entry requirements. Continue west for 2 mi. to the marked turnoff for Garden Canyon. Turn left (south) and go 4 mi. or so to the entrance of the canyon where the road bends to the southwest. Proceed another 2.5 mi. to picnic areas and parking. Continue another 0.7 mi. past the end of the paved road to the trailhead for Scheelite Canyon.

Scotia Canyon, Huachuca Mountains—From the jct. of AZ 82 and AZ 83 in Sonoita, go south on AZ 83 about 28 mi. to jct. with FS 48 at the turnoff for Parker Canyon Lake. Continue southeast on FS 48 2.2 mi. to jct. with FS 228. Turn left (northeast) on FS 228 and go 2.6 mi. where the road ends at a "T". Turn and go about 0.2 mi. and park. Walk up trail to the north to descend into Scotia Canyon.

Sells Highway—From I-19 in Tucson, take Exit 99 west onto Ajo Way (AZ 86). Follow AZ 86 56 mi. to Sells.

Shannon-Broadway Desert, Tucson—From I-10 in Tucson, take Exit 257A and go west on St. Mary's Rd. (becomes Anklam Rd.). Go 2.8 mi. west to jct. with Shannon Rd. Turn left (south) on Shannon Rd. and go 0.3 mi. to jct. with Broadway. Park here and explore desert habitat to the west.

Shannon Campground, Mount Graham—From I-10 east of Willcox, take Exit 352 and go north on US 191. Continue north for 27 mi. on US 191 to jct. with AZ 366. Turn left (west) on AZ 366, and go 21.5 mi. to Shannon Campground.

Sierra Vista Wastewater Ponds—From the jct. of I-10 and AZ 90 (Exit 302) west of Benson, go south on AZ 90 about 34 mi. to the jct. with AZ 92 and Fry Blvd. in Sierra Vista. Turn left (east) and continue on AZ 90 about 3 mi. to the sewage treatment plant. Turn left (north) to enter the site.

Ski Run Road, Mount Lemmon—See Molino Canyon and Mount Lemmon entries. The Ski Run section of the road is near the top of Mount Lemmon, about 30 mi. from Tucson.

Sonoita—From I-10 east of Tucson, take Exit 281 to AZ 83. Proceed south on AZ 83 about 26 mi. to jct. of AZ 83 and AZ 82 at the town of Sonoita.

Sonoita Creek—Sonoita Creek parallels AZ 82 between Sonoita (see Sonoita entry) and Patagonia. The best access to the creek is at the Patagonia-Sonoita Preserve (see entry).

Sonoita Grassland—Grassland habitat borders AZ 82 going east from Sonoita (see entry).

South Fork, Cave Creek Canyon—See Cave Creek Canyon entry. At the FS 42B/42 jct., proceed on FS 42 about 2 mi. to where the road for South Fork branches off to the left.

Spitler Land and Cattle Company alfalfa fields, Elfrida—From I-10, 9 mi. south of Willcox, take Exit 331 onto US 191 south. Follow US 191 about 23 mi. to Pearce. Continue on US 191 east for 9 mi., then south for 13 mi. to Elfrida. Fields along this section of road are good for wintering, open-country birds.

Sycamore Canyon, Nogales—See California Canyon entry. At the Sycamore Canyon turnoff, turn left and drive to the parking lot at Hank and Yank Springs. This is the trailhead for Sycamore Canyon. Park and proceed south on the trail up the canyon.

Tanque Verde Wash, Tucson—In Tucson, take Exit 256 from I-10 east onto E. Grant Rd. and continue east about 10.7 mi. to jct. with Tanque Verde Rd. Bear left on Tanque Verde Rd. Continue east on Tanque Verde 6.8 mi. to jct. with Wentworth Rd. Turn right (south) on Wentworth Rd. and proceed 0.7 mi. to wash.

Teec Nos Pos—The trading post town of Teec Nos Pos is located at the jct. of US 160 and US 64 on the Navajo Indian Reservation in extreme northeastern Arizona. Pull-offs from US 64 provide access to surrounding high desert habitat.

Terry Flat—See Escudilla Mountain entry.

Tonto Natural Bridges State Park—From I-17 55 mi. south of Flagstaff, take Exit 287 onto AZ 260. Go east on AZ 260 about 23 mi. to jct. with AZ 87. Turn right (west) on AZ 87 and go west and south about 17 mi. to jct. with FS 583. Turn right (west) on FS 583 and go about 2 mi. to the park.

Tumacacori National Monument—See Santa Cruz River Valley entry.

Turkey Creek—From I-10 southwest of Willcox, take Exit 331 and follow US 191 south 26 mi. to jct. with AZ 181 at Sunizona. Turn left (east) on AZ 181 and go about 12.5 mi. until AZ 181 makes a sharp left turn. Continue straight (east) on Turkey Creek Rd. (FS 41) for 11 mi. or so. Examine habitats along the road

Upper Carr Canyon, Huachuca Mountains—See Carr Canyon entry.

Vermilion Cliffs—From I-40 east of Flagstaff, take Exit 201 north onto US 89. Follow US 89 north 104 mi. to Bitter Springs. Bear left at Bitter Springs on US 89

Alt., and proceed 14 mi. to Marble Canyon. Continue south on US 89 Alt. The Vermilion Cliffs parallel US 89 Alt. northwest of the road for the next 20 mi.

White Mountains—See Big Lake Loop entry.

Willcox Lake—At Willcox, take Exit 344 off from I-10 onto Haskell Rd. Go southwest on Haskell Rd. 4 mi. to jct. with AZ 186. Turn left (southeast) on AZ 186. Proceed 0.5 mi. on AZ 186 to jct. with Rex Allen Dr. (and a sign for the Municipal Golf Course). Turn right on Rex Allen Dr. and proceed 1.2 mi. to the lake.

CALIFORNIA (136)

Andree Clark Bird Refuge—In the California coast city of Santa Barbara, take Cabrillo Blvd. Exit from US 101 and go south on Cabrillo Blvd. one block. Turn right on Los Patos Way and proceed to the refuge parking lot.

Angeles Crest Highway—From I-210 take Hwy 2 (Angeles Crest Hwy) north into the San Gabriel Mts. Highlands providing views of the San Fernando Valley also can be excellent for viewing migrating raptors in April.

Anza-Borrego Desert State Park—The hq. for this huge park is in Borrego Springs. The quickest way to get there depends on where you are coming from. From Los Angeles, take I-10 to I-215. Go south on I-215 until it merges with I-15. Continue south on I-15 to the Temecula Exit. Go east on CA 79 about 40 mi. to jct. with S22. Go east on S22 to Borrego Springs. The park hq. is off S22 on the west side of town.

Baldwin Lake—From Victorville on I-15, go east on CA 18 through Lucerne (at about 21 mi.) and on to the vicinity of the lake (at 35 mi. or so). The road turns west here. Look for an unmarked, dirt road to the left (south) that goes around the lake, and provides access.

Ballinger Canyon Road—From jct. of I-5 and CA 99 28 mi. south of Bakersfield, go north on I-5 4 mi. and exit to the west on CA 166. Go west on CA 166 23 mi. to Maricopa then south 14 mi. to jct. with CA 33. Turn left (south) on CA 33 and proceed 3.5 mi. to jct. with Ballinger Canyon Rd. Turn left (east) on Ballinger Canyon Rd. and go another 3.3 mi. to the campground at the road's end.

Big Canyon—From the jct. of I-405 and CA 55 in Costa Mesa, go southwest on CA 55 6 mi. to jct. with CA 1. Turn left (east) on CA 1 and go about 2.5 mi. to jct. with Jamboree Rd. Turn left (north) on Jamboree Road. Go about 1 mi. on Jamboree Rd. to jct. with San Joaquin Hills Rd. Turn left (west) on San Joaquin Hills Rd. Go about 0.2 mi. to jct. with Back Bay Dr. Turn right (north) on Back Bay Dr. The drive here goes through Big Canyon along the east border of Upper Newport Bay. Park in dirt parking lot for birding.

Big Morongo Canyon Preserve—From I-10 northwest of Palm Springs, exit north on CA 62. Continue north on CA 62 about 10 mi. to the town of Morongo Valley. At the jct. of CA 62 and East Drive in Morongo Valley. Turn right (southeast) on East Drive and proceed 3 blocks to the preserve.

Black Mountain Campground—From I-10 at Banning, exit south on CA 243. Proceed south on CA 243 about 16.5 mi. to a dirt road to the left that goes to Black Mountain. Turn left (east) on this road and proceed to the campground.

Bluff Lake—From Victorville on I-15, go east on CA 18 through Lucerne (at about 21 mi.) and on to the vicinity of Baldwin Lake (at 35 mi. or so) where CA 18 turns west. Follow CA 18 around the north end of Baldwin Lake and through Bear City. From Bear City, continue on CA 18 along the south shore of Big Bear Lake about 5 mi. to jct. with Mill Creek Road (2N10). Stay on Mill Creek Road for the next 8 mi. or so as it winds around until you come to the jct. with 2N11. Turn right on 2N11, and proceed to parking lot.

Bob's Gap—From the jct. of CA 2 and N 4 (Big Pines Highway) northwest of the town of Wrightwood, proceed northwest on N 4 about 6.8 mi. to jct. with Bob's Gap Road. Turn right on Bob's Gap Road and proceed 2.2 mi. to jct. with dirt road to the right. Turn right on dirt road and park along road.

Bolsa Chica State Ecological Reserve—From the jct. of I-405 and CA 55 in Costa Mesa, go southwest on CA 55 6 mi. to jct. with CA 1. Turn right on CA 1 and go about 9 mi. to a parking lot on the right for the reserve.

Border Field State Park—From the jct. of I-5 and CA 905 south of San Diego, go west on CA 905 about 0.7 mi. to jct. with Hollister St. Turn left (south) on Hollister St. and go about 1.5 mi. to jct. with Monument Rd. Turn right (west) on Monument Rd. and proceed about 2.5 mi. to the park.

Borrego Palm Canyon Campground—From the I-15 Temecula Exit, go east on CA 79 about 40 mi. to jct. with S22. Go east on S22 to Borrego Springs. The Anza-Borrego Desert State Park Visitor Center is on your left coming into Borrego. Go to the center for maps and information. The campground is located a mile or so north of the center.

Buckhorn Flat Campground—From the jct. of CA 2 and N 4 (Big Pines High-way) northwest of the town of Wrightwood, proceed west on CA 2 about 21 mi. to the campground (sign on left, entrance on right).

Buena Vista Lagoon—From I-5 at Oceanside, take the east exit for CA 78. Go east on CA 78 about 0.6 mi. to jct. with Jefferson St. Turn right on Jefferson St., and take an immediate right down to the north side of the lagoon.

Burnt Rancheria Campground—From I-8 41 mi. east of San Diego, take the exit for S1 (Sunrise Hwy.). Go north on S1 about 10 mi. to the campground, just before (0.2 mi.) entering the village of Mount Laguna.

Butterbredt Spring Wildlife Sanctuary—From the southern jct. of CA 58 and CA 14 in the town of Mojave, go north about 1.2 mi. until CA 14 branches off to the right. Follow CA 14 northeast for about 20 mi. to the jct. with Jawbone Canyon Rd. Turn left (west) on Jawbone Canyon Rd. and go 5.2 mi. to the turnoff for Butterbredt Spring. Bear right and proceed 0.9 mi. to the spring.

Cabrillo National Monument—In San Diego, at the jct. of I-5 and I-8 (Ocean Beach Freeway), exit west onto Ocean Beach Freeway. Proceed west on the freeway about 2 mi. until the road bends southwest and becomes Sunset Cliffs Blvd. Go about 1.5 mi. on Sunset Cliffs Blvd. to jct. with Point Loma Ave. Turn left on Point Loma Ave., go about 0.8 mi., then right on Catalina Blvd. Follow this south (it becomes Cabrillo Memorial Dr.) about 4 mi. to the monument.

Carrizo Plain—On I-5 just west of Bakersfield, exit west on CA 58 and proceed 44 mi. to jct. with Soda Lake Rd. Turn left (south) on Soda Lake Rd. The road (part paved, part dirt) extends 50 mi. across the Carrizo Plain, finally exiting onto CA 166.

Casper's Wilderness Park—On I-5 at San Juan Capistrano, exit east onto CA 74 (Ortega Hwy.). Continue east about 7.5 mi. to the park visitor center for maps and information.

Cedar Canyon Road, Cima—On I-15 26 mi. east of Baker, exit south on Cima Rd. Continue south 17 mi. to Cima. At Cima, turn right on the Cima-Kelso Rd. and go 4.5 mi. to jct. with Cedar Canyon Rd. Turn left (east) on Cedar Canyon Rd. and continue for 6 mi. or so, examining habitat along the route.

Channel Islands National Park—Made up of Santa Barbara, Santa Rosa, San Miguel, Anacapa, and east end of Santa Cruz Islands. The park headquarters may be reached by proceeding northwest from the jct. of CA 1 and US 101 north of Oxnard on US 101. Go 5.3 mi. to Seaward Ave. Exit in Ventura. Exit south onto Seaward Ave. and turn left in Ω block onto Harvard Blvd. Proceed on Harvard Blvd. 1.6 mi. to jct. with Spinnaker Dr. Turn right on Spinnaker Dr. and go to the end of the road for the park hq. The islands can be reached by various charters, including Island Packers (office at 1867 Spinnaker Dr, Ventura, CA, tel. 805-642-7688) (Holt 1990:169).

Charlton Flat Picnic Area—From I-210 take CA 2 (Angeles Crest Hwy.) north into the San Gabriel Mountains. Follow CA 2 about 21 mi. to Charlton Flat Picnic Area (left side of road).

Chilao Recreation Area—From I-210 take CA 2 (Angeles Crest Hwy.) north into the San Gabriel Mountains. Follow CA 2 about 23 mi. to the entrance to the recreation area (visitor center with maps and information).

Cibola National Wildlife Refuge—On I-10 at Blythe, exit south on CA 78 and proceed about 24 mi. south to the refuge.

Clark Mountain—On I-15 15 mi. west of the Arizona border, take the Bailey Rd. Exit north. Mine roads and trails (4-wheel-drive) climb north from there toward Clark Mountain (3 mi.).

Crystal Cove State Park—From the jct. of I-405 and CA 55 in Costa Mesa, go southwest on CA 55 6 mi. to jct. CA 1. Turn left (southeast) on CA 1. Go about 5 mi. southeast along the coast and look for park signs on your right.

Cuyamaca Rancho State Park—About 30 mi. east of San Diego on I-8, take CA 79 north 8 mi. to the park museum (maps and information available).

Date Palm Grove, Brawley—From I-8 at El Centro, take CA 86 north 16 mi. to Brawley. At the jct. of CA 86 and CA 78, turn left on CA 86 and go 1 block to jct. with Western Ave. Turn right on Western Ave., then left on "D" St. Follow "D" St. to Las Flores Dr. At Las Flores, park and walk north to palm grove.

Dawson Saddle, San Gabriel Mountains—From I-210 north of Burbank, take Hwy 2 (Angeles Crest Hwy) north into the San Gabriel Mts. Continue on the Angeles Crest Hwy for about 42 mi. to Dawson Saddle, at 7, 091', the highest point on Angeles Crest Hwy.

Devereux Slough—From US 101 west of Santa Barbara, Exit south on Storke Rd. Proceed about 1.5 mi. south to jct. with Colegio Dr. Turn right at this intersection and proceed a few hundred yards to the slough.

Dorothy May Tucker Wildlife Sanctuary—From I-5 at Costa Mesa, take the S18 Exit east (El Toro Rd.) about 9 mi. to jct. with Modjeska Grade Rd. Turn right on Modjeska Grade Rd. and continue about 2.3 mi. to the sanctuary. Visitor center is on your left and cabin with feeders is on the right.

El Cariso Campground—From I-15 at Lake Elsinore, exit southwest on CA 74. Follow CA 74 southwest as it winds through Lake Elsinore to the jct. with Grand Ave. From where CA 74 turns right off from Grand Ave. to the turn for El Cariso Campground is about 5.6 mi.

El Dorado Nature Center—From the jct. of I-5 and I-605, go south on I-5 about 10 mi. to the Spring St. Exit. Exit west on Spring St., and watch for the center entrance on the left (7550 East Spring St.).

Fairmount Park, Riverside—From the jct. of I-215 and CA 91 in Riverside, go southwest on CA 91 about 1 mi. to jct. with University Ave. Turn right on University Ave. and go about 1 mi. to jct. with Redwood Dr. Turn right on Redwood Dr. and go a little more than a half mile to the park.

Forrestal Drive, Palos Verdes Peninsula—From the jct. of I-405 and US 110, take US 110 south about 10 mi. to jct. with 25th St. Turn right (west) on 25th St. Go about 3 mi. on 25th to jct. with Forrestal Dr. Turn right on Forrestal Dr. and park by the school on the left. Foot paths go up into the hills on the right.

G13 near Bitterwater—From US 101 at King City, exit on G13 Hwy. From about 10 mi. east of King City to the jct. with CA 25 (15 mi.), the habitat is good for Yellow-billed Magpie and other oak savanna species.

Generals Highway, Sequoia National Park—From CA 99 near Visalia, exit east on CA 198. Go east on CA 198 about 33 mi. to the entrance of Sequoia National Park. Continue into the park. Giant Forest Village is 19 mi., at an elevation of 6,409 feet.

Goleta Point—Driving west from Santa Barbara on US 101, exit south on CA 217. Follow CA 217 southwest all the way to the end (CA 217 becomes Lagoon Rd. on the University of California, Santa Barbara campus). The road ends in a parking lot. Walk west from here to Goleta Point.

Greenspot Picnic Ground—From Victorville on I-15, go east on CA 18 through Lucerne (at about 21 mi.) and on to the vicinity of the lake (at 35 mi. or so) where CA 18 turns west. Look for Baldwin Lake Rd. here, an unmarked, dirt road to the left (south). Follow Baldwin Lake Rd. 4.7 mi. around the east and south ends of the lake then west after merging with Shay Rd. to jct. with CA 38. Turn left on CA 38 (Greenspot Blvd.) and go 3.8 mi. to Greenspot Picnic Ground.

Grout Bay Campground—From Victorville on I-15, go east on CA 18 through Lucerne (at about 21 mi.) and on to the vicinity of Baldwin Lake (at 35 mi. or so). The road turns west here. Follow CA 18 around the north end of Baldwin Lake and through Bear City to jct. with CA 38. Follow CA 38 west along the north shore of Big Bear Lake 2.9 mi. to the campground.

Guadalupe Dunes County Park—At the jct. of US 101 and CA 166 west in Santa Maria, exit west onto CA 166. Follow CA 166 (West Main St.) about 13 mi. to the mouth of the Santa Maria River and Guadalupe Dunes County Park.

Harbor Regional Park—From the jct. of I-405 and US 110, take US 110 south about 4.4 mi. to jct. with CA 1 (Pacific Coast Hwy.). Exit west onto CA 1 and proceed about 0.5 mi. to jct. with Vermont Ave. Turn left (south) on Vermont Ave. The park is on the left.

Havasu Lake—From I-40 at Needles, exit south on CA 95. Follow CA 95 south about 20 mi. to jct. with Havasu Lake Rd. Turn left (east) on Havasu Lake Rd., and proceed about 16 mi. to the lake.

Hi Mountain Road—About 15 mi. south of San Luis Obispo, take the Grand Ave. Exit from US 101 east onto Lopez Dr. and CA 227. At the split of CA 227 and Lopez Dr. (0.8 mi.) continue west on Lopez Dr. for about 10 mi. to the jct. with Hi Mountain Rd. (immediate right turn after crossing southeast arm of Lopez Lake). Turn right on Hi Mountain Rd. and stop at appropriate habitat. Road goes 13 mi. to the top of Hi Mountain.

Huntington Central Park (Lake Talbert)—From the jct. of I-405 and CA 55 in Costa Mesa, go north on I-405 4.7 mi. to the Brookhurst St. Exit. Turn right from the off ramp, then immediately left onto Slater St. Continue on Slater St. for 2.9 mi. One hundred yards before reaching Golden West St., turn left into the Huntington Central Park parking lot (Gallagher in Holt 1990:63).

Imperial Dam—Take Exit 2 off from I-8 and go north on US 95 18 mi. to jct. with Imperial Dam Rd. Turn left (west) on Imperial Dam Rd. and go about 8 mi. following signs to the dam.

Imperial National Wildlife Refuge—See Arizona Imperial National Wildlife Refuge entry.

Irvine Regional Park—From the jct. of I-5 and CA 55 in Santa Ana, go north on CA 55 5 mi. to jct. with S18 (Villa Park Rd.). Turn right (east) on S18. Proceed on S18 (becomes Santiago Canyon Rd.) about 5.5 mi. to jct. with Chapman Ave. Turn left and proceed to the park.

Joshua Tree National Monument—From I-10 northwest of Palm Springs, exit north on CA 62. Continue north and east on CA 62 about 27 mi. to the town of Joshua Tree. Watch for sign for right turn at Park Blvd. to monument hq. for information, maps, and checklist.

La Cumbre Fire Lookout—At the jct. of US 101 and CA 154 (San Marcos Pass Rd.) on the west side of Santa Barbara, take CA 154 north. Proceed 9.3 mi. or so to San Marcos Pass and the jct. with East Camino Cielo Rd. Turn right on East Camino Cielo Rd. and proceed about 9 mi. to La Cumbre Peak and fire lookout tower.

La Jolla Beach—Coming north from San Diego on I-5 (you can't take this route coming south), Exit I-5 at Ardath Rd. Follow Ardath Rd. for 1.2 mi. where it becomes Torrey Pines Rd. From there continue on Torrey Pines Rd. another mile and follow signs from there for the "Scenic Route" to the lifeguard station parking area at La Jolla Beach.

Lake Cachuma—At the jct. of US 101 and CA 154 (San Marcos Pass Rd.) on the west side of Santa Barbara, take CA 154 north. Proceed about 19 mi. to Lake Cachuma County Park.

Lake Crowley—Technically speaking, the Crowley Lake area is 40 miles north of the coverage of this book. Nevertheless, I include it because it is the nearest place for a decent chance to see Sage Grouse. The instructions are modified from Childs (1993:76). From the town of Bishop on US 395, proceed north about 32 mi. to jct. with Benton Crossing Rd. Turn right (east) on Benton Crossing Rd., and go 1.1 mi. to jct. with an unpaved road. Turn right on this road and proceed 0.8 mi. to a fork. Take the right fork and proceed another 1.0 mi. Turn right, proceed 0.3 mi. and park. Arrive well before dawn from mid-March through April for best chance of seeing and hearing birds.

Lake Elsinore State Recreation Area—From the jct. of I-15 and CA 74 at Lake Elsinore, take CA 74 west and proceed about 3 mi. to the entrance to the recreation area on the left. Lake Elsinore State Park is at the south end of the lake.

Lake Fulmor—From I-10 at Banning, exit south on CA 243. Proceed south on CA 243 about 15 mi. to the lake.

Lake Hemet—From I-10 at Banning, exit south on CA 243. Proceed south on CA 243 about 31 mi. to jct. with CA 74 at Mountain Center. Turn left (south) on CA 74 and go 3.7 mi. to Lake Hemet (right) and Hurkey Creek Campground (left).

Lake Perris State Recreation Area—From the jct. of I-215 and CA 60 east of

Riverside, go south on I-215 about 7.5 mi. to the Ramona Expressway Exit. Go east on Ramona Expressway about 2.6 mi. to jct. with Lake Perris Dr. Turn left (north) on Lake Perris Dr. and proceed about 4 mi. to the recreation area.

Lawler Park, San Jacinto Mountains—From I-10 at Banning, exit south on CA 243. Proceed south on CA 243 about 18.3 mi. to the trailhead for Dark Canyon Trail, which climbs up past Lawler Lodge into Dark Canyon.

Little Corona City Beach (Corona del Mar State Beach)—From the jct. of I-405 and CA 55 in Costa Mesa, go southwest on CA 55 6 mi. to jct. CA 1. Turn left (east) on CA 1 and go about 4.6 mi. to jct. with Poppy Ave. Turn right (south) on Poppy Ave., drive to the end (0.3 mi.) and park. Walk to the beach.

Lopez Lake County Park—See Hi Mountain Road entry. Continue straight ahead on Lopez Dr. to the park entrance.

Lost Palms Oasis—See Joshua Tree National Monument entry. Get maps and information for specific sites at the monument hq.

Louis Rubidoux Nature Center—From the jct. of I-215/CA 60 and CA 91 in Riverside, go west on CA 60 2.7 mi. to jct. with Rubidoux Blvd. Turn left on Rubidoux Blvd., and go 0.6 mi. to jct. with Mission Blvd. Turn right on Mission Blvd. and proceed 0.3 mi. to jct. with Riverview Dr. Follow Riverview Dr. 1.8 mi. to the nature center (modified from McGaugh in Holt 1990:151).

Lower San Juan Picnic Ground—On I-5 at San Juan Capistrano, exit east onto CA 74 (Ortega Hwy.). Continue east about 16.4 mi. to the picnic ground on the left.

Malibu Creek State Park—From the jct. of I-405 and US 101 northwest of Los Angeles, go west on US 101 about 14 mi. to the jct. with N1. Go south on N1 about 4 mi. to the park (entrance on the right).

Malibu Lagoon State Beach—See Malibu Creek State Park entry above. Go south on N1 about 9 mi. to the jct. with CA 1. Turn left on CA 1 and proceed for a few hundred yards to the Malibu Lagoon Beach entrance.

McGill Campground—From I-5 south of Bakersfield, exit west on Frazier Mountain Rd. toward Frazier Park. Proceed west on Frazier Mountain Rd. 7 mi. to Lake of the Woods where the road splits. Take the right fork (Cuddy Valley Rd.), and go 5.2 mi. to where Cuddy Valley Rd. turns to the left to climb up Mount Pinos. Potrero Hwy. goes to the right. Follow Cuddy Valley Rd. up the mountain 5.3 mi. to McGill Campground.

Mill Creek Canyon, Big Falls Picnic Area—From the jct. of I-10 and CA 30 in Redlands, exit north on CA 30. Take the first right on Lugonia Ave. This becomes CA 38 in about 1.0 mi. Continue on CA 38 about 13 mi. to jct. with Forest Falls Rd. CA 38 makes a sharp turn to the left (north). Continue ahead on Forest Falls Rd. up Mill Creek Canyon to Big Falls Picnic Area.

Montaña de Oro State Park—South of San Luis Obispo at the jct. of US 101 and Los Osos Valley Rd., go west on Los Osos Valley Rd. about 11.5 mi. to jct. with

Pecho Valley Rd. Turn left (south) on Pecho Valley Rd. and proceed 4 mi. to the park hq.

Mount Pinos Road—See McGill Campground entry. Follow Cuddy Valley Rd. up the mountain 7 mi. to the parking lot at the end of the paved road. Mount Pinos Rd. (dirt) continues another 1.2 mi. to the top.

Morro Bay—From CA 1 east of the town of Morro Bay, exit south on South Bay Blvd. Go south on South Bay Blvd. about 1.0 mi. until the road splits. Take the right fork (State Park Rd.) about 1.5 mi. to the bay and park hq.

Morro Rock, Morro Bay—For a good look at Morro Rock, exit from CA 1 on Morro Bay Blvd. Go about 1.0 mi. on Morro Bay Blvd. until it ends in a "T". Turn right (north) at the "T" and follow the road to its end as it curves around the north end of the bay.

Nojoqui Falls County Park, Santa Barbara—From the jct. of CA 1 and US 101 at Gaviota, go north about 2.3 mi. Turn right (east) and proceed about 1.9 mi. to the park entrance.

Oak Canyon Nature Center, Santa Ana Mountains—From the jct. of I-5 and CA 55 in Santa Ana, go north on CA 55 7.5 mi. to jct. with CA 91. Go right (east) on CA 91 about 2.5 mi. to jct. with CA 90. Go south on CA 90 until the road ends at Nohl Ranch Rd. Turn left on Nohl Ranch Rd. and continue to jct. with Walnut Canyon Rd. Turn left on Walnut Canyon Rd. and proceed 0.5 mi. to the nature center.

Ocean Beach County Park, Lompoc—From the jct. of CA 1 and US 101 west of Santa Barbara, go north on CA 1 19 mi. to Lompoc. In Lompoc, follow CA 1 as it turns left on Ocean Ave., but continue west on Ocean Ave. when CA 1 turns north in 1.0 mi. Follow Ocean Ave. all the way to the park (10 mi.).

Oceano Campground, Oceano—In Arroyo Grande, take the Grande Ave. Exit on US 101. Continue west on Grand Ave. to jct. with CA 1 at 2.7 mi. Turn left (south) on CA 1 and go 0.9 mi. to jct. with Coolidge Dr. Turn right (west) on Coolidge Dr., proceed to the end of the street, and park.

O'Neill Regional Park, Santa Ana Mountains—From I-5 at Costa Mesa, take the S18 Exit east (El Toro Rd.) about 7.8 mi. to Cook's Corner at the jct. of S18 with S19 (Live Oak Canyon Rd.). Turn right on Live Oak Canyon Rd., and go 3.2 mi. to the park.

Otay Lakes, San Diego—From the jct. of I-5 and I-805 near the California-Mexico border south of San Diego, proceed north on I-805 for 5.8 mi. to jct. with Telegraph Canyon Rd. Turn right (east) on Telegraph Canyon Rd. and proceed 5.5 mi. to jct. with Otay Lakes Rd. Bear right (east) onto Otay Lakes Rd., and proceed to lakes (about 2 mi.).

Palomar Mountain State Park—From I-15, 11 mi. south of Temecula, exit east onto CA 76. Follow CA 76 for 16 mi. to Rincon and the jct. with S6. Continue east from Rincon 5.3 mi. until S6 (South Grade Rd.) branches off to the left. Follow S6 6.8 mi. to jct. with S7. Turn left (northwest) on S7 (State Park Rd.) and proceed 3 mi. to the park.

Palos Verdes Peninsula—See Forrestal Dr. entry. Go about 3 mi. on 25th to the peninsula. Twenty-fifth St. becomes Palos Verdes Dr., which follows the perimeter of the peninsula.

Parker Dam, Colorado River—At the western Arizona border, take Exit 9 off from I-40 and follow AZ 95 south 45 mi. to Parker Dam.

Pine Cove Road, San Jacinto Mountains—From I-10 at Banning, exit south on CA 243. Proceed south on CA 243 about 19 mi. to the town of Pine Cove. Turn right at the gas station onto Pine Cove Rd. (Holt 1990:134).

Piute Mountain Road, Kern County—From the southern jct. of CA 58 and CA 14 in the town of Mojave, go north about 1.2 mi. until CA 14 branches off to the right. Follow CA 14 northeast for about 20 mi. to the jct. with Jawbone Canyon Rd. Turn left (west) on Jawbone Canyon Rd. and go 5.2 mi. to the turnoff for Butterbredt Spring. Bear right and proceed 8.5 mi. to jct. with Kelso Valley Rd. Turn right on Kelso Valley Rd., and proceed 1.3 mi. to jct. with Piute Mountain Rd. at Sageland. Turn left on Piute Mountain Rd., which goes on for another 13 mi., to Piute Peak.

Placerita Canyon State Park—From the jct. of I-5 and CA 14 northwest of Los Angeles, follow CA 14 northeast about 3 mi. to the Placerita Canyon Rd. Exit. Go about 2 mi. east on Placerita Canyon Rd. to the park.

Point Fermin Park—From the jct. of I-405 and US 110, take US 110 south about 11 mi. to its end at Point Fermin.

Point La Jolla Lifeguard Station, San Diego—See La Jolla entry.

Point Mugu State Park—From the jct. of CA 1 and US 101 south of Ventura, go south on CA 1 about 16 mi. to the turnoff for the park (to the left).

Point Vicente Park, Palos Verdes Peninsula—See Forrestal Dr. entry. Go about 7 mi. on 25th (becomes Palos Verdes Dr. South) to the park and interpretive center.

Quatal Canyon, Ventucopa—From the jct. of I-5 and CA 99 south of Bakersfield, take I-5 north 4 mi. to jct. with CA 166. Exit west on CA 166 and go 23 mi. to the jct. with CA 33 at Maricopa. Continue south on CA 166/33 from Maricopa 14 mi. until CA 33 branches off to the left. Follow CA 33 left (south) 8.2 mi. to jct. with Quatal Canyon Rd. Turn left (east) on Quatal Canyon Rd.

Red Box Ranger Station, San Gabriel Mountains—From I-210 take CA 2 (Angeles Crest Hwy.) north into the San Gabriel Mts. Follow CA 2 about 12 mi. to the ranger station (right side of road just west of the Mount Wilson turnoff).

S6 Hwy, Summit Grove, Palomar Mountain—From I-15, 11 mi. south of Temecula, exit east onto CA 76. Follow CA 76 for 16 mi. to Rincon and the jct. with

S6 (South Grade Rd.). Continue east from Rincon 5.3 mi. until S6 branches off to the left. Follow S6 6.8 mi. to jct. with S7 at Summit Grove.

Salton Sea National Wildlife Refuge—From I-8 at El Centro, take CA 86 north 16 mi. to Brawley. At the jct. of CA 86 and CA 78, turn left and follow CA 86/78 7 mi. to Westmorland. In Westmorland, turn right (north) on Forrester Rd. (S30). Go north on Forrester Rd. about 2.7 mi. to jct. with Walker Rd. Turn right (east) on Walker Rd. and proceed 0.5 mi. to jct. with Gentry Rd. Turn left (north) on Gentry Rd. and go 7.5 mi. north to the refuge hq. for maps, information, and checklist.

San Elijo Lagoon Sanctuary, Solana Beach—From the jct. of CA 78 and I-5 in Oceanside, go south on I-5 about 11 mi. to the Santa Fe Dr. Exit. Travel west on Santa Fe Dr. about 0.5 mi. to jct. with San Elijo Ave. Turn left on San Elijo Ave. and proceed south about 1.8 mi. to the lagoon.

San Jacinto Wildlife Area—From the jct. of I-215 and CA 60 east of Riverside, go east on CA 60 about 9 mi. to jct. with Theodore St. Turn right (south) on Theodore St. (becomes Davis Rd.) and proceed about 6 mi. to the turnoff to the left for the wildlife area.

San Juan Forestry Station—On I-5 at San Juan Capistrano, exit east onto CA 74 (Ortega Hwy.). Continue east about 12.6 mi. to the forestry station on the left.

Santa Anita Canyon, Los Angeles Region—"To reach the canyon, go east from Pasadena to Santa Anita Ave. Turn left (north) to the end of the road." (Holt 1990:180).

Santa Barbara Museum of Natural History—In the California coastal city of Santa Barbara, take the Cabrillo Blvd. Exit from US 101 and go west on Cabrillo Blvd. about 3.5 mi. to jct. with State St. Turn right on State St. and proceed about 2.2 mi. to jct. with Los Olivos St. Turn right on Los Olivos St. and proceed about 0.5 mi. until Mission Canyon Rd. bears off to the left. Follow Mission Canyon Rd. 0.5 mi. to the museum (on the left).

Santa Clara River Estuary, Ventura—From the jct. of CA 1 and US 101 north of Oxnard on US 101, go 5.3 mi. to the Seaward Ave. Exit in Ventura. Exit south onto Seaward Ave. and turn left in Ω block onto Harvard Blvd. Proceed on Harvard Blvd. about 2 mi. to the Santa Clara River Bridge. Park off the road before reaching the bridge to survey the river mouth and estuary.

Santa Clara River Mouth, Ventura—See Santa Clara River Estuary entry.

Santa Maria Municipal Dump—At the jct. of US 101 and CA 166 West (Main St.) in Santa Maria, exit east onto Main St. and proceed about 2 mi. to the municipal dump (on your left).

Santa Maria River Mouth—See Guadalupe Dunes County Park entry. The river mouth can be reached on foot from the park.

Santa Rosa Plateau Preserve—From the jct. of I-15 and CA 74 at Lake Elsinore, go west on CA 74 to Lakeshore Dr. Turn left (south) on Lakeshore Dr. and follow this road until it merges with Palomar-Washington St. Continue southeast on Palomar-Washington St. to jct. with Clinton-Keith Rd. Turn right on Clinton-Keith Rd. and proceed to the preserve.

Santiago Oaks Regional Park—From the jct. of I-5 and CA 55 in Santa Ana, go north on CA 55 5 mi. to jct. with S18 (Villa Park Rd.). Turn right (east) on S18. Proceed on S18 (becomes Santiago Canyon Rd.) about 3.5 mi. to jct. with Windes Dr. Turn left and proceed to the park.

Sequoia National Park—From CA 99 near Visalia, exit east on CA 198. Go east on CA 198 about 33 mi. to the entrance of Sequoia National Park. The Foothills Visitor Center is less than a mile ahead on the right.

Shell Beach—From the jct. of CA 1 and US 101 north of Oceano, continue on US 101 northwest about 1.5 mi. to the Shell Beach Rd. Exit. Proceed northwest on Shell Beach Rd. 0.3 mi. to tennis courts where parking is available.

Shipley Nature Center, Huntington Beach—See Huntington Central Park entry. To get to the nature center, exit the park by making a left on Slater St. Continue on Slater St. 0.6 mi. to jct. with Edwards St. Turn left on Edwards St. Proceed 0.4 mi. on Edwards St. to the park entrance on the left. Turn left into the park entrance road and proceed 0.3 mi. to the parking lot. At the north end of the lot is a trail to the nature center (Gallagher in Holt 1990:64).

Silverwood Audubon Sanctuary—From I-8 east of San Diego, exit onto Jennings Par Rd. (becomes Maple View St.) Continue on Maple View St. to jct. with Ashwoco St. Turn right on Ashwoco St. (becomes Wildcat Canyon Rd.) and go to 13003 Wildcat Canyon Rd. where the sanctuary is located.

Silverwood Lake State Recreation Area—From the jct. of I-15 and I-215 at San Bernardino, go north 8 mi. on I-15 to the CA 138 Exit. Go east on CA 138 about 8 mi. to the recreation area.

Soda Lake, Carrizo Plain—See Carrizo Plain entry. Soda Lake is on the left side of Soda Lake Rd. about 11 mi. southeast of the jct. of CA 58 and Soda Lake Rd.

South Coast Botanic Garden, Palos Verdes Peninsula—From the jct. of I-405 and US 110, take US 110 south about 4.4 mi. to jct. with CA 1 (Pacific Coast Hwy.). Exit west onto CA 1 and proceed about 0.5 mi. to jct. with Vermont Ave. Turn left (south) on Vermont Ave. Proceed on Vermont Ave. about 1.2 mi. to jct. with Anaheim St. and Palos Verdes Dr. Go west from this intersection on Palos Verdes Dr., and continue 3.5 mi. to jct. with Crenshaw Blvd. Turn right on Crenshaw Blvd. and go 0.3 mi. to the garden.

South Bay Marine Biological Study Area—From the jct. of I-5 and I-805 near the Mexican border, proceed north on I-5 about 3.7 mi. to jct. with CA 75 (Palm Ave.). Exit onto CA 75 west and proceed about 2 mi. west, then, as CA 75 bends north, continue north for another 1.5 mi. or so to the study area on the right.

South Kern River Reserve—From the jct. of CA 99 and CA 204 north of Bakersfield, follow CA 204 southeast 2.5 mi. to jct. with CA 178. Take CA 178 east and proceed about 54 mi. to the town of Weldon. Look for a sign on the left for the reserve hq. where maps and information about the reserve are available.

Summit Grove, Palomar Mountain—See S6 Hwy. entry.

Sunrise Hwy., Laguna Mountains—See Burnt Rancheria Campground entry. Sunrise Hwy. (S1) winds through much of the Laguna Mountain highlands.

Switzer Picnic Area, San Gabriel Mountains—From the jct. of CA 2 and N 4 (Big Pines Hwy.) northwest of the town of Wrightwood, proceed west on CA 2 about 10 mi. to the road that goes off to the right, down to the picnic area. The turn is marked.

Tapia County Park—From the jct. of I-405 and US 101 northwest of Los Angeles, go west on US 101 about 14 mi. to the jct. with N1. Go south on N1 about 5.3 mi. to the park (entrance on the right).

Tijuana Estuary National Wildlife Refuge—From the jct. of I-5 and I-805 near the Mexican border, proceed north on I-5 about 3.7 mi. to jct. with CA 75 (Palm Ave.). Proceed west on Palm Ave. about 3 mi. to jct. with Seacoast Dr. Turn left (south) on Seacoast Dr. and continue 1.5 mi. until the road ends at the estuary.

Torrey Pines State Reserve—Coming north from San Diego on I-5, exit I-5 west at S21. Follow S21 west about 1.0 mi. to the reserve.

Upper Newport Bay—From the jct. of I-405 and CA 55 in Costa Mesa, go southwest on CA 55 6 mi. to jct. with CA 1. Turn left (east) on CA 1 and go about 2.5 mi. to jct. with Jamboree Rd. Turn left (north) on Jamboree Rd. Go about 0.2 mi. on Jamboree Rd. to jct. with Back Bay Dr. Turn left (west) on Back Bay Dr. and proceed to the shore of the bay. Landslides closed the drive north of the parking lot in 1998.

Valle Vista Campground, Mount Pinos—From the jct. of I-5 and CA 99 south of Bakersfield, take I-5 north 4 mi. to jct. with CA 166. Exit west on CA 166 and go 23 mi. to the jct. with CA 33 at Maricopa. Continue south on CA 166/33 from Maricopa 14 mi. until CA 33 branches off to the left. Follow CA 33 left (south) 8.2 mi. to jct. with Quatal Canyon Rd. Turn left (east) on Quatal Canyon Rd. Proceed east on Quatal Canyon Rd. 14.8 mi. to jct. with Portrero Hwy. Turn left on Portrero Hwy. and go 6.5 mi. to the entrance to the campground (on right).

Vivian Meadows, San Bernardino Mountains—See Mill Creek Canyon, Big Falls Picnic Area entry. From the falls, hike upstream to Vivian Meadows.

West Fork, San Gabriel River—See Red Box Ranger Station entry. A hiking trail from the station goes to the river.

West Pond, Imperial National Wildlife Refuge—See Imperial National Wildlife Refuge entry. Get maps and information at refuge hq.

Wister Unit, State Imperial Wildlife Area, Salton Sea—From El Centro, proceed east 3 mi. on I-8 to jct. with CA 111. Exit onto CA 111 and go north 39 mi. to the Wister Unit (entrance road on the left).

Wyman Canyon, White Mountains—This site is a bit north of the defined region (20 mi.), but provides a southern California site for the Broad-billed Hummingbird. From the jct. of US 395 and CA 168 at Big Pine, go northeast on CA 168 about 27 mi. to the turnoff to the right for Deep Springs College. Continue on CA 168 past this turnoff about 3 mi. to the turnoff on the left (dirt road for 4-wheel drive vehicles) that follows Wyman Creek into Wyman Canyon.

Yaqui Well, Anza-Borrego Desert State Park—See Anza-Borrego State Park entry. Get maps and information at park hq.

NEVADA (22)

Bonanza Trailhead—From the jct. of US 95 and I-15 in downtown Las Vegas, take Exit 42 off I-15 and go northwest on US 95 (Tonopah Hwy., follow signs to Reno). Continue on US 95 about 35 mi. to jct. with Cold Creek Rd. (turnoff for the Correctional Center). Go west on Cold Creek Rd. 13 mi. to Bonanza Trailhead.

Cold Creek, Spring Mountains—See Bonanza Trailhead entry above. Go west on Cold Creek Rd. 12.6 mi. to a sharp right (marked "Willow Creek 3 miles"). Turn right and go 0.7 mi. to Cold Creek.

Corn Creek, Desert National Wildlife Range—From the jct. of US 95 and I-15 in downtown Las Vegas, take Exit 42 off I-15 and go northwest on US 95 (Tonopah Hwy., follow signs to Reno). Continue on US 95 about 17 mi. to the turnoff for the Desert National Wildlife Range on the right (sign). Turn right and follow signs to the visitor center (about 5.5 mi.) for maps, information, and checklist. Corn Creek is located near the visitor center.

Davis Dam—From the jct. of US 95 and US 93 west of Boulder, go south on US 95 about 55 mi. to jct. with NV 163. Turn left (east) on NV 163 and go 21 mi. to Davis Dam.

Desert National Wildlife Range—See Corn Creek entry. Visitor center has maps and information on habitats and localities on this huge refuge.

Floyd Lamb State Park—See Bonanza Trailhead entry. Continue on US 95 about 8 mi. to jct. with Durango Dr. Bear right onto Durango Dr. and continue 1.3 mi. until the road splits. Take the right fork and go 0.9 mi. to the park entrance (modified from Titus 1991:22).

Kyle Canyon—See Bonanza Trailhead entry. Continue on US 95 about 15 mi. to jct. with NV 157 (Kyle Canyon Rd.). Turn left (west) and proceed up Kyle Canyon Rd. toward Mount Charleston.

Lake Mead—From the jct. of US 95 and US 93 west of Boulder, go east on US 93 7 mi. to the Lake Mead Visitor Center for maps, information, and checklist.

Lake Mojave—From the jct. of US 95 and US 93 west of Boulder, go south on US 95 about 36 mi. to jct. with NV 164. Turn left (east) on NV 164 and go 14 mi. to Cottonwood Cove on Lake Mojave.

Las Vegas Wash—From I-515 in east Las Vegas, take Exit 70 onto Las Vegas Valley Dr. Go east on Las Vegas Valley Dr. about 3.4 mi. to jct. with S. Hollywood Blvd. Turn right (south) onto S. Hollywood Blvd. About 1.0 mi. south, this road comes very close to the wash, and parallels it for the next 2.0 mi. Park and examine the wash habitat.

Lee Canyon Ski Area, Mount Charleston—See Bonanza Trailhead entry. Continue on US 95 about 30 mi. to jct. with Kyle Canyon Rd. (NV 156). Go left on NV 156 and go about 16 mi. to the ski area.

Mount Charleston—See Bonanza Trailhead entry. Continue on US 95 about 15 mi. to jct. with NV 157 (Kyle Canyon Rd.). Turn left (west) and proceed up Kyle Canyon Rd. about 21 mi. to Mount Charleston Wilderness Area.

Overton Wildlife Management Area—From the jct. of US 95 and I-15 at Exit 42 in downtown Las Vegas, go north on I-15 about 33 mi. to jct. with NV 169. Turn right (east) on NV 169 and go 24 mi. to a "T" jct. The right branch is SSR 12 to Overton Beach. Take the left turn onto NV 169 going north. Continue about 6 mi. to the entrance to the management area. Turn right and proceed 0.3 mi. to parking area.

Pahranagat National Wildlife Refuge—These wetlands are a bit north of the defined region, but provide excellent habitat for water birds and shorebirds, and so are included. To reach them, take Exit 64 off from I-15 about 20 mi. north of Las Vegas onto US 93. Proceed north on US 93 about 63 mi. to the entrance road for the refuge hq. (sign).

Potosi Mountain—From I-15 about 9 mi. south of Las Vegas, take Exit 33 onto NV 160 and go west 18.6 mi. to jct. with Potosi Mountain Rd. Turn left (south) on Potosi Mountain Rd. and explore highland desert habitats along road.

Red Rock Canyon National Monument—From I-15 in downtown Las Vegas, take Exit 41B west onto Charleston Blvd. (NV 159). Proceed west on Charleston Blvd. about 15 mi. to the entrance of the monument. Follow signs to visitor center for maps, information, and checklist.

Sunset Park, Las Vegas—From I-15 in south Las Vegas, take Exit 37 onto Tropicana Ave. Proceed east on Tropicana Ave. about 3.5 mi. to jct. with Eastern Ave. Turn right (south) on Eastern Ave. and continue 2 mi. to jct. with Sunset Rd. Turn left (east) on Sunset Rd. Proceed 0.3 mi. east on Sunset and look for sign to park on right.

Valley of Fire State Park—From the jct. of US 95 and I-15 at Exit 42 in downtown Las Vegas, go north on I-15 about 33 mi. to jct. with NV 169. Turn right (east) on NV 169 and go 18 mi. (through the park) to the visitor center for maps and information.

NEW MEXICO (120)

American Canyon Spring, Mount Taylor—Take Exit 79 off I-40, 76 miles west of Albuquerque, onto NM 605 north. Follow NM 605 to San Mateo. At San Mateo, take FS 456 to its junction with FS 239. Turn left on 239 and continue to the junction with FS 453. Turn right on 453 and continue on this road for about 27 miles to American Canyon Spring. Good for Band-tailed Pigeon.

Animas—The town of Animas is located on NM 338, 24 miles south of I-10's Exit 11 in southwestern New Mexico. Aplomado Falcons used to occur in the vicinity of Animas, but have not been seen in recent years.

Artesia Cemetery—The town of Artesia is located at the jct. of US 285 and US 82 in southeastern New Mexico. The cemetery is located on the south side of town, east of US 285. Broadleaf woodlands here and elsewhere in and around the town are attractive to rare, eastern migrants.

Bandelier National Monument—At the jct. of US 285 and NM 502 in Pojoaque, 18 mi. north of Santa Fe, take NM 502 west 11 mi. to jct. with NM 4. Turn left on NM 4 and follow signs for about 12 mi. to the entrance of Bandelier National Monument. The monument has beautiful pinyon-juniper, ponderosa pine, spruce-fir, and riparian habitats, with all of the associated species.

Bill Evans Lake—From Silver City in southwestern New Mexico, take US 180 25 mi. north to Bill Evans Road. Turn left on Bill Evans Road and continue about 3.5 miles to a turnoff to the left for Bill Evans Lake. Neotropic Cormorants, Western Grebes, and other wetland species can be found here. Stop along the road in to examine Gila River riparian habitats.

Bitter Lake National Wildlife Refuge—From the jct. of US 285 and US 380 in the southeastern New Mexico city of Roswell, go east on US 380 about 3 mi. to NM 265 (Red Bridge Rd.). Turn left on NM 265 and go north 3 mi. to East Pine Lodge Rd., turn right and proceed to the refuge headquarters for bird lists and information. The refuge is excellent for migrating waterfowl.

Bluewater Canyon—Take Exit 53 off I-40 31 mi. east of Gallup in western New Mexico. Take NM 612 south out of Thoreau about 17 mi. Here the road begins to climb, paralleling Bluewater Creek for the next 6 mi. or so. Watch for Belted Kingfisher, MacGillivray's Warbler, and other streamside species.

Bluewater Lake State Park—Take Exit 63 off I-40 at Prewitt. Head south on NM 412 about 6 mi. to the park hq. The lake is good for migrating waterfowl and shorebirds.

Bosque del Apache National Wildlife Refuge—Near the town of San Antonio, take Exit 139 off from I-25 onto US 380. Proceed east on US 380 about 0.5 mi. to jct. with NM 1. Turn right (south) on NM 1 and go 9 mi. to the refuge.

Bottomless Lakes State Park—From the US 285/380 jct. in Roswell, go east about

10 mi. on US 380 to Bottomless Lakes Rd. (NM 409). Turn right, and head south on NM 409 to the state park (about 4 mi.).

Caballo Lake State Park—From the southwestern New Mexico town of Truth or Consequences, take I-25 south about 20 mi. to Exit 59, and head east from the exit to the park and lake.

Canjilon Mountain—From the old state capital of Española in north-central New Mexico, head north on US 84 50 mi. to jct. with NM 115. Turn right (east) on NM 115 and go about 2.5 mi. to the Canjilon Ranger Station (south side of road). Get maps and information here. Continue on NM 115 a few hundred yards to jct. with FS 559. Turn left (north) on FS 559 and follow signs to Canjilon Mountain, Carson National Forest. You will climb through ponderosa pine, mountain meadows, and mixed aspen-conifer habitat (April–September, when the road isn't snowed in).

Capulin Volcano National Monument—Take Exit 451 off from I-25 near the northeastern New Mexico town of Raton, and head east 27 mi. on US 87 to Capulin. Turn left (north) at Capulin on NM 325 and proceed about 2.5 mi. to the national monument.

Carlsbad—The City of Carlsbad is in the southeastern corner of New Mexico at the jct. of US 285 and US 180. Blue Jays, Chimney Swifts, Northern Flickers, and other birds of the Great Plains can be found flying over the city and in its parks, cemeteries, and along the Pecos River. The Living Desert Museum, located 3 mi. north of Carlsbad on US 285, also provides good birding sites.

Carlsbad Caverns National Park—From Carlsbad, go south on US 180 16 mi. to Whites City. Turn right on NM 7 and go 7 mi. to the park hq.

Catwalk, Glenwood—From Silver City, go northwest on US 180 about 61 mi. to Glenwood. At Glenwood, turn right (east) on FS 95 toward the Catwalk over Whitewater Creek. Fish hatchery is .25 mi. east on FS 95; the catwalk and picnic area are at the end of the road (about 5 mi.).

Ceremonial Cave Trail—See Bandelier National Monument entry. Get map at entrance.

Cherry Creek Campground—From the US 180/90 jct. in Silver City, go east on US 180 a little more than a mile to the jct. with NM 15. Turn left (north) on NM 15. There is a turnoff for Cherry Creek Campground on the east side of NM 15 about 13 miles north of Silver City.

Cibola National Forest Hawk Watch Site—"This station, in the Cibola National Forest, is reached by traveling east on I-40 from Albuquerque. Take the Carnuel Exit 170, continue east on US 66 for 1.8 miles, and turn left into the Montecello subdivision. Follow FS 522 to the Three Gun Spring Trailhead (Forest Service Trail 194). The Hawk Watch trail begins at the Forest Service boundary fence, from which a spur trail forks eastward across an arroyo and up the ridge to the observation point. This route is about two miles long and steep in places, with a total elevation gain of 900 feet." (Zimmerman et al. 1992:91–92).

Clayton—The City of Clayton is located at the US 56/87 jct. in extreme northeastern New Mexico.

Clayton Lake State Park—Take NM 370 north from Clayton about 10 mi. Turn left (west) at the jct. of NM 370 and NM 455, and follow NM 455 to the park.

Clayton Municipal Airport—The airport is east of town.

Coal Mine Campground—From the western New Mexico town of Grants (I-40 Exit 85), take NM 547 (Lobo Canyon Rd.) north out of town for 11 mi. to Coal Mine Campground.

Cochiti Lake Reservoir—From I-25 Exit 264 (18 mi. southwest of Santa Fe) head west on NM 16 about 6 mi. to a right turn for Cochiti Lake. Follow this road to the dam across the Rio Grande that forms Cochiti Lake.

Conchas Lake—From I-40, take Exit 300 (30 mi. west of the eastern New Mexico town of Tucumcari). Follow NM 129 north about 20 mi. to NM 432. Turn off to the left for Conchas Lake State Park.

Cottonwood Campground, Simon Canyon—From the northwestern New Mexico city of Farmington, go east on US 64 36 mi. to jct. with NM 539. Turn left (north) on NM 539 and go 6 mi. to jct. NM 173. Turn left (west) on NM 173 and go about 5 mi. to jct. CH 4280. Turn right (north) on CH 4280, and follow road 3 mi. to parking area.

Cottonwood Canyon—From I-40, take Exit 33 (11 mi. east of Gallup in western New Mexico) and follow NM 400 about 10 mi. to McGaffey. From there take FS 50 about 7 mi. to Page. Turn left at Page and continue on FS 50 14 rough mi. to Cottonwood Canyon.

Cox Ranch Visitors' Center—In the southern New Mexico city of Las Cruces, take I-25 Exit 1 (University Ave.) and continue east about 8 mi., following signs for Cox Ranch.

Dome Meadow—From the northern New Mexico town of Los Alamos, head west on NM 501 about 4 mi. to jct. with NM 4. Turn right on NM 4 and proceed about 4 mi. to jct. with FS 289. Turn left (south) on FS 289, and continue 4 mi. or so to Dome Meadow.

Dripping Springs Natural Area—See Cox Ranch entry. Continue past Cox Ranch Visitors' Center another mile or so to reach Dripping Springs.

Dry Cimarron River—From Clayton, go east 2.5 mi. on US 64 to jct. with NM 406. Turn left (north) on NM 406 and proceed 38 mi. to jct. with NM 456. Turn left (west) on NM 456, which stretches for the next 50 mi. along the Dry Cimarron River Valley.

Dulce Lake—From the northeastern New Mexico town of Dulce, head south on US 64 about 4 mi. to Dulce Lake, which you will see on the right (west) side of the road. Park along the road. These and other lakes on the Jicarilla Apache Reservation are excellent for waterfowl and shorebirds, and the surrounding uplands are good for sage and pinyon-juniper species.

Echo Amphitheater—Take US 84 about 17 mi. northwest of the northern New Mexico town of Abiquiu to Echo Amphitheater Campground (west side of road).

Elephant Butte Reservoir—Take Exit 79 off I-25 into the southern New Mexico town of Truth or Consequences. From there, head east on NM 51 2.5 mi. to "T" intersection. Go left at "T" and proceed 2 mi. to another "T". Turn left and go 0.3 mi. to state park and access to lake.

El Malpais National Monument—Take Exit 89 from I-40 (70 mi. west of Albuquerque) onto NM 117 into El Malpais National Monument. Stop at BLM Ranger Station at about 8 mi. for maps, information, and checklist.

Embudito Canyon—In Albuquerque, take the Tramway Blvd. Exit off I-40, and head north on Tramway Blvd. about 5 mi. to jct. with Montgomery Blvd. Turn right (east) on Montgomery Blvd. and proceed about 0.5 mi. to jct. with Glenwood Hills Dr. Turn left (north) on Glenwood Hills Dr. Bear left after 0.5 mi. or so onto Trailhead Rd., and drive to the end of this road for the parking area for the Embudito Trailhead parking area. Walk up the trail to the canyon.

Fort Stanton—From the jct. of US 380 and US 54 in Carrizozo, go east on US 380 about 20 mi. to Fort Stanton. Proceed east through Fort Stanton on US 380 to the bridge over the Rio Bonito, east of town.

Fort Sumner State Monument—Take US 84 58 mi. west of the eastern New Mexico town of Clovis. About 2 mi. east of Fort Sumner, turn left (south) on NM 272 and proceed about 6 mi. to Fort Sumner National Monument. Explore grasslands and streamside woodlands for Northern Bobwhite, Blue Jay, Red-headed Woodpecker, and occasional Dickcissels.

Frijoles Canyon—See Bandelier National Monument entry. Get map at entrance.

Gila Cliff Dwellings National Monument—From Silver City, take NM 15 north 44 miles to the monument.

Grasslands Turf Ranch—From Albuquerque, go 20 mi. south on I-25 to Exit 203. Take NM 6 west and turn right (north) on the first dirt road, and proceed roughly 1 mi. to the entrance of the ranch (Zimmerman et al. 1992:106).

Guadalupe Canyon—See Arizona entry.

Harroun Lake—From Carlsbad, go south on US 285 17 mi. to Malaga. Turn left (east) in Malaga. Proceed east about a mile and take the left branch of the road, which winds around, crosses the Pecos River, and eventually reaches Harroun Lake in 2 mi. or so.

High Rolls Country Store—From the south-central New Mexico town of Alamogordo, take US 70 north about 4 mi. to the jct. with US 82. Turn right (east) on US 82 and proceed 9 mi. to High Rolls.

Holloman Lakes Wildlife Refuge—From Alamogordo, take US 70 south about 11 mi. (0.6 mi. past mile marker 204). Turn right (north) to enter the refuge (Zimmerman 1992:148).

Hyde Memorial State Park—From I-25 Exit 282 for Santa Fe, go north on US 285 4 mi. to the exit for NM 475 (Paseo de Peralta). Follow Paseo de Peralta east about 1 mi. to Washington Ave. Turn left (north) on Washington, then, after 0.2 mi. or so, right on Artist Rd. (still on NM 475). Follow NM 475 10 mi. or so to Hyde Memorial State Park.

Iron Creek Campground—South of Truth or Consequences, take Exit 63 off I-25 and proceed west on NM 152 for about 35 mi. to Iron Creek Campground.

Isleta Lakes and Recreation Area—About 10 mi. south of Albuquerque, take I-25 Exit 215. Take the left fork (NM 47). A few hundred yards along this road take the first right, following a sign to the Isleta Lakes and Recreation Area. Proceed a mile or so to the recreation area.

Jackson Lake State Game Refuge—From the jct. of US 64 and US 550 in Farmington, go west on US 64 about 2.5 mi. to jct. NM 170. Go north on NM 170 about 5 mi. to the refuge.

Juniper Campground—See Bandelier National Monument entry. Get map at entrance.

Laguna Grande—From Carlsbad, go south on US 285 to jct. with NM 31. Turn left (east) on NM 31. Go about 7 mi. until the road splits into NM 31 (left) and NM 128 (right). Take the right branch and proceed about 2 mi. to best viewing point of salt lakes.

Lake Roberts—From Silver City, go north on NM 15 26 mi. to jct. with NM 35. Go east on NM 35 about 4 mi. to Lake Roberts.

Langmuir Laboratory—Take Exit 147 from I-25 to the western New Mexico town of Socorro. From Socorro, go west on US 60 16 mi. to jct. with FS 235. Turn left (south) on FS 235 and go to the end of the road (about 10 mi.) at the top of South Baldy Peak (10,783 feet) where the laboratory is located.

Las Vegas National Wildlife Refuge—From I-25 take Exit 345 at the northern New Mexico town of Las Vegas onto NM 104. Go east on NM 104 a little over a mile and turn right (south) on NM 281. Follow NM 281 about 5.5 mi. to the refuge hq.

La Ventana, El Malpais National Monument—See El Malpais entry. Get map at Ranger Station. La Ventana is about 8 mi. south of the Ranger Station on NM 117.

Lions Park, San Juan River—From the jct. of NM 170 and US 64 in Farmington, go west on US 64 about 3.5 mi. to a left turn onto CH 489 (the old Kirtland Hwy.), which parallels US 64. Go west on this road about 1 mi. to a sign for Lions Park (Zimmerman et al. 1992:5).

Little Walnut Picnic Area—From US 180 in Silver City, go north on Little Walnut Rd. 4 mi. to the picnic area.

Los Alamos Canyon—See Bandelier National Monument entry. Get map at entrance.

Lower Mimbres River Valley—From the jct. of US 90 and US 180 in Silver City, go east on US 180 7 mi. to jct. with NM 152. Take NM 152 east 14 mi. to jct. with NM 61. Take NM 61 south. The road parallels the river. Stop and examine riparian habitat from the road.

Maxwell National Wildlife Refuge—From I-25, take Exit 426 at the northeastern New Mexico village of Maxwell. From Maxwell, go north on NM 445 about 1 mi. Turn left (west) and proceed about 2.5 mi. to refuge hq.

Middle Rio Grande Conservancy District—From I-25 20 mi. south of Albuquerque, take Exit 203. Go east on NM 6. Take levee roads that parallel the river along either side to examine riparian habitat. This area can be dangerous, so birding should not be done alone (Zimmerman et al. 1992:71–72).

Morgan Lake—From the jct. of NM 170 and US 64 in Farmington, go west on US 64 about 3.5 mi. to a left turn onto CH 489 (the old Kirtland Hwy.), which parallels US 64. Go west on this road about 4 mi. to Fruitland. Turn left (south) to cross San Juan River, and continue winding south and west on IR 6675 for about 5 mi. to the lake.

Navajo Dam—From Farmington, go east on US 64 36 mi. to jct. with NM 539. Turn left (north) on NM 539 and go 6 mi. to Navajo Dam and Navajo Lake State Park.

Navajo Indian Irrigation Project—From Farmington, go south on NM 371 about 6 mi. to IR 3003. Turn left (east) on IR 3003 and go about 8 mi. to IR 4047. Turn right (south). Drive 4 to 5 mi. south on this and other roads to pass through best raptor areas (Nelson in Zimmerman et al. 1992:8).

Navajo Lake State Park—See Navajo Dam entry.

NM 26 between Hatch and Deming—38 mi. north of Las Cruces, take Exit 41 off I-25 to Hatch. Go west on NM 26 48 mi. to Deming. Scan along road for raptors.

NM 152 between Central and Santa Rita—From Silver City, go east on US 180 8 mi. to jct. NM 152 at Central. Go east on NM 152 toward Santa Rita (7 mi. or so). The road passes through grasslands and pinyon-juniper.

NM 338 to Animas—From the western New Mexico town of Lordsburg, go west on I-10 11 mi. to Exit 11. Go south on NM 338 to Animas (24 mi.). Stop along the road to examine mesquite desert scrub for typical species, e.g., Bendire's Thrasher, Black-throated Sparrow, and Scott's Oriole.

NM 464 to Redrock—At Lordsburg, take Exit 22 off I-10 and go north on US 70. Bear left on US 70 when NM 90 splits to the right (2 mi. or so). Go a little over a mile and take NM 464 to the right (north). Follow this road about 20 mi. to Redrock. Stop along the road for birding in appropriate habitat.

NM 511, Reese Canyon—From the northwestern New Mexico town of Bloomfield, go 10 mi. east on US 64 to jct. with NM 511. Turn left (north) on NM 511, and proceed about 21 mi. (15 mi. past Navajo Dam) until the road drops into Reese Canyon.

Old Refuge, Las Cruces—In Las Cruces, take I-10 west from jct. with I-25 to Exit 140. Take NM 28 southwest from here a little less than a mile to jct. with NM 359. Take 359 west about 2 mi. Immediately after crossing the Rio Grande, pull off the road and park. From here, walk south on the levee paralleling the river (Zimmerman et al. 1992:141).

Oliver Lee Memorial State Park—From Alamogordo, go south 10 mi. on US 54 to jct. CH A16. Turn left on A16 and proceed 3 mi. or so to park.

Oxbow Lake, Rio Grande Nature Center—See Rio Grande Nature Center entry. Get maps and information at visitor center.

Pajarito Mountain Ski Area—See Bandelier National Monument entry. Get maps and information at entry. The ski area is actually located about 8 mi. north and west of the monument (follow NM 501 north about 4 mi. from jct. NM 4 to ski area road).

Pecos River north of Brantley Lake—From Carlsbad, go north on US 285 about 20 mi. to jct. NM 381. Turn right (east) on NM 381 for about 2 mi. to Lakewood where NM 381 turns north. Go north about 3.5 mi. to a road heading east. Take this road to riparian habitat along the Pecos River (Bixler et al. in Zimmerman et al. 1992:157).

Percha Dam State Park—From I-25 16 mi. south of Truth or Consequences, take Exit 59. Head south on NM 185 for about 2 mi. to a left (east) turn to the park.

Perico Creek—From the jct. of US 56 and US 87 in Clayton, head south on US 87 a block or two to the jct. with NM 402. Take NM 402 south 3 mi. to where it crosses Perico Creek. Scan river bottom from the bridge. The bottom is private property and should not be entered without permission (see Zimmerman et al. 1992:43 for details).

Picnic Area, State Fish Hatchery, Glenwood—See Catwalk entry. Fish hatchery is .25 mi. east on FS 95, and the picnic area is at the end of the road (about 5 mi.).

Pine Tree Trail, Cox Ranch Visitors' Center—See Cox Ranch Visitors' Center entry. Get map at center.

Ponderosa Campground—See Bandelier National Monument entry. Get map at entrance.

Portales—The eastern New Mexico town of Portales is 91 mi. northeast of Roswell on US 70. The parks, cemeteries, golf courses, and residential areas are home to Great Plains and eastern species such as Blue Jays.

Randall Davey Audubon Center—From I-25 in Santa Fe, take Exit 284 north onto NM 466 (Old Pecos Trail) for a little more than a mile to where the road splits. Follow the right fork (Old Pecos Trail), and continue about 2 mi. to the jct. with Alameda St. Turn right (east) on Alameda and continue a little more than a mile until the road makes a sharp right and crosses the Santa Fe River. About 0.1 mile beyond the river turn left on Upper Canyon Rd. Almost immediately, the road splits. Take the right fork (Apodaca Hill) and follow it 0.6 mi. to the end where the center is located.

Rattlesnake Springs—From Carlsbad, go south 25 mi. on US 180 to jct. with CH 418. Turn right on CH 418 (sign for "Rattlesnake Springs") and continue 3 mi. to springs.

Redrock Wildlife Area—From Lordsburg, take I-10 Exit 22 north on US 70. Proceed 3 mi. on US 70 to NM 464. Turn right on NM 464 and proceed 21 mi. to Redrock. Go another 0.5 mi. or so to a left turn crossing a bridge over the Gila River. Take this left, bear right after crossing the river, and proceed 1.5 mi. to the New Mexico Game and Fish Department's Wildlife Area.

Rio Grande Nature Center—From the jct. of I-25 and I-40 in Albuquerque, go west on I-40 about 3 mi. to Exit 157 (Rio Grande Blvd.). Go north on Rio Grande Blvd. about 1.5 mi. to jct. with Candelaria Rd. Turn left (west) on Candelaria Rd. and proceed to nature center (about ¾ mi.).

Rio Pueblo Valley—From Española, go north on NM 68 20 mi. to jct. NM 75. Turn right (east) on NM 75 and proceed 21 mi. to jct. NM 518. Take the right fork (south) on NM 518 following Embrudo Creek and, after Tres Ritos, the Rio Pueblo Valley. Examine willow thickets along road for typical high country riparian birds.

Rocky Arroyo—From the jct. of US 285 and US 180 in Carlsbad, go north on US 285 12 mi. to jct. NM 137. Turn left (west) on NM 137, and go 10 mi. to the arroyo.

Roswell South Park Cemetery—From the jct. of US 380 and US 285 in Roswell, go south on US 285 (Main St.) about 2.5 mi. Look for the cemetery on the right (west) side of the road. Jaffa Ave. runs through the cemetery.

Roswell Spring River Golf Course—From the US 380/285 jct., go west on US 380 (2nd St.) about 1.5 mi. to Nevada. Turn right (north) on Nevada and proceed about 0.2 mi. to Spring River Golf Course.

Roswell Zoo—From the US 380/285 jct., go east on US 380 (2nd St.) about 1 mi. to NM 265 (Atkinson Ave.). Turn left (north) on NM 265 and go 1 mi. to the Roswell Zoo.

Rutherford Tract—From the jct. of NM 44 and US 64 in Bloomfield go east on US 64 2.5 mi. to jct. with CH 4901. Turn right (south) on CH 4901 and proceed 0.5 mi. to the New Mexico Game and Fish Department's Rutherford Tract—riparian habitat bordering the San Juan River (Nelson in Zimmerman et al. 1992:9).

San Rafael Ponds—From I-40 80 mi. west of Albuquerque, take Exit 81 south onto NM 53. Go about 2.5 mi. south on NM 53 to the ponds.

Sandia Crest—From I-40 Exit 175, east of Albuquerque, go north on NM 14 about 7 mi. to jct. NM 536. Turn left on NM 536 and proceed about 14 mi. to the crest.

Sandia Park Pond—See Sandia Crest entry above. Turn left on NM 536 and proceed about 0.6 mi. to the pond (on left side of road).

Sandstone Bluffs Overlook—Take Exit 89 from I-40 (70 mi. west of Albuquerque) onto NM 117 into El Malpais National Monument, and go 10 mi. to the overlook.

Santa Fe Baldy—See Hyde Memorial State Park entry. Follow NM 475 16 mi. to the Santa Fe Ski Basin parking lot. From here, a trail leads to Santa Fe Baldy, 7.5 mi.

Signal Peak Road—From the US 180/90 jct. in Silver City, go east on US 180 about a mile to the jct. with NM 15. Turn left on NM 15. There is a turnoff to the right (east) for Signal Peak Road (FS 154) about 16 mi. north of Silver City. A rough road climbs the next seven miles up Signal Peak through montane coniferous habitat.

Sitting Bull Falls—From the US 285/180 jct. in Carlsbad, go north on US 285 12 mi. to jct. NM 137. Turn left (west) on NM 137, and go 31 mi. to jct. FS 276 (Sitting Bull Falls Rd.) and proceed 8 mi. to the falls.

NM 14 at San Marcos—Take I-25 Exit 276 (6 mi. west of Santa Fe) and head south on NM 14. From here to San Marcos (about 6 mi. to jct. NM 586), the road passes off and on through grasslands, with typical species.

Tesuque River Bottom—The Tesuque River "flows" (usually there isn't much water) under NM 502 just west of the jct. of NM 502 and US 285 at Pojoaque, 18 mi. north of Santa Fe. You could park on the shoulder of NM 502, and walk under the bridge and from there along the wooded river bottom. Another possibility is to take the exit ramp off US 285 and get on the east frontage road going north. Take the first left past NM 502 off the frontage road (CH 84), and follow this through Pojoaque out west of town 0.7 miles until the road crosses the Tesuque River. Park along the road, and walk along the river bottom into the woods.

Tsankawi Section—See Bandelier National Monument entry. Get map at entrance.

US 380 Bridge over the Pecos River—From the US 380/285 jct. in Roswell, go east on US 380 about 7 mi. to the bridge over the Pecos River.

US 380 Roadside Rest—From US 380/285 jct. in Roswell, go east on US 380 42 mi. to roadside rest on the south side of the road.

Valle Vidal Alpine Sites—At the town of Questa, 43 mi. north of Taos on NM 522, turn right on NM 196 to Amalia. Proceed 16 mi. until the road splits. Take the right fork on FS 1950 (4-wheel-drive required). From here the road ascends through alpine habitat.

Water Canyon Campground—Take Exit 147 from I-25 to Socorro. From Socorro, go west on US 60 16 mi. to jct. with FS 235. Turn left (south) on FS 235 and go about 5 mi. to the campground.

Willow Creek Campground—From Silver City, take US 180 northwest 66 mi. to jct. with NM 159 to the right (east) toward the ghost town of Mogollon. Proceed 26 mi. to Willow Creek Campground (road closed Oct–Apr).

Photographers

Bogusch: 456 (from author's collection)

Vernon Grove: 2, 4, 6, 17, 18, 23, 25, 30, 31, 33, 35, 37, 39, 44, 49, 51, 53, 65, 69, 70, 73, 74, 77, 82, 96, 97, 99, 104, 105, 109, 110, 111, 112, 113, 114, 117, 118, 119, 120, 121, 122, 124, 126, 128, 130, 131, 132, 133, 135, 138, 142, 145, 147, 148, 150, 153, 167, 173, 175, 177, 185, 188, 189, 192, 193, 197, 201, 203, 204, 207, 219, 220, 226, 229, 230, 232, 233, 234, 263, 265, 269, 270, 271, 272, 275, 287, 299, 304, 313, 315, 318, 319, 325, 331, 346, 350, 355, 356, 380, 382, 384, 390, 398, 399, 400, 401, 403, 412, 415, 416, 419, 420, 422, 428, 429, 431, 432, 433, 434, 443, 448

William Paff: 7, 21, 27, 28, 43, 140, 159, 163, 176, 202, 215, 218, 298, 305, 314, 322, 396, 454

David Parmalee: 1, 8, 81, 136, 141, 144, 149, 151, 152, 157, 161, 162, 165, 166, 172

John Rappole: 20, 34, 45, 46, 50, 59, 63, 64, 66, 67, 71, 78, 79, 80, 84, 87, 88, 89, 94, 103, 116, 123, 129, 137, 139, 158, 168, 170, 174, 187, 199, 212, 223, 224, 238, 240, 241, 253, 261, 268, 273, 284, 285, 291, 293, 294, 295, 296, 300, 301, 306, 320, 321, 324, 330, 332, 342, 351, 354, 374, 388, 402, 404, 407, 414, 436, 447

Barth Schorre: 26, 29, 32, 40, 41, 42, 48, 52, 54, 56, 57, 143, 154, 155, 156, 160, 169, 190, 191, 221, 222, 246, 247, 277, 282, 283, 286, 290, 333, 335, 336, 337, 338, 341, 344, 347, 357, 359, 362, 363, 365, 369, 370, 371, 372, 373, 375, 378, 381, 383, 393, 394, 408, 410, 411, 413, 421, 423, 425, 427, 435, 437, 438, 439, 440, 441, 449, 451, 455

VIREO/S. Armistead: 244

VIREO/R. Behrstock: 213

VIREO/R. & N. Bowers: 38, 194, 196, 200, 209, 216, 250, 252, 257, 259, 288, 309, 348, 352, 364, 368, 376, 377, 391, 424

VIREO/John Cancalos: 95

VIREO/H. Clarke: 100, 106, 214, 251, 339, 349, 397, 406, 442, 445

VIREO/A. J. Clay: 195

VIREO/H. Cruickshank: 210

VIREO/R. Curtis: 102, 206, 236, 242, 297, 379, 395, 446

VIREO/R. & S. Day: 125

VIREO/G. Dremeaux: 310

VIREO/J. Dunning: 274, 279

VIREO/D. Fischer: 262, 307

VIREO/S. Fried: 329, 405

VIREO/ J. Fuhrman: 76, 312, 358, 386

References

Abbey, E. 1973. *Cactus Country.* Time-Life Books, New York.

Alcorn, J. R. 1988. *The Birds of Nevada.* Fairview West Publishing, Fallon, Nevada. 418 pp.

American Ornithologists' Union. 1998. *Check-List of North American Birds.* American Ornithologists' Union, Allen Press, Lawrence, Kansas.

Anderson, A. H. 1934. *The Arizona State List since 1914.* Condor 36:78–83.

Bache-Wiig, J. 1996. *Nogales, Arizona Christmas Bird Count.* John Bache-Wiig, Nogales, Arizona.

Bailey, F. M. 1928. *Birds of New Mexico.* New Mexico Department of Game and Fish, Santa Fe, New Mexico. 807 pp.

———. 1939. *Among the Birds in the Grand Canyon Country.* U.S. Government Printing Office, Washington, D. C. 211 pp.

Baker, M. E. 1940. Annotated hypothetical checklist of birds observed along the Green and Colorado Rivers from Green River, Wyoming to Lake Mead. Unpub. manuscript, Grand Canyon National Park, Grand Canyon, Arizona.

Behle, W. H., and H. G. Higgins. 1959. The Birds of Glen Canyon. Pp. 107–33 *in Ecological Studies of the Flora and Fauna of Glen Canyon* (A. M. Woodbury, Ed.), University of Utah Anthropological Papers No. 40.

Brown, B. T., P. S. Bennett, S. W. Carothers, L. T. Haight, R. R. Johnson, and M. M. Riffey. 1978. *Birds of the Grand Canyon Region: An Annotated Checklist.* Grand Canyon Natural History Association Monograph No. 1, Grand Canyon, Arizona. 64 pp.

Brown, B. T., S. W. Carothers, and R. R. Johnson. 1986. *Grand Canyon Birds.* University of Arizona Press, Tucson, Arizona.

Bureau of Land Management. nd. *Bird Checklist: Red Rock Canyon National Conservation Area.* Bureau of Land Management, Las Vegas District, Stateline Resource Area, Nevada.

Childs, H. E., Jr. 1993. *Where Birders Go in Southern California.* Los Angeles County Audubon Society, Los Angeles, California.

Clark, J. L. 1993. *Nevada Wildlife Viewing Guide.* Falcon Press, Helena, Montana. 87 pp.

Clark, W. S., and B. K. Wheeler. 1987. *A Field Guide to the Hawks of North America.* Houghton Mifflin, Boston.

Clement, P., A. Harris, and J. Davis. 1993. *Finches and Sparrows: an Identification Guide.* Princeton University Press, Princeton, New Jersey.

Cooke, W. W. 1915. *Bird Migration.* USDA Bulletin 185:1–47.

Coues, E. 1876. *Birds of the Colorado River Valley.* U.S. Government Printing Office, Washington, D.C.

Curson, J., D. Quinn, and D. Beadle. 1994. *New World Warblers.* A&C Black, London.

Davis, B. L. 1997. *A Field Guide to the Birds of the Desert Southwest.* Gulf Publishing Co., Houston, Texas.

Davis, W. A., and S. M. Russell. 1990. *Birds in Southeastern Arizona.* Tucson Audubon Society, Tucson, Arizona.

Dawson, W. L. 1923. *The Birds of California.* Volumes 1–4. South Moulton Company, San Diego, California. 2,120 pp.

DeGraaf, R. M., and J. H. Rappole. 1995. *Neotropical Migratory Birds: Natural History, Distribution, and Population Change.* Cornell University Press, Ithaca, New York. 676 pp.

DeGraaf, R. M., V. E. Scott, R. H. Hamre, L. Ernst, and S. H. Anderson. 1991. *Forest and Rangeland Birds of the United States: Natural History and Habitat Use.* Forest Service, U.S. Department of Agriculture, Agriculture Handbook 688. 625 pp.

Dunn, J. L., and K. L. Garrett. 1987. The Identification of North American Gnatcatchers. *Birding* 19:17–29.

Dunne, P., and C. Sutton. 1989. *Hawks in Flight: Flight Identification of North American Migrant Raptors.* Houghton Mifflin, Boston.

Edison, J., M. Malone, R. Ruisinger, R. O. Russell, J. Tweit, R. Tweit, and D. Yetman. 1995. *Davis and Russell's Finding Birds in Southeast Arizona.* Tucson Audubon Society, Tucson, Arizona.

Edwards, E. P. 1972. *A Field Guide to the Birds of Mexico.* Privately Published, Sweet Briar, Virginia.

Fettig, S. M. 1996. *A Checklist of Birds of Bandelier National Monument.* Southwest Parks and Monuments Association, Tucson, Arizona.

Fisk, E. J. 1983. *The Peacocks of Baboquivari.* W. W. Norton & Co., New York, New York.

Folse, L. J., and K. Arnold. 1976. "Secondary Sex Characteristics in Roadrunners." *Bird-Banding* 47:115–18.

Gaines, D. 1992. *Birds of the Yosemite and the East Slope.* Second edition, with updates by Sally Gaines. Artemesia Press, Lee Vining, California.

Garrett, K., and J. Dunn. 1981. *Birds of Southern California: Status and Distribution.* Los Angeles Audubon Society, Los Angeles, California.

Grant, P. J. 1982. *Gulls: a Guide to Identification.* Poyser, Calton, Stoke-on-Trent, United Kingdom.

Grinnell, J., and A .H. Miller. 1944. *The Distribution of Birds in California.* Pacific Coast Avifauna #27 (Reprinted, 1986, Artemesia Press, Lee Vining, California).

Groschupf, K., B. T. Brown, and R. R. Johnson. 1987. *A Checklist of the Birds of Organ Pipe Cactus National Monument.* Southwest Parks and Monuments Association, Tucson, Arizona.

———. 1988. *An Annotated Checklist of the Birds of Organ Pipe Cactus National Monument, Arizona.* Cooperative National Park Resources Studies Unit, University of Arizona, Tucson, Arizona.

Harrison, G. H. 1976. *Roger Tory Peterson's Dozen Birding Hot Spots.* Simon and Schuster, New York.

Harrison, P. 1983. *Seabirds: An Identification Guide.* Houghton Mifflin Company, Boston, Massachusetts. 448 pp.

Hasty, G. M., and D. P. Fletcher. 1998. *A Checklist of Wildlife of Canyon De Chelly National Monument.* Southwest Parks and Monuments Association, Tucson, Arizona.

Hayman, P., J. Marchant, and T. Prater. 1986. *Shorebirds: an Identification Guide to the Waders of the World.* Houghton Mifflin Company, Boston, Massachusetts. 412 pp.

Hines, R. W. 1985. *Ducks at a Distance: a Waterfowl Identification Guide.* U.S. Fish and Wildlife Service, Washington, D.C.

Holt, H. 1989. *A Birder's Guide to Southeastern Arizona.* American Birding Association, Colorado Springs, Colorado.

————. 1990. *A Birder's Guide to Southern California.* American Birding Association, Colorado Springs, Colorado. 238 pp.

Hubbard, J. P. 1978. *Revised Check-list of the Birds of New Mexico.* New Mexico Ornithological Society Publ. No. 6.

Hunt, C. B. 1967. *Physiography of the United States.* W. H. Freeman and Company, San Francisco, California. 480 pp.

James, E. 1823. *An Account of an Expedition from Pittsburgh to the Rocky Mountains.* Three volumes and atlas. H. C. Carey and J. Lea, Philadelphia, Pennsylvania.

Jenks, R. 1931. *Ornithology of the Life Zones: Summit of San Francisco Peaks to the Bottom of Grand Canyon.* Grand Canyon Natural History Association, Grand Canyon, Arizona. 31 pp.

Johnsgard, P. A. 1979. *A Guide to North American Waterfowl.* Indiana University Press, Bloomington, Indiana. 274 pp.

Koford, C. B. 1966. *The California Condor.* Dover Publishing, New York. 154 pp.

Küchler, A. W. 1975. *Potential Natural Vegetation of the Conterminous United States.* American Geographical Society, Washington, D.C.

Lane, J. A. 1974. *A Birder's Guide to Southeastern Arizona.* Privately Published, Denver, Colorado.

Ligon, J. S. 1961. *New Mexico Birds, and Where to Find Them.* University of New Mexico Press, Albuquerque, New Mexico. 360 pp.

Marshall, J. T., Jr. 1957. *Birds of Pine-oak Woodland in Southern Arizona and Adjacent Mexico.* Pacific Coast Avifauna 32:1–125.

McMillon, W. 1995. *Birding Arizona.* Falcon Press, Helena, Montana. 206 pp.

Mearns, E. A. 1886. *Some Birds of Arizona.* Auk 3:289–307.

Merriam, C. H. 1890. *Results of a Biological Survey of the San Francisco Mountain Region and Desert of the Little Colorado, Arizona.* North American Fauna No. 3, U. S. Government Printing Office, Washington, D.C. 136 pp.

Miller, A. H. 1951. *An Analysis of the Distribution of the Birds of California.* University of California Publications in Zoology 50:531–644.

Mohave County Parks Department. 1998. *Hualapai Mountain Park Wildlife.* Mohave County Parks Department, Kingman, Arizona.

Monson, G., and A. R. Phillips. 1981. *Annotated Checklist of the Birds of Arizona.* 2nd Ed. University of Arizona Press, Tucson, Arizona.

Muir, J. 1911. *My First Summer in the Sierra.* Houghton Mifflin, Boston, Massachusetts.

National Geographic Society. 1987. *Field Guide to the Birds of North America.* 2nd Ed. National Geographic Society, Washington, D.C. 464 pp.

New Mexico Ornithological Society. 1995. *Field Checklist of New Mexico Birds*. New Mexico Ornithological Society, Santa Fe, New Mexico.

Norris, L. L. 1991. *Checklist of Birds: Sequoia and Kings Canyon National Parks*. Sequoia Natural History Association, Three Rivers, California.

Norris, L. L., and W. Schreier. 1982. *A Checklist of the Birds of Death Valley National Monument*. Death Valley Natural History Association, Death Valley, California.

Oberholser, H. 1974. *The Bird Life of Texas*. University of Texas Press, Austin, Texas.

Peterson, R. T. 1961. *A Field Guide to the Birds of Texas*. Houghton Mifflin Company, Boston, Massachusetts. 366 pp.

———. 1963. *A Field Guide to Western Birds*. Houghton Mifflin Company, Boston, Massachusetts. 304 pp.

———. 1990. *A Field Guide to Western Birds*. 3rd Ed. Houghton Mifflin Company, Boston, Massachusetts.

Petrified Forest National Park. 1998. *Bird Checklist*. National Park Service, Petrified Forest National Park, Arizona.

Phillips, A. R. 1975. "Semipalmated Sandpiper Identification, Migration, Summer and Winter Ranges." *American Birds* 29:799–806.

———. 1986. *The Known Birds of North and Middle America, Part I: Hirundinidae to Mimidae; Certhiidae*. Privately published, Denver, Colorado. 259 pp.

———. 1991. *The Known Birds of North and Middle America, Part II: Bombycillidae; Sylviidae to Sturnidae; Vireonidae*. Privately published, Denver, Colorado. 259 pp.

Phillips, A. R., J. Marshall, and G. Monson. 1964. *The Birds of Arizona*. University of Arizona Press, Tucson, Arizona. 220 pp.

Pyle, R. L., and A. Small. 1961. *Birds of Southern California: Annotated Field List*. Otis Wade, Los Angeles, California. 64 pp.

Rappole, J. H., and G. W. Blacklock. 1994. *Birds of Texas: A Field Guide*. Texas A&M University Press, College Station, Texas. 280 pp.

Red Rock Audubon Society. 1991. *A Checklist of the Birds of Lake Mead National Recreation Area*. Southwest Parks and Monuments Association, Tucson, Arizona.

Rising, J. D. 1996. *A Guide to the Identification and Natural History of the Sparrows of the United States and Canada*. Academic Press, New York.

Robbins, C. S., B. Brunn, and H. S. Zimm. 1983. *Birds of North America: A Guide to Identification*. Revised Edition. Golden Press, New York, New York. 340 pp.

Rosenberg, G. H., and D. Stejskal. 1994. *The Arizona Bird Committee's Field Checklist of the Birds of Arizona*. Arizona Bird Committee, Phoenix, Arizona.

Sams, J. R., and K. Stott, Jr. 1959. *Birds of San Diego County, California: an Annotated Checklist*. San Diego Society of Natural History Occasional Papers 10:1–49.

San Diego Audubon Society. 1997. *Checklist of Southern California Birds*. Blue-footed Press, San Diego, California.

Sanchez, F. 1995. *Spring Count of Birds on Canjilon Mountain*. Carson National Forest, Taos, New Mexico

Sexton, C. W. 1972. *Avian Use of Upper Newport Bay and Other Parts of the Estuary/coastal Lagoon Ecosystem of Southern California*. Department of Population and Environmental Biology, University of California, Irvine. 13 pp.

Sexton, C. W., and G. L. Hunt, Jr. 1979. *An Annotated Checklist of the Birds of Orange County, California.* Privately Published, Irvine, California.

Shimer, J. A. 1972. *Field Guide to Landforms in the United States.* Macmillan Co., New York, New York.

Small, A. 1975. *The Birds of California.* Winchester Press, New York, New York. 310 pp.

Stepniewski, A. 1971. *Birds of the San Joaquin Marsh.* Department of Population and Environmental Biology, University of California, Irvine. 30 pp.

Stokes, D. W., and L. Q. Stokes. 1996. *Stokes Field Guide to Birds: Western Region.* Little, Brown and Company. Boston, Massachusetts.

Swarth, H. S. 1914. "A Distributional List of the Birds of Arizona." *Pacific Coast Avifauna* No. 10, Cooper Ornithological Society, Berkeley, California. 85 pp.

Taylor, R. C. 1995. *A Birder's Guide to Southeastern Arizona.* American Birding Association, Inc., Colorado Springs, Colorado.

Titus, C. K. 1991. *Southern Nevada Birds: A Seeker's Guide.* Privately Published, Las Vegas, Nevada.

————. 1996. *A Field List of the Birds of Nevada.* Red Rock Audubon Society, Las Vegas, Nevada.

Tulare County Audubon Society. 1997. *A Checklist of the Birds of Tulare County, California.* Tulare County Audubon Society, Visalia, California.

U.S. Fish and Wildlife Service. 1994. *Birds of Imperial National Wildlife Refuge.* Imperial National Wildlife Refuge, Yuma, Arizona.

————. 1995. *Birds of Desert National Wildlife Range, Nevada.* Desert National Wildlife Range Complex, Las Vegas, Nevada.

————. 1997. *Salton Sea National Wildlife Refuge: Watchable Wildlife.* Salton Sea National Wildlife Refuge, Calipatria, California.

————. 1997. *Birds of the Gila National Forest: a Checklist.* Gila National Forest, Silver City, New Mexico.

————. 1997. *Birds of the Sangre De Cristo Mountains: a Checklist.* Carson National Forest, Taos, New Mexico.

Weathers, W. W. 1983. *Birds of Southern California's Deep Canyon.* University of California Press, Berkeley, California. 266 pp.

Willet, G. 1912. "Birds of the Pacific Slope of Southern California." *Pacific Coast Avifauna* #7. 122 pp.

————. 1933. "Revised List of the Birds of Southwestern California." *Pacific Coast Avifauna* #21. 204 pp.

Zimerman, D. A., M. A. Zimmerman, and J. N. Durrie (Eds.). 1992. *New Mexico Bird Finding Guide.* Revised Edition. New Mexico Ornithological Society, Albuquerque, New Mexico. 170 pp.

Index

Birds are listed separately in the index by common and scientific name (following the AOU Check-List, 7th Edition), with common names for species for which there are Species Accounts in **bold**. The plate number for birds in the photo gallery are shown in **bold** with the abbreviation pl. The page within the Species Accounts on which the bird is described is shown in *italics*.

For habitats, pages on which a habitat is pictured are shown in **bold.**

For localities, the page on which the locality is described in the Site Locator is shown in **bold,** and in those cases in which the site is featured in a photo, the page on which that photo appears is shown in **bold.** Note that all geographic references are included in the Index that are mentioned in the text, except for most roads.

Lordsburg, 292, 294
Los Alamos, 289
Los Alamos Canyon, 139, **292**
Los Angeles, 133, 170, 273, 279, 281, 282, 284
Los Padres National Forest, 129
Lost Palms Oasis, 158, **279**
Louis Rubidoux Nature Center, 51, 62, 90, 146, 207, 215, 230, **279**
Lower Mimbres River Valley, 69, **292**
Lower San Juan Picnic Ground, 181, **279**
Loxia curvirostra, 249, **pl. 450**
Lucerne, 273, 274, 277

Madera Canyon, 66, 127, 131, 134, 135, 147, 152, 155, 178, 194, 215, 216, **266**, 271
Magpie, Black-billed, 12, 159, *171*, **pl. 291**
  Yellow-billed, *171*, 191, 276, **pl. 292**
Malaga, 290
Malibu Creek State Park, 67, 170, 179, 197, **279**
Malibu Lagoon State Beach, 79, **279**
Mallard, *49*, 93, **pl. 49**
Many Farms, 266
Many Farms Lake, xi, 93, **266**
Manzana Mountains, 194
Marana Pecan Grove, 123, 127, 212, 213, 221, 237, 251, **266**
Marble Canyon, 273
Maricopa, 273, 281, 284
Martin, Purple, *173*, **pl. 297**
Martinez Lake, 90, **267**
Massai Point, 178, **267**
Maxwell, 292
Maxwell National Wildlife Refuge, 61, 62, 92, 127, 142, 162, 222, 228, **292**
McGaffey, 289
McGill Campground, 75, 123, 125, 129, 144, 145, 171, 174, 246, 248, 249, **279**, 280
Meadowlark, Eastern, 240, **pl. 431**
  Western, *9*, 240, **pl. 432**
Melanerpes erythrocephalus, 142, **pl. 232**
  formicivorus, 143
  lewis, 142, **pl. 231**
  uropygialis, 143, **pl. 234**
Melanitta fusca, 55, **pl. 61**

nigra, 55, **pl. 62**
  perspicillata, 54, **pl. 60**
Meleagris gallopavo, 74, **pl. 99**
Melospiza georgiana, 230, **pl. 409**
  lincolnii, 229, **pl. 408**
  melodia, 229, **pl. 407**
Melville, Herman, 7
Merganser, Common, 57, **pl. 67**
  Hooded, 57, **pl. 66**
  Red-breasted, 59, **pl. 68**
Mergus merganser, 57, **pl. 67**
  serrator, 59, **pl. 68**
Merlin, 8, 69, **pl. 90**
mesquite, honey, 13, 14
Micrathene whitneyi, 125, **pl. 200**
Middle Rio Grande Conservancy District, 25, 26, 153, 230-32, 242, **292**
migration: raptor, 273; Rufous Hummingbird, 17, 18; seabird, 18; species from eastern North America, 17, 287; waterfowl, 287; Virginia's Warbler, 17; Western Tanager, 17
Mill Creek Canyon, 132, 274, **279**, 284
Miller Canyon, 124, **267**
Mimidae, 197
Mimus polyglottos, 197, **pl. 342**
Mittry Lake, 27, 40, 65, 78-80, 89, 91, 92, 207, 220, 241, **267**
Mniotilta varia, 212, **pl. 369**
Mockingbird, Northern, 16, *197*, **pl. 342**
Mogollon, 296
Mogollon Mountains, 170
Mojave, 275, 281
Molino Basin Campground, 178, 181, 189, **267**
Molino Canyon, 180
Molothrus aeneus, 243
  ater, 243
Montaña de Oro State Park, xi, 30, 46, 99, 102, 104, 116, 155, 178, 221, **279**
Montecello subdivision, 288
Monterrey Bay, 16
Moorhen, Common, 79, **pl. 110**
Morgan Lake, 83, 85, 88, 95, 96, 101, 105, 202, **292**
Mormon Lake, 71, 130, 176, 184, 219, **267**

Pyrocephalus rubinus, 157, **pl. 263**
Pyrrhuloxia, 11, *235,* **pl. 420**

Quail, California, 12, *76,* 170, **pl. 102**
    Gambel's, 10, 11, 13, *76,* 126, **pl. 103**
    Montezuma, *77,* **pl. 105**
    Mountain,   12, *75,* **pl. 100**
    Scaled, 47, *75,* **pl. 101**
Quartzite, 266
Quatal Canyon, 152, 246, 251; Area 14, 157,
    158, 160, 161, 163, 221, 229, 230, 234, 235,
    281
Quercus, 12
    agrifolia, 12
    douglasii, 12
    keloggii, 12
    wislizenii, 12
Questa, 295
Quiscalus mexicanus, 242, **pl. 436**
    quiscula, 242, **pl. 435**

Rail, Black, 70, *78,* **pl. 106**
    Clapper, *78,* 93, **pl. 107**
    Virginia, 8, *78,* **pl. 108**
    Yellow, 255
Rallidae, 77
Rallus limicola, 78, **pl. 108**
    longirostris, 78, **pl. 107**
Ramsey Canyon Preserve, 75, 134, 135, 147,
    169, 225, 235, 262, **269**
Ramsey Vista Campground, 211, 263, **269**
Randall Davey Audubon Center, 172, **293**
raptor, 292
Raton, 288
Rattlesnake Springs, 157, 164, 192, 217, 244-
    46, **294**
Raven, Chihuahuan, *172,* **pl. 294**
    Common, 10, 16, 47, 148, *172,* **pl. 295**
Recurvirostra americana, 87, **pl. 122**
Recurvirostridae, 86
Red Box Ranger Station, 127, **281**
Red Butte, 76, 172, **269**
Reddington Pass, 165, **269**
Redhead, *53,* **pl. 56**
Redlands, 279

Red Mountain, 154, **269**
Redpoll, Common, 257
Redrock, 293, 294
Red Rock Canyon Conservation Area, xi,
    63, 67-69, 72, 124, 133, 136, 146, 181, 184,
    185, 189, 200, 210, 224, 226, 236, 244,
    249, 251, 126, **286**
Redrock Wildlife Area, 66, 235, 245, **294**
Redstart, American, 15, *212,* **pl. 370**
    Painted, 148, *215,* **pl. 377**
    Slate-throated, 256
Reese Canyon, 293
Regulidae, 187
Regulus calendula, 188, **pl. 327**
    satrapa, 187, **pl. 326**
Remizidae, 179
Rincon, 281
Rio Grande, 21, 22, 81, 289, 293, 294
Rio Grande Nature Center, 53, 177, 293,
    294
Rio Pueblo Valley, 194, **294**
Riparia riparia, 175, **pl. 301**
Rissa tridactyla, 110, **pl. 167**
Riverside, 276, 279, 282
Roadrunner, Greater, 10, 11, 115, *122,* **pl.**
    192
Robin, American, *195,* **pl. 338**
    Rufous-backed, 256
Rockies, 9
Rocky Arroyo, 238, **294**
Rocky Mountains, 5
Roosevelt Lake, 140, **269**
Roosevelt Lake Wildlife Area, 51, 139, 209,
    269
Rose Canyon Lake, 174, **269**
Rose Well, 261
Roswell, 121, 287, 293-295
Roswell South Park Cemetery, 242, **294**
Roswell Spring River Golf Course, 61, 132,
    194, **294**
Roswell Zoo, 168, 235, 253, **294**
Rosy-Finch, Black, 257
    Brown-capped, 16, *247,* **pl. 445**
    Gray-crowned, *246,* **pl. 444**
Round Rock, 203

Ruby town site, 262
Rucker Canyon, 135, **269**
Ruff, 256
Rustler Park Recreation Area, 178, 215, **270**
Rutherford Tract, 90, 177, 229, **294**
Rynchops niger, 114, **pl. 177**

S6 Hwy, Summit Grove, **281**
Sabino Canyon Recreation Area, 134, 156,
    234, **270**
Sacramento River, 6
Safford, 262
sage, 10
sagebrush, 12, 47
Sageland, 281
saguaro, 11
Saguaro National Park, 10, 65, 138, 143, 157,
    160, 190, 205, 220, **270**
Salix, 14
Salpinctes obsoletus, 184, **pl. 319**
saltbush, 10
salt cedar, 13
Salton Sea. *See* Salton Sea National Wild-
    life Refuge
Salton Sea National Wildlife Refuge, xi, 8,
    28, 33, 39, 41, 44-46, 52, 53, 56, 70, 72, 78,
    85-87, 89, 92, 95, 96, 98, 99, 103, 107,
    108, 110-114, 121, 174, 175, 181, 186, 190,
    200, 234, 241, 243, **282**
Salvia, 12
San Antonio, 287
San Bernardino, 283
San Bernardino Mountains, 284
San Bernardino National Wildlife Refuge,
    69, **270**
Sanchez, 262
Sanderling, *95,* 114, **pl. 137**
Sandia Crest, 151, **295**
Sandia Park Pond, 204, 207, 214, 219, **295**
San Diego, 17, 274-76, 278, 280, 281, 283, 284
San Diego Bay, 3
Sandpiper, Baird's, *97,* **pl. 141**
    Buff-breasted, 256
    Curlew, 255
    Least, *96,* **pl. 140**

Pectoral, *97,* **pl. 142**
Semipalmated, *95,* **pl. 138**
Sharp-tailed, 255
Solitary, 8, *89,* **pl. 125**
Spotted, *90,* **pl. 128**
Stilt, *98,* **pl. 144**
Upland, *91,* **pl. 129**
Western, *96,* **pl. 139**
White-rumped, 255
Sandstone Bluffs Overlook, 198, **295**
San Elijo Lagoon Sanctuary, 136, **282**
San Fernando Basin, 159
San Fernando Valley, 273
San Francisco Bay, 6
San Gabriel Mountains, 66, 273, 275, 276,
    281, 284
San Gabriel Mts. Highlands, 273, 275, 276,
    281, 284
Sangre de Cristo Mountains, xiv, 5, 191
San Jacinto Mountains, 279, 281
San Jacinto Wildlife Area, 42, 48, 50, 83, 85,
    88, 89, 97, 127, 128, 239, **282**
San Joaquin River, 6
San Juan Capistrano, 275
San Juan de los Caballeros, 3
San Juan Forestry Station, 144, 149, **282**
San Juan River, 291, 292, 294
San Luis Obispo, 16, 277, 279
San Marcos, 292
San Marcos Pass, 278
San Mateo, 287
San Miguel Island, 275
San Pedro House, 161, 220, 227, **270**
San Pedro Riparian National Conserva-
    tion Area, 50, 141, **270**
San Pedro River, 125, 214, 237, 264, 265,
    268, **270**
San Rafael Grassland, 202, **270**
San Rafael Ponds, 194, **294**
San Rafael Wilderness, 43
Santa Ana, 278, 280, 283
Santa Ana Mountains, 280
Santa Anita Canyon, 132, **282**
Santa Barbara, 17, 47, 273, 275-77, 279, 280,
    284